Principles
of
Project
Finance

Principles of Project Finance

E. R. Yescombe
Yescombe Consulting Ltd.
London, U.K.
(www.yescombe.com)

ACADEMIC PRESS
An Imprint of Elsevier

Amsterdam   Boston   London   New York   Oxford   Paris
San Diego   San Francisco   Singapore   Sydney   Tokyo

Cover photo credit: © Digital Vision, 2002.
This book is printed on acid-free paper. ∞

Copyright © 2002, Yescombe Consulting, Ltd.
All Rights Reserved.
No part of this publication may be reproduced or transmitted in any form or by any means,
electronic or mechanical, including photocopy, recording, or any information storage and
retrieval system, without permission in writing from the publisher.

Permissions may be sought directly from Elsevier's Science and Technology Rights Department in
Oxford, UK. Phone: (44) 1865 843830, Fax: (44) 1865 853333, e-mail: permissions@elsevier.co.uk.
You may also complete your request on-line via the Elsevier homepage: http://www.elsevier.com by
selecting "Customer Support" and then "Obtaining Permissions".

Academic Press
An Imprint of Elsevier
525 B Street, Suite 1900, San Diego, California 92101-4495, USA
http://www.academicpress.com

Academic Press
84 Theobolds Road, London WC1X 8RR, UK
http://www.academicpress.com

Library of Congress Catalog Card Number: 2002104613

ISBN-13: 978-0-12-770851-5
ISBN-10: 0-12-770851-0

PRINTED IN THE UNITED STATES OF AMERICA
07   MM   9   8   7   6   5

Contents

Chapter 6

Project Contracts: (1) The Project Agreement 69

Chapter 7

Project Contracts: (2) Ancillary Contracts   105

Chapter 8
Commercial Risks   137

Chapter 12
Financial Modeling and Evaluation   251

Chapter 13

Financial Structuring and Documentation 283

Chapter 1

Introduction

Project finance is a method of raising long-term debt financing for major projects through "financial engineering," based on lending against the cash flow generated by the project alone; it depends on a detailed evaluation of a project's construction, operating and revenue risks, and their allocation between investors, lenders, and other parties through contractual and other arrangements. Project finance is a relatively new financial discipline that has developed rapidly over the last 20 years. In 2001, some $190 billion of investments in projects around the world were financed using project finance techniques (cf. §2.1).

"Project finance" is not the same thing as "financing projects," because projects may be financed in many different ways. Traditionally, large scale public-sector projects in developed countries were financed by public-sector debt; private-sector projects were financed by large companies raising corporate loans. In developing countries, projects were financed by the government borrowing from the international banking market, multilateral institutions such as the World Bank, or through export credits. These approaches have begun to change, however, as privatization and deregulation have changed the approach to financing investment in major projects, transferring a significant share of the financing burden to the private sector.

Unlike other methods of financing projects, project finance is a seamless web that affects all aspects of a project's development and contractual arrangements, and thus the finance cannot be dealt with in isolation. If a project uses project finance, not only the finance director and the lenders but also all those involved in the project (e.g., project developers, governments and other public authorities, engineers, contractors, equipment suppliers, fuel suppliers, product offtakers, and other parties to Project Contracts) need to have a basic understanding of how

1

project finance works, and how their part of the project is linked to and affected by the project finance structure.

This book is therefore intended to provide a guide to the principles of project finance and to the practical issues that can cause the most difficulty in commercial and financial negotiations, based on the author's own experience both as a banker and as an independent adviser in project finance. The book serves both as a structured introduction for those who are new to the subject, and as an *aide mémoire* for those developing and negotiating project finance transactions. No knowledge of the financial markets or financial terms is assumed or required.

"The devil is in the detail" is a favorite saying among project financiers, and a lot of detailed explanation is required for a book on project finance to be a practical guide rather than a generalized study or a vague summary of the subject. But with a systematic approach and an understanding of the principles that lie behind this detail, finding a way through the thickets becomes a less formidable task.

The subject of project finance is presented in this book in much the same way that a particular project is presented to the financing market (cf. §5.1.8), i.e.:

- *A general background on the project finance market and the roles of the main participants:*
  - Chapter 2 explains the recent development of project finance, its key characteristics and how these differ from other types of finance, and why project finance is used.
  - Chapter 3 provides information on the markets for raising project finance debt.
  - Chapter 4 explains how Sponsors (lead investors) and the Project Company develop projects as well as the competitive-bidding procedures for project development by public authorities.
  - Chapter 5 sets out the procedures for raising finance from private-sector lenders.
- *A review of the commercial contracts that can form a framework for raising project finance:*
  - Chapter 6 reviews the main Project Agreement, usually an Offtake Contract or Concession Agreement, which plays the central role in many project finance structures.
  - Chapter 7 looks at the other important Project Contracts—including those for construction and operation of the project, provision of raw materials and other input supplies, and insurance.
- *An explanation of project finance risk analysis:*
  - Chapter 8 explains how lenders analyze and mitigate the commercial risks inherent in a project.
  - Chapter 9 similarly examines the effect of macroeconomic risks (inflation,

and interest rate and exchange rate movements) on project financing and how these risks are mitigated.

- Chapter 10 analyzes political risks and how these may affect a project.
- Chapter 11 reviews how political risks unacceptable to private-sector lenders may be dealt with using insurance, guarantees, or loans from export credit agencies and development banks, as well as private-sector insurance.
- *A description of how the financing structure for a project is created:*
  - Chapter 12 summarizes the inputs used for a financial model of a project and how the model's results are used by investors and lenders.
  - Chapter 13 demonstrates how the process of review and risk analysis concludes in a negotiation of the project's finance structure and terms.

Technical terms used in this book that are mainly peculiar to project finance are capitalized, and briefly explained in the Glossary, with cross-references to the sections in the main text where fuller explanations can be found; other specialized financial terms are also explained and cross-referenced in the Glossary, as are the various abbreviations.

Spreadsheets with the detailed calculations on which the tables in Chapters 9, 12, and 13 are based can be downloaded from www.yescombe.com.

Unless stated otherwise, "$" in this book refers to U.S. dollars.

Chapter 2

What Is Project Finance?

This chapter reviews the factors behind the recent rapid growth of project finance (cf. §2.1), its distinguishing features (cf. §2.2), and relationship with privatization (cf. §2.3), and also with other forms of structured finance (cf. §2.4). Finally, the benefits of using project finance are considered from the point of view of the various project participants (cf. §2.5).

§2.1 DEVELOPMENT OF PROJECT FINANCE

The growth of project finance over the last 20 years has been driven mainly by the worldwide process of deregulation of utilities and privatization of public-sector capital investment. This has taken place both in the developed world as well as developing countries. It has also been promoted by the internationalization of investment in major projects: leading project developers now run worldwide portfolios and are able to apply the lessons learned from one country to projects in another, as are their banks and financial advisers. Governments and the public sector generally also benefit from these exchanges of experience.

Private finance for public infrastructure projects is not a new concept: the English road system was renewed in the 18th and early 19th centuries using private-sector funding based on toll revenues; the railway, water, gas, electricity, and telephone industries were developed around the world in the 19th century mainly with private-sector investment. During the first half of the 20th century, however, the state took over such activities in many countries, and only over the last 20 years has this process been reversing. Project finance, as an appropriate method of long-term financing for capital-intensive industries where the investment financed has

5

Table 2.1

Private-Sector Project Finance Loan Commitments, 1996–2001

($ millions)	1996	1997	1998	1999	2000	2001
Power	18,283	18,717	21,663	37,262	56,512	64,528
Telecommunications	13,296	19,864	16,275	24,929	36,735	25,445
Infrastructure	5,037	7,436	9,006	12,673	16,755	14,473
Oil and gas	3,417	15,386	10,666	7,792	12,552	12,638
Real estate and leisure	290	465	369	1,573	1,638	6,530
Petrochemicals	4,100	4,603	3,129	5,356	3,337	3,898
Industry (process plant)	1,964	2,144	2,641	1,396	3,538	3,646
Mining	1,234	6,307	2,694	1,377	629	2,323
Total	**47,621**	**74,922**	**66,443**	**92,358**	**131,696**	**133,481**

Adapted from: *Project Finance International,* issues 113 (January 13, 1997), 137 (January 28, 1998), 161 (January 27, 1999), 185 (January 26, 2000), 209 (January 24, 2001), 233 (January 23, 2002).

a relatively predictable cash flow, has played an important part in providing the funding required for this change,

Some successive waves of project finance can be identified:

- Finance for natural resources projects (mining, oil, and gas), from which modern project finance techniques are derived, developed first in the Texas oil fields in the 1930s; this was given a considerable boost by the oil price increases, and the development of the North Sea oil fields in the 1970s, as well as gas and other natural resources projects in Australia and various developing countries.
- Finance for independent power projects ("IPPs") in the electricity sector (primarily for power generation) developed first after the Private Utility Regulatory Policies Act ("PURPA") in the United States in 1978, which encouraged the development of cogeneration plants, electricity privatization in the United Kingdom in the early 1990s, and the subsequent worldwide process of electricity privatization and deregulation.
- Finance for public infrastructure (roads, transport, public buildings, etc.) was especially developed through the United Kingdom's Private Finance Initiative ("PFI") from the early 1990s; such projects are now usually known as public–private partnerships ("PPPs").
- Finance for the explosive worldwide growth in mobile telephone networks developed in the late 1990s.

An analysis by industry sectors of the project finance loan commitments provided by private-sector lenders in recent years illustrates these trends (Table 2.1). The effects of recent electricity deregulation in parts of the United States and the upsurge in worldwide investment in mobile phone networks are especially evident in these figures. The steady growth in PPP-related project finance (infrastructure and real estate) is also notable. (For a fuller analysis on a geographical basis, cf. Chapter 3.)

Assuming that debt averages 70% of total project costs, in 2001 on the basis of these figures some $190 billion of new investments worldwide were financed with project finance from private-sector lenders.

It should be noted that these statistics do not include direct lending for projects by export credit agencies and multilateral development banks (cf. Chapter 11) or other public-sector agencies. In addition, because (a) it is debatable whether certain structured finance loans should be classified as project finance or not (cf. §2.4), and (b) the borderline between project finance and financing projects (cf. Chapter 1) is not always clear, market statistics compiled by different sources can vary considerably;[1] however, the overall trends in and scale of project finance are reasonably clear.

§2.2 FEATURES OF PROJECT FINANCE

Project finance structures differ between these various industry sectors and from deal to deal: there is no such thing as "standard" project finance, since each deal has its own unique characteristics. But there are common principles underlying the project finance approach.

Some typical characteristics of project finance are

- It is provided for a "ring-fenced" project (i.e., one which is legally and economically self-contained) through a special purpose legal entity (usually a company) whose only business is the project (the "Project Company").
- It is usually raised for a new project rather than an established business (although project finance loans may be refinanced).
- There is a high ratio of debt to equity ("leverage" or "gearing")—roughly speaking, project finance debt may cover 70–90% of the cost of a project.
- There are no guarantees from the investors in the Project Company ("non-recourse" finance), or only limited guarantees ("limited-recourse" finance), for the project finance debt.
- Lenders rely on the future cash flow projected to be generated by the project for interest and debt repayment (debt service), rather than the value of its assets or analysis of historical financial results.
- The main security for lenders is the project company's contracts, licenses, or ownership of rights to natural resources; the project company's physical assets are likely to be worth much less than the debt if they are sold off after a default on the financing.

---

[1] For example, Euromoney's Loanware database estimated the total project finance market in 2001 at $145 billion, $12 billion higher than the figure in Table 2.1

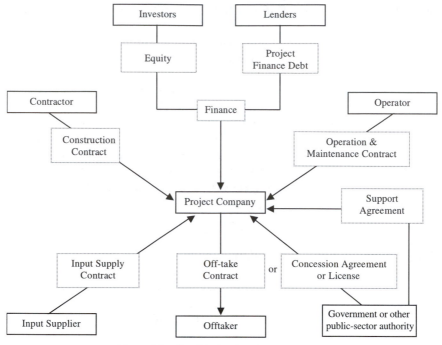

Figure 2.1   Simplified project finance structure.

- The project has a finite life, based on such factors as the length of the contracts or licenses or the reserves of natural resources, and therefore the project finance debt must be fully repaid by the end of this life.

Hence project finance differs from a corporate loan, which is primarily lent
against a company's balance sheet and projections extrapolating from its past cash
flow and profit record, and assumes that the company will remain in business for
an indefinite period and so can keep renewing ("rolling over") its loans.

Project finance is made up of a number of building blocks, although all of these
are not found in every project finance transaction (cf. §2.4), and there are likely to
be ancillary contracts or agreements not shown in Figure 2.1.

The project finance itself has two elements:

- Equity, provided by investors in the project
- Project finance-based debt, provided by one or more groups of lenders

The project finance debt has first call on the project's net operating cash flow; the
equity investors' return is thus more dependent on the success of the project.

The contracts entered into by the Project Company provide support for the
project finance, particularly by transferring risks from the Project Company to the

other parties to the Project Contracts, and form part of the lenders' security package. The Project Contracts may include the following:

- A Project Agreement, which may be

  either an Off-take Contract (e.g., a power purchase agreement), under which the product produced by the project will be sold on a long-term pricing formula

  or a Concession Agreement with the government or another public authority, which gives the Project Company the right to construct the project and earn revenues from it by providing a service either to the public sector (e.g., a public building) or directly to the general public (e.g., a toll road)

  Alternatively, the project company may have a license to operate under the terms of general legislation for the industry sector (e.g. a mobile phone network).

- Other project contracts, e.g.:
  - A turnkey Engineering, Procurement and Construction (EPC) Contract, under which the project will be designed and built for a fixed price, and completed by a fixed date
  - An Input Supply Contract, under which fuel or other raw material for the project will be provided on a long-term pricing formula in agreed quantities
  - An Operating and Maintenance (O&M) Contract, under which a third party will be responsible for the running of the project after it has been built
  - A Government Support Agreement (usually in a developing country), which may provide various kinds of support, such as guarantees for the Offtaker or tax incentives for the investment in the project.

Project Agreements are discussed in detail in Chapter 6 and other Project Contracts in Chapter 7. Of course none of these structures or contractual relationships are unique to project finance: any company may have investors, sign contracts, get licenses from the government, and so on; however, the relative importance of these matters, and the way in which they are linked together, is a key factor in project finance.

§2.3 PROJECT FINANCE AND PRIVATIZATION

Project finance should be distinguished from privatization, which:

either conveys the ownership of public-sector assets to the private sector— this does not necessarily involve project finance: a privatized former state-owned company may raise any finance required through a corporate loan

or   provides for services to be supplied by a private company that had pre-
          viously been supplied by the public sector (e.g., street cleaning)—
          again, this does not necessarily involve project finance: the private com-
          pany may not have to incur major new capital expenditure and so not
          require any finance at all, or may use a corporate loan to raise the finance
          to make the investment required to provide the service.

Project finance may come into the picture if a company needs finance for the construction of public infrastructure on the basis of a contract or licence, e.g.:

* An Off-take Contract, based on which a project will be constructed to sell its
  output to a public-sector body (e.g., construction of a power station to sell
  electricity to a state-owned power company)
* A Concession Agreement under which a project will be constructed to provide a service to a public-sector body (e.g., provision of a public-sector hospital building and facilities)
* A Concession Agreement under which a project will be constructed to provide a service to the general public normally provided by the public sector
  (e.g., a toll road)
* A Concession Agreement or licence under which a project will be constructed to provide new services to the public (e.g., a mobile phone
  network).

Such Project Agreements with the public sector, which provide a basis for project finance, can take several different forms:

Build-own-operate-transfer ("BOOT") projects: The Project Company
    constructs the project and owns and operates it for a set period of time, earn-
    ing the revenues from the project in this period, at the end of which owner-
    ship is transferred back to the public sector. For example, the project com-
    pany may build a power station, own it for 20 years during which time the
    power generated is sold to an Offtaker (e.g., a state-owned electricity distri-
    bution company), and at the end of that time ownership is transferred back
    to the public sector.
Build-operate-transfer ("BOT") projects (also known as design-build-
    finance-operate ["DBFO"] projects). In this type of project, the Project
    Company never owns the assets used to provide the project services. How-
    ever the Project Company constructs the project and has the right to earn rev-
    enues from its operation of the project. (It may also be granted a lease of the
    project site and the associated buildings and equipment during the term of
    the project—this is known as build-lease-transfer ("BLT") or build-lease-
    operate-transfer ("BLOT"). This structure is used where the public nature
    of the project makes it inappropriate for it to be owned by a private-sector

company—for example, a road, bridge, or tunnel—and therefore ownership remains with the public sector.

Build-transfer-operate ("BTO") projects. These are similar to a BOT project, except that the public sector does not take over the ownership of the project until construction is completed.

Build-own-operate ("BOO") projects. These are projects whose ownership remains with the Project Company throughout its life—for example, a power station in a privatized electricity industry or a mobile phone network. The Project Company therefore gets the benefit of any residual value in the project. (Project agreements with the private sector also normally fall into this category.)

There are other variations on these acronyms for different project structures, and the project finance market does not always use them consistently—for example, "BOT" is often used to mean "Build-Own-Transfer," i.e., the same as "BOOT."

Clearly a Project Company would always prefer to own the project assets, but whether or not the ownership of the project is transferred to the public sector in the short or the long term, or remains indefinitely with a private-sector company, or is never held by the private-sector company, makes little difference from the project finance point of view. This is because the real value in a project financed in this way is not in the ownership of its assets, but in the right to receive cash flows from the project. But although these different ownership structures are of limited importance to lenders, any long-term residual value in the project (as there may be in a BOO but not a BOOT/BOT/BTO project) may be of relevance to the investors in assessing their likely return.

§2.4 PROJECT FINANCE AND STRUCTURED FINANCE

Although there are general characteristics or features to be found in what the market calls "project finance" transactions, as already mentioned, all of the "building blocks" shown in Figure 2.1 are not found in every project financing, for example:

- If the product of the project is a commodity for which there is a wide market (e.g., oil), there is not necessarily a need for an Offtake Contract.
- A toll-road project has a Concession Agreement but no Offtake Contract.
- A project for a mobile phone network is usually built without a fixed price, date-certain EPC Contract, and has no Offtake Contract.
- A mining or oil and gas extraction project is based on a concession or license to extract the raw materials, but the Project Company may sell its products into the market without an Offtake Contract.

- A project that does not use fuel or a similar raw material does not require an Input Supply Contract
- Government Support Agreements are normally only found in projects in developing countries.

There is, therefore, no precise boundary between project finance and other types of financing in which a relatively high level of debt is raised to fund a business. The boundaries are also blurred as transactions that begin as new projects become established and then are refinanced, with such refinancing taking on more of the characteristics of a corporate loan.

Lenders themselves draw the boundaries between project finance and other types of lending based on convenience rather than theory, taking into account that skills used by loan officers in project finance may also be used in similar types of financing. Many lenders deal with project finance as part of their "structured finance" operations, covering any kind of finance where a special-purpose vehicle (SPV) like a Project Company has to be put in place as the borrower to raise the funding, with an equity and debt structure to fit the cash flow, unlike corporate loans, which are made to a borrower already in existence (cf. §5.1). As a result, project finance market statistics have to be treated with some caution, as they may be affected by inclusion or exclusion of large deals on the borderline between project finance and other types of structured finance.

Examples of other types of structured finance and their differences from project finance include the following:

Receivables financing. This is based on lending against the established cash flow of a business and involves raising funds through an SPV similar to a Project Company (but normally off the balance sheet of the true beneficiary of the cash flow). The cash flow may be derived from the general business (e.g., a hotel chain) or specific contracts that give rise to this cash flow (e.g., consumer loans, sales contracts, etc.). The key difference with project finance is that the latter is based on a projection of cash flow from a project yet to be established.

   Although telecommunication financing is often included under the heading of project finance, it has few of the general characteristics shared by other types of project finance. It could be said to come halfway between such receivables financing and "true" project finance, in that the financing may be used towards construction of a project (a new telephone network), but loans are normally not drawn until the initial revenues have been established (cf. §8.8.7).

Securitization. If receivables financing is procured in the bond market (cf. §5.2), it is known as securitization of receivables. (There have also been a few securitizations of receivables due from banks' project finance loan books, but so far this has not been a significant feature in the market.)

Leveraged buyout ("LBO") or management buyout ("MBO") financing. This highly leveraged financing provides for the acquisition of an existing business by portfolio investors (LBO) or its own management (MBO). It is usually based on a mixture of the cash flow of the business and the value of its assets. It does not normally involve finance for construction of a new project, nor does this type of financing use contracts as security as does project finance.

Acquisition finance. Probably the largest sector in structured finance, acquisition finance enables company A to acquire company B using highly leveraged debt. In that sense it is similar to LBO and MBO financing, but based on the combined business of the two companies.

Asset finance. Asset finance is based on lending against the value of assets easily saleable in the open market, e.g., aircraft or real estate (property) financing, whereas project finance lending is against the cash flow produced by the asset, which may have little open-market value.

Leasing. Leasing is a form of asset finance, in which ownership of the asset financed remains with the lessor (i.e., lender) (cf. §3.4).

§2.5 WHY USE PROJECT FINANCE?

A project may be financed by a company as an addition to its existing business rather than on a stand-alone project finance basis. In this case, the company uses its available cash and credit lines to pay for the project, and if necessary raise new credit lines or even new equity capital to do so (i.e., it makes use of corporate finance). Provided it can be supported by the company's balance sheet and earnings record, a corporate loan to finance a project is normally fairly simple, quick, and cheap to arrange.

A Project Company, unlike a corporate borrower, has no business record to serve as the basis for a lending decision. Nonetheless, lenders have to be confident that they will be repaid, especially taking account of the additional risk from the high level of debt inherent in a project finance transaction. This means that they need to have a high degree of confidence that the project (a) can be completed on time and on budget, (b) is technically capable of operating as designed, and (c) that there will be enough net cash flow from the project's operation to cover their debt service adequately. Project economics also need to be robust enough to cover any temporary problems that may arise.

Thus the lenders need to evaluate the terms of the project's contracts insofar as these provide a basis for its construction costs and operating cash flow, and quantify the risks inherent in the project with particular care. They need to ensure that project risks are allocated to appropriate parties other than the Project Company, or, where this is not possible, mitigated in other ways. This process is known as

Table 2.2

Benefit of Leverage on Investors' Return

			Low leverage	High leverage
	Project cost		1,000	1,000
(a)	Debt		300	800
(b)	Equity		700	200
(c)	Revenue from project		100	100
(d)	Interest rate on debt (*p.a.*)		5%	7%
(e)	Interest payable	[(a) × (d)]	15	56
(f)	Profit	[(c) − (e)]	85	44
	Return on equity	[(f) ÷ (b)]	12%	22%

"due diligence." The due-diligence process may often cause slow and frustrating progress for a project developer, as lenders inevitably tend to get involved—directly or indirectly—in the negotiation of the Project Contracts, but it is an unavoidable aspect of raising project finance debt. (The issues covered during due diligence are discussed in Chapters 8 to 10.)

Lenders also need to continue to monitor and control the activities of the Project Company to ensure that the basis on which they assessed these risks is not undermined. This may also leave the investor with much less independent management of the project than would be the case with a corporate financing. (The controls imposed by lenders are discussed in Chapter 13.)

Besides being slow, complex, and leading to some loss of control of the project, project finance is also an expensive method of financing. The lenders' margin over cost of funds may be 2–3 times that of corporate finance; the lenders' due diligence and control processes, and the advisors employed for this purpose (cf. §5.4), also add significantly to costs.

It should also be emphasized that project finance cannot be used to finance a project that would not otherwise be financeable.

§2.5.1 Why Investors Use Project Finance

Why, despite these factors, do investors make use of project finance? There are a variety of reasons:

High leverage. One major reason for using project finance is that investments in ventures such as power generation or road building have to be long term but do not offer an inherently high return: high leverage improves the return for an investor.

Table 2.2 sets out a (very simplified) example of the benefit of leverage on an investor's return. Both the low-leverage and high-leverage columns relate to the same investment of 1,000, which produces revenue of 100 *p.a.* If it is financed with 30% debt, as in the low-leverage column (a typical level of debt for a good corporate credit), the return on equity is 11%. On the other hand, if it is financed with 80% (project finance-style) leverage, the return on the (reduced level) of equity is 22%, despite an increase in the cost of the debt (reflecting the higher risk for lenders):

Project finance thus takes advantage of the fact that debt is cheaper than equity, because lenders are willing to accept a lower return (for their lower risk) than an equity investor. Naturally the investor needs to be sure that the investment in the project is not jeopardized by loading it with debt, and therefore has to go through a sound due diligence process to ensure that the financial structure is prudent. Of course the argument could be turned the other way around to say that if a project has high leverage it has an inherently higher risk, and so it should produce a higher return for investors. But in project finance higher leverage can only be achieved where the level of risk in the project is limited.

Tax benefits. A further factor that may make high leverage more attractive is that interest is tax deductible, whereas dividends to shareholders are not, which makes debt even cheaper than equity, and hence encourages high leverage. Thus, in the example above, if the tax rate is 30%, the after-tax profit in the low leverage case is 60 (85 × 70%), or an after-tax return on equity of 8.5%, whereas in the high-leverage case it is 31 (44 × 70%), or an after-tax return on equity of 15.4%.

In major projects there is, however, likely to be a high level of tax deductions anyway during the early stages of the project because the capital cost is depreciated against tax (cf. §12.7.1), so the ability to make a further deduction of interest against tax at the same time may not be significant.

Off-balance-sheet financing. If the investor has to raise the debt and then inject it into the project, this will clearly appear on the investor's balance sheet. A project finance structure may allow the investor to keep the debt off the consolidated balance sheet, but usually only if the investor is a minority shareholder in the project—which may be achieved if the project is owned through a joint venture. Keeping debt off the balance sheet is sometimes seen as beneficial to a company's position in the financial markets, but a company's shareholders and lenders should normally take account of risks involved in any off-balance-sheet activities, which are generally revealed in notes to the published accounts even if they are not included in the balance sheet figures; so although joint ventures often raise project finance for other reasons (discussed below), project finance should not usually be undertaken purely to keep debt off the investors' balance sheets.

Borrowing capacity. Project finance increases the level of debt that can be borrowed against a project: nonrecourse finance raised by the Project Company is not normally counted against corporate credit lines (therefore in this sense it may be off-balance sheet). It may thus increase an investor's overall borrowing capacity, and hence the ability to undertake several major projects simultaneously.

Risk limitation. An investor in a project raising funds through project finance does not normally guarantee the repayment of the debt—the risk is therefore limited to the amount of the equity investment. A company's credit rating is also less likely to be downgraded if its risks on project investments are limited through a project finance structure.

Risk spreading / joint ventures. A project may be too large for one investor to undertake, so others may be brought in to share the risk in a joint-venture Project Company. This both enables the risk to be spread between investors and limits the amount of each investor's risk because of the nonrecourse nature of the Project Company's debt financing.

As project development can involve major expenditure, with a significant risk of having to write it all off if the project does not go ahead (cf. §4.2), a project developer may also bring in a partner in the development phase of the project to share this risk.

This approach can also be used to bring in "limited partners" to the project (e.g., by giving a share in the equity of a Project Company to an Offtaker who is thus induced to sign a long-term Offtake Contract, without being required to make any cash investment, or with the investment limited to a small proportion of the equity.)

Creating a joint venture also enables project risks to be reduced by combining expertise (e.g., local expertise plus technical expertise; construction expertise plus operating expertise; operating expertise plus marketing expertise). In such cases the relevant Project Contracts (e.g., the EPC Contract or the O&M Contract) are usually allocated to the partner with the relevant expertise (but cf. §4.1).

Long-term finance. Project finance loans typically have a longer term than corporate finance. Long-term financing is necessary if the assets financed normally have a high capital cost that cannot be recovered over a short term without pushing up the cost that must be charged for the project's end product. So loans for power projects often run for nearly 20 years, and for infrastructure projects even longer. (Oil, gas, and minerals projects usually have a shorter term because the reserves extracted deplete more quickly, and telecommunication projects also have a shorter term because the technology involved has a relatively short life.)

Enhanced credit. If the Offtaker has a better credit standing than the equity investor, this may enable debt to be raised for the project on better terms than the investor would be able to obtain from a corporate loan.

Unequal partnerships. Projects are often put together by a developer with an

Table 2.3

Effect of Leverage on Offtaker's Cost

		Low leverage	High leverage
	Project cost	1,000	1,000
(a)	Debt	300	800
(b)	Equity	700	200
(c)	Return on equity[(b) × 15%]	105	30
(d)	Interest rate on debt (*p.a.*)	5%	7%
(e)	Interest payable[(a) × (d)]	15	56
	Revenue required[(c) + (e)]	120	86

idea but little money, who then has to find investors. A project finance structure, which requires less equity, makes it easier for the weaker developer to
maintain an equal partnership, because if the absolute level of the equity in the
project is low, the required investment from the weaker partner is also low.

§2.5.2 THE BENEFITS OF PROJECT FINANCE TO THIRD PARTIES

Equally, there are benefits for the Offtaker or end user of the product or service
provided by the Project Company, and also for the government of the country
where the project is located:

Lower product or service cost. In order to pay the lowest price for the project's product or service, the Offtaker or end user will want the project to raise
as high a level of debt as possible, and so a project finance structure
is beneficial. This can be illustrated by doing the calculation in Table 2.2
in reverse: suppose the investor in the project requires a return of at least
15%, then, as Table 2.3 shows, to produce this, revenue of 120 is required using low-leverage finance, but only 86 using high-leverage project finance,
and hence the cost to the Offtaker or end user reduces accordingly. (In
finance theory, an equity investor in a company with high leverage would expect a higher return than one in a company with low leverage, on the ground
that high leverage equals high risk. However, as discussed above, this effect
cannot be seen in project finance investment, since its high leverage does not
imply high risk.) (Also cf. §13.1 for other issues affecting leverage.)

So if the Offtaker or end user wishes to fix the lowest long-term purchase
cost for the product of the project and is able to influence how the project is
financed, the use of project finance should be encouraged, e.g., by agreeing
to sign a Project Agreement that fits project finance requirements.

Additional investment in public infrastructure. Project finance can provide

funding for additional investment in infrastructure that the public
sector might otherwise not be able to undertake because of economic or
financial constraints on the public-sector investment budget.

Of course, if the public sector pays for the project through a long-term Project Agreement, it could be said that a project financed in this way is merely
off-balance sheet financing for the public-sector, and should therefore be included in the public-sector budget anyway. Whether this argument is a valid
one depends on the extent to which the public sector has transformed real project risk to the private sector.

Risk transfer. A project finance contract structure transfers risks of, for example, project cost overruns from the public to the private sector. It also
usually provides for payments only when specific performance objectives
are met, hence also transferring to the private sector the risk that these are
not met.

Lower project cost. Private finance is now widely used for projects that
would previously have been built and operated by the public sector (cf. §2.3).
Apart from relieving public sector budget pressures, such PPP projects also
have merit because the private sector can often build and run such investments more cost-effectively than the public sector, even after allowing for the
higher cost of project finance compared to public-sector finance.

This lower cost is a function of:

- The general tendency of the public sector to "overengineer" or "gold-
  plate" projects
- Greater private-sector expertise in control and management of project construction and operation (based on the private sector being better able to offer incentives to good managers)
- The private sector taking the primary risk of construction and operation
  cost overruns, for which public-sector projects are notorious
- "Whole life" management of long-term maintenance of the project, rather
  than ad hoc arrangements for maintenance dependent on the availability
  of further public-sector funding

However, this cost benefit can be eroded by "deal creep" (i.e., increases in
costs during detailed negotiations on terms or when the specifications for the
project are changed during this period—cf. §4.6.3).

Third-party due diligence. The public sector may benefit from the independent due diligence and control of the project exercised by the lenders, who will
want to ensure that all obligations under the Project Agreement are clearly
fulfilled and that other Project Contracts adequately deal with risk issues.

Transparency. As a project financing is self-contained (i.e., it deals only with
the assets and liabilities, costs, and revenues of the particular project), the
true costs of the product or service can more easily be measured and monitored. Also, if the Sponsor is in a regulated business (e.g., power distribu-

tion), the unregulated business can be shown to be financed separately and on an arm's-length basis via a project finance structure.

Additional inward investment. For a developing country, project finance opens up new opportunities for infrastructure investment, as it can be used to create inward investment that would not otherwise occur. Furthermore, successful project finance for a major project, such as a power station, can act as a showcase to promote further investment in the wider economy.

Technology transfer. For developing countries, project finance provides a way of producing market-based investment in infrastructure for which the local economy may have neither the resources nor the skills.

Chapter 3

The Project Finance Markets

This chapter reviews the private-sector debt markets for project finance, in particular commercial banks (cf. §3.1) and bond investors (cf. §3.2). The uses of mezzanine or subordinated debt (cf. §3.3), leasing (cf. §3.4), and vendor finance (cf. §3.5) are also considered. Loans and guarantees provided by export credit agencies and multilateral and bilateral development banks, mainly for projects in developing countries where the private sector is not willing to assume the credit risk in the country concerned, are discussed in Chapter 11 (but cf. §3.6).

Private-sector project finance debt is provided from two main sources—commercial banks and bond investors. Commercial banks provide long-term loans to project companies; bond holders (typically long-term investors such as insurance companies and pension funds) purchase long-term bonds (tradable debt instruments) issued by project companies. Although the legal structures, procedures, and markets are different, the criteria under which debt is raised in each of these markets are much the same. ("Lender" is used in this book to mean either a bank lender or a bond investor.)

In 2001 (according to market statistics collected by the journal *Project Finance International*), the total amount of project finance debt raised from private-sector lenders was approximately $133 billion, of which $108 billion was raised through bank loans and $25 billion through bonds. Around a third of the total, $47 billion, was raised for projects in the United States, and $38 billion went to projects in Western Europe.

The World Bank estimates that total bank debt provided to developing countries in 2000 was $125 billion and bond debt $77 billion.[1] Based on the *Project Finance International* statistics (which are not entirely comparable), developing

---

[1] World Bank: *Global Development Finance 2000* (World Bank, Washington D.C., 2001).

countries (notably in Latin America) raised approximately $35 billion of project finance debt in 2000, of which some $31 billion was raised from banks and $4 billion in the bond market. The World Bank also estimates that total private-sector infrastructure investment in developing countries in 1999 (i.e., excluding natural resources projects) was $68 billion,[2] which compares with some $20 billion of project finance debt to developing countries in the same year. The importance of project finance for developing countries is therefore evident.

It should be noted that the *Project Finance International* statistics do not include direct lending to private-sector projects by export credit agencies and multilateral development banks, although they do include loans guaranteed by them. They also do not include loans by national (bilateral) development banks and some domestic commercial banks in developing countries. The figures therefore understate somewhat the level of project finance for developing countries. The figures for bank loans also relate to amounts committed during the year, rather than those actually lent, and the figures include refinancings of other loans on a project finance basis.

§3.1 COMMERCIAL BANKS

Commercial banks are the largest providers of project-finance (cf. §5.1), with 82% of the private-sector project finance debt raised in 2001. The division between different market sectors set out in Table 2.1 for the private-sector funding market as a whole is broadly reflected *pro rata* in the banking market.

§3.1.1 AREAS OF ACTIVITY

As can be seen from the figures set out in Table 3.1, bank project finance activity is heavily concentrated in the Americas (especially the United States) and Western Europe.

The following comments can be made on recent project finance developments in some of the more active markets:

- *United States:* Project finance business in 2000/1 was driven primarily by large investment in the power sector, as well as telecommunications.
- *Brazil:* The sharp increase in Brazilian loans in 2000 was based mainly on some major oil and gas projects, continuing at a lower level in 2001 along with power projects.

[2]A.K. Izaguirre & G. Rao: *Public Policy for the Private Sector, Note N° 215—Private Infrastructure,* (World Bank, Washington D.C., 2000).

Table 3.1

Bank Project Finance Loan Commitments, 1996–2001

($ millions)	1996	1997	1998	1999	2000	2001
Americas—of which:	8,917	15,500	25,121	37,532	52,795	47,447
U.S.A.	*5,710*	*5,301*	*9,630*	*27,605*	*33,573*	*31,254*
Canada	*288*	*280*	*3,030*	*3,087*	*2,526*	*622*
Argentina	*44*	*1,275*	*482*	*1,658*	*1,895*	*1,051*
Brazil	*336*	*2,318*	*4,482*	*761*	*9,217*	*4,561*
Chile	*500*	*2,033*	*631*	*540*	*1,618*	*2,721*
Mexico	*1,066*	*560*	*1,128*	*2,416*	*2,153*	*3,162*
Western Europe—of which:	15,709	18,843	14,669	15,764	33,612	37,392
Germany	*558*	*398*	*1,482*	*110*	*12,806*	*4,721*
Italy	*2,506*	*2,500*	*856*	*989*	*5,310*	*13,787*
Netherlands	*281*	*550*	*690*	*1,772*	*300*	*1,176*
Portugal	*500*	*994*	*500*	*2,041*	*1,537*	*1,536*
Spain	*891*	*52*	*572*	*826*	*567*	*6,031*
Sweden			*624*	*156*		*2,343*
U.K.	*10,098*	*9,930*	*7,088*	*8,151*	*11,490*	*6,089*
Central Europe and CIS— of which:	702	6,883	2,205	624	4,588	1,059
Russia		*5,535*	*501*		*2,077*	*225*
Poland	*100*	*518*	*474*	*180*	*1,561*	*436*
Middle East and North Africa— of which:	5,847	7,072	4,435	5,596	7,255	8,939
Kuwait	*1,197*	*1,200*				*900*
Oman		*2,072*		*60*	*513*	*2,030*
Qatar	*1,911*	*350*	*1,114*	*914*		*1,132*
Saudi Arabia	*1,810*	*2,200*	*845*	*600*	*852*	*2,176*
Turkey	*929*		*576*	*351*	*2,834*	*362*
UAE			*1,178*	*1,096*		*1,638*
Sub-Saharan Africa— of which:		546	398	427	550	2,269
South Africa		*386*		*87*	*127*	*718*
Asia—of which:	7,309	10,853	3,667	4,401	7,787	7,191
China	*621*	*1,412*	*1,440*	*49*		
Hong Kong	*724*	*435*			*1,371*	*514*
India	*523*	*583*	*205*	*1,151*	*129*	*114*
Indonesia	*3,384*	*4,272*		*116*	*303*	
Japan				*49*	*550*	*131*	*2,265*
Philippines	*261*	*1,661*	*515*		*1,510*	*1,519*
Singapore			*148*	*1,135*	*1,857*	*700*
Thailand	*395*	*1,960*	*504*		*1,718*	*536*
Australasia—of which:	4,346	7,728	6,156	8,048	4,298	4,170
Australia	*4,346*	*7,728*	*5,406*	*7,746*	*3,806*	*3,999*
Total	**42,830**	**67,425**	**56,651**	**72,392**	**110,885**	**108,447**

Adapted from *Project Finance International* (for references see Table 2.1).

- *Mexico:* A high level of activity in the power and telecommunications sectors.
- *Germany:* A sharp increase in 2000, based mainly on mobile phone and cable projects.
- *Italy:* The growth in 2000/1 reflects the beginning of Italy's PPP program, as well as a number of major power project telecommunications financings.
- *Portugal:* Figures reflect an active program of PPPs in road construction
- *United Kingdom:* A major user of project finance for its PFI (PPP) program, as well as for telecommunications and power projects.
- *Turkey:* Project finance has mainly been for power-generation projects.
- *Spain:* 2001 figures reflect some major financings in the telecommunications and infracture sectors, as well as power projects.
- *Australia:* Like the United Kingdom, Australia has a substantial PPP program, and project finance is also used for natural resources and power-generation projects
- *Japan:* The development of Japan's PPP program is reflected in the 2001 figures.

In the Middle East, project finance has been used for petrochemical, LNG, and (more recently) power-generation projects, and it tends to fluctuate from year to year based on relatively few large projects. Project finance was used heavily in Asia in 1996–1997 for power-generation projects, many of which suffered badly from the catastrophic currency devaluations of 1997 (cf. §9.3.5), and by 2001 the overall level of project finance business in Asia was still low compared to similar markets in Latin America. In particular, after promising initial growth in the power sector, development of project finance in China and India has so far been limited. Similarly, the effect of the Russian debt repudiation of 1998 is evident.

§3.1.2 BANKS IN THE MARKET

It is usually preferable for a project in a particular country to raise its funding from banks operating in that country, first because they have the best understanding of local conditions, and second because the funding can be provided in the currency of the country, so avoiding foreign exchange risks (cf. §9.3, but note also 10.3.1). Thus in developed countries projects are normally financed by local banks or foreign banks with branch or subsidiary operations in the country concerned. Such financing constitutes the largest proportion of the project finance market.

In some developing countries, however, this approach may not be possible. There may be no market for long-term loans in the domestic banking market, or the domestic banks may have no experience in project finance. In some developing countries (such as India and Brazil), there are public-sector local development

Table 3.2

Major Lead Managers of Bank Project Finance Loans, 2001 [a]

Lead Manager	Country	Amount ($ millions)	Number of Loans	Average Loan ($ millions)
Citigroup	U.S.A.	15,512	54	287
West LB	Germany	8,235	27	305
BNP Paribas	France	6,429	29	222
Société Générale	France	5,301	17	312
Credit Suisse First Boston	Switzerland	4,742	8	593
JP Morgan	U.S.A.	4,333	18	241
Dresdner Kleinwort Wasserstein	Germany	4,038	17	238
ABN Amro	Netherlands	4,019	19	212
Deutsche Bank	Germany	3,623	14	259
Barclays Bank	U.K.	3,612	18	201
Mizuho Financial Group	Japan	3,187	20	159
Intesa BCI	Italy	2,621	5	524
Bank of America	U.S.A.	2,282	13	176
Crédit Lyonnais	France	2,019	12	168
Royal Bank of Scotland	U.K.	1,1911	16	119
SEB	Sweden	1,582	2	791
Bank of Tokyo-Mitsubishi	Japan	1,573	18	87
ANZ Bank	Australia	1,532	12	128
Santander Central Hispano	Spain	1,465	10	147
Crédit Agricole Indosuez	France	1,366	10	137

Adapted from *Project Finance International* (for references see Table 2.1).
[a]These are banks which arranged and underwrote loans (cf. §5.1.2), subunderwriters and participating banks are not included; loans with more than one lead manager are divided *pro rata*.

banks that can help to fill the gap if the local commercial banks are not able to provide the funding needed, but their capacity is also limited. Thus the international banking market also plays a major role in project finance for developing countries.

It can be said that there is an inner circle of some 20 major banks that put together project finance transactions as Lend Managers on a worldwide basis, with reasonably large project finance operations concentrated in key locations around the world. At a minimum, a leading international project finance bank will have one project finance office in the United States (covering the Americas), one in Europe (covering Europe, the Middle East, and Africa), and one in Asia/Australasia, and perhaps 50 professional staff (at least) in these offices. The top 20 banks in 2001 are set out in Table 3.2.

In 2001 a total of 123 banks were Lead Managers of project finance loans, the majority of these working jointly in groups of banks (cf. §5.1.5). By comparing the figures for the top 20 in Table 3.2 with those in Table 3.1, it can be seen that these banks with some $80 billion of transactions, accounted for over 70% of the bank project finance loan market.

There is a considerable difference in the volume of project finance business arranged by the banks at the top of the table and those lower down. The top banks are involved in the complete range of project finance products and arrange:

- Domestic project finance in their own countries (e.g., a loan for a U.S. project in US$, lent from the New York branch of a U.S. bank)
- Domestic project finance in other countries in which they have branch operations (e.g., a loan for an Australian project in Australian $, lent from the Sydney branch of a U.S. bank)
- Cross-border loans (e.g., a loan for an Australian project in US$, lent from the New York branch of a U.S. bank).

Some of the banks lower in Table 3.2 tend to specialize more in a particular country, region, or type of financing, and therefore play a major role in such specialized areas.

There are many other banks participating in the project finance market at the next level down as subunderwriters or participants in syndicated loans. Some of these participate in domestic lending in their own countries, others in syndications of a wider range of loans around the world originally arranged and underwritten by

Table 3.3

Project Finance Bond Issues, 1996–2001

($ millions)	1996	1997	1998	1999	2000	2001
Americas—of which:	1,475	5,116	6,958	16,070	16,099	21,056
U.S.A.	*1,142*	*2,551*	*4,018*	*11,944*	*11,313*	*16,334*
Canada			*335*	*1,863*	*489*	
Argentina		*610*	*513*	*296*	*625*	*363*
Brazil					*875*	*1,050*
Chile	*162*		*362*		*430*	*1,289*
Mexico		*309*	*770*	*892*	*1,831*	*1,250*
Western Europe—of which:	1,230	936	1,334	2,364	2,790	945
U.K.	*1,230*	*936*	*1,034*	*1,212*	*2,498*	*240*
Central Europe and CIS	0	150	0	0	363	0
Middle East and North Africa	1,350	0	300	750	175	0
Sub-Saharan Africa	0	0	0	158	0	51
Asia—of which:	736	615	40	132	0	2,631
Indonesia	*651*	*400*				
Malaysia						*1,709*
South Korea				*132*		*652*
Australasia—of which:	0	680	1,160	492	1,384	590
Australia		*680*	*1,160*	*492*	*1,293*	*460*
Total	**4,791**	**7,497**	**9,792**	**19,966**	**20,811**	**25,003**

Adapted from *Project Finance International* (for references see Table 2.1).

the larger players in the market (cf. §5.1.8). Therefore, actual project finance lending, as opposed to loan arrangement, is spread among a reasonably wide range of banks.

§3.2 BOND ISSUES

A bond issued by a Project Company is basically similar to a loan from the borrower's point of view, but it is aimed mainly at the nonbanking market and takes the form of a tradable debt instrument (cf. §5.2). The issuer (i.e., the Project Company) agrees to repay to the bond holder the amount of the bond plus interest on fixed future installment dates. Buyers of project finance bonds are investors who require a good long-term fixed-rate return without taking equity risk, in particular insurance companies and pension funds. (Note that a bond in this context has nothing to do with "bonding" or "bonds" issued as security, e.g., in an EPC Contract—cf. §7.1.10. Bonds may also be referred to as "securities," "notes," or "debentures.") The market for project finance bonds is far narrower in scope than that for bank loans, but significant in certain countries.

The figures for the bond market in Table 3.3 show that no less than $16 billion of the total of $25 billion of project finance bonds issued in 2001 were placed for projects in the United States, but in addition to this bond financing is also raised in the United States for projects outside the country, especially in Latin America. The recent growth of the U.S. market for project finance bonds primarily reflects a lower continuing demand for bonds in the power sectors.

A few other countries have developed domestic bond markets where investors are prepared to invest in project finance bonds; this is the case with Canada, the United Kingdom, and Australia, and (in 2001) Malaysia and South Korea. As can also be seen in Table 3.3, the development of the project bond market in Asia was badly hit by the 1997 crisis.

Nor surprisingly, given the U.S. preponderance in the bond market, the investment banks most active in placing project finance bonds are also mainly U.S.-based, or with strong New York operations (Table 3.4). As can be seen by comparison with Table 3.3, these "top ten" in Table 3.4 accounted for 90% of the total market for bond placements in 2001.

§3.3 MEZZANINE AND SUBORDINATED DEBT

Subordinated debt is debt whose repayment ranks after repayments to senior bank lenders or bond investors (senior debt), but before distributions of profits to investors. It is usually provided at a fixed rate of interest higher than the cost of senior debt.

Table 3.4

Major Lead Managers of Project Finance Bond Issues, 2001

Manager	Country	$ million	No. of issues
Lehman Brothers	U.S.A.	7,621	13
Citigroup	U.S.A.	4,966	17
Credit Suisse First Boston	Switzerland	4,640	11
Goldman Sachs	U.S.A.	1,825	2
Bank of America	U.S.A.	1,045	3
Korea Development Bank	South Korea	555	1
ABN Amro	Netherlands	474	2
Morgan Stanley	U.S.A.	421	1
Banco Bilbao Vizcaya Argentaria	Spain	418	2
Bank Utarna	Malaysia	398	1

Adapted from *Project Finance International* (for references see Table 2.1).

Subordinated debt may be provided by investors as part of their equity investment (for the reasons set out in 12.7.2); as between lenders and investors, such debt is treated in the same way as equity.

Other subordinated debt (often referred to as "mezzanine debt" in this context) may be provided by third parties, usually non-bank investors, such as insurance companies or specialized funds, in cases where either there is a gap between the amount that senior lenders are willing to provide and the total debt requirements of the project, or in lieu of part of the equity to produce more competitive pricing for the Project Company's output or service. Mezzanine debt may also be provided by institutional investors as part of a debt package including bond financing.

Bringing subordinated debt into the financing package obviously creates issues of repayment priority and control over the project between the different levels of lenders (cf. 13.13.5).

§3.4 LEASE FINANCE

In a lease finance structure, the equipment being financed is owned by the lessor (lender) rather than the lessee (borrower). The lessee pays lease rentals instead of interest and principal payments (debt service) on a loan, but other things being equal (e.g., assuming the implied interest rate for the financing included in the lease rental payments is the same as the loan interest rate), payments under a lease or a loan should be the same.

It should be noted that in this context leasing means a lease of equipment to the project company as a way of raising finance. This has to be distinguished from a property (real estate) lease in a BLT/BLOT structure, which as already mentioned is one way of giving the Project Company control of the project instead of full ownership, but does not imply the provision of any finance (cf. §2.3).

Leasing is most commonly used for financing vehicles, factory machinery, and similar equipment, and it tends either to offer finance to clients who cannot otherwise raise funding, based on the security offered by the value of the equipment, or allows the lessee to use the equipment for a short period of time and then return it, with the lessor taking the residual value risk. Both of these types of finance are expensive compared to direct loans, and neither of them are normally relevant to a project finance situation.

The merit of linking lease finance with project finance comes from the use of tax benefits. In some countries (e.g., the United States, the United Kingdom, and Japan) lessors can take advantage of accelerated tax depreciation through their ownership of the equipment that is the subject of the project finance (cf. §12.7.1). Accelerated tax depreciation is only useful if the owner of the equipment has taxable profits that this depreciation can be used to reduce, but in the early years of a project's operation this may not be the case. If so, it may be better for the equipment to be owned by a lessor who can take advantage of the tax depreciation by offsetting it against its other taxable revenue, and pass part of this benefit back to the Project Company (as lessee), in the form of a reduced cost of finance (i.e., the lease rentals are lower than debt service payments would be under a loan). In deciding whether to use lease finance, the Project Company has to assess whether the benefit of this reduced financing cost outweighs the loss of the tax depreciation.

If the project assets are being used to provide a service to the public sector, however, there is an issue whether lease finance should be encouraged, as the apparent lower cost produced is obviously at the expense of tax revenues.

Two structures can be used to bring lease finance into a project:

Leveraged lease. The equipment is purchased using equity provided by a lease investor, which may be a lease finance company or another company (or even individuals in some countries) that can use the tax depreciation from this investment to shelter their tax liabilities, together with debt provided by banks (without recourse to the lease equity investor). Leveraged leases are used in countries such as the United States and Japan.

Guaranteed lease. In some countries, such as the United Kingdom, the leveraged lease structure is not possible for tax reasons, and the lessor provides the whole of the finance. As lease finance companies generally are not equipped to assess project finance risks, the lessor is often guaranteed by banks, who thus take the same kind of risk as if they were lenders, but without actually providing funding directly. (The level of risk they take may, however, be higher than if they were lending directly; if the lease is terminated early, additional tax liabilities will need to be covered.)

It is sometimes claimed that an additional merit of leasing is that it provides 100% finance: this is correct in the sense that 100% of the cost of the equipment being financed is covered; however, this does not mean that 100% of the project's overall costs are financed:

- Lease finance is unlikely to be available to pay for land acquisition.
- Tax leasing for buildings is usually less attractive than leasing of equipment.
- "Soft" costs such as development costs and interest during construction are often not covered—and thus even if no other debt is raised investor equity will still be needed. Furthermore, the loss of the residual value of the equipment which may occur with some lease structures is an additional hidden cost.

"Synthetic" leveraged leases have been used for some project finance transactions in the United States. These are leases that for tax purposes transfer ownership and hence tax benefits to the lessee (thus leaving the lessee in the same position for tax purposes as a borrower), but for accounting purposes are treated as off-balance-sheet "operating" leases, i.e. leases where ultimate economic ownership theoretically lies with the lessor, because the lessee has the right to return the equipment after a period of use, although in reality this right will not be exercised. (To make the return option unattractive, at the end of the lease period the lessee may either have to renew the lease or exercise an option to purchase the equipment for the outstanding debt and lease equity; if neither of these happens, the lessee must pay a large lump-sum rental payment and the equipment is sold.) This type of lease finance may be used as a way of manipulating reported earnings, if the lease rental payments in the early years of the project are structured to be lower than the total of accounting depreciation (cf. §12.7.1) and interest payments on a loan, while minimising tax payments. It is therefore more suitable for relatively short-term financing (typically up to 5–7 years) during construction and early operation of a project, which may then be refinanced. It has been especially used for "warehousing" gas turbines which have been ordered in advance for use in power generation projects.

In summary, however, lease finance is a "bolt-on" to the basic finance structure whose primary merit is a reduction in financing costs, or an improvement in reported earnings; it does not change the fundamental approach to the finance by either Sponsors or financiers.

§3.5 VENDOR FINANCE

In some cases, finance may be offered by a seller of equipment, an EPC Contractor, or a supplier of services to the project (a vendor in this context). An equipment supplier, for example, may have a better understanding of the technical risks of the project, or of the industry concerned, than a commercial lender, and therefore be willing to take risks unacceptable to the financial markets. Vendor finance may thus enable a supplier to increase sales and open up new markets.

Vendor finance may take the form of a loan (i.e., selling the equipment on credit), a lease of equipment, or even a guarantee of a bank financing. A vendor just introducing banks to provide finance to the project (without any guarantee) is not providing vendor finance, which in this context means finance provided at the vendor's risk, not the banks' risk.

It has to be said, however, that finance is sometimes offered by the vendor as part of a bid to secure a contract, with little understanding of the real risks and difficulties involved, and time may be wasted by the sponsors pursuing a financing plan that turns out not to be viable when the vendor has a fuller understanding of the project structure and risks.

Therefore the security structure and risk analysis for any vendor finance should largely mirror that provided by the bank and bond financing markets, to ensure that:

- A coherent financial structure is achieved.
- The vendor is not taking excessive or unexpected risks that could affect the ability or willingness to perform under the contract.
- The vendor finance can be refinanced in due course in the general financing markets, so relieving pressure on the vendor's balance sheet.

The vendor finance option is often examined by sponsors when looking at financing alternatives, but its role in the project finance market has been limited, being primarily confined to finance for construction of mobile phone networks.

§3.6 PUBLIC-SECTOR FINANCE

Public-sector debt is sometimes provided to projects as a kind of subsidy, often on a subordinated basis to that provided by the commercial financing markets. Repayment in such cases, as with any subordinated debt, will come in second place to the senior lenders. Alternatively public-sector grants may be provided to the Project Company—these may be without any obligation for repayment (so long as the money is in fact used for the project), or may be repaid if the project reaches an agreed level of success (e.g., as reflected in its cash flow). Where there is no obligation for repayment, or repayment is highly contingent in nature, such grants may be considered by commercial lenders as equity rather than debt (cf. §4.1).

Paradoxical as it may seem, there is a wider argument for financing public infrastructure projects with private-sector equity but public-sector debt. As set out in §2.5.2, one of the reasons for using project finance for public infrastructure is that the private sector is more efficient about managing the construction and whole-life maintenance of projects, which therefore produces a lower cost for private-sector funded projects, despite the fact that the private sector (project finance) debt raised for such projects costs more than public-sector funding.

It could therefore be argued that to get the benefit of both worlds the public sector should provide the project with debt, in partnership with private equity. Private-sector lenders would say that this method loses the discipline of the due diligence and control from a third party lender that is inherent in project finance, as well as the financing creativity that the private sector can offer; however, the public sector can still get the private-sector finance market to take the risk of the project in areas where these controls may prove useful (e.g., by providing a completion guarantee), and if creativity adds value private-sector finance can still be used.

Apart from funding for developing countries from multilateral and bilateral development banks, which is not really relevant in this context, the only significant example of this type of structure to date in developed countries is the use of European Investment Bank finance (cf. §11.6.9). A similar result can be achieved by using a "double-wrapped" bond (cf. §5.2.3).

Chapter 4

Project Development and Management

The life of a project can be divided into three phases:

- *Development.* The period during which the project is conceived, the Project Contracts are negotiated and signed, and the equity and the project finance debt are put in place and available for drawing—the end of this process is known as "Financial Close" (or the "Effective Date").
- *Construction.* The period during which the project finance is drawn down and the project is built—the end of this process is often known as the "commercial operation date" (or "COD").
- *Operation.* The period during which the project operates commercially and produces cash flow to pay the lenders' debt interest and principal repayments and the investors' equity return.

The Sponsors (cf. §4.1) play the primary role during the development phase of the project, managing this process (cf. §4.2) and making use of external advisers (cf. §4.3). Where more than one Sponsor is involved, a joint-venture structure has to be agreed to (cf. §4.4). The Project Company is usually set up towards the end of the development phase and manages the project from Financial Close (cf. §4.5). The project may also be developed initially by parties other than the Sponsors through a bidding (public procurement) process for a Project Agreement, organized by the Off-taker or a public-sector authority (cf. §4.6).

§4.1 SPONSORS AND OTHER INVESTORS

In order to obtain project finance debt, the investors have to offer priority payment to the lenders, thus accepting that they will only receive their equity return after lenders have been paid their amounts due. Therefore, investors assume the highest financial risk, but at the same time they receive the largest share in the project's profit (*pro rata* to the money they have at risk) if it goes according to plan.

The active equity investors in a project are usually referred to as the Sponsors (or promoters or developers), meaning that their role is one of promotion, development, and management of the project. Even though the project finance debt may be nonrecourse (i.e., have no guarantees from the Sponsors), their involvement is important. One of the first things a lender considers when deciding to participate in a project financing is whether the Sponsors of the project are appropriate parties.

Lenders wish to have Sponsors with:

- Experience in the industry concerned and, hence, the ability to provide any technical or operating support required by the project
- A reasonable amount of equity invested in the project, which gives them an incentive to provide support to protect their investment if it gets into difficulty
- A reasonable return on their equity investment: if the return is low there may be little incentive for the Sponsors to continue their involvement with the Project Company
- Arm's-length contractual arrangements with the Project Company
- An interest in the long-term success of the project
- The financial ability (although not the obligation) to support the project if it runs into difficulty

Typical Sponsors in projects using project finance include:

- Companies who wish to improve their return on equity, or spread their risks among a wider portfolio in the relevant industry than could be financed on balance sheet with corporate debt (cf. §2.5.1)
- Companies in industries that are regulated in their own market, or in which there is limited room for expansion, and which therefore need to expand elsewhere (e.g., power utilities)
- Contractors, who use the investment in a project as a way of developing "captive" contracting business
- Equipment suppliers, again using their investment to develop "captive" business
- Operators, here also using the investment to develop their business
- Offtakers of the project's products (e.g., electricity) who do not wish (or are not able) to fund the construction of the project directly, or who are constrained from doing so by government policy, but who have the resources to invest in part of the equity (or are offered equity in return for signing an Offtake Contract)

- Fuel or other Input Suppliers, who use the project as a way of selling their products (e.g., a company supplying natural gas to a power project)

Lenders normally require the original Sponsors of the project to retain their shareholdings at least until the construction of the project is complete and it has been operating for a reasonable period of time; otherwise the perceived benefits of the particular Sponsors being involved in the project would be lost.

Sponsors may bring in other types of investors such as:

- Investment funds specializing in project finance equity
- Institutional investors, such as insurance companies and pension funds
- Shareholders in quoted equity issued by the Project Company on a local or international stock exchange
- Governments, government agencies, or other public authorities
- Local partners
- Multilateral institutions, such as International Finance Corporation (cf. §11.6.2)

Lenders will be uneasy if a significant share of the equity in a project is held by passive investors who take no active role in its promotion, development, or operation, although this concern reduces when the project has been built and is seen to be operating successfully.

Apart from Sponsors and other investors, the other possible source of "equity" for the project is public-sector grants, subsidies, or subordinated loans, which may also entitle the public sector to a share of the profits from the project (cf. 3.6).

It is evident that a Sponsor may have potential conflicts of interest between its position as a Sponsor and as a party with other contractual relationships with the Project Company. If the project is to pass the lenders' due diligence, these contractual relationships need to be conducted on an arm's-length basis. A Project Company that signs a construction contract with a contractor shareholder that is widely out of line with the market (either in its pricing or its detailed terms) is unlikely to find financing. Sponsors such as contractors and equipment suppliers may not have an obvious long-term interest in the project; in such cases lenders will be more comfortable if these Sponsors are in partnership with other Sponsors who have a long-term interest and can ensure that contracts with the equipment supplier or contractor are set up and run on an arm's-length basis.

It is not just the lenders who are concerned about the Sponsors. Other parties contracting with the Project Company may be taking a higher than normal risk of payment, in the absence of corporate guarantees. For example, the EPC Contractor knows that if the lenders turn off the tap to the Project Company, amounts outstanding under the EPC Contract are not likely to be paid. The presence of the Sponsors, with whom the EPC Contractor may have other relationships and have completed EPC Contracts on other projects, is clearly relevant, as is the extent of their financial commitment to the project (cf. §8.5.3). Similarly, the Offtaker or end-user of the project's products or services will want to ensure that it will be properly developed, financed, and operated, and the Offtaker or end user will therefore be concerned that the Sponsors can provide this technical and financial expertise to the project company (cf. §8.8.8).

In summary, a project that looks viable but does not have credible Sponsors— even if the project finance is nonrecourse—will probably not get financed. (The Sponsors' financial credibility is also of importance because they may have to fill up any gaps in the project risk by providing limited-recourse guarantees, as discussed in §8.12.)

§4.2 PROJECT DEVELOPMENT

Like any other activity in project management, using project finance requires a systematic and well-organized approach to carrying out a complex series of inter-related tasks. The additional factor in project finance is that the sponsors must be ready for outside parties—the lenders and their advisors—to review and perhaps get closely involved in what the Sponsors have been and are doing, a process that will take extra work and time. Finance can thus become a major critical-path item.

As with any new investment, the Sponsors normally undertake a feasibility study when initially considering the investment. However, if project finance is being used, then structural requirements resulting from this (e.g., the terms of the Project Contracts) also need to be considered at this early stage since these may affect the commercial approach to and hence the feasibility of the project.

Once active development of the project is under way, the Sponsors need to set up a development team with a mixture of disciplines, depending on the nature of the project:

- Engineering and construction
- Operation
- Legal, covering site acquisition, Permits, Project Contracts, loan documentation, etc.
- Accounting and tax
- Financial modeling
- Financial structuring

It is important that this team is well coordinated: one of the most common errors during project development is for the Sponsors to agree on a Project Contract that is commercially sound, but not acceptable from a project finance point of view: for example, the fuel may be cheap, but the supply contract does not cover the loan period; or the EPC Contract may be at a low price, but the financial penalties on the EPC Contractor for failure to build on time or to specification are not adequate for lenders.

As the development process on all projects runs into months, and on many projects into years, Sponsors should not underestimate the scale of costs involved. High costs are unavoidable, with the Sponsor's own development staff working for long periods of time on one project, perhaps traveling extensively or setting up a local office. The costs of external advisers (cf. §4.3) have to be added to this. Development costs can reach 2.5–5% of the project cost, and there is always a risk that the project will not move forward and all these costs will have to be written off. Cost-control systems are therefore essential. (There are also limited economies of scale—large projects also need to be more complex in structure, so the development costs also remain relatively high.)

§4.3 THE ROLE OF ADVISERS

Various external advisers are usually used by the Sponsors during the project development and financing process. They can play a valuable role, especially if the Sponsor has not undertaken many such projects in the past, since they will probably have had greater experience in a variety of projects than the sponsors' in-house staff; if a sponsor is not developing a continuous pipeline of projects, employing people with the necessary expertise just to work on one project may be difficult. Using advisers with a good record of working in successful projects also gives the project credibility with lenders.

External advisers working on the project may include:

Legal. Legal advisers have to deal not only with the Project Contracts, but also with how these interact with project finance requirements, as well as being familiar with project finance documentation. This work tends to be concentrated in a small pool of major American and English law firms who have built up the necessary mixture of expertise. However, outside the United States and United Kingdom it is also necessary to employ local legal advisers with the expertise in doing business in the country concerned, so it may be necessary to coordinate two sets of lawyers.

Because so much of project finance is about the structuring of contracts, legal advisers play a key role. But since they are usually paid for the time they spend working rather than by a fixed fee, their time needs to be used effectively. For example, the lawyer should not be unnecessarily involved in making decisions about the commercial structure of the project, and should not begin drafting contracts until the outline of the commercial deal is decided. On the other hand, lawyers' experience of commercial solutions in previous transactions can be very helpful to the Sponsors in their negotiations.

Engineering. For the role of the Owner's Engineer, cf. §7.1.5

Environmental. In most countries an environmental impact assessment

("EIA") is needed before any major project can proceed (cf. §7.4.1), for which the Sponsors will probably have to engage specialized advisers. Environmental issues are of considerable importance to many lenders, who do not want to be associated with projects causing environmental harm, even if they as lenders have no legal liability for this.

Market. Market advisers are needed for aspects of the project not covered by contracts (e.g., fuel supply, product offtake, or traffic risks) if the Sponsors do not have their own expertise in the product concerned. The expertise of these advisers, and the degree of their involvement in the project, may be significant factors for the lenders' due-diligence process.

Accountants. Accountants are often retained to advise on the accounting and tax aspects of the project, both for the Project Company itself and for the Sponsors.

Insurance. For the role of the insurance broker, cf. §7.6.

Financial advisers. cf. §5.1.2.

In addition to these advisers, the lenders use a parallel set of advisers to those employed by the Sponsors as part of their due-diligence process (cf. §5.4).

The Sponsors may also make use of other project counterparts in an advisory capacity—e.g. an O&M Contractor (cf. §7.2) may offer advice on the design of the project based on the practical experience of operating similar projects.

§4.4 JOINT-VENTURE ISSUES

Project finance is often used where the equity investment in the Project Company is split between several Sponsors (cf. §2.51).

Developing project through a joint venture adds a further layer of complexity to the process: one partner may have a good understanding of project finance while the other does not; cultural differences become more acute under the heat of a project finance scrutiny; or negotiations with the lenders may be undertaken before all intrapartnership issues have been clearly resolved. Indeed, it is not unusual for the development of a project financing to be held up, not because the lenders raise problems, but because the Sponsors have not agreed on key issues among themselves.

Good communication between sponsors is therefore especially important when using project finance. They need to form a real joint team and ensure that the divisions of roles and responsibilities is clearly defined. For example, one Sponsor may be primarily responsible for finance, another for the EPC Contract. If one of the Sponsors is going to sign a contract with the Project Company, another Sponsor should ideally control the negotiation of this contract from the Project Company side of the table to avoid the obvious conflict of interest (cf. §4.1).

Sponsors developing a project together usually sign a Development Agreement, which covers matters such as:

- The scope and structure of the project.
- An exclusivity commitment.
- Management roles and responsibilities.
- A program for feasibility studies, appointment of advisers, negotiations with EPC Contractors and other parties to the Project Contracts, and approaches to lenders.
- Rules for decision making.
- Arrangements for funding of development costs or the crediting of these costs against each Sponsor's allocation of equity (taking account of both the amount of the costs and the timing of when they were incurred).
- Adjustments of equity interests to reflect the timing of each Sponsor's investment (cf. §12.12.2).
- Provisions for "reserved roles" (if any) (e.g., if one of the Sponsors is to be appointed as the EPC Contractor without being subject to third-party competition); this is a difficult provision unless the scope and pricing basis can be agreed at the same time.
- Arrangements for withdrawal from the project and sale of a Sponsor's interest.

Major decisions on the project have to be taken unanimously, because if the project develops in a direction not acceptable to one partner, that partner will not wish to keep funding it. Lesser issues—such as appointment of an adviser—may be taken on a majority-vote basis. If a Sponsor wishes to withdraw, the other Sponsors usually have a right to purchase its share.

The Development Agreement is usually superseded by a Shareholder Agreement when the Project Company has been set up and takes over responsibility for the project (cf. §4.5.2).

§4.5 THE PROJECT COMPANY

§4.5.1 STRUCTURE

The Project Company lies at the center of all the contractual and financial relationships in project finance. These relationships have to be contained inside a project finance "box," or SPV (cf. §2.4) which means that the Project Company cannot carry out any other business which is not part of the project (since project finance depends on the lenders' ability to evaluate the project on a stand-alone basis). Thus in most cases a new company is incorporated specifically to carry out the project. The corporate form of borrower (i.e., a Project Company) is generally preferred by lenders for security and control reasons (cf. §13.7.2).

The Project Company may not always be directly owned by the Sponsors; for tax reasons the Sponsors often use an intermediary holding company in a favorable third-country tax jurisdiction (e.g., to ensure that withholding tax is not deducted from dividends).

In some projects a form other than that of a limited company is used (e.g., so that the income of the project is taxed directly at the level of the Sponsors, or tax depreciation on its capital costs can be deducted directly against Sponsors' other income rather than in the Project Company). This is usually some form of limited partnership, so the Sponsors' liability remains limited in the same way as if they were shareholders in a limited company.

For example, in oil and gas field developments, the Sponsors may use an unincorporated joint venture as a vehicle to raise funding. The Sponsors sign an operating agreement, which usually provides for one of them to be the operator, dealing with day-to-day management, subject to an operating committee. The operator enters into the Project Contracts (e.g., for construction of a rig) and makes cash calls on the other Sponsors on an agreed basis. If a Sponsor defaults, the others may undertake to pay, and the interest of a defaulter who does not remedy the situation is forfeited. The liability of the operator to third parties needs to be made clear in the Project Contracts: is the operator directly liable and relying on being reimbursed by cash calls, or acting as an agent for the other Sponsors, incurring liability on their behalf? In this structure the Sponsors usually participate through individual special-purpose companies, and may raise funding individually through these companies to cover their share of the project costs, rather than raising finance collectively for the project. This structure is beneficial for Sponsors with a good credit rating who wish to raise funds on a corporate basis, while other financially weaker partners go ahead with project finance for their share. (However, the lenders' security position may be less than ideal in such cases.)

The Project Company is usually incorporated in the country in which the project is taking place, although it may occasionally be possible, and beneficial for tax purposes, to incorporate it outside the country concerned (but cf. §10.2).

§4.5.2 SHAREHOLDER AGREEMENT

If there is more than one Sponsor, once the Project Company has been set up and is responsible for managing the implementation of the project, the Development Agreement previously signed by the Sponsors (cf. §4.2) is normally superseded by a Shareholder Agreement (although it is possible to have one agreement for both phases of the project). The Shareholder Agreement covers issues such as:

- Percentage share ownership
- Procedure for future equity subscriptions
- Voting of shares at the annual general meeting
- Board representation and voting
- Provisions to deal with conflicts of interest (e.g., if the EPC Contractor is a Sponsor, participation in board discussion or voting on issues relating to the EPC contract are not allowed.)
- Appointment and authority of management
- Distribution of profits
- Sale of shares by Sponsors (usually with a first refusal right being given to the other Sponsors)

Some of these provisions may be included in the Project Company's corporate articles rather than a separate Shareholder Agreement. The Sponsors may also have a separate agreement with the Project Company to pay in their agreed levels of equity; if so, this agreement is assigned to the lenders as part of their security.

Fifty-fifty joint ventures are not uncommon in the project finance field, and they give rise to obvious problems in decision making. In cases with more Sponsors, it may still not be possible to get a consensus where a minority partner can block a vote on major issues. Arbitration or other legal procedures are seldom a way forward in this context. Clearly, if there is a deadlock one partner will have to buy out the other, for which a suitable process has to be established.

§4.5.3 MANAGEMENT AND OPERATIONS

The Project Company should have no assets or liabilities except those directly related to the project, which is why a new company should be formed rather than reusing an existing one that may have accrued liabilities. The Project Company also agrees with the lenders not to take on any extraneous assets or liabilities in future (cf. §13.10.2).

The Project Company is often formed at a late stage in the project development process (unless project Permits have to be issued earlier, or it has to sign Project Contracts), because it normally has no function to perform until the project finance is in place. Sponsors may even sign some of the project contacts to begin with (e.g., an EPC Contract) and transfer them in due course to the Project Company. However, even if the project company comes into formal existence late in the development process (as mentioned previously), arm's-length arrangements need to be in place from an early stage for negotiating any contracts which it is going to sign with its Sponsors.

Similarly, the Project Company may not have a formal organization and management structure until a late stage, as the Sponsors' staff will be doing the project development work. There is, however, only a limited overlap between the skills needed at this development stage and those needed once the Project Company is set up and the project itself is under way, and arrangements must be made to ensure a smooth transition between the two phases of the project.

Sponsors are generally well organized in ensuring that all the engineering and construction management expertise is in place when the project begins, but sometimes they neglect the finance side of the Project Company's organization. The new Project Company needs to have in place a finance director and an accounting department who have an immediate grasp of the complex requirements of the finance documentation, not just in relation to drawing and spending the money provided under these arrangements, but also to deal with matters such as the lenders' reporting requirements.

The Project Company's personnel to manage the construction of the project may be a combination of its own staff and outside advisers such as an Owner's Engineer (cf. §7.1.5). Operation of the project may be carried out by Project Company personnel or by a third-party operator under an O&M Contract (cf. §7.2).

§4.6 PUBLIC PROCUREMENT

This description of the project development process assumes that it is entirely under the control of the Sponsors, but this is often not the case. Projects involving provisions of products or services to the public sector under a Project Agreement are often initially developed by a national or local government or other public-sector agency, which then calls for competitive bids to finance and construct the project and provide the product or service. A public procurement (competitive bidding) process is a legal requirement in many countries where public funding is being provided, or services are being provided to the public (e.g., within the European Union), and it is generally also required if project finance funding or guarantees are provided by multilateral development banks, such as the World Bank. In such cases the bidding process has to follow specific procurement procedures, as discussed below. A private-sector Offtaker (e.g., an industrial plant that requires a power plant to be built to supply its needs) may also choose to go through the same process.

The bidding process is normally carried out in several stages: prequalification (cf. §4.6.1), a request for proposals to the prequalified bidders (cf. §4.6.2); and negotiations on the bid leading to signing of the Project Agreement (cf. §4.6.3). In some cases the Project Company's own Project Contracts may have to go through a similar process (cf. §4.6.4).

§4.6.1 PREQUALIFICATION

The project is advertised in official publications and the financial and trade press. Interested bidding groups are provided with a summary of the project and its requirements, and they are invited to set out their qualifications to undertake the project, demonstrating:

- The technology proposed
- Technical capacity to carry out the project
- Experience of the personnel to be involved
- Experience and performance with similar project
- Financial capacity to carry out the project

Bidders who do not meet minimum criteria at this stage are then excluded, and the other bidders invited to bid.

Prequalification may go a stage further by drawing up an initial short list of bidders (preferably no more than around four to six), if the relevant procurement rules allow this (World Bank procurement rules, for example, do not). This procedure is often desirable because if there are too many bidders for the project the chances of winning the bid may be too small to make it worth the prospective bidders' while, given the considerable time and cost involved in preparing and submitting a bid. Of course fewer bidders also make managing the whole process easier.

§4.6.2 REQUEST FOR PROPOSALS

A formal request for proposals (RFP—also known as an invitation to tender (ITT) or invitation to negotiate (ITN)) is then sent out to the prequalified or short-listed bidders. This is accompanied with an information package that sets out, e.g.:

- General legislative background
- Project *raison d'être*
- Data on the market, traffic flows, and so on (for some types of infrastructure projects)
- Availability, service, and other output requirements
- Proposed pricing formula
- Draft Project Agreement (or summarized terms)
- The basis of the bid evaluation
- The form of bid required
- Bid deadline

It is important that the RFP does not overspecify what is required. In particular, the output—a product or service—should be ideally specified, not the input, or how the output is delivered. Thus if bids are requested for a power station, the RFP should specify the capacity in megawatts, but not the model of turbine that should be used to generate the power. In some projects, however, especially if the project assets have a longer useful life and are taken over at the end of the contract period under a BOT/BOOT/BTO structure, there will also inevitably be a degree of input specification.

The response to the RFP is likely to be required to cover aspects such as:

- Technology
- Design and engineering
- Construction program
- Details of works or services to be provided
- Management structures for both the construction and operation phases
- Quality and safety assurance procedures
- Commercial viability (e.g., traffic or demand projections)
- Operation and maintenance policy
- Insurance coverage
- Project costs (both construction, and operation and maintenance). These may be required to assess the overall financial feasibility of the bid, though concerns about commercial confidentiality may arise.
- Financing strategy and structure (cf. §5.1.4)
- Qualifications to RFP contract or other requirements
- Proposals for the Tariff, tolls, or other charges for the project

Apart from responding to specific requirements in the RFP, bidders' proposals need to demonstrate:

- An understanding of the requirements of the project
- How the bidder will achieve these requirements, including staffing
- Any advantages the bidder's approach may have over the competition

Fairness and transparency in the bidding process are essential; if bidders do not understand or trust the process, or do not believe there is a genuine competition in which they have a good prospect of winning, it is evident that the best results will not be achieved. Thus, a full and detailed record should be kept of the bid comparisons and why a particular bidder was chosen. Particular issues that may arise on the bidding process include:

Bid-evaluation system. If the bidding procedure is to have any real value, the bids have to be compared with each other. This means that bids must be submitted using common assumptions where this is appropriate (e.g., as to the cost of fuel, raw materials, interest rates, etc.). The prequalification process should have already eliminated bidders for whom there are questions about financial capacity (as Sponsors), technology, or ability to undertake the project, so further fundamental qualitative comparisons of this nature should be limited in scope.

There are two main approaches for comparing the bids:

- *Price comparison.* If the bids can be submitted on virtually identical bases, then the final decision may be a question of simply comparing the bid prices.

  If the price bases of different bids fluctuate over time (i.e., payments under a long-term Project Agreement), it is necessary to discount the amounts payable in future to a net present value (NPV) (cf. §12.8.1) to compare like with like.

- *Scoring.* A more complex system may be needed: such a system is often based on scoring different aspects of the bid—giving points for price, speed of completion, reliability, quantity or quality of whatever is being provided, risk assumption by the bidder (i.e., transfer of risk away from the public sector), and any other characteristics that are important to the project, and further adjusting for bids that are considered overambitious in their projections of performance, financing plans, as well as for the cost of exceptions to the proposed terms of the Project Agreement thus identifying the bid that is both realistic and the most economically advantageous to the project.

  Scoring systems can be beneficial in that—like a simple comparison on price—they should be relatively transparent and the weight given to different factors can be set out in the RFP, however, it may be difficult to reduce different aspects of the bid to common numerical formulæ.

Some bids are not based on the price to be charged for the product or service but the level of subsidy to be provided by the public sector. This approach is relevant if the bid relates to a service provided to the general public in return for the payment of tolls or fares, the levels of which are fixed and which do not produce sufficient revenue to cover the funding required for the project.

The technical and financial competence of the bidders normally should not be a basis for decision on the bids, as this should have already been considered at the prequalification stage. However, the overall financing plan for the project (i.e., the terms on which project finance debt is to be raised) does need to be examined (cf. §5.1.4).

Nonconforming bids. It is often beneficial not to be too prescriptive about the bid requirements, since bidders may then use their imagination to come up with innovative solutions for the project which, although not previously considered, may actually be more beneficial.

A standard procedure is that bidders must make at least one bid that conforms to the requirements of the RFP, but they may also offer alternative bids that do not conform. The recipient then has the option to choose a nonconforming bid if it offers a better solution.

Communication with bidders. The same information should be made available to all bidders. This can be achieved in several ways: (a) by holding meetings and site visits which all builders attend, which helps to flush out any major issues that bidders may have with the project; and (b) written answers to questions or issues raised by one bidder can also be copied to all of them, without indicating who asked the original question.

Modifications. Discussions with bidders may lead to modifications in the bid requirements: in such cases the bid schedule may have to be delayed to give bidders enough time to deal with these modifications.

Bid consortium changes. After a particular bidding consortium has been prequalified, one of its members may not wish to proceed, and the consortium may wish to introduce a new member, perhaps a bidder in a consortium that previously did not prequalify. Other bidders may object to this, but it may be preferable not to exclude changes of this kind completely and to leave some discretion on the matter (e.g., if the new member can demonstrate it is as well qualified as the one it is succeeding). An alternative approach is to allow changes in the consortium only after the winning bid has been selected; however, no bidder should be allowed to participate in more than one consortium at the same time, as this could lead to leakages of information or collusion between consortia.

Bonding. Bidders are commonly required to provide bid bonds from their bankers, as security for their proceeding with the bid once it has been made. The bond is released when the contract documentation is signed, or when construction of the project begins. The amount of the bond may be quite significant in absolute terms (e.g., 1–2% of the project value). This helps to deal with the problem of deliverability (i.e., presentation of an aggressive bid that cannot be financed, or where the bidders hope to improve their position once they are the preferred bidder).

Compensation for cancellation. The corollary of bonding for bidders is an agreement by the public authority conducting the bid that if the process is canceled at any stage bidders should be compensated for the costs they have incurred, perhaps up to a certain limit. Losing bidders may even be given some compensation for their costs in any case, to encourage competition in a complex project.

§4.6.3 Bid Negotiation to Contract Signing

A further stage of bidding may be gone through, in which discussions on the bids and the detailed terms of the Project Agreement take place and the project specifications and contract terms are clarified, and a final decision may be made at this stage. (This is not acceptable under some procurement procedures, on the basis that such issues should be settled before the initial bid, and negotiations of this type cloud the transparency of the procedure.) Alternatively, two or three of the short-listed bidders may then be invited to submit revised "best and final offers" ("BAFOs"), taking account of revised project specifications and documentation that reflect these discussions (again assuming procurement procedures allow this second round of bids).

When the bid recipient has chosen a preferred bidder, a letter of intent (LOI, or memorandum of understanding—MOU) is signed setting out the basic terms of the transaction, as the first step to concluding a final contract. Negotiation of the MOU and the detailed contract should theoretically be quick and simple if model contracts were included in the RFP package and bidders were required to raise any exceptions (i.e., objections) to anything in the contracts at the time of their bid.

Some bidders, however, may not raise exceptions in the bid, but do so by way of "clarifications" after they have been appointed as the preferred bidder. Pressure to get the project under way may seriously affect the ability of the bid recipient to resist the preferred bidder making changes to the Project Agreement in this way. This danger of "deal creep" becomes much greater if the requirements for the project are not initially specified in enough detail, or are changed after the preferred bidder has been appointed, which is especially likely in a large and complex project. Much of the benefit for the public sector of using private-sector finance may be eroded in this way. Ideally, one or more other bidders should be required to keep their bids on the table in case the preferred bidder tries to take advantage of this position.

It must also be borne in mind that where bidding has been carried out under public procurement rules, significant changes to the winning bid cannot be agreed without reopening the competition to new bids.

§4.6.4 COMPETITIVE BIDDING FOR OTHER PROJECT CONTRACTS

As to the Project Company's other contracts, under European Union procurement law a Project Company does not have to go through a competitive bidding procedure where it is signing a contract for services with a controlling shareholder, but may have to do so in other cases, including an EPC Contract if it has a Project Agreement with the public sector.

Under the World Bank's procurement rules, if the Project Company itself (or its Sponsors) has gone through a competitive bid to secure the Project Agreement, then the Project Company does not have to put its own contracts (such as the EPC

Contract) out for bidding, but if not, any Project Contracts to be financed by the World Bank have to go through a bidding procedure.

If such competitive bidding for other Project Contracts is required by law, a prospective bidder who is excluded or unfairly treated in the bidding process has the right to sue the Project Company for damages (e.g., loss of profit), or in some cases have the contract canceled. Therefore lenders will want to ensure that correct procedures were followed in placing all Project Contracts.

Chapter 5

Working with Lenders

This chapter covers the procedures for raising project finance from private-sector lenders, in particular commercial banks (cf. §5.1) and bond investors (cf. §5.2), with a comparison between the two (cf. §5.3).

The financing and additional credit support that can be obtained from public-sector sources, in particular export credit agencies (such as U.S. EximBank) and multilateral development banks (such as the World Bank) are discussed in Chapter 11.

The nature and roles of the various external advisers used by lenders are also considered (cf. §5.4).

§5.1 COMMERCIAL BANKS

Most commercial banks in the project finance field have specialist departments that work on putting project finance deals together. There are three main approaches to organizing such departments:

Project finance department. The longest standing approach is to have a department purely specializing in project finance transactions. Larger departments are divided into industry teams, covering sectors such as energy, infrastructure, and telecommunications. Concentrating all the project finance expertise in one department ensures an efficient use of resources and good cross-fertilization, using experience of project finance for different industries; however, it may not offer clients the best range of services.

Structured finance department. As mentioned in §2.4, the divisions between project finance and other types of structured finance are becoming increas-

49

ingly blurred, and therefore project finance often forms part of a larger structured finance operation. Again there may be a division into industry teams.
This approach may offer a more sophisticated range of products, but there is
some danger that project finance may not fit easily into the operation if other
business is based on a much shorter time horizon.

Industry-based departments. Another approach is to combine all financing
for a particular industry sector (e.g., electricity, oil and gas, or infrastructure)
in one department; if this industry makes regular use of project finance, project finance experts form part of the team. This provides one-stop services
to the bank's clients in that particular industry, but obviously may dimin-
ish cross-fertilization between project finance experience and different
industries.

In the end good communication and cooperation within the bank are probably
more important than the formal organization.

In general, the project finance personnel in these departments have banking or
finance backgrounds, although some banks employ in-house engineers and other
specialists, including people with relevant industry experience. Even though most
of the personnel are not experts in construction, engineering, or other nonfinancial
disciplines, by working on a variety of transactions over time they develop experience and expertise in various industries and the technical and practical issues
that can affect the viability of a project; however, banks also rely extensively on
specialized external advisers (cf. §5.4).

Project finance is a time-consuming process for banks and uses well-qualified
and therefore expensive staff; some past market leaders have withdrawn from the
business because the bank has come to the decision that a better return on capital can be obtained from other types of structured finance or from concentrating
on retail banking. Nonetheless as Table 3.2 illustrates, most major international
banks remain active in the market.

Projects need to be of a reasonable minimum size to provide banks with enough
revenue to make the time spent on them worthwhile. Arranging debt for a project
much under, say, $25 million, is unlikely to be economic (unless it is part of a pro-
duction line of very similar projects for which the same template can be used), and
most major banks would prefer to work on projects of, say, $100 million or more.

§5.1.1 ADVISERS AND LEAD MANAGERS

There are two different financial roles in the project-development process:
financial adviser and lead manager.

The financial adviser. Unless the sponsors are experienced in project development, problems are highly likely to be caused by negotiation (or even signature) of Project Contract arrangements that are later found to be unac-

ceptable to the banking market. Therefore Sponsors without in-house project finance expertise need financial advice to make sure they are on the right track as they develop the project.

Financial advisory services can be provided to Sponsors by major banks, such as the "top 20" listed in §3.2, or other banks with specialized knowledge of a particular market, as well as investment banks (i.e., banks that arrange finance but that do not normally lend money themselves), major international accounting or management consulting firms, specialist project finance advisory firms or individual advisers.

The Financial Adviser in project finance has a more wide-ranging role than would be the case in general corporate finance. The structure of the whole project must meet project finance requirements, so the Financial Adviser must anticipate all the issues that might arise during the lenders' due-diligence process, ensuring that they are addressed in the Project Contracts or elsewhere.

The terms of the Financial Adviser's engagement are set out in an Advisory Agreement, usually signed with the Sponsors. (The Sponsors may transfer the Advisory Agreement to the Project Company in the latter stages of the project development process.) The Financial Adviser's scope of work under an Advisory Agreement includes:

- Advising on the optimum financial structure for the project
- Assisting in the preparation of a financial plan
- Advising on sources of debt and likely financing terms
- Assisting in preparing a financial model for the project
- Advising on the financing implications of Project Contracts and assisting in their negotiation
- Preparing an information memorandum to present the project to the financial markets
- Advising on assessing proposals for financing
- Advising on selection of commercial bank lenders or placement of bonds
- Assisting in negotiation of financing documentation

Financial Advisers are usually paid by a combination of fixed or time-based retainer fees, and a success fee on conclusion of the financing. Major out-of-pocket costs, such as travel, are also paid by the Sponsors. These costs are charged on to the Project Company in due course as part of the development costs.

The Financial Adviser obviously needs to have a good record of achieving successful financing on projects of the same type, and (if possible) in the same country as the project concerned. Sponsors also need to ensure that the individual actually doing the work has this experience, rather than just relying on the general reputation and record of the Financial Adviser.

These financial advisory services may be essential to the successful development of the project, but they are necessarily expensive (costing around 0.5–1% of the debt amount on an average-sized project; however a large part of this may be successed-based). Costs may be reduced by using smaller advisory boutiques or individual consultants, but less experienced developers may feel uneasy about not using a big name adviser. There is also always some risk that the Financial Adviser—however well qualified—thinks a project is financeable but the banking market does not agree.

Lead manager(s). The normal approach to arranging a project finance loan is to appoint one or more banks as Lead Manager(s), who will ultimately underwrite the debt and place it in the market. (Other terms are used for this role, such as arranger or lead arranger.) As with a Financial Adviser, experience of lending to the type of project and in the country concerned are key factors in selecting a Lead Manager; a wider banking relationship with one or more of the Sponsors is often another element in the decision. Lead Managers' fees are predominately based on a successful conclusion of the financing, although there may be a small retainer, and advisers' (cf. §5.4) and other out-of-pocket costs, such as travel, are usually covered by the Sponsors.

One of the first questions Sponsors have to consider on the financing side is when the Lead Managers should be brought into the transaction. Ideally, to ensure the maximum competition between banks on the financing terms, the whole of the project package should be finalized (including all the Project Contracts) and a number of banks then invited to bid in a competition to underwrite and provide the loan as Lead Managers. This implies either that the Sponsors make use of a Financial Adviser to put this package together, or do it themselves if they have the experience (cf. §5.4.6).

The alternative approach is to agree with one or more banks at an early stage of the project development process that they will act both as Financial Adviser and Lead Manager. This should reduce the cost of the combined financial advisory and banking underwriting fees, and also ensure that the advice given is based on what the banks are themselves willing to do, and therefore that the project should be financeable.

In this case a mandate letter is normally signed between the Sponsors and the Lead Manager(s), which provides for services similar to those of the Financial Adviser set out above, but also expresses the banks' intention—subject to due diligence, credit clearance, and agreement on detailed terms—to underwrite the debt required; some indication of pricing and other debt terms may also be given, although this may be difficult at an early stage of the transaction. This mandate letter usually does not impose a legal obligation on the bank(s) to underwrite or lend money for the project.

The obvious problem with this approach is that the banks are not in a competitive position (even if there may have originally been some kind of bidding process for the mandate), and therefore the Sponsors will probably not get the most aggressive final terms for the financing. However, this may be a reasonable price to pay for the greater efficiency of the process and greater certainty of obtaining finance that this method affords. Clearly the general relationship between the Sponsors and the banks concerned may also affect this decision.

It is also possible for the Sponsors to stipulate that they will have the right to "market test" the final financing package by asking for competitive bids from other banks, and if the original Lead Managers are found not to be competitive, the financing will be moved to new banks. (However, this may hold up conclusion of the financing and therefore not be practical unless the original Lead Managers have become so out of line with the market that it is worth the loss of time and extra legal and other costs that are likely to be involved in going elsewhere.)

In major projects, both a Financial Adviser and Lead Manager(s) may be appointed separately at an early stage to provide more balanced advice, although obviously this adds to development costs.

Throughout the due-diligence process, the Financial Advisers or Lead Managers are likely to play an active role in the negotiation of Project Contracts, such as the Project Agreement, EPC Contract, Input Supply Contract, etc., to ensure that financing implications of these contracts are taken into account. Any changes in the Project Contracts that are good for the Sponsors are generally good for the banks too, and so the banks are also frequently used by Sponsors to improve their commercial position in these negotiations.

§5.1.2 LETTERS OF INTENT

Banks commonly provide letters of intent (or letters of interest) to Sponsors early in the development of a project. These are usually short—1–2 pages long—and confirm the banks' basic interest in getting involved in the project. If the letter requires the Sponsors to deal exclusively with the banks concerned, this may amount to a Lead Managers' mandate letter as described in §5.1.2. Alternatively, the Sponsors may collect a number of such letters from different banks. Letters of this nature provide the Sponsors with initial reassurance that the financing market is interested in their project, and help to give the Sponsors credibility with other prospective Project Contract counterparts, such as fuel suppliers, product purchasers, governments, etc.

Although some banks treat them more seriously than others, such letters should not be regarded as any kind of commitment on the banks' part. Many banks issue these letters without going through any internal credit approval procedure. They are primarily used by banks to ensure they keep their foot in the door of the project, and they should not be interpreted as anything stronger than that.

§5.1.3 LENDERS AND THE PUBLIC-PROCUREMENT PROCESS

Rather than independently developing their own project, Sponsors may have to bid in a public-procurement process for a Project Agreement (cf. §4.6).

Financial Advisers and Lead Managers are normally involved in this process. When the bid is submitted, bidders may have to provide proof that financing can be arranged. This may be no more than letters of intent from banks expressing their willingness to provide finance to the bidder for the project, but which do not commit the banks to do so (see above). If a separate Financial Adviser is used, the adviser normally also provides a support letter for the bid, confirming that in their view the project can be successfully financed.

At the other end of the scale, banks may be required to go through a full due-diligence process, put together a detailed financing package, obtain credit approvals, and perhaps even have agreed documentation with the bidders, to demonstrate that the financing can be provided and thus the project can begin without delay. The disadvantage of the latter is that a full underwriting commitment by banks may involve fee payments (and higher legal costs), and bidders may be unwilling to pay for this with no certainty that they will win the bid—in such cases it is not uncommon for losing bidders' costs to be covered up to an agreed level by the bid recipient.

It is also possible for the bid for the project to be separated from the bid for the financing—i.e., the bid process is carried out on preset common financing assumptions, and once the preferred bidder has been appointed and the Project Contracts agreed to, the financing itself is put out for competitive bidding in the market. The payments under the Project Agreement are then adjusted from the bid pricing to take account of the actual financing costs and structure.

§5.1.4 BANK ROLES

Larger loans may require more than one bank to underwrite the financing. When several banks are involved as Lead Managers, they normally divide up responsibilities for various aspects of the transaction, which enables them to use their resources more effectively. Typical divisions of roles between the banks are:

- Documentation, in conjunction with the banks' lawyers (perhaps with banks subdividing between Project Contracts and the financing documentation); however, unless there are a lot of banks involved, all the banks in the transaction normally want to be closely involved in this area.
- Engineering (in liaison with the Lenders' Engineer—cf. §5.4.2)

- Financial modeling (cf. §5.1.6)
- Insurance (in liaison with the insurance adviser—cf. §5.4.3)
- Market or traffic review (in liaison with the banks' market or traffic advisers—§5.4.5)
- Preparation of the information memorandum (cf. §5.1.8)
- Syndication (cf. §5.1.8)
- Loan agency (cf. §5.1.9)

There are varying degrees of perceived prestige (and in some cases division of the arrangement fees) involved with these various roles, and the Sponsors may have to intervene to decide who is doing what if the banks cannot agree between themselves. However banks are used to working in teams in this way in the project finance market, which is more "cooperative" than some other forms of financing—banks that compete against each other in one deal may be working together in the next, and people from different banks working together on a deal for a prolonged period of time may well get to know each other better than they do their fellow employees in their own banks. Thus the banks should be able to work together smoothly without too much intervention from the Sponsors. The Sponsors should of course try to ensure that the banks with the best experience in the relevant field undertake the work.

§5.1.5 FINANCIAL MODEL

Throughout the due-diligence process, the Financial Adviser or Lead Manager develops a financial model for the project (if it is developed by a Financial Adviser, it is normally passed on to the banks for their use). The structure and inputs required for a financial model, and the ways in which its output is used, are discussed in detail in Chapter 12.

The development of the financial model should ideally be a joint operation between the Sponsors and the Financial Adviser or Lead Manager, probably with each assigning one or two people to work in a joint team. Although the Sponsors should have already developed their own model at an early stage of the project's development to assess its basic feasibility, it is usually better for there to be one model for the project so all concerned are working from the same base. This may make it more efficient to abandon the development model and start again when the banks come into the picture.

§5.1.6 TERM SHEET, UNDERWRITING, AND DOCUMENTATION

As the financing structure develops, a term sheet is drawn up, setting out in summary form the basis on which the finance will be provided (cf. Chapter 13). This can develop into quite an elaborate document, especially if the bank lawyers are involved in drawing it up, which can add substantially to the Sponsors' legal costs. It is preferable for term sheet discussions to concentrate on commercial rather than legal issues, although the dividing line may be difficult to draw.

A term sheet may be used in a PIM (cf. §5.1.8) by the Financial Adviser as a basis for requesting financing bids from prospective Lead Managers, or at a later stage for the Lead Managers to crystallize their commitment to the financing.

The final term sheet provides the basis for the Lead Managers to complete their internal credit proposals and obtain the necessary approvals to go ahead with the loan. The work of a bank's project finance team, and the consequent proposal for a loan, is normally reviewed by a separate credit department, and it may be presented to a formal credit committee for approval. Banks must have a well-organized interface between the credit team and the project finance team, especially where a bank is acting as a Lead Manager: it may take a long time to develop a project finance transaction, and if the loan is turned down at the end of that process on credit grounds, this obviously has serious consequences for the Sponsors (and does not help the bank's project finance department very much). On the other hand, the bank cannot obtain credit approval at the beginning of the development process, because the structure of the transaction will probably not be sufficiently finalized. The Sponsors therefore need to have confidence that a Lead Manager has the experience and credibility to manage this internal review process.

After obtaining their credit approval, Lead Managers "underwrite" the debt, usually by signing the agreed term sheet. The term sheet provides for a final date by which documentation should be signed, as banks usually have to reapply for internal credit approval if their loan is not signed within a reasonable period.

This signature of a term sheet is still normally no more than a moral obligation, as the commitment by the banks is usually subject to further detailed due diligence of the project documentation and agreement on financing and security documentation. Bank technical or other advisers may also still have due-diligence work to do. Nonetheless, a term sheet is treated seriously, and banks normally only withdraw from an underwriting if there is a major change of circumstances, either in relation to the project itself, the country in which it is situated, or the market in general.

The next phase in the financing is the negotiation of financing documentation, typical terms for which are discussed in Chapter 13; when this is signed the Sponsors finally have obtained committed financing for the Project Company. Even at this stage, the banks may not actually provide the funding, as there are numerous conditions precedent that have to be fulfilled before the project reaches Financial Close (cf. §13.8), and a drawing can be made.

It is evident from this description that arranging project finance is not a quick process. If the project is presented to potential Lead Managers as a completed package, with all the Project Contracts in place, it is likely to take a minimum of

3 months before signature of the loan documentation by the Lead Managers. But there is clearly a lengthy process to go through before such a package can be completed, and issues may well arise during banks' due diligence that further slow down the matter. Finance is therefore often the main critical-path item for the project, and it is not uncommon for banks to work for a year or more on the financing side of a major project.

§5.1.7 INFORMATION MEMORANDUM AND SYNDICATION

The Lead Managers (and any subunderwriters they may bring in) usually reduce their own exposure by placing part of the financing with other banks in the market. As has been seen, a large proportion of project finance loans are arranged and underwritten by a small number of Lead Managers (cf. §3.1.2), but these banks depend on being able to place out a significant share of this underwritten debt with other banks, while retaining arranging and underwriting fees.

The Lead Managers prepare a package of information to facilitate this syndication process, at the heart of which is an information memorandum. This final information memorandum ("FIM") used for syndication may be based on a preliminary information memorandum ("PIM") originally prepared by the Sponsors or their Financial Adviser to present the project to prospective Lead Managers.

The FIM (usually around 100 pages long) provides a detailed summary of the transaction, including:

- A summary overview of the project, its general background, and *raison d'être*
- The Project Company, its ownership, organization, and management
- Financial and other information on Sponsors and other major project parties, including their experience in similar projects and the nature of their involvement in and support for the current project
- Market situation (the commercial basis for the project) covering aspects such as supply and demand, competition, etc.
- Technical description of the construction and operation of the project
- Summary of the Project Contracts (cf. Chapters 6 and 7)
- Project costs and financing plan (cf. §12.4)
- Risk analysis (cf. Chapters 8, 9, and 10)
- Financial analysis, including the Base Case financial model (cf. §12.10) and sensitivity analyses (cf. §12.11)
- A detailed term sheet for the financing (cf. Chapter 13)

In other words, the information memorandum provides a synopsis of the structure of the project and the whole due-diligence process, which speeds up the credit analysis by prospective participant banks. (If well organized and written, it also provides the Project Company's staff with a useful long-term reference manual on the project and its financing.)

The FIM is accompanied by supplementary reports and information:

- A hard copy or disk of the financial model, with the Model Auditor's report (cf. §5.4.4)
- A technical report from the Lenders' Engineer (cf. §5.4.2), summarizing their due diligence review
- Adviser's report on the market in which the project is operating (cf. §5.4.5), and its revenue projections (if sales of its product or services are not covered by a long term Project Agreement—even then background information on the market is useful)
- A similar market report on fuel or raw material input supplies may be relevant
- The legal advisers (cf. §5.4.1) may provide a summary of legal aspects of the project
- A report on insurances from the insurance adviser (cf. §5.4.3)
- A copy of the environmental impact assessment (usually prepared by the Project Company—cf. §4.3) may also be provided
- Annual reports or other information on the various parties to the project

The Sponsors and the Project Company are actively involved in the production of the information memorandum, which is normally subject to their approval and confirmation of its accuracy (but cf. §13.9).

A formal presentation is often made to prospective participant banks by Lead Managers, the Sponsors, and other relevant project parties, sometimes through a "road show" in different financial centers.

Prospective participant banks are usually given 3–4 weeks to absorb this information and come to a decision whether to participate in the financing. They are generally given the documentation to review after they have taken this decision in principle to participate, and may sign up for the financing 2–3 weeks after receiving this.

The Project Company does not usually take any direct risk on whether the syndication is successful or not; by then the loan should have been signed and thus underwritten by the Lead Managers. Sponsors should resist delay tactics by Lead Managers, who try to avoid signing the financing documentation until after they have syndicated the loan and thus eliminated their underwriting risk.

§5.1.8 AGENCY OPERATION

Once the financing documentation has been signed, one of the Lead Managers acts as agent for the bank syndicate as a whole: this agent bank acts as a channel between the Project Company and the banks, as otherwise the Project Company could find it is spending an excessive amount of time communicating with individual banks. The agent bank performs the various tasks:

- Collects the funds from the syndicate when drawings are made and passes these on to the Project Company
- Holds the project security on behalf of the lenders (This function may be carried out by a separate security trustee, acting on the instructions of the agent bank.)
- Calculates interest payments and principal repayments
- Receives payments from the Project Company and passes these on to the individual syndicate banks
- Gathers information about the progress of the project, in liaison with the lenders' advisers, and distributes this to the syndicate at regular intervals
- Monitors the Project Company's compliance with the requirements of the financing documentation and provides information on this to the syndicate banks
- Arranges meetings and site visits as necessary for the Project Company and the Sponsors to make more formal presentations to the syndicate banks on the project's progress
- Organizes discussions with and voting by the syndicate if the Project Company needs to obtain an amendment or waiver of some term of the financing
- Takes enforcement action against the Project Company or the security after a default

The agent bank seldom has any discretion to make decisions about the project finance (for example, as to placing the Project Company in default), but acts as directed by a defined majority of the banks (cf. §13.12). Requiring collective voting by the banks in this way ensures that one rogue bank cannot hold the rest of the syndicate (and the Project Company) for ransom.

§5.2 BOND ISSUES

As has been seen (cf. §3.2), bonds provide an important source of project finance in certain specific markets, such as the United States, Latin America, the United Kingdom, and Australia.

The key difference in nature between loans and bonds is that bonds are tradable instruments and therefore have at least a theoretical liquidity, which loans do not. This difference is not as great as it at first appears, because many bonds are sold on a private placement basis, to investors who do not intend to trade them in the market, whereas loans are in fact traded on an *ad hoc* basis between banks.

Bonds are purchased by investors looking for long-term, fixed-rate income — typically life insurance companies and pension funds. (Inflation-linked bonds

Table 5.1

Investment Grade Ratings

Standard & Poor's	Moody's
AAA	Aaa
AA+	Aa1
AA	Aa2
AA−	Aa3
A+	A1
A	A2
A-	A3
BBB+	Baa1
BBB	Baa2
BBB−	Baa3

have also been issued for some projects—cf. §9.1.1.) Project finance bonds provide an attractive alternative to buying government or corporate bonds, since the return is higher.

§5.2.1 THE INVESTMENT BANK AND THE RATINGS AGENCIES

Investors in bonds generally do not get directly involved in the due-diligence process to the extent that banks do, and rely more on the project's investment bank and a ratings agency to carry out this work.

An investment bank (i.e., a bank that arranges and underwrites financing but does not normally provide the financing itself, except on a temporary basis) is appointed as Lead Manager and assists in structuring the project in a similar way to a Financial Adviser on a bank loan (cf. §5.1.2). The investment bank then makes a presentation on the project to a credit-rating agency (the leaders in the field as far as project finance bonds are concerned are Standard & Poor's and Moody's Investors Services), which assigns the bond a credit rating based on its independent review of the risks of the project, including legal documentation and independent advisers' reports (cf. §5.4). This review considers the same risk issues as a commercial bank would do.

Gradations of credit ratings by Standard & Poor's and Moody's from the prime credit level of AAA/Aaa down to the minimum "investment grade" rating of BBB-/Baa3 (below which most major bond investors will not purchase a bond issue) are as listed in Table 5.1. Most project finance ratings are at the lower end of this range. (Below the investment grade level the ratings continue from BB+/Ba1, etc.)

Some bank loans are also rated by the ratings agencies, to assist in a wider syndication, and because some institutional investors are beginning to participate in bank syndicate loans. However, this is not as yet a widespread practice in the project finance market.

The investment bank finally prepares a preliminary bond prospectus that covers similar ground to an information memorandum for a bank syndication (cf. §5.1.8). The work done by the investment bank and the rating agency reduces the need for detailed due diligence by bond investors; provided the bond rating fits the bond investor's maximum risk profile, such investors can just decide to buy it without having to do a lot of work. Major bond investors, however, carry out their own review of the project information in the prospectus besides relying on the credit rating.

After any necessary preliminary testing of the market (which may include a road show of presentations to investors), the investment bank issues the final bond prospectus and underwrites the bond issue through a subscription agreement. The coupon (interest rate) and other key conditions of the bond are fixed based on the market at the time of underwriting, and the bond proceeds are paid over to the Project Company a few days later. The investment bank places (or resells) the bonds with investors, and may also maintain a liquid market by trading in the bond.

§5.2.2 RULE 144A

Bonds may either be public issues (i.e., quoted on a stock exchange and—at least theoretically—quite widely traded), or private placements, which are not quoted and are sold to a limited number of large investors. It is possible for a private placement to take place without the intervention of an investment bank (i.e., the Sponsors can deal directly with investors, as they can deal direct with banks, without the use of an adviser), although this seldom occurs.

The importance of the U.S. market for project finance bond issues is based on rule 144a, adopted by the Securities and Exchange Commission in 1990. A private placement of a bond issue does not have to go through the SEC's lengthy full registration procedure, but under normal SEC rules such a private placement cannot be sold on to another party for two years. This lack of liquidity is generally not acceptable to U.S. bond investors. Rule 144a allows secondary trading (i.e., reselling) of private placements of debt securities, provided sales are to "qualified institutional buyers" (QIBs). The latter are defined as entities that have a portfolio of at least $100 million in securities. Rule 144a bonds are therefore sold by the Project Company to an investment bank, which then resells them to QIBs. Thus Rule 144a provides an efficient and effective way of raising project finance in the world's largest bond market, and it is the main basis on which project finance bonds are issued in that market, whether they are limited private placements or more widely traded issues.

Rule 144a bond issues have to be relatively large in size—in the $100–200 million range. (Other types of public bond issue can be for smaller amounts, but as with bank loans, a small financing is unlikely to be economic.)

§5.2.3 WRAPPED BONDS

An alternative structure for raising finance in the bond market is the "wrapped" bond (i.e., a project bond that is guaranteed by a "monoline" insurance company), a structure that was originally used to insure municipal bonds in the United States. The insurance companies active in this field are primarily based in the United States. Theoretically, the bond investors need to pay little attention to the background or risks of the project itself and can rely on the credit rating of the insurance company (usually AAA); the insurance company has to go through its own due-diligence process, and projects generally have to secure a "shadow" investment grade rating in their own right to obtain wrapped cover, as monoline insurers have to convince the ratings agencies that their portfolio meets the credit standards required for it to maintain their AAA ratings.

This structure may offer benefits of greater certainty, speed, and flexibility, a better repayment profile if the monoline insurer is willing to take more long-term risk than direct bond investors, and savings in cost if the monoline insurer is willing to take a lower return for the credit risk than direct investors. It also ensures a greater demand and hence liquidity for the bonds, which should also be reflected in the bond pricing. There may be a question, however, whether bond investors should rely only on this guarantee—which may last for 20 years or more—without considering the underlying project being guaranteed.

A significant proportion of the project bond financing in the United Kingdom, for example, for key public infrastructure, such as roads and other PPPs, has been on a wrapped basis, which has thus encouraged the development of the largest project finance bond market outside the United States.

A further refinement is the "double wrap," where the government sponsoring a PPP counterguarantees the obligations of the monoline insurer; this involves little risk for the government if the Project Agreement is with a public-sector body, but further reduces the cost of finance and hence the cost of the product or service under the Project Agreement.

§5.2.4 BOND PAYING AGENTS AND TRUSTEES

Paying agents and trustees (also known as fiscal agents) are appointed for the bond issue (except in a private placement to a single bond investor), with similar roles to that of an agent bank for a loan. The paying agent pays over the proceeds of the bond to the borrower and collects payments due to the bond investors. The bond trustee holds the security on behalf of the investors and calls meetings of bond holders to vote on waivers or amendments of the bond terms.

§5.3 LOANS VERSUS BONDS

Various factors affect whether a project should use commercial bank loans or bonds (or a combination of the two) for its financing (Table 5.2).

Because of some of the uncertainties about the final availability or terms of bond financing, Sponsors may arrange a bank loan as an insurance policy in case the bond issue falls through, or put together a bank loan with the intention of refinancing it rapidly with a bond. Obviously this involves extra costs.

In general, bonds are suitable for developed markets and "standard" projects. They are also especially suitable if a project is being refinanced after it has been built and has operated successfully for a period. Conversely, the greater flexibility of bank loans tends to make them more suitable for the construction and early operation phases of a project, projects where there are likely to be changes in the Offtaker's or end-user's requirements, more complex projects, or projects in more difficult markets.

§5.4 THE ROLES OF THE LENDERS' ADVISERS

Lenders use their own external advisers, largely paralleling and checking the work done by the Sponsors' external advisers (cf. §4.3). The costs of all these advisers are payable by the Sponsors, and can add considerably to the total development costs—they are payable whether or not the financing is concluded. It follows from this that the terms of reference and fees for these advisers must be approved by the Sponsors.

Advisers appointed by the lenders may include legal advisers, lenders' engineers, insurance advisers, model auditors, and others.

§5.4.1 LEGAL ADVISERS

The lenders' legal advisers carry out due diligence on the project contracts, and in due course they assist the banks in negotiating the financing documentation. Both local and international lawyers may be engaged for this purpose.

§5.4.2 LENDERS' ENGINEER

One of the major international engineering firms, which are now well used to providing this type of advice, is appointed as lenders' engineer (also known as the Independent Engineer, or Technical Adviser ("TA")). Their work is in two stages:

Table 5.2

Bank loans versus Bonds

Bank loans	Bonds
Can be provided (either on a domestic or crossborder basis) to any credit-worthy market	Only available in certain markets (cf. Table 3.3);
The Sponsors' corporate banking lines may be used up in project finance loans.	Bonds rely on a different investor base, thus avoiding the need to tie up bank credit lines.
In some markets (e.g., U.S.) banks will not offer long-term maturities (cf. §13.6.3)	Generally offer a longer term of repayment
Generally only offer fixed interest rates through hedging arrangements (cf. §9.2)	Fixed rates of interest
Inflation-linked loans generally not available	Some markets can offer bonds with the interest rate linked to inflation, if the Project Company's revenues are linked to inflation.
Funds from the loan drawn only when needed	Funds from the bond have to be drawn all at once and then redeposited until required to pay for project capital costs — there may be a loss of interest (known as "negative arbitrage") caused by the redeposit rate being lower than the coupon (interest rate) on the bond (cf. §9.2.5).
Banks tend to maintain longer-term policies towards lending.	More affected by short-term sentiment — as a result an economic crisis in, say, Thailand may immediately close off the international market for new bond issues in Mexico.
Although banks do not formally commit to loan terms in advance, they are more likely to stand by the terms they offer at an early stage.	The terms for the bond and the market appetite for it are only finally known at a late stage in the process, when the underwriting takes place.
Project Contracts kept confidential, in a loan syndicated to a restricted number of banks	The terms of Project Contracts may have to be published in listing particulars or a bond prospectus: this may not be acceptable to the Sponsors for reasons of commercial confidentiality (e.g., they may not wish to reveal the terms of a fuel supply contract).
Banks exercise control over all changes to Project Contracts and impose tight controls on the Project Company.	Bond investors only control matters that significantly affect their cash flow cover or security; events of default leading to acceleration of the financing are more limited in bond issues.
Banks tightly control the addition of any new debt and are unlikely to agree the basis for this in advance.	It is generally easier to add a limited amount of new debt (e.g., for a project expansion) to bond financing as bond investors will agree the terms for this in advance.
It is easier to negotiate with banks if the project gets into difficulty.	Bonds may be less flexible if major changes in terms are required (e.g., if the project gets into serious trouble), as it can be difficult to have direct dialogue with bond holders, who are more passive in nature than a bank syndicate; banks are often wary of lending in partnership with bond holders for this reason.
If a project gets into difficulty, negotiations with banks should remain private.	Negotiations with bond holders may be publicized.
Low penalties for prepayment (e.g., because the debt can be refinanced on more favourable terms) (cf. §13.6.3)	High penalties for prepayment

Due diligence. The Lenders' Engineer reviews and reports to the lenders on matters such as:
- Suitability of project site
- Project technology and design
- Experience and suitability of the EPC Contractor
- Technical aspects of the EPC Contract
- Construction costs and the adequacy of the allowance for contingencies
- Construction schedule
- Construction and operating Permits
- Technical aspects of any Input Supply Contract or Project Agreement
- Suitability of the Project Company's management structure and personnel for construction and operation
- Any particular technical issues or risks in operation of the project
- Projections of operating assumptions (output, likely availability, etc.)
- Projections of operating and maintenance costs

Monitoring. Once the project construction is under way, the Lenders' Engineer is provided with regular information on progress by the Project Company, the Owner's Engineer, and the EPC Contractor, and provides regular reports to the lenders, highlighting any particular problems. The Lenders' Engineer may also be required to certify that claims for payment by the EPC Contractor have been properly made, and that the required performance tests on completion of construction have been passed, but otherwise is not in any way supervising or controlling the construction process, which remains the responsibility of the Project Company.

When construction is complete and the project is operating, the Lenders' Engineer continues to monitor and report on operating performance and maintenance.

For process plant projects such as a refinery, an engineering company may also carry out a "hazop" (hazard and operations) study for the lenders, which looks at the possibilities for damage caused by the processes used in the plant and the effect of the layout of the plant on its safety.

§5.4.3 INSURANCE ADVISER

The insurance adviser (usually a department of a major international insurance broker, specializing in providing this service for lenders) reviews and reports on any insurance provisions in the project documentation, the proposed insurance package for the construction period of the project, and renewals of insurances during operation (cf. §7.6). If any claims are made, the insurance adviser monitors these on behalf of the lenders.

§5.4.4 MODEL AUDITOR

When the financial model (cf. §5.1.6) is virtually complete, a Model Auditor (usually one of the major firms of accountants) is appointed to review the model, including tax and accounting assumptions, and confirm that it properly reflects the Project Contracts and financing documentation and can calculate the effect of various sensitivity scenarios.

§5.4.5 OTHER ADVISERS

Depending on the needs of the project, various other advisers may be appointed in areas such as:

Market. If the product produced by the Project Company is not being sold on a long-term contract, or if it is a commodity whose sale price is dependent on market conditions, market advisers are appointed to review the reasonableness of the projections for the sale volume and price.

Fuel or raw material. The same principle applies if fuel or raw material required for the project is not being purchased on a long-term contract, or at a price that can be passed on to the product Offtaker.

Traffic. Traffic advisers are needed for an infrastructure project where revenues are dependent on traffic flows.

Natural resources. In a project that depends on the extraction of natural resources, whether as an input to or output from the project, lenders require a reserve report (for a mining project) or a reservoir report (for a hydrocarbon project), together with an engineering report that confirms the feasibility, timing, and costs of extracting the reserves.

Similarly, lenders to a wind power generation project need advice on wind patterns, and on water supply for a water supply or hydropower project.

§5.4.6 PREAPPOINTMENT OF LENDERS' ADVISERS

It is possible for Sponsors to appoint lenders' advisers before there are any lenders, i.e., if it is intended that there will be competitive bids from prospective Lead Managers after the Project Contracts have been negotiated and project structuring is largely complete (cf. §5.1.2). In this case the lenders' advisers act as devil's advocates in checking the project specifications and documentation, to ensure that issues normally raised by lenders are adequately covered, and prepare due-diligence reports for prospective lenders. Once the lenders have been appointed, they continue to work with these advisers on a normal basis. The benefits of this procedure are that it helps to ensure the project remains financeable as it is being developed, and it reduces the amount of time spent on due diligence by lenders when they finally bid for the finance, although it obviously increases Sponsors' development costs.

§5.4.7 USE OF ADVISERS' TIME

Lenders work primarily on fixed fees (cf. §13.4), whereas their advisers are likely to work on time-based fees. The lenders therefore have every incentive to try to shift due-diligence work to their advisers to get a better return on the time of their staff involved in the project. Typical examples of this are the use of lawyers to act as secretaries of meetings that are primarily discussing commercial or financial (rather than legal) issues, or to draw up the term sheet (cf. §5.1.7).

Sponsors therefore must agree to the lenders' advisers' scope of work and carefully supervise time spent to keep these costs under control.

Chapter 6

Project Contracts: (1) The Project Agreement

The Project Contracts provide a basis for the Project Company's construction and operation of the project (cf. §2.2). The most important of these is the Project Agreement (i.e., a contract that provides the framework under which the Project Company obtains its revenues). (Other important Project Contracts are discussed in Chapter 7.)

The only types of projects that do not operate under a Project Agreement are those that sell a product or service to private-sector buyers in a commodity-based or open competitive market, such as mining or telecommunications projects, or "merchant" power plants (cf. §8.8.6), although they usually have some form of license to allow them to do this in lieu of a Project Agreement.

There are two main models for a Project Agreement:[1]

- An *Offtake Contract,* under which the Project Company produces a product and sells it to an Offtaker (cf. §6.1)
- A *Concession Agreement,* under which the Project Company provides a service to a public authority or directly to the general public (cf. §6.2)

These models have many characteristics in common: some of the issues that relate to both types of contract are discussed in §6.3–§6.9.

[1]For some standard forms of Project Agreements and their legal framework, cf. United Nations Industrial Development Organisation: *Guidelines for Infrastructure Development through Build-Operate-Transfer (BOT) Projects* (UNIDO, Vienna, 1996); United Nations Economic Commission for Europe: *Negotiation Platform for Public-Private Partnerships in Infrastructure Projects* (UN ECE, Geneva, 2000); United Nations Commission on International Trade Law: *UNCITRAL Legislative Guide on Privately Financed Infrastructure Projects* (United Nations, New York, 2001); U.K. Treasury Taskforce: *Standardisation of PFI Contracts* (Butterworths, London, 1999)—a new edition is to be published by the U.K. Office for Government Commerce in 2002.

It should be said that although many legal issues are discussed in this and the following chapters, they are not intended as a commentary on all the legal ramifications of Project Contracts and the associated financing documentation, but concentrate on the key issues likely to emerge in commercial negotiations between the Project Company and its project counterparts and lenders.[2]

§6.1 OFFTAKE CONTRACT

An Offtake Contract is used for a project that produces a product (e.g., a power purchase agreement is used for a project producing electricity). Such agreements provide the Offtaker (purchaser) with a secure supply of the required product and the Project Company with the ability to sell its products on a preagreed basis.

Going back to first principles, if a high ratio of project finance debt is to be raised, the risks taken by the Project Company in selling its product must be limited; an Offtake Contract is the easiest way of limiting these risks.

§6.1.1 TYPES OF OFFTAKE CONTRACT

Offtake Contracts can take various forms:

Take-or-pay contract. This provides that the Offtaker (i.e., the purchaser of the project's product) must take (i.e., purchase) the project's product or make a payment to the Project Company in lieu of purchase. The price for the product is based on an agreed Tariff (cf. §6.1.5).

It should be noted that such contracts are seldom on a "hell-or-highwater" basis, where the Offtaker is always obliged to make payments whatever happens to the Project Company. The Project Company is only paid if it performs its side of the deal; in general, if it is capable of delivering the product.

BOT/BOOT/BTO/BOO contracts (cf. §2.3) involving sale of a product are usually on a take-or-pay basis.

Take-and-pay contract. In this case the Offtaker only pays for the product taken, on an agreed price basis. Clearly this has limited relevance for an Offtake Contract in a project financing, as it provides no long-term certainty that the product will be purchased. It may be found, however, in Input Supply Contracts for fuel or other raw materials (cf. §7.3.1).

---

[2]For discussion of various legal aspects of project finance, cf. Scott L. Hoffman, *The Law and Business of International Project Finance* (Kluwer Law International, The Hague, 2001 [2nd ed.]); Graham D. Vinter, *Project Finance: A Legal Guide* (Sweet & Maxwell, London, 1998 [2nd ed.]); Philip R. Wood, *Project Finance, Subordinated Debt and State Loans* (Sweet & Maxwell, London, 1995).

Long-term sales contract. In this case the Offtaker agrees to take agreed-upon quantities of product from the project, but the price paid is based on market prices at the time of purchase or an agreed market index. The Project Company thus does not take the risk of demand for the project's product, but takes the market risk on the price. This type of contract is commonly used in, for example, mining, oil and gas, and petrochemical projects, where the Project Company wants to ensure that its product can easily be sold in international markets, but Offtakers would not be willing to take the commodity price risk.

This type of contract may have a "floor" (minimum) price for the commodity, as has been the case in some LNG projects—if so, the end result equates to a take-or-pay contract at this floor price and has the same effect as a hedging contract.

Hedging contract. Hedging contracts are found in the commodity markets; it is possible to enter into various kinds of hedging contracts with market traders, such as:

- A long term forward sale of the commodity at a fixed price (this is effectively the same as a take-or-pay agreement)
- An agreement that if the commodity's price falls below a certain floor level the product can be sold at this floor price; if the price does not fall to this level the product is sold in the open market
- An agreement similar to this, but also establishing a ceiling price for the commodity, so that if the market price rises above this level the product will also be sold at this ceiling level; if the price is below the ceiling or above the floor, the product is sold in the open market (this is similar in concept to an interest rate collar—cf. §9.2.2)

   Thus, for example, an oilfield project may enter into an agreement to hedge its expected production such that if the oil price is below $20/bbl, it can sell its production at $20 to the hedging counterpart, and if it is above $25/bbl, the hedging counterpart can buy it at $25. In this way the project knows that its oil can always be sold for at least $20; however, if the price goes over $25 the project will not benefit from this.

   These types of hedging contracts should be distinguished from financial hedging described in Chapter 9, although similar principles are involved.

Contract for Differences ("CfD"). Under a CfD structure the Project Company sells its product into the market and not to the Offtaker. If however, the market price is below an agreed level, the Offtaker pays the Project Company the difference, and vice versa if it is above an agreed level. The effect of this is that both the Project Company and the Offtaker have hedged their respective sale and purchase prices against market movements; however, a Contract for Differences differs from a hedging contract in that the product is always sold in the market and not to the hedging counterpart; it is thus purely a financial contract. The end result is a contract with a similar practical effect as a take-or-pay contract with an agreed Tariff.

Long-term CfDs are especially used in the electricity market: in fact, in some countries these contracts have to be used rather than a PPA (see below) because all power produced has to be sold into the country's electricity pool rather than to end-users.

Throughput contract. (also known as a transportation contract). This is used, e.g., in pipeline financings. Under this agreement a user of the pipeline agrees to use it to carry not less than a certain volume of product, and to pay a minimum price for this. (This type of contract is similar to a service contract—cf. §6.2.1.)

(It should be noted that there is considerable confusion of terminology in the market, especially on the definition of take-and-pay and take-or-pay contracts; in this book the terms are used as set out previously.)

In §6.1.2–§6.1.7, typical provisions in a take-or-pay Offtake Contract are discussed. A power purchase agreement ("PPA") is used as an example, as it is the most common type of Offtake Contract in the project finance context, and other contracts tend to follow the PPA model. Where different issues arise in a Contract for Differences these are noted. (The effect of the lesser coverage from a take-and-pay or long-term sales contract is considered in the context of more general risk analysis in §8.8.5, and projects where there are no long term sales arrangements are discussed in §8.8.6.)

§6.1.2 PPA Structure

The place of a PPA in the structure for an independent power plant ("IPP") project (for a gas-fired power plant) is set out in Figure 6.1. A PPA provides for the Project Company to construct a power station, with agreed technical characteristics as to, for example,

- Output (in megawatts [MW])
- Heat rate (the amount of fuel required to produce a set amount of power)
- Emissions or other environmental requirements

The PPA requires the plant to be constructed by an agreed-upon date (cf. §6.1.3) and to be operated on an agreed-upon basis (cf. §6.1.4). The power from the completed plant is sold under a long-term Tariff (cf. §6.1.5–§6.1.6) to the Power Purchaser, who may be a public-sector transmission and distribution company, a local distribution company, or a direct end-user of the power (e.g., an industrial plant). The Tariff is based on a minimum required availability of the power plant (i.e. the number of days in a year the plant will be able to operate at the specified output, after making allowances for routine maintenance and

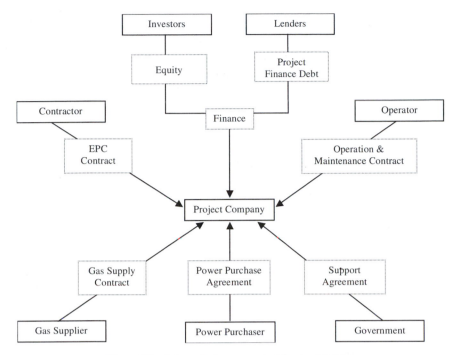

Figure 6.1   Independent power project finance structure.

unexpected plant outages) and deductions are made or penalties paid if the plant does not meet minimum availability or output requirements (cf. §6.1.7).

The Power Purchaser needs to be satisfied that the Project Company and its Sponsors have the necessary technical and financial capacity to construct and operate the plant as required, have an appropriate EPC Contractor and a secure fuel supply, and that the terms of the project finance do not indirectly expose the Power Purchaser to undue risks. The Power Purchaser may therefore restrict the ability of the Sponsors to sell their shares to ensure the continuing involvement of appropriate parties in the project.

§6.1.3 COMPLETION OF THE PLANT

The Tariff is payable from the date the plant is completed (often known as the "Commercial Operation Date" ["COD"]). To reach COD the Project Company has to demonstrate completion to the Power Purchaser by undertaking performance tests. These performance tests will at least demonstrate the actual output the plant can achieve (since the Tariff is based on the output capacity); in a BOT/BOOT/BTO project, the Power Purchaser, as the eventual owner of the plant, may also be concerned to ensure that other technical and performance requirements are fulfilled. The Power Purchaser's representative may join the performance tests being carried out under the EPC Contract, or the PPA performance tests may be carried out separately. (Obviously the PPA tests should not be more stringent than those under the EPC Contract—cf. §7.1.6.)

The Project Company may be required to fulfill other conditions to achieve COD, such as:

- Obtaining operating Permits
- Confirmation that emissions requirements are met
- Confirmation that operating phase insurances are in place on the agreed basis
- Demonstrating reserve stocks of fuel are in place

§6.1.4 OPERATION OF THE PLANT

The parties agree detailed operating procedures; for example, the Power Purchaser notifies the Project Company in advance of its expected requirements for power, and the Project Company advises the Power Purchaser of any changes in output or availability, for example, due to routine maintenance or an emergency shutdown, and as far as possible carries out maintenance in times of low demand. This does not imply that the Power Purchaser has any right to intervene directly in the operation or maintenance of the plant, except in the case of a default by the Project Company (cf. §6.7).

The dispatch risk (i.e., the risk of whether or not the power station's electricity is required by the Power Purchaser—either directly or through the grid transmission system) is the responsibility of the Power Purchaser. The Project Company only has to ensure that it is ready and available to produce power when required; as will be seen, the Tariff that the Power Purchaser pays provides an adequate return to the Project Company whether the plant is dispatched (generates power) or not. Since the Power Purchaser is taking the dispatch risk, it follows that it has the right to decide when the plant actually produces power.

In the case of a Contract for Differences, the Project Company may not get paid unless it actually sells its electricity into the market (i.e. the dispatch risk remains with the Project Company). In such cases the Project Company has to bid an appropriate price into the market to ensure that it always sells its power.

§6.1.5 TARIFF

The Tariff is usually paid on a monthly basis by the Power Purchaser to the Project Company and generally consists of two main elements: a fixed Availability Charge (also known as the Capacity Charge or Fixed Charge), and an Energy

Charge, which varies with usage of the plant (also known as the Variable Charge). In addition, certain other charges may be payable.

Availability charge. The Availability Charge element of the Tariff is paid even if plant is not dispatched, since it represents the fixed costs that the Project Company incurs just by building the plant and making it available to the Power Purchaser.

This element of the Tariff is thus intended to cover:

- *Fixed operating costs,* e.g. land rental, staff costs, insurance premiums, scheduled maintenance and replacement of spare parts, fixed (or capacity) payments to a fuel supplier for a fuel pipeline, taxes, etc. Accounting depreciation of the plant (cf. §12.7.1) is not a fixed operating cost for this purpose, nor is it taken into account in calculating the equity return, as it is not a cash flow item; however, the debt service and equity return elements cover this and the other capital costs of the project.
- *Debt service* (interest payments and principal repayments), usually based on preagreed assumptions as to the level of debt to be incurred by the Project Company and the interest rate on the debt.
- *Equity return,* i.e., the Project Company's free cash flow after debt service and fixed operating costs, and taxes, again based on a pre-agreed assumption about the level of equity required.

The Availability Charge may be split into three elements as above, or two, combining the debt service and equity elements, thus leaving the Project Company to decide the best financial structure for funding the project or even combined as one payment. (The extent to which the Availability Charge is split is affected by the extent to which these different elements are indexed separately—cf. §6.1.6.)

The Availability Charge is normally fixed when the PPA is signed (i.e., the Project Company takes the risk of the costs of the project being higher than the original costs assumed when the Tariff was calculated). Sometimes there are exceptions to this, e.g., the Project Company is compensated for the actual costs of operating insurances.

Energy Charge. This element of the Tariff is intended to cover a project's variable costs, of which the most important is fuel. The Energy Charge takes into account:

- The quantity of fuel that should have been used (on preagreed heat rate assumptions) to generate the electricity actually produced by the plant
- The actual cost of this fuel to the Project Company (or the cost based on an index of fuel costs)
- Any other O&M costs that vary with usage of the plant

The Energy Charge makes an allowance for the degradation in performance (and hence gradual increase in fuel consumption) that takes place between each major maintenance of the plant (cf. §8.7.6).

In general, if the plant is not dispatched the Energy Charge is not payable, but if the Project Company has take-or-pay obligations for fuel, and it does not need the expected level of fuel because of a low level of dispatch of the plant, the Power Purchaser would need to cover this cost (unless the low level of dispatch is because the plant has not been available).

In other types of process plant projects, the cost of raw materials being processed is dealt with through a Variable Charge in a similar way to the Energy Charge.

Other charges. Various other charges may be payable as part of the Tariff, e.g., costs for more than a certain number of start-ups of the plant every year (which use extra fuel and cause higher maintenance costs), or the extra costs of running on a partial load (cf. §8.7.6).

Payments may also be received for the sale of waste steam from the plant for use in industrial processes at an adjacent site or for district heating. (In some countries steam from power generation is being increasingly used for water desalination, to the extent that this is the main reason for constructing the plant.)

Tariff charges may take account of the Power Purchaser's varying requirements for power, so that in a northern location more may be paid for power generated in winter evenings.

Measurement of the power produced is through meters at the plant controlled by both parties.

If this type of "fixed/variable" Tariff structure is used, the Project Company may be obliged to sell the whole of the power output to the Power Purchaser, even if this output turns out to be greater than originally anticipated (e.g., because the project operates at above its design capacity).

This Tariff structure thus leaves various key risks with the Project Company (cf. §8.3), for example:

Project cost overrun. If the project costs more to construct than expected, and as a result incurs more debt and equity financing, this is not taken into account in the Tariff calculations.

Availability. If the plant is not able to operate so as to produce the quantity of power required over time, revenue is lost (or penalties are paid) (cf. §6.1.7).

Operating costs. If the plant does not operate as well as expected, and, e.g., it takes more fuel to generate the electricity, or maintenance costs are higher than expected, this also does not change the Tariff payment.

§6.1.6 TARIFF INDEXATION

The various elements of the Tariff are normally indexed (i.e., increased over time against agreed published economic indices).

The Availability Charge payments are dealt with as follows:

- *Fixed operating costs:* indexed as appropriate against the consumer price index (CPI) or industry price indices in the country where the relevant costs are to be incurred, or in limited respects may be based on actual costs (e.g., for insurance)
- *Debt service:* not normally indexed
- *Equity return:* may be indexed against CPI

If any of the fixed operating costs are to be incurred in a foreign currency, or if the equity or debt is raised in a foreign currency, calculations of the Tariff may be made in that currency to that extent. In such cases payments normally continue to be made in the local currency, but are indexed against the exchange rate with the foreign currency concerned (cf. §9.3.1).

If the Energy Charge is calculated based on actual fuel costs, no further indexation is required. In some cases the Energy Charge may be based on a published index for the cost of the fuel concerned, and in which case the Project Company takes the risk of not being able to obtain fuel at this price.

There can be some timing problems with indexation, since economic indices are often published after a considerable lag, and hence there may be a need for retrospective adjustment of Tariff payments to catch up with such indices. If foreign currency adjustments are being made, it may be necessary to take account of the exchange rate movements between the time the monthly Tariff bill is calculated and presented, and when it is finally paid.

Other adjustments that may be made to the Tariff are discussed below in §6.5.

§6.1.7 PENALTIES

The Tariff as set out above is only paid by the Power Purchaser if the Project Company's power plant performs as required under the power purchase agreement. If it does not, the Project Company will be liable to penalties, which may be deducted from Tariff payments or paid separately by the Project Company to the Power Purchaser.

These penalties are liquidated damages, that is, the agreed level of loss for the Power Purchaser, and therefore the only damages that can be recovered. (In this sense the use of the expression "penalties" is misleading, as contractual penalties that are not calculated to cover a real loss generally cannot be recovered in many legal systems—cf. §7.1.8.)

Typical penalties include:

Late completion. The Power Purchaser should bear in mind that the Project
Company has every incentive to complete on time whether or not penalties
are payable: the ability of any highly geared Project Company to sustain a
prolonged delay in completion is limited, because the loss of revenue from
such a delay is significant (obviously no Tariff payment is made if the project is not complete). If the Power Purchaser suffers no loss from the delay,
payment of penalties by the Project Company is not appropriate, may not be
legally enforceable, and will only add to project costs as the Power Purchaser
will, if possible, pass on this extra risk to the EPC Contractor, who will build
it into the contract price and timing.

   If, however, the plant is completed later than the agreed-upon date, and as
a result the Power Purchaser expects to have to generate or buy in power
from another more expensive source, the Project Company may be made
liable (subject to extensions for *force majeure*—cf. §6.6) to a penalty payment reflecting this loss, at an appropriate rate for each day of delay. The
Project Company will of course try to ensure that this penalty is mirrored in
the liquidated damages (LDs) under the EPC Contract (cf. §7.1.8), and that
there is a cap on the PPA penalties that also reflects the position in the EPC
Contract.

   To avoid a prolonged period of uncertainty about whether the project is
ever going to happen or not, there is normally also a final termination date
(as with the EPC Contract) by which if COD has not taken place the Power
Purchaser has the right to terminate the PPA.

   If the Power Purchaser is also the transmission grid owner, it must ensure
that the grid connection to the plant is provided. If the connection is not provided, and the construction of the plant is complete but it cannot be tested
for performance without a grid connection, this cannot be used as a basis for
charging penalties for late completion, and the Power Purchaser is obliged
to begin paying the Availability Charge element of the Tariff.

   Provision may also be made for a bonus to be paid to the Project Company
for early completion, if this would be beneficial to the Power Purchaser.

Low initial output. If the plant is supposed to have an output of x MW, and
when completed it actually produces $(x - y)$ MW, a lump-sum penalty is
payable, or the Availability Charge reduced, to allow for this. Again this
penalty should be taken into account in the LDs under the EPC Contract.

High initial heat rate. If at the performance tests the plant uses more fuel than
expected to produce a given amount of electricity, this can be dealt with in
two ways: either the difference in heat rate is ignored in the Energy Charge
calculations, and the Project Company bears the cost of the extra fuel required, or the Energy Charge assumptions for fuel consumption can be adjusted, and an initial penalty paid to the Power Purchaser to compensate for

this. In either case the EPC Contract LDs should cover the cost of the extra fuel consumption or the initial penalty.

Low availability. If the plant is required to be available to produce, say, 100 MW for 90% of the year (i.e., 329 days), this means that the plant must produce 32,900 MWh in a year. Therefore if the plant is not capable of producing this total output level, whether because the plant is unavailable, or the output of the plant deteriorates below the agreed level, the Project Company is liable for a penalty payment (or the Availability Charge is reduced).

In setting the original availability and output requirements, allowance is made for routine maintenance, and an agreed level of unexpected shutdowns (outages) in calculating the period for which the plant is to be made available each year, and for the natural deterioration in output that takes place between major maintenance overhauls. These allowances are translated into detailed availability and production schedules agreed to in advance, usually on a broad annual basis, adjusted as necessary on a shorter term basis. Penalties may be greater when the power is most needed (e.g., during the winter evenings in a northern country), and similarly the Project Company is required to undertake routine maintenance in a period of low demand for power.

To a certain extent it may be possible to pass these penalties on to the O&M Contractor (cf. §7.2.4).

The Power Purchaser may require security for penalty payments through a bank guarantee, which is often provided by the lenders as part of the total financing package for the project.

There may also be a bonus payable to the Project Company if either the availability of the plant or the actual amount of power produced are above certain levels.

§6.2 CONCESSION AGREEMENT

A Concession Agreement is a contract between a public-sector entity and the Project Company, under which a project is constructed to provide a service (rather than a product as under an Offtake Contract) to the public-sector entity, or directly to the public. Concession Agreement is the traditional name for this type of contract, but it now also goes under various different names, such as Service Agreement or Project Agreement. Obviously a Concession Agreement has many characteristics in common with the Off-take Contract already described.

The public-sector entity with whom the Concession Agreement is signed may be a national or regional government, a municipality, a state agency, a state-owned company, or a special-purpose entity set up by the state to grant the concession. (There is no generally agreed term for the public sector entity under a Concession Agreement: it will be referred to hereafter as the Contracting Authority.)

A contract to construct a project to provide a service, similar to a Concession

Agreement, can also be signed with a private-sector counterpart, although this is less common; where such contracts exist they follow the same principles as the public-sector contracts discussed here.

Examples of Concession Agreements include contracts for construction and operation of:

- A toll road, bridge, or tunnel for which the public pays tolls
- A road, bridge, or tunnel where tolls are not paid by the public, but a Contracting Authority makes payments (known as "shadow tolls") based on usage by the public
- A transportation system (e.g., a railway or metro) for which the public pays fares
- A transportation system (or parts of the system, such as trains or signaling), where payments are made by a public-sector system operator (as Contracting Authority) for availability of the system rather than by the public for usage
- Water and sewage systems, where payments are made by a municipality or by end-users
- Ports and airports, usually with payments made by airlines or shipping companies
- Public-sector buildings such as schools, hospitals, prisons, and government offices, where payments are made by the Contracting Authority for availability

Such Agreements are usually on a BOOT/BOT/BTO but in some cases a BOO basis may be appropriate. These "public-private partnerships" (PPPs) are now a major growth area in project finance.

It should be noted that PPPs do not necessarily involve project finance:

- A typical form of PPP is for publicly owned land (e.g., a school) to be made available to a private property developer who builds, say, an office block on it, but as payment for the land also builds a new school on part of the site; the financing of the project (i.e., building the office and the school) does not involve any long-term Concession Agreement-type obligation by the public sector, and the security for the lenders is the value of the (now privately owned) office block—hence, this is asset finance (cf. §2.4) not project finance.
- PPPs may not involve any major long-term capital expenditure where they relate only to the private sector taking over a service—such as street cleaning—that had previously been provided by the public sector (cf. §2.3).

As can be seen from the list above, Concession Agreements can be divided into two classes:

"Service" contracts (cf. §6.2.1). The Project Company constructs a project to provide a service for which the Contracting Authority pays—in such cases the usage risk is transferred to the Contracting Authority, in the same way that the dispatch risk is transferred to the Power Purchaser in a PPA. (It is perhaps misleading to refer to these as service contracts, in that the contract is mainly based on payments by the Contracting Authority for the finance and construction of a project—e.g., a water supply system—although the project is required to supply a service while these payments are being made.)

"Toll" contracts (cf. §6.2.2). The Project Company constructs a project to provide a service for which private-sector users pay, with revenues thus being entirely dependent on usage. (This is the classic kind of Concession Agreement.) A toll road, bridge, or tunnel, a public transportation system (where the Project Company earns fare revenues), or a port or airport (where revenues come from usage by shipping companies or airlines) all come into this category, as does a mobile phone or cable TV system.

Alternatively, the Project Company is paid by the Contracting Authority, but on the basis of usage of the project by the general public: this is the case in "shadow" toll projects—here again the usage risk is transferred to the Project Company.

There are also hybrid contracts, where tolls paid by the general public may not be sufficient to support the project, and the government provides a fixed subsidy, or a guarantee of a minimum base revenue. (In such cases the bid for the project involves bidders specifying how much public subsidy or support they require to undertake it.)

§6.2.1 SERVICE CONTRACTS

A Concession Agreement, under which a service is provided to a Contracting Authority, but where usage risk remains with the Contracting Authority, is very similar in structure to an Offtake Contract for a process plant such as the PPA discussed previously.

Payments are made for availability of the project (i.e. for the service provided); unlike a process plant, however, a split between an Availability Charge and a Variable Charge (cf. §6.1.5) is not usually appropriate, and one payment is made for provision of the facility as a whole (a Unitary Charge). However, the Unitary Charge usually has subelements which cover the fixed costs (including debt service and equity return) and the service provision. The Unitary Charge is adjusted for any periods of nonavailability, and penalties are payable if the services provided are not at the required standard. The level of the Unitary Charge is indexed against appropriate inflation or other indices (cf. §6.1.6).

The main issue that arises in a service contract that differs from those already discussed for a PPA relate to the definitions of availability or service. The availability of a power station is easily measured—its ability to generate the agreed level of power when required by the Power Purchaser; availability and service are the same thing, and the Availability Charge element of the Tariff is easily calculated based on this. In a service contract, the definitions of both availability and the quality of the service are more difficult and more specific to the project concerned.

Availability is relatively easy to measure if a specific piece of equipment or service is being provided—(e.g., a transportation system, an air traffic control system, or flight training simulator) but more difficult to measure, for a public service building such as a prison, hospital, or school, or a number of buildings such as accommodation units. Calculation of the *pro rata* share of this loss of availability is complex (and very project-specific) if part of the building or facility provided may still be available or usable for part of its required purposes, or if some parts of the building or facility are more important than others. Therefore, to determine the percentage of availability that has been achieved in a building or other facility, a weighting has to be agreed to for factors such as:

- The building not providing shelter from wind and rain
- Inability to use any part of the building or facility (based not only on, say, floor space, but the relative importance of each part of the building or facility)
- Nonprovision of heating, light, water, or other utilities
- Nonprovision of key equipment, communications, or information technology (IT) infrastructure
- Failure to provide any other specified element required to keep the building or facility in operation
- The relative importance of different parts of the building or facility

In addition to the basic availability requirements, there may also be requirements for a certain quality of service (i.e., a performance régime). Services that may be subject to a performance régime include matters such as provision of disposable equipment in a hospital, catering in a prison, or cleaning or security in any kind of public building. Again, measurement of service performances may be highly complex, with a requirement to specify standards of performance in great detail. If the Project Company does not provide an adequate level of service, penalties are paid or deducted from the Unitary Charge. Such penalties are intended to encourage the Project Company and its investors to improve performance, but do not usually result in the Unitary Charge becoming so low that the Project Company cannot cover its operating costs and debt service. However, serious and persistent breach of the performance requirements (e.g., the Project Company's being subject to more than a certain level of penalties for several years in succession) could be grounds for termination of the Concession Agreement (cf. §6.8.1).

As with a Tariff under an Offtake Contract such as a PPA, the service contract structure therefore leaves certain limited risks with the Project Company:

Project cost overrun. If the project costs more to construct than expected and as a result incurs more debt and equity financing, this is not taken into account in the Unitary Charge calculations.

Availability. If the project is not able to operate so as to produce the service required over time, revenue is lost (or penalties are paid).

Operating costs. If the operating or maintenance costs are higher than expected, this also does not usually change the Unitary Charge.

Having said this, however, where "soft" services such as building management are being provided by outside contractors to the Project Company (who may often also be Sponsors as well), a process of review of these costs against the market ("benchmarking"), or direct market testing of the costs by calling for competitive bids, may take place at intervals (say every 5 years). Insofar as the costs that emerge from this review are higher or lower than the originally agreed base, the Unitary Charge is adjusted accordingly. This mechanism can be used:

- To give the Project Company protection against an unexpectedly large shift in operating costs because of factors that were not fully foreseeable at the time the contract was signed
- To provide the public-sector user with the assurance that a fair market rate is still being paid for the continuing services
- To give flexibility to make changes in the service arrangements, which can then be repriced based on current market costs

A similar procedure can also be used to deal with the situation where future capital costs have to be incurred, and the Project Company (or its lenders) is not prepared to fix (or fund) these costs far in advance. But the procedure is unlikely to be appropriate in relation to maintaining long-life assets, as it encourages a short-term view of maintenance of such assets.

It follows that under these procedures either adequate data must be available for benchmarking (which it may not be) or other companies in the market must be prepared to bid even though the current incumbent (a) is in a preferred position and (b) may seek to impose undue risk transfer or other onerous terms on its subcontractor. (The cost of the services concerned also obviously has to be separately identifiable in the original service contract.)

Finally lenders will not accept the possibility that this process could reduce the service contract revenue to such an extent that debt service is jeopardized.

§6.2.2 TOLL CONTRACTS

"Real" tolls. A Concession Agreement giving a right to collect tolls or fares from the general public ("real" tolls) is a long-established contractual structure for a PPP. It has been used extensively in project finance for infrastructure projects such as roads, bridges, tunnels, and railways (Figure 6.2). Typical terms for such a Concession Agreement are:

- The Project Company is obliged to complete the project to an agreed specification by an agreed back-stop date. (In some cases an independent engineer may be appointed as *maître d'œuvre* to confirm that the plant is being built to the required specification, but this should not translate into a right for the public sector to approve the construction—cf. §6.4.)
- The Contracting Authority makes available the land and rights of way required for the concession.
- Ownership of the project facilities (other than moveable assets) remains with the public sector (i.e., a BOT/BTO project).
- The concession is granted for a fixed period of time, during which the Contracting Authority agrees not to allow the construction of competing concessions (or only to allow them under specific conditions including payment of compensation to the Project Company).
- Operation and management of the concession is in the hands of the Project Company.

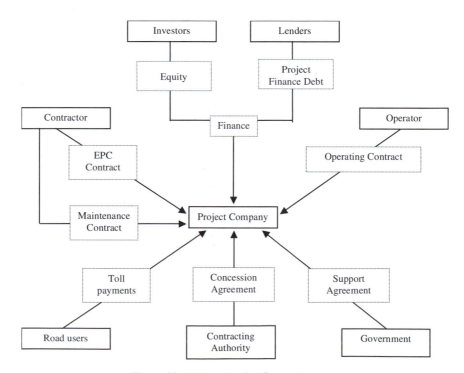

Figure 6.2   Toll road project finance structure.

- A maximum toll or fare is set, with indexation for inflation (and currency movements if appropriate), within which the Project Company has flexibility to fix tolls or fares, but subject to provisions preventing discrimination against any particular class of user.
- Minimum service provisions are specified—these usually include a required level of availability and other provisions on quality of service, similar to those for service contracts discussed above—and the Project Company may have to pay penalties for failure to provide the service.
- The Project Company is also subject to penalties for failing to maintain safety standards.
- Other provisions are similar to those for an Offtake Contract, or a service contract where the Contracting Authority takes usage risk.

Possible variations on the basic structure include:

- Although the maximum term of the concession is fixed, if the debt is repaid and the investors have attained an agreed rate of return, the concession may be terminated at that point. (This takes account the fact that if traffic growth, for example, is well over the original projections, this is probably not due to the merit of the individual project but a factor of growth in the whole regional and national economy; therefore investors should not earn excessive profits from this.)
- The traffic or other usage level may not be adequate to support a financing of the whole project; therefore the Contracting Authority provides a "fare box" guarantee (i.e., a guarantee of a minimum level of usage), or alternatively may guarantee part of the project finance debt, so that the remaining revenues are sufficient to cover the unguaranteed debt, or provide a grant towards the capital cost (cf. §3.6).

Shadow tolls. The alternative structure of the Contracting Authority paying "shadow" tolls, which leaves the usage risk with the Project Company, but with payment by the Contracting Authority instead of the end-users, is used in cases where

- Direct levying of tolls would be too complex because, for example, of the layout of connecting roads;
- Traffic flows would be distorted by drivers using unsuitable roads to avoid paying the tolls;
- Traffic flows are too small to produce an adequate level of toll payments;
- There is public opposition to payment of tolls;
- The project involves part of an integrated transport system (e.g., a mass transit system) and therefore usage of the part of the system provided by the Project Company cannot be directly charged for separately.

In this case the Project Company is paid according to usage (e.g., so much per passenger or car kilometer). The payment formula is often on a diminishing sliding scale (i.e., the highest rate is paid for the first x car kilometers,

then a lower rate for the next *y* car kilometres, and eventually payment may
be zero for the top band of usage). This structure serves two purposes:

- The first band of payment, which is based on a relatively low level of usage risk, covers the Project Company's operating costs and debt service
  (this may be split into two bands).
- The second band of payment provides the equity return to the investors
  (again this may be split into bands providing a basic return and a bonus
  return).
- Once usage has exceeded the level from which payments cover operating
  costs, debt service and equity return the government's liability is capped
  (i.e., the marginal cost to the public sector above this level is zero).

As with a "real" toll project, the Project Company may also have to pay
penalties for failure to maintain the required availability or quality of service.

§6.3 TERM OF PROJECT AGREEMENT

Having dealt with the particular features of an Offtake Contract or Concession
Agreement, the remainder of this chapter covers issues which are common to any
type of Project Agreement.

The term (duration) of the Project Agreement is normally measured from
COD, subject to a back-stop date (i.e., the term is calculated from this back-stop
date even if the project is completed later). Alternatively, the Project Agreement
may run for a fixed period from signature of the Project Agreement, leaving the
Project Company to bear the risk of a later completion but take the benefit of an
earlier one.

Various factors influence the length of the term:

The useful life of the project. Clearly there is little value in continuing
to pay for a product or service from a project that can no longer operate
safely, effectively, or efficiently, and so the useful life of the project sets the
maximum term of the Project Agreement. Possible future changes in technology may also make it inefficient to have a very long term in certain types
of Project Agreements (e.g., provision of IT services), unless the Project
Agreement allows for upgrading and renewal of the technology concerned.

The likely term of the debt. If the Project Agreement runs for a comparatively short period, the debt must be repaid and the investors must secure
their return over this shorter period, which could force up the cost of the
product or service from the project to an uneconomic level (cf. §2.5.2) (i.e.,
the "affordability" of the Tariff is affected by the debt structure).

Conversely, if the Project Agreement runs for a long period, the cost of the
product or service should be lower, although if the Project Agreement runs

for much longer than the debt the investors may make windfall profits at the Power Purchaser's expense from refinancing the debt already paid for in the Tariff (cf. §6.9).

Therefore the ideal term is probably about 1–2 years longer than the expected term of the debt, to leave lenders with a "tail" (cf. §12.9.4 and §13.2).

The residual value of the plant. In a BOOT/BOT/BTO project, the Power Purchaser may be happy with a shorter term for the Project Agreement since the plant is taken over at the end of the term and the Power Purchaser can thus benefit from its residual value (i.e., ability to continue to operate efficiently and profitably) at that time.

Conversely, in a BOO project the Offtaker or Contracting Authority loses this residual value, and a longer term contract may therefore be preferable; alternatively the Project Company may build an assumed residual value into its Tariff, and so reduce the Tariff below a level that fully recovers debt service and an equity return, thus taking the risk that the project assets can be redeployed or sold at the end of the Project Agreement.

§6.4 CONTROL OF PROJECT DESIGN AND CONSTRUCTION, CONTRACTS, AND FINANCING

The Project Company is fully responsible for designing the project to meet the required performance specifications, and arranging construction to meet the required completion schedule. The Offtaker or Contracting Authority must specify the product or service required in sufficient detail to ensure what is required is delivered but the way in which it is delivered is primarily the Project Company's responsibility; the Offtaker or Contracting Authority should satisfy itself that the way proposed is viable before signing the Project Agreement. It follows from this that the Offtaker or Contracting Authority has no right to require changes in design, to supervise, or otherwise get involved in the construction process. Having said this, the Offtaker or Contracting Authority's experience elsewhere may be helpful when detailed design issues are being considered, and it is therefore not unreasonable for the Offtaker or Contracting Authority to have the right to review designs, visit the site, and be kept informed on progress. And the Offtaker or Contracting Authority clearly has an interest in ensuring that the project is constructed to the agreed specifications. This should not, however, be transformed into an approval process — if the Offtaker or Contracting Authority does insist on subsequent approval of any aspect of the design or construction, it follows that the Project Company should not be penalized if this later goes wrong.

Similarly, the Offtaker or Contracting Authority should not be concerned with the terms of other Project Contracts except insofar as the costs of these (e.g., fuel purchase) are being passed through directly under the Project Agreement.

The same principle applies to financing arrangements, where the primary concern of the Offtaker or Contracting Authority should be to ensure that a credible financing plan is in place that ensures the project is completed. It may be necessary to control some aspects of the financing (e.g., increasing the debt burden, which could jeopardize the viability of the financing) (cf. §6.9.1).

For a discussion of risks for the Offtaker or Contracting Authority under a Project Agreement, cf. §8.8.8.

§6.5 COMPENSATION FOR ADDITIONAL COSTS

Apart from indexation (cf. §6.1.6), the Availability or Unitary Charge may also be adjusted under the Project Agreement to compensate the Project Company for additional costs in other limited circumstances, or a compensation payment may be made in lieu of changing the Availability or Unitary Charge:

§6.5.1 BREACH BY THE OFFTAKER OR CONTRACTING AUTHORITY

If the Offtaker or Contracting Authority is obliged, e.g., to provide access to the site and does not do so, and the Project Company suffers a loss of revenue or extra cost caused by the delay, compensation would be payable.

§6.5.2 CHANGE IN SPECIFICATIONS

A procedure may also be agreed for the Offtaker or Contracting Authority to make changes in the specification of the project (e.g., to convert an oil-fired power plant to gas firing), or to change the basis on which the project operates, again with additional costs being compensated. The project could also be reduced in specification and hence cost.

If extra capital cost is incurred in this way, it will obviously not have been taken into account in the original funding plan—a standard approach is to require the Project Company to raise additional funding and adjust the Tariff accordingly, but if funding cannot be raised, or the Offtaker or Contracting Authority is not happy with the effect the terms offered have on the Tariff, the costs are paid directly by the Offtaker or Contracting Authority.

The Project Company needs to ensure that it has a corresponding right to make changes in the EPC Contract specifications.

If changes affect the Project Company's operating revenues or costs, these should be taken into account by revising the Tariff.

Where changes in the project requiring capital expenditure are required after COD the Offtaker or Contracting Authority may have the right to require the Project Company to go through a competitive procurement procedure for this work; financing is then covered as above.

§6.5.3 CHANGES IN LAW

A change in the law may involve the Project Company in additional capital or operating costs for which compensation may be payable by the Offtaker or Contracting Authority (cf. §10.6).

§6.5.4 LATENT DEFECTS

In some projects the Offtaker or Contracting Authority may transfer the project site or other project assets (e.g., an existing power plant, transportation system, or road) to the Project Company. Usually the Offtaker or Contracting Authority requires the Project Company to complete the necessary due diligence and thus take the risk of any latent (hidden) defects in the transferred assets, or other unforeseeable costs (such as unexpected ground conditions on the site). This may not be appropriate when the condition of the assets cannot be easily ascertained (e.g., underground mine workings near the project site, latent defects in buildings, bridges, or tunnels): in such cases the Project Company may agree to take the risk of unexpected costs (or loss of revenue from delays) up to a certain limit, but expect to pass the costs on under the Project Agreement thereafter.

§6.6 *FORCE MAJEURE*

A *force majeure* event is something that affects the ability of one party to fulfill its contract, but which is not the fault of, and could not reasonably have been foreseen by, that party. In principle the results of *force majeure* are:

- A party subject to *force majeure* should not be penalized for nonperformance as a result of this.
- If the product or service is not being delivered because of *force majeure,* no payments are due from the Offtaker or Contracting Authority.
- A party subject to *force majeure* remains liable to make any monetary payments due under the contract.
- If *force majeure* makes it permanently impossible for the contract to be carried out it is canceled.

Force majeure provisions are found in most Project Contracts, and coordination between the provisions of the different Project Contracts in this respect is important (cf. §8.11).

Force majeure events can be divided into two main classes:

- Natural *force majeure* (also known as acts of God)—e.g. fire, explosion, flood, unusual weather conditions, etc.
- Political *force majeure*—e.g. war, terrorism, or civil unrest (also known as "political violence") (cf. §10.5)

The precise list of *force majeure* events is usually much discussed in the negotiations on the various Project Contracts. Other events may be added to the list such as:

- Unforeseen ground conditions during construction
- Delay in obtaining Permits or licenses
- Sabotage
- Blockade or embargo
- National strikes
- Strikes at suppliers' plants

The Sponsors naturally prefer where possible to have these types of events classified as ones for which compensation is payable (cf. §6.5), with *force majeure* being a fall-back position in negotiations.

Force majeure events may have a temporary effect on the project, preventing it being completed or operating properly or make it permanently impossible to complete or operate the project. As will be seen, most of the events listed above would normally come into the temporary category, as once any damage is repaired or obstruction to construction or operation removed, the project should be able to pick up where it had left off.

Temporary *force majeure* events that prevent the completion of construction of the project—also known as "relief events"—relieve the Project Company from the obligation to pay any penalties under the Project Agreement for delay in completion (but obviously no Availability or Unitary Charge payments are due). The term of the Project Agreement may also be extended by the time lost due to temporary *force majeure*.

If temporary *force majeure* events affect the operation of the project, this usually means that the Project Company loses its Availability or Unitary Charge payment to this extent. However, the Offtaker or Contracting Authority may agree that political *force majeure* events are not the Project Company's risk, and therefore any delay or inability to operate for this purpose is ignored and the Availability or Unitary Charge is payable, at least to the extent necessary to cover debt service and operating costs.

Temporary *force majeure* affecting an Offtaker or Contracting Authority (e.g.

a Power Purchaser's grid line going down) does not relieve it from the obligation to pay the Availability or Unitary Charge, since the project is obviously still available even if unusable.

Loss of income or additional capital costs caused by temporary *force majeure* should generally be covered by insurance (cf. §7.6), but this is usually a matter for the Project Company to sort out, taking account of the provisions of the Project Agreement.

Force majeure that makes it permanently impossible to complete or operate the project is dealt with under the termination provisions discussed in §6.8.3.

§6.7 STEP-IN BY THE OFFTAKER OR CONTRACTING AUTHORITY

As an interim measure on a default by the Project Company, the Offtaker or Contracting Authority may also have the right to step in and operate the project itself to ensure continuity of supply or service. The Offtaker or Contracting Authority may also have this right in the case of an emergency, even if the Project Company is not in default. If the Offtaker or Contracting Authority operates the plant, whether the Project Company is in default or not, the Tariff continues to be payable (after deducting reasonable costs incurred), and the Offtaker or Contracting Authority must indemnify the Project Company for any loss or damage.

Clearly both investors and lenders will be uneasy about the terms on which such a step-in right can be allowed, and it has to be coordinated with the lenders' step-in rights (cf. §7.7).

§6.8 TERMINATION OF THE PROJECT AGREEMENT

The Project Agreement may be terminated before the end of its normal term because of a default by the Project Company (cf. §6.8.1) or the Offtaker or Contracting Authority (cf. §6.8.2), or be made necessary because a *force majeure* event has made it impossible to complete or continue operating the project (cf. §6.8.3). The Offtaker or Contracting Authority may also have an option to terminate the Project Agreement early and take over the project (§6.8.4). Allowance may have to be made for the tax status of a payment on early termination (§6.8.5). Provisions also need to be agreed to for the handover of the project at the end of a BOOT/BOT/BTO contract (§6.8.6).

One difficult area in negotiating Project Agreements is the provisions concerning what happens after a early termination, especially of a BOOT/BOT/BTO project. The key issue is whether a compensation payment (known as the Termination Sum) should be made by the Offtaker or Contracting Authority in all circumstances (as it usually inherits the project), and if so, how this should be calculated. Market practice in this respect is quite variable, especially when the Project Company is in default. Not surprisingly, lenders have strong views on the matter and may be more concerned about it than the Sponsors, who may take the view that if the Project Company goes into default there will be little or no equity value left in the project anyway. Therefore, even though the lenders are not parties to the Project Agreement, negotiation on this issue often becomes a dialogue between the lenders and Offtaker or Contracting Authority, with the Sponsors on the sidelines.

§6.8.1 EARLY TERMINATION: DEFAULT BY THE PROJECT COMPANY

Events of default by the Project Company that give the Offtaker or Contracting Authority the right to terminate the Project Agreement should clearly only be of so fundamental a nature that the project is really no longer delivering the product or service required. A short-term failure to perform to the required standard can generally be dealt with by penalties (cf. §6.1.7) rather than a termination. Events that come under the "fundamental" heading may include:

- Project completion does not take place by an agreed backstop date.
- Failure to develop the project or to be available for operation for prolonged periods of time ("abandonment")
- Operating performance cannot meet minimum required standards.
- Nonpayment of penalties
- Bankruptcy of the Project Company
- Failure to adhere to other obligations agreed to be fundamental under the Project Agreement (e.g. maintaining a minimum quality of service—cf. §6.2.1), subject to a reasonable grace period to remedy the default (unless the failure is a deliberate act by the Project Company)

The consequences of such a termination depend on whether the project is on a BOO or BOT/BOOT/BTO basis.

In a BOO project, ownership of the project usually remains with the Project Company; the Offtaker or Contracting Authority can normally just walk away from the Project Agreement if it goes into default and may have a claim for damages. The Project Company is then left to try to make use of the project's assets as best it can. The Offtaker or Contracting Authority may have an option to purchase the project on termination, in which case the purchase price is likely to be calculated on a similar basis to a BOOT project.

In a BOOT project, at the end of the Project Agreement's term, the project is transferred to the Offtaker or Contracting Authority for no or nominal payment. If the contract is terminated early, the transfer of ownership is also likely take to place early, because the Offtaker or Contracting Authority will probably wish to take over operation of the project, assuming it can sort out the problems that caused the default (if not, it may have the right to walk away as for a BOO project, and it is then up to the Project Company and its lenders to realize some value from the project). Similarly, in a BOT/BTO project, the Off-taker or Contracting Authority owns the project anyway, and automatically takes it over if the Project Agreement comes to an end.

It appears unreasonable for the Off-taker or Contracting Authority to get the project early for nothing after a default, if this results in a windfall gain at the expense of lenders and investors. A variety of approaches have been taken in the market to deal with this situations; there is certainly no clear market standard.

Dealing first with termination after the project has started operating, the most common options are:

- A Termination Sum payment based on outstanding equity and debt, less the costs to the Offtaker or Contracting Authority of remedying the default
- A Termination Sum payment equal to the outstanding debt
- Sale of the project with its Project Agreement in the open market
- No payment at all

To look at these in more detail:

- **Payment based on outstanding equity and debt, less the costs to the Off-taker or Contracting Authority of remedying the default.** The first step in this process is to establish the outstanding equity and debt level—finding out what the outstanding debt is should be quite easy, but establishing the outstanding equity level may not be such an obvious calculation. There are two approaches to this:
  (1) A formula based on the past, i.e.:
  (a) The outstanding debt (excluding any loans from the investors)
  plus   accrued unpaid interest (but not any extra penalty interest payable on default)
  plus   breakage costs for fixed-rate debt, interest rate swaps, or repayment of a floating rate loan before the interest date (cf. §9.2.1), insofar as these represent real costs to the lenders (i.e., prepayment fees or other penalties of this type should not be covered)
  minus any breakage profits
  minus any amounts held in Reserve Accounts (cf. §13.5.2—the lenders can recover these amounts directly as they have security over them)
  plus
  (b) the total required to give investors an equity IRR (§12.8.2) at a preagreed rate to the date of termination, taking account of (i) the timing and amounts of the original equity investments (including any investors' subordinated debt) and (ii) all amounts already received as dividends or payments on investors' subordinated debt

or

the outstanding balance of shareholder subordinated debt and unredeemed equity

(2) A formula based on the future, i.e.:
The NPV (cf. §12.8.1) of the finance (equity return and debt service) elements of future Availability or Unitary charges, discounted at the Project IRR (cf. §12.8.2—thus removing the equity return and financing costs elements from these future revenues, and giving the current equity and debt outstandings)

or

The NPV of the total Tariff or Unitary Charges, *minus* the originally projected costs of operating the project, discounted at the Project IRR

Having established by one of these formulae how much the Project Company's current investment in the project is, this amount then has to be reduced by any extra costs incurred by the Offtaker or Contracting Authority to complete or operate the project, or restore it to the required performance level, or any other loss suffered as a result of the default (e.g., obtaining products or services from elsewhere).

If the original negotiations between the Sponsors and the Offtaker and Contracting Authority have been transparent as to capital and operating costs, it is relatively easy to identify any increases in such costs. The NPV of these increases, discounted at the Offtaker or Contracting Authority's cost of capital (not the project IRR, as the Offtaker or Contracting Authority can only earn its cost of capital on payments set aside to cover these future extra costs), is then deducted from the formula, along with any identifiable losses such as having to buy a more expensive product from elsewhere. In the absence of transparency on costs, the parties simply have to negotiate capital and operating costs caps, above which a deduction is made from the Termination Sum in the same way.

This formula can cause problems with lenders, however, as it is possible any deductions could be greater than the outstanding balance of the equity, and therefore all the debt would not get repaid.

Having said this, in some cases the Termination Sum is the *lesser* of the amount calculated under this formula and the outstanding debt, to ensure that under no circumstances do the investors get paid anything if the Project Company defaults. The problem with this is that it may allow the Offtaker or Contracting Authority to take over the project at an artificially low value, and does not help the situation with the lenders.

- **Payment equal to outstanding debt.** An alternative is for the payment to be simply equal to the outstanding debt (calculated as set out in 1(a) above), with no deductions, but no payment to be made for the equity component.

Investors may find this acceptable on the grounds that if the project goes into default there is likely to be little equity value left anyway. This approach is quite common for projects in developing countries; for example, it was the basis on which the first generation of BOT projects in Turkey (where the term BOT was invented in the 1980s) were undertaken. However, in such cases the project must be completed to the required standard.

A problem that applies to any formula involving repayment of debt is what level of debt should be covered by this Termination Sum payment—the debt originally scheduled to be outstanding at the time of the default, or the actual level at that time? If the project has been having problems it may have failed to repay debt as expected and so have more debt outstanding than expected. Should the Offtaker or Contracting Authority have any responsibility for this? The issue becomes even more acute if extra debt has been incurred through refinancing (cf. §6.9.1).

An Offtaker or Contracting Authority who is expected to cover this extra debt may want the ability to approve it, which both investors and lenders may feel inhibits their ability to deal flexibly with problems should they arise. A compromise may be to allow extra debt up to an agreed limit (say 110–120% of the originally scheduled amounts), and for amounts above this to be subject to the Offtaker's or Contracting Authority's approval. The same problem of course also applies to any additional amounts of equity if this is being covered by the Termination Sum formula.

It is evident that if outstanding debt is automatically repaid on a Project Company default, the lenders' due diligence and control over the project should be reduced to take account of their lower level of risk.

These formulæ also imply that any interest rate hedging or fixed-rate borrowing has to be agreed to in advance by the Offtaker or Contracting Authority, as they are responsible for the breakage costs (cf. §9.2.1).

- **Sale in the market.** In the "market value" approach, the Project Agreement is offered for sale "as is." This obviously assumes that there will actually be a market when the time comes, and that a new owner of the project can do something to sort out whatever caused the Project Company to default and continue to operate the project profitably.

  This clearly exposes both lenders and investors to a much higher risk, and it is quite possible that when the time comes there may not be a real market for the project. Therefore a further refinement is for the Project Company and its lenders to have the option of selling in the open market but receiving a Termination Sum based on one of the options above if the open market sale cannot take place, or produce a price any higher.

- **No Termination Sum.** Default by a Project Company under its Project Agreement once it has begun operations is actually very rare. The most likely scenario is a position where, because of increased costs or poor operation, the investors have lost hope of any equity return and therefore walk away from their investment and the project. (Obviously where usage risk is involved, default is more likely.)

The argument for no Termination Sum payment from the Offtaker or Contracting Authority in this situation is that even if the problem that caused the Project Company to default is serious enough to eliminate the equity return and therefore the investors' continuing interest in a solution, the project can be taken over by the lenders (e.g., by exercising their substitution right under the Direct Agreement—cf. §7.7) who will do their best to sort it out to protect their loan. Thus the Project Agreement should never actually terminate. Therefore whatever the circumstances, working out a formula that involves the Offtaker or Contracting Authority in the problem is unnecessary.

The argument against this, as already stated, is that the Offtaker or Contracting Authority could get something for nothing by taking over the project facilities on a default, however unlikely the possibility.

If the Project Company default occurs before the project is complete, the choice is normally between:

- No payment if the Offtaker or Contracting Authority chooses not to take over the project assets, or
- Paying the cost incurred on the project to date, less an amount by which this cost and the NPV of the cost to complete exceed an originally agreed amount

Although the lenders may be at risk of not being repaid in full, this type of completion risk is one that they are normally willing to accept (cf. §8.5).

Finally, if the Offtaker or Contracting Authority originally provided the land for the project site, care needs to be taken that the Project Company has no incentive to go into default and sell the land rather than continue with the project. Further adjustment to the Termination Sum may be needed to ensure this.

§6.8.2 EARLY TERMINATION: DEFAULT BY THE OFFTAKER OR CONTRACTING AUTHORITY

In a BOOT project, because the open-market value of the project is likely to be low, the Project Company needs to be compensated for the Offtaker's or Contracting Authority's failure under the Project Agreement. In a BOT/BTO project, the Project Company does not own the project assets and cannot benefit from any open-market value anyway, and therefore depends on a Termination Sum payment for compensation.

The most likely cause of default by the Offtaker or Contracting Authority is an inability to pay the Tariff, so it might be thought that negotiating a Termination Sum payment is a waste of time. The Termination Sum may, however, be guaranteed (e.g., by the government), and even if it is not, a large Termination Sum will still discourage the Offtaker or Contracting Authority from default. A Termination Sum payment also discourages other fundamental breaches of obligations under the Project Agreement, which make it impossible for the project to be constructed or to operate as intended (e.g., providing site access or rights of way).

In this case the Termination Sum should take into account the Project Company's loss of profit. If future loss of profit is not taken into account, the Offtaker or Contracting Authority could default shortly after completion of the project as a way of purchasing it at cost, leaving the investors with little monetary return for their risk.

A reasonable formula for this is therefore:

(a) The outstanding debt (excluding any loans from the investors)—in this case there can be less objection to payment of the actual debt outstandings as the Project Company is not in default

plus accrued unpaid interest (including any extra penalty interest payable on default)

plus breakage costs for fixed-rate debt, interest rate swaps or repayment of a floating rate loan before the interest date (cf. §9.2.1), including prepayment fees or other penalties

minus any breakage payments to the Project Company

minus any amounts held in Reserve Accounts

plus

(b) *either* if there is an identifiable equity component in the Availability or Unitary Charge rather than one amount covering both equity and debt, the NPV of the equity component of future Availability or Unitary Charges, discounted at the cost of long-term debt (thus enabling the investors to recover the present value of their equity return less their cost of capital)

or if there is an agreed Base Case projection of equity returns (cf. §12.10), the NPV of future returns discounted in the same way. (However, if the equity return is not separately identified in the Tariff, it is often not acceptable to the Sponsors to show these projections to the Offtaker or Contracting Authority.)

or what the market value of the investors' equity would have been if there had been no default (as the market value should reflect the value of future profits).

Another alternative—less favorable to the investors—is for a payment to be made sufficient to repay debt and ensure that the investors receive an agreed IRR to the date of payment (i.e., not taking loss of future profits into account). The danger of this formula is again that it may encourage default or an optional termination of the Project Agreement (cf. §6.8.4) soon after the project has begun operations, thus enabling the Offtaker or Contracting Authority to buy out the project more or less at cost without paying very much for the completion risk taken by the equity investors. (This can be dealt with by requiring a higher IRR for an early termination.)

As for a default during the construction period, the simplest approach is to compensate for all costs incurred to date, plus an agreed return on equity invested (and a return can also be paid on equity committed but not yet drawn, by deducting the cost of capital from the agreed equity return).

If this payment is made the project is transferred to the Offtaker or Contracting Authority.

In a BOO project, a similar payment applies, but if the Project Company maintains ownership of the project, its open-market value should be deducted from this payment.

§6.8.3 EARLY TERMINATION: *FORCE MAJEURE*

Various types of *force majeure* events may lead to termination of the Project Agreement because it is no longer possible to complete or operate the plant:

- A natural *force majeure* event that destroys the project or permanently prevents its operation, and its restoration is not financially viable (taking account of insurance—cf. §7.6). The choices here are:
  - No payment—insurance should cover the Project Company's loss (but cf. §8.10.1)
  - A Termination Sum payment by the Offtaker or Contracting Authority equal to the debt, deducting any insurance proceeds (with no repayment for equity because *force majeure* is an equity risk)
- A political *force majeure* event such as war, terrorism or civil unrest, or action by the host government itself (e.g., expropriation or blocking the transfer or exchange of currency) (cf. Chapter 10) may be treated in developing countries as a default by the Off-taker or Contracting Authority under a Project Agreement, or the government under a Government Support Agreement (cf. §7.5), with any insurance proceeds deducted from the Termination Sum payment; in developed countries it is treated in the same way as a natural *force majeure* event.

§6.8.4 OPTIONAL TERMINATION

The Offtaker or Contracting Authority may also have an option to terminate "for convenience" (i.e., because it wants to take over the project). In this case a similar formula applies for the Termination Sum to that payable on default by the Offtaker or Contracting Authority.

§6.8.5 Tax Implications of a Termination Sum Payment

Finally, the tax implications of any Termination Sum need to be considered; if the Termination Sum is taxable the amount received by the investors and lenders may be insufficient to compensate them as intended, and it therefore needs to be "grossed up" (i.e., increased as necessary to produce the net amount required after tax).

Such a gross-up provision would not apply, however, if the Termination Payment relates to a Project Company default.

§6.8.6 Final Maturity of a BOOT/BOT/BTO Contract

In a BOOT/BOT/BTO contract, provisions are required for the transfer of the project to the Offtaker or Contracting Authority at the end of the contract (assuming it still has some remaining useful life). There is an obvious temptation for the Project Company to neglect maintenance during the final years of operation. A maintenance régime therefore has to be agreed to in the Project Agreement and monitored in good time before the end of the contract, but by the time the Project Agreement comes to an end, the Project Company may have paid over all its remaining cash to its shareholders, and ceased to have any financial substance to pay compensation for poor maintenance.

Therefore if the Offtaker or Contracting Authority wishes to ensure that maintenance is properly carried out in the latter years of the Project Agreement, this can be achieved by:

- A right to survey the condition of the project
- Part of the Tariff or tolls is paid for the last few years into a maintenance reserve account under the control of both the Project Company and the Offtaker or Contracting Authority; this fund is used for maintenance as required, and any final surplus is returned to the Project Company
- The Project Company provides security—a Sponsor or bank guarantee—to ensure that the final maintenance obligations are carried out

Provisions are also needed for the transfer of operating information, manuals, etc.

Most BOOT projects for process plant assume there will be little residual value at the end of the Offtake Contract period, but in a Concession Agreement the Contracting Authority may have a continuing use for the facilities being provided or they may have a value in the open market. The possible alternatives where there is such a potential residual use or value are:

(1) Acquisition of the facilities for a nominal sum, as in a standard BOOT contract
(2) Acquisition of the facilities for a preagreed fixed sum

(3) Acquisition of the facilities for the then current market value (if the facilities being provided have an alternative private sector use such as housing or office accommodation), perhaps with a cap on the price, since there is an obvious danger that the Contracting Authority could effectively end up paying twice, once under the Project Agreement and again in the residual value payment

(4) Option to renew the contract instead of taking over the project facilities

(5) Option to put a renewed contract out for a new competitive bid (in which the existing Project Company may participate); the winner of the bid may purchase the facilities provided by the Project Company (at a preagreed price), or provide new facilities

Alternatives (1)–(3) may be structured as an option to purchase, in which case it could be said that technically it is a BOO rather than BOOT contract. If this option is not exercised, the land on which the project is situated may revert to the Offtaker or Contracting Authority, and the Project Company may be obliged to remove its plant, equipment, and buildings from the site and restore it to its original state. Again security for this obligation may be needed in the Project Agreement.

Any assumption of a residual value (especially if the Contracting Authority agrees to acquire the possibilities for a minimum sum) will enable the Project-Company to reduce the Tariff, but less so if the Contracting Authority only has an option to purchase at the end of the contract, as the Project Company is taking the "downside" risk on the residual value.

Alternatives (4) and (5) encourage the Project Company to maintain and update the project as it comes to the end of the initial contract period.

§6.9 EFFECT OF DEBT REFINANCING OR EQUITY RESALE ON THE PROJECT AGREEMENT

§6.9.1 DEBT REFINANCING

Refinancing of the debt, once the project has been completed and is seen to be operating as expected, is a common phenomenon in project finance, reflecting the reduction in risk as the project progresses, and benefits the investors in the Project Company (cf. §12.12.4). It can take various forms:

- Increasing the debt amount (so allowing an immediate repayment of part of the equity)
- Extending the debt repayment term
- Reducing the interest costs
- Otherwise improving loan terms (e.g., by reducing Reserve Account requirements—cf. §13.5.2)

The refinancing may be undertaken by the original lenders, or the original debt may be prepaid (cf. §13.6.3), and new debt raised on improved terms. Conversely, refinancing may also be necessary because the project has got into trouble.

This raises some issues for the Offtaker or Contracting Authority:

- A refinancing may affect the Project Company's ability to perform under the Project Agreement if the debt level increases or the repayment term is lengthened
- Performance may also be affected if the Sponsors recover most of their original investment via the refinancing, and so have a limited continuing financial interest in the success of the project
- A refinancing may increase the amount payable as a Termination Sum following default by the Project Company or a *force majeure* event, if this is calculated including debt outstandings (cf. §6.8.1–§6.8.3)

The Offtaker or Contracting Authority may therefore wish to exercise some control over a refinancing, or even go so far as to forbid any refinancing, especially if it is for the benefit of the investors rather than made necessary by problems with the project.

The Offtaker's or Contracting Authority's interest in the refinancing may be wider than this. The Project Company is selling its product or providing its service at a Tariff or toll pricing based on an assumed rate of return, which is itself partly a product of the debt repayment schedule. A refinancing that improves the investors' return may be made possible not because the project has been well-operated, but because the financial markets' view of the risk in this type of Project Agreement has improved. This is simply a "windfall" gain for the investors, and the Offtaker or Contracting Authority may wish to claim that a share of this benefit should be passed through in a reduction of the Tariff or toll or a lump-sum refund.

§6.9.2 EQUITY SALE

Similarly, the Sponsors may want to take the opportunity early in the project's operating life to sell some of their equity at a premium, reflecting the reduction in risk in the project once it has reached that stage (cf. §12.12.3).

The Offtaker or Contracting Authority may be concerned that performance of the Project Company may be affected because the Sponsors are no longer involved and consider that this early sale of equity is likely to bring the Sponsors a windfall benefit in the form of a higher return than that on which they were originally happy to base their investment. Here again the Off-taker or Contracting Authority may wish to claim to share in this windfall.

§6.9.3 DOES IT MATTER?

The process of bringing private capital into public infrastructure may face political attack if windfall benefits from refinancing or a resale of equity are seen to be made by private-sector investors at the expense of the taxpayer. This is not beneficial to the particular project as it may increase the general political risk (cf. §10.1), and it may also affect the public sector's ability to undertake similar projects in the future. Therefore there is clearly a case for the Offtaker or Contracting Authority sharing in these benefits. But it must be borne in mind that it may also be difficult to define precisely what such a windfall refinancing really means:

- It is difficult to distinguish legally between a *windfall* refinancing and a *rescue* refinancing, where a loan agreement may need to be amended (or terms waived) rather than replaced with a new one because the Project Company has got into financial difficulty (although one possible way to do so is to demonstrate that the investors' return on the project has gone down rather than up). Lenders will be unwilling to accept a restriction under the Project Agreement on their ability to agree to a rescue package with the Project Company.
- A "synthetic" refinancing structure can be used:
  - A flexible repayment schedule can be introduced into the original loan documentation, allowing a much longer repayment schedule if the project is completed and achieves certain operating results.
  - The lenders may agree to vary the interest rate based on the performance of the project.
  - Cash retention requirements (Reserve Accounts) may be loosened, allowing more cash to be taken out of the project.
- Finance may be channeled via a holding company and so refinanced "behind the curtain." (However such finance may not be able to benefit from Direct Agreements—cf. §7.7.)
- Sponsors' affiliates' service subcontracts with the Project Company can be amended to drain out cash at the operating level.

And the same problems apply to a disposal of equity interests:

- Equity may be held via an intermediate holding company, and the shares in this holding company sold rather than those in the Project Company
- Subordinated debt from shareholders can be sold to third parties or converted to senior debt from commercial lenders
- The investors may sell warrants to subscribe for shares, or an interest in the revenues of the company, which do not formally count as a sale of their equity

- The investors may conceal the sale by acting as nominees for the new buyers of the shares

The Offtaker or Contracting Authority thus is likely to spend a lot of unproductive time trying to second-guess whether the Sponsors' particular financing structure is intended to avoid sharing any windfall benefits, establishing the "real" base return for investors against which to measure any such benefits, distinguishing between windfall benefits and an improved return because of greater efficiency on the part of the Project Company, and trying to stop up any potential holes in the drafting of the Project Agreement to deal with these issues.

Furthermore, the Offtaker or Contracting Authority must take into account the fact that these refinancing or equity sale benefits may be factored into the pricing proposed by the Sponsors in the first place; the Sponsors may be willing to accept a lower initial return for their original risk than they really require, on the assumption that a higher return will be obtained through a refinancing or equity sale at a later stage. This is quite likely if the bidding for the Project Agreement has been very competitive. Therefore, if the Offtaker or Contracting Authority insists on sharing in these benefits, the only result may be to increase the original bid pricing under the Project Agreement. Similarly, the ability to sell equity helps to creates a greater availability of capital for new investments, and creates a liquid market that itself can reduce the cost of equity.

The Sponsors may also claim that an Offtaker or Contracting Authority who wants to share in the upside if the project goes well must also be prepared to share in the downside if the project goes badly.

This therefore suggests that it is only necessary for the Offtaker or Contracting Authority to try to share in these windfall benefits if:

- Competition for the Project Agreement has been limited
- There has been "deal creep" (i.e., lengthy negotiation with a preferred bidder, during which contract terms have shifted in the latter's favor)
- The terms of the financing are affected because it is for a new type of project or in a new market, and once the market has become used to the risk a sharp improvement in terms (e.g., higher leverage, a longer loan repayment term, or a lower return on equity) can be expected

Chapter 7

Project Contracts: (2) Ancillary Contracts

This chapter summarizes the key provisions usually found in the Project Contracts that may be signed by the Project Company apart from the Project Agreement discussed in the last chapter, namely

- Construction contract (cf. §7.1)
- Operation and maintenance (O & M) contracts (cf. §7.2)
- Fuel or other input supply contract (cf. §7.3)
- Permits — not a contract as such but an important underpinning for all the Project Contracts (cf. §7.4)
- Government Support Agreement (cf. §7.5)
- Insurance (cf. §7.6)
- Direct Agreements, which link the lenders to the Project Contracts (cf. §7.7)

As already mentioned (cf. §2.4), all of these contractual building blocks are not found in every project financing, but one or more of them usually are, and it is important to understand their general scope, purpose, and structure as they usually form a major element of the foundation on which the project financing is built.

§7.1 EPC CONTRACT

In the conventional contracting procedure for a major project, the project developer has a consulting engineer draw up the design for the project, based on which a bid for the construction is invited with detailed drawings, bill of quantities, etc.; any specific equipment required is procured separately. But even if the Sponsors have the experience to arrange the work under separate contracts and coordinate different responsibilities between different parties, this is not usually acceptable to lenders in project finance who want there to be "one-stop" responsibility for completing the project satisfactorily, since they do not want the Project Company to be caught in the middle of disputes as to who is responsible for a failure to the do the job correctly.

Therefore the construction contract in a project-financed project is usually in the form of a contract to design and engineer the project, procure or manufacture any plant or equipment required, and construct and erect the project (i.e. a "turnkey" responsibility to deliver a complete project fully equipped and ready for operation). This is known as an engineering, procurement, and construction (EPC) contract. (It is also known as a design, procurement, and construction or DPC contract.)

Another approach to contracting for major projects is to appoint a contracting or engineering company as construction manager, with the responsibility of handling all aspects of the construction of the project, against payment of a management fee. The fee may vary according to the final outcome of the construction costs. Although this may be an economically efficient way of handling major projects, a variable construction cost is not acceptable to lenders because of the risk of a cost overrun for which there may not be sufficient funding, or which adds so much to the costs that the project cannot operate economically (cf. §8.5.4). The EPC Contract therefore also provides for the work to be done by the EPC Contractor at a fixed price and to be completed by a fixed date.

Such a fixed-price, date-certain, turnkey EPC Contract transfers a significant amount of responsibility (and thus risk) to the EPC Contractor, which is clearly likely to be reflected in the EPC Contractor building more contingencies into the contract costings, and hence a higher contract price than the price if the work were done on a cost-plus basis.

Fixed-price, date-certain EPC Contracts are standard in power and infrastructure projects. Sponsors who want to adopt a different approach normally have to give lenders completion guarantees, thus diluting the nonrecourse nature of the transaction (cf. §8.12). Certain types of projects do not or cannot usually use such contracts—for example mining and oil and gas extraction projects, as well as projects involving a gradual investment in a network, influenced by changing demand, such as in telecommunications projects (cf. §8.5.9).

It should be noted that standard forms of EPC Contracts, such as those produced by the International Federation of Consulting Engineers (FIDIC) are generally not suitable for project finance, first because they tend to be too "contractor friendly," and second because there are some differences of structure compared to project finance requirements.[1]

---

[1] A useful detailed commentary on construction contracts can be found in United Nations Commission on International Trade Law: *UNCITRAL Legal Guide on Drawing up International Contracts for the Construction of Industrial Works* (United Nations, New York [1988]).

Key aspects of an EPC Contract from the project finance point of view are:

* Contract scope (cf. §7.1.1)
* Commencement of the works (cf. §7.1.2)
* The Project Company's responsibilities and risks (cf. §7.1.3)
* Contract price, payments, and variations (cf. §7.1.4)
* Construction supervision (cf. §7.1.5)
* Definition of completion (cf. §7.1.6)
* *Force majeure* (cf. §7.1.7)
* Liquidated damages (cf. §7.1.8)
* suspension and termination (cf. §7.1.9)
* Security (cf. §7.1.10)
* Dispute resolution (cf. §7.1.11)

§7.1.1 SCOPE OF CONTRACT

The EPC Contract sets out the design, technical specifications, and performance criteria for the project. Nonetheless the EPC Contractor remains responsible for constructing a project that is capable of performing as specified, even if something has been omitted from the detailed description.

An EPC Contract offers a "fast-track" route to construction of the project, since the contract is signed and construction can begin before all the detailed design work is complete; however, the Project Company has the right to object to detailed designs as these are produced by the EPC Contractor.

The EPC Contractor is responsible for employing (and paying) any necessary subcontractors or equipment suppliers, although the Project Company may have a right of prior approval over major subcontractors or equipment suppliers, to ensure that appropriately qualified subcontractors or suppliers with relevant technology are being used.

Work "outside the fence," such as fuel and grid connections for a power station, or road or rail connections being built by the Offtaker or Contracting Authority under a Project Agreement, or a third party, is not normally within the scope of the EPC Contract. Therefore, if noncompletion of this work affects the completion or operation of the project the EPC Contractor is not liable.

Another exception to the turnkey responsibility of the EPC Contractor arises where the project is being constructed using technology licensed by a third party, which is commonly the case in refinery or petrochemical plant projects. The EPC Contractor does not take responsibility for the operation of the plant insofar as this depends on such a third-party license.

Construction insurance should normally be excluded from the scope of the EPC Contract price (cf. §7.6.1).

For tax reasons EPC Contracts with international contractors are sometimes broken into separate parallel contracts, e.g. for provision of services (such as design) and equipment, or into an "offshore" contract for work outside the country of the project, and an "onshore" contract for the rest. This is acceptable provided the contracts are clearly linked together and effectively form one whole.

§7.1.2 COMMENCEMENT OF THE WORKS

There is often a gap between the time the EPC Contract is signed and the point at which Financial Close has been reached, and usually the EPC Contractor does not begin work until the latter date, when there is assurance that the financing is in place. The EPC Contract therefore often provides for a Notice to Proceed (NTP) (i.e., a formal notice to begin the works), which can be issued by the Project Company at Financial Close. In such cases the required completion date is calculated as a date that is a period of time after the NTP is issued, rather than a fixed date.

A delay in reaching Financial Close may affect the EPC Contract price; there is likely to be a final date for NTP, after which the EPC Contractor may increase the price or is no longer bound to undertake the works. Similarly, a delay in starting the work will lead to a delay in completion, which could jeopardize the project as a whole. In such cases, the Sponsors may be willing to take the risk of asking the EPC Contractor to begin work under their guarantee, based on the assumption that Financial Close will catch up with events, enabling the guarantee to be canceled at that point. For this purpose, an optional procedure for "pre-NTP" works may be included in the EPC Contract: this work may cover just the (relatively low cost) preliminary design work, or allow the EPC Contractor to place orders for (high-cost) long lead-time equipment.

The Project Company should have the right to terminate the EPC Contract if at any time a decision is taken not to proceed further with the project (this is known as a "termination for convenience"), against an agreed formula for paying compensation to the EPC Contractor.

§7.1.3 OWNER'S RISKS

Apart from making payments under the EPC Contract when these fall due, the Project Company (often called the "owner" in the context of the EPC Contract) is responsible for only limited matters such as:

- Making the project site available
- Ensuring access to the site
- Obtaining construction and similar Permits (where these have to be obtained by the Project Company rather than the EPC Contractor—cf. §7.4.1)

- Providing access to utilities needed for construction (such as electricity and water)
- Providing fuel or other materials required for testing the plant
- Ensuring that third-party contracts (e.g., a fuel pipeline to the site, an access road, etc.) are carried out as required
- Extra costs caused by having to remove hidden pollution or hazardous waste from the site, other than any pollution caused by the EPC Contractor (this is known as "site legacy" risk)

These are generally known as Owner's Risks.

§7.1.4 CONTRACT PRICE, PAYMENTS, AND VARIATIONS

Payment of the contract price is normally made in stages: after an initial deposit, payments are made against the EPC Contractor reaching preagreed milestones, relating to items such as completing a major stage of the works or delivery of a major piece of equipment, or alternatively against the overall value of the work performed as a proportion of the total contract value.

Payments may be made directly by the lenders to the EPC Contractor, rather than passing the funds through the Project Company's bank account (cf. §13.3.2).

If export credits or other tied funding (cf. Chapter 11) are being used, the EPC Contractor cannot change the arrangements for sourcing of equipment or services (as otherwise the Project Company may not have enough finance available).

Although in principle the EPC Contract price is fixed, there are some exceptions to this that usually allow the EPC Contractor to increase the price, e.g.:

- If the Project Company changes the required design or performance of the plant, or adds other new elements to the contract
- If Owner's Risks cause additional costs (including the cost of delays to the construction program)
- If extra costs are caused by delays due to the discovery of fossils or archæological remains
- If changes in law require the design or construction of the project to be changed

The EPC Contractor normally remains responsible for any problems with the geology of the site that cause extra costs, although the EPC Contractor may not accept liability for problems with projects being built in locations where mining has taken place and underground site conditions are uncertain.

The way in which the EPC Contract price is made up has in principle nothing to do with the Project Company, which is just paying a lump-sum price; however, it is sometimes necessary for the price to be broken up by the EPC Contractor for tax purposes (cf. §12.7.1).

§7.1.5 CONSTRUCTION SUPERVISION

Although the EPC Contractor is responsible for completing the project as agreed, the Project Company still supervises the construction process closely to ensure that it is built to the agreed specifications.

An outside engineering firm is often employed as Owner's Engineer to draw up the specifications for the project plant, to assist in the process of calling for bids for and negotiating the EPC Contract, to supervise the EPC Contractor's work construction of the plant, and to certify that claims for payment are in order. (The Lenders' Engineer may also be required to certify payments.)

The EPC Contract may also provide for an independent checker (also known as a *Maître d'Oeuvre*) to certify that the various stages of the works have been properly completed, who may also perform the same function under the Project Agreement.

Key EPC Contractor personnel working on the project are also designated and cannot be changed without the Project Company's consent.

§7.1.6 COMPLETION

The EPC Contract sets out the basis on which the project will be accepted by the Project Company as complete: this may involve running tests to check the performance of the project against preagreed standards.

Completion is often in several stages:

- *Mechanical completion,* when the project is ready for start-up and testing
- *Initial acceptance* (i.e., COD, also known as "substantial completion") when the project meets the basic requirements of the EPC Contract (or liquidated damages—cf. §7.1.8—have been paid), at which point the project is handed over to the Project Company for operation
- *Final acceptance* (also known as "final completion") which is dependent on resolution of "punch list" items, which are part of the agreed scope of the EPC Contract but do not prevent the project operating (e.g., landscaping).

The Lenders' Engineer (cf. §5.4) is usually involved in the process of certifying completion.

A final date for COD is set out in the EPC Contract and can only be extended in limited circumstances, e.g. if delays are caused to the EPC Contractor's work by:

- The Project Company failing to carry out its responsibilities under the EPC Contract (cf. §7.1.3)
- The discovery of fossils, archæological remains, or pollution in the site (where this is not caused by the EPC Contractor), which delay progress of the construction work
- *Force majeure* (see below)

§7.1.7 FORCE MAJEURE

Force majeure is an event which could not reasonably have been anticipated by and is outside the control of a prudent and experienced EPC Contractor (cf. §6.6), and which therefore excuses the EPC Contractor from liability for delay in completing the project. However, the EPC Contractor cannot claim compensation for extra costs caused by a *force majeure* event.

Typical events of *force majeure* that would excuse the EPC Contractor for a delay in completion ("relief events") are:

- War, civil unrest, or terrorism
- A nationwide strike (but not labor disputes that are specific to the EPC Contractor or the subcontractors or that occur only at the project site)
- Unusually adverse weather conditions at the site or on the route of equipment being delivered
- Fire, flood, earthquake, and other natural disasters

An adverse change in market conditions (e.g., making the cost of equipment much higher than expected) is not *force majeure.*

Some aspects of site condition (e.g., hidden pollution) may be designated as *force majeure* rather than Owner's Risks, thus in effect sharing the risk between the Project Company and the EPC Contractor; the EPC Contractor is not compensated for the problem but is not penalized with LDs (cf. §7.1.8) because of it.

Title to the equipment or works passes from the EPC Contractor to the Project Company when it is delivered or paid for, but the EPC Contractor remains responsible for any losses of equipment or other damage at the site until the project is taken over by the Project Company. (Some of these losses as well as certain *force majeure* events may be covered by insurance—cf. §7.6.1.)

§7.1.8 LIQUIDATED DAMAGES AND TERMINATION

Liquidated damages (LDs) are fixed amounts that both sides agree are sufficient to cover the Project Company's financial losses resulting from late completion of the project or failure of the project to perform as specified. If specific amounts are not agreed to in this way there would be lengthy disputes about loss in each case: the uncertainty involved in this would not be acceptable to lenders, and the time spent in dispute could be financially disastrous for the Project Company.

LDs are not intended as a penalty (indeed, many legal systems make a penalty payment of this type unenforceable), but a fair compensation for the loss suffered.

Apart from the LD amounts, the Project Company cannot make claims against the EPC Contractor for loss of profits or extra costs, except on termination of the EPC Contract. LDs are important for lenders, who tend to require higher levels of LDs than might be found in a construction contract that is not being project financed. LDs may also be needed to cover penalties payable under the Project Agreement (cf. §6.1.7). Obviously the EPC Contractor takes the risk of providing high levels of LDs into account when proposing a construction schedule and pricing the contract.

Delay LDs. LDs for delay in completion, subject to events excusing late completion (cf. §7.1.6) or *force majeure* (cf. §7.1.7) are standard in most EPC Contracts.

Delay LDs are calculated on a daily basis, at a rate that is a matter for negotiation but should at the minimum be sufficient to cover the Project Company's debt interest costs and fixed overheads, plus any penalties payable to an Offtaker or Contracting Authority for late completion (i.e., the costs incurred as a result of the delay); ideally they should be high enough to cover the total loss of revenue (less any variable overheads, e.g., for fuel).

The total sum payable as delay LDs is capped; lenders expect this cap to be at a high enough level to cover at least 6 months of delay in completion. A typical cap for delay LDs would be 15–20% of the EPC Contract value.

Performance LDs. Performance LDs are appropriate where the project involves some form of process plant (e.g., a power station, refinery or petrochemical plant), or the performance of a system. For example a contract for a power station will specify that it must produce at least x megawatts of power, and should not burn more than y units of fuel for each z megawatts of power production. Performance LDs are also referred to as "buy-down amounts" the lump sums paid are to compensate for the failure to build a project that operates as agreed.

The calculation of LDs in such cases is done by projecting the loss of revenue or increase in operating costs resulting from failure to meet the specification over the life of the project. These amounts are then discounted to an NPV, which is the level of the LDs. Again there will be an overall cap on the performance LDs of say 10% for each particular requirement.

Overall LD cap. An overall cap is established for LDs for all types, typically around 25–30% of the contract value, again a figure that is higher than that usually found in nonproject financed EPC Contracts.

It is important to note, therefore, that LDs do not provide compensation for a complete inability by the EPC Contractor to complete the contract: termination of the contract (see below) may provide further remedies in this case.

Environmental guarantees. The EPC Contractor may also provide guarantees of the environmental effect of the project (e.g., emissions from a plant). If meeting emissions limits is a legal requirement, LDs are usually not relevant—the standards have to be met or the EPC Contract is not complete.

Bonus. The EPC Contractor may also be paid a bonus for completing the project ahead of schedule: this should divide the benefit of earlier revenue between the Project Company and the EPC Contractor.

Termination by the Project Company. LDs alone may not cover the Project Company against poor performance by the EPC Contractor, especially as these are limited in amount: the Project Company therefore also has the right to terminate the contract if the EPC Contractor fails to complete the project by an agreed long-stop date. In this context failure to reach minimum performance standards (i.e., where performance LDs are exhausted) or environmental requirements would be a failure to complete the project.

In such cases the Project Company has the right to terminate the contract and to employ another contractor to finish the project, in which case any extra costs of doing so would be payable by the original EPC Contractor. Alternatively the Project Company may require the EPC Contractor to restore the site to its original condition, and repay all sums the Project Company has paid under the EPC Contract.

§7.1.9 Suspension and Termination by the EPC Contractor

The EPC Contractor has the right to terminate the contract and obtain compensation for any losses if the Project Company defaults by failing to pay amounts due under the contract, or in any other fundamental way under the contract (e.g., by failing to give access to the project site).

As an interim measure, the EPC Contractor is normally required to suspend work for a period of time before finally terminating the contract. For example, if the Project Company defaults in a payment, the EPC Contractor may suspend work 30 days after the payment was due, but not terminate the EPC Contract for another three months. This suspension period is normally extended further under the terms of the Direct Agreement with the lenders (cf. §7.7).

If work resumes because the Project Company has cured the default, the suspension period is added on to the period for completion of the project, and the Project Company may also have to pay costs incurred in keeping the project in suspension (e.g., personnel costs or storage of equipment).

§7.1.10 SECURITY

The EPC Contractor provides the Project Company with various types of security for fulfilment of the obligations under the EPC Contract (known generally as "bonding"):

Retainage. A percentage (usually around 5–10%) of each contract payment is retained by the Project Company until satisfactory final completion of the project. This ensures that the EPC Contractor will deal expeditiously with outstanding smaller items of work at the end of the contract. Alternatively, the EPC Contractor may be paid this "retainage" (retention amount) and instead provide a retention bond for the same amount.

Performance bond. The EPC Contractor is usually required to provide a bond for around 15% of contract value as security for general performance under the contract. This also provides further security to cover the obligation to pay LDs, insofar as the retention amount is not sufficient for this purpose.

Advance payment guarantee. If any payments have been made in advance of the work being done (for example, an initial deposit of say 10%, which is quite common) the EPC Contractor provides an advance payment guarantee, under which the amounts concerned will be repaid *pro rata* if the contract is terminated before the work is complete.

Warranties. After completion of the project, the EPC Contractor usually provides warranties, e.g., against failure of equipment (also known as a maintenance bond), running for several years.

These obligations should be secured by bank letters of credit or insurance company bonds that enable the Project Company to make an immediate drawing of cash rather than having to go through a dispute procedure or legal action before being paid anything (if they are not covered by cash retainage). If this is not the case the Project Company may face a cash crisis if the events being covered by the security arise and payment cannot be obtained immediately.

§7.1.11 DISPUTE RESOLUTION

Resolution of disputes in an EPC Contract is often by an arbitration procedure rather than court action, which is preferable, as otherwise construction could be unduly delayed. Smaller issues in dispute may be dealt with by an expert agreed by both sides.

Even if there is a dispute, the EPC Contractor is required to keep working on the project.

§7.2 OPERATION AND MAINTENANCE CONTRACT(S)

An O&M Contract helps to ensure that project O&M costs stay within budget and that the project operates as projected. Because the Project Company has no track record of operating at the beginning of a project, lenders often prefer established companies, with the necessary experience of similar projects as well as more financial substance, to take this responsibility.

Even if the project is going to be operated by one of its Sponsors (a fairly common scenario), a separate agreement for this purpose is necessary, to define the scope of the Sponsor's involvement.

§7.2.1 SCOPE OF CONTRACT

O&M may be dealt with under one contract with a single contractor, if this is appropriate to the type of project (e.g., a power station). Alternatively, the O & M responsibilities may be split (e.g., for a toll road, where toll operations involve one type of expertise and road maintenance another). Another approach is for the EPC Contractor or equipment supplier to provide long-term major maintenance (cf. §7.2.5), while minor maintenance and general operations are undertaken by an O&M Contractor.

§7.2.2 SERVICES

The scope of work for the O&M Contractor needs to be clearly defined to ensure that the division of responsibility with the Project Company is clear. The Project Company must have an adequate ability to monitor what the O&M Contractor should be doing; corporate functions should normally remain under the control of the Project Company rather than the O&M Contractor. In summary, the O&M Contractor should deal only with the project and the Project Company at least with general administration, finance, insurance, and personnel issues (other than O&M personnel).

Under a standard O&M Contract, the O&M Contractor provides the key staff (e.g., a plant manager). Other more junior staff may be employed by the Project Company or the O&M Contractor. The O&M Contractor may also make further staff available from its own organization to provide initial training and help in starting up the project (in liaison with the EPC Contractor, who may also have responsibilities in this respect), and to deal with operating problems as they arise.

Services are usually divided into three phases:

Planning. The O&M Contractor provides input into the design of the project on operational issues and projections of operating parameters and costs.

Mobilization. The O&M Contractor is responsible for a smooth handover from the EPC Contractor and transition into operation when the project has reached the end of construction, and may therefore provide support during the start-up and testing of the project.

Operation. The O&M Contract obviously comes into full effect when the project is ready to begin operations. Responsibilities thereafter may include:

- Securing operating Permits
- Operating the project to general industry standards, and on a day-to-day basis as required under the Project Agreement
- Annual budgeting
- Ordering and handling input supplies
- Maintaining a stock of spare parts
- Keeping operating costs within the annual budget
- Maintaining health and safety standards
- Keeping operating, maintenance, and personnel records
- Keeping the operating manuals up-to-date (the original manual will probably have been prepared by the EPC Contractor)
- Scheduling and carrying out routine inspections and maintenance, taking account of the EPC Contractor's warranty obligations
- Carrying out emergency repairs

§7.2.3 FEE BASIS

The O&M Contractor's fees may be on a fixed or a "cost plus" basis plus a profit margin, the latter being the normal approach where the O&M Contractor has responsibility for major maintenance. Fixed fees may therefore just cover staff costs and a profit margin, with other costs (e.g., materials or replacement parts) reimbursed by the Project Company as incurred. Fixed fees are normally indexed against CPI or an industry price index.

§7.2.4 INCENTIVES AND PENALTIES

The O&M Contractor is usually paid a bonus if the project operates at better than initially agreed levels, and conversely may suffer penalties (LDs) if it operates below agreed levels. (As with the EPC Contract, there are exceptions from penalties in case of *force majeure*.)

Penalties are normally limited to the equivalent of one or two year's fees; any bonus is calculated so as to share the extra revenue from better operation between the Project Company and the O&M Contractor.

§7.2.5 MAJOR MAINTENANCE CONTRACT

In some cases the manufacturer may be willing to assume responsibility for performance and maintenance of major elements of the project in a project (e.g., for the turbines in a power station) against payment of fixed maintenance fees over a period of time.

The benefit of this type of arrangement is that it fixes maintenance costs for such items, and so helps in long-term budgeting. However, as with an O&M Contract, the manufacturer may be unwilling to compensate the Project Company for consequential loss (i.e., loss of revenue or payment of penalties) if the plant is not maintained adequately. (There may also be difficulty in establishing whose fault it is that the project did not work if the operator is not maintaining it or if part of it is being maintained separately.)

§7.3 FUEL OR OTHER INPUT SUPPLY CONTRACT

Fuel or raw materials (referred to below as "input supplies") are likely to be the main operating cost for a project selling an output product (as opposed to providing a service), whether under an Offtake Contract or into the open market. Security of the input supplies, on an appropriate pricing basis, is therefore an important building block for this type of project finance, usually achieved through a long-term Input Supply Contract.

If a Project Company has an Offtake Contract, an Input Supply Contract is usually signed which, as far as possible, matches the general terms of the Off-take Contract such as the length of the contract, *force majeure,* etc. In the absence of an Offtake Contract, the Input Supply Contract should normally run for at least the term of the debt.

Of course an Input Supply Contract for the Project Company is an Offtake Contract for the Input Supplier, and therefore it may share many of the characteristics of an Offtake Contract.

§7.3.1 SUPPLY BASIS

The Project Company normally purchases its input supplies on an exclusive basis from the seller. The Input Supply Contract sets out the technical specifications for the input supplies, with metering or other methods for measuring delivery volumes and quality, and a right to reject supplies if they do not meet the required standard.

The start-up date for supply is generally COD. This date should have some flexibility to allow for delays in completion. (Provision may also be needed for input supplies to be made available to the project before COD when required for testing purposes. Volumes and timing are obviously likely to be uncertain, and therefore arrangements for this have to be flexible.)

The volume of input supplies required by the Project Company is linked to the project's output. The Project Company may not be in control of that output, since demand for its product may depend on a long-term Offtake Contract, such as a PPA where a Power Purchaser who does not require power can tell the Project Company to shut down the power plant and continue to pay the Availability Charge — in such cases the Project Company needs to ensure that its obligations to buy fuel can be reduced in parallel.

An Input Supply Contract is an Offtake Contract for the Input Supplier, and so as with Offtake Contracts (cf. §6.1.1) different contractual approaches are used, involving different levels of commitment by the Project Company to purchase input supplies:

> **Take-or-pay contract.** (also called a Put-or-Pay Contract, to distinguish it from a Take-or-Pay contract signed with an Offtaker—cf. §6.1.1).
>
> A Take-or-Pay Contract requires the Project Company to buy a specified minimum volume of input supplies. If the Project Company does not require the input supplies, they may be sold in the open market by the Project Company or the Input Supplier, where this is possible.
>
> An Input Supplier who fails to deliver as contracted is liable to penalties (subject to being excused because of *force majeure*); however, in an arm's-length Input Supply Contract (i.e., where there is no relationship between Input Supplier and the Project Company or the Offtaker), these penalties may be limited to the extra cost of obtaining alternative supplies rather than any loss of revenue for the Project Company.
>
> **Take-and-pay contract.** In this case the Project Company pays only for input supplies actually needed. Here the risk of disposing of unwanted input supplies remains with the Input Supplier.
>
> **Tolling Contract.** In a Tolling Contract the input supplies are provided at no cost. In effect, the Project Company is paid a "toll" (through an Availability Charge) for processing the raw material into another product (whether or not the raw material is delivered). There are two types of Tolling Contracts:
> - *Pull tolling.* The Offtaker prefers to handle and take the risk of securing input supplies, (e.g., a Power Purchaser may provide the gas for the Project Company's power plant); here, since the raw material supplier and the Offtaker are the same person, there is no benefit in this person paying for the

product while charging for the raw material, since this is just moving money from one pocket to the other.

- *Push tolling.* The product is sold into a competitive market, and the Input Supplier is willing to take the price risk. In this case the Availability Charge is paid by the Input Supplier rather than an Offtaker, and sales revenues flow directly to the Input Supplier (e.g., an oil company paying a refinery project to refine crude oil, or a metal company paying a smelter project to smelt copper).

The degree of commitment by the Input Supplier can also vary:

Fixed or variable supply. The Input Supplier agrees to provide a fixed quantity of supplies to the Project Company, on an agreed schedule (which may have some flexibility in timing), or a variable supply between an agreed maximum and minimum, as required by the Project Company. In either case the Input Supplier is responsible for ensuring it has enough supplies, and the supply may be under a take-or-pay or take-and-pay arrangement.

Output dedication. The Input Supplier dedicates the entire output from a specific source (e.g., its own plant) to the Project Company; again, this can be under a take-or-pay or take-and-pay arrangement. It should be noted that the Input Supplier may have no obligation (other than a general requirement to act in good faith) to produce any output, unless agreed otherwise with the Project Company.

Reserve dedication. This is similar to output dedication—the Input Supplier owns, say, a coal mine, and dedicates the entire output of the mine to the Project Company. Again the Input Supplier may have no more than a good faith obligation to produce anything, but anything that is produced cannot be sold to anyone other than the Project Company without the latter's agreement.

Interruptible supply. Some input supplies, such as gas, are offered on a lower-cost "interruptible" basis—often via a pipeline supplying other users. If the Project Company agrees that input supplies can be interrupted for specified maximum periods each year, the price for the supplies is reduced. So long as these arrangements can be kept parallel with Offtake Contract requirements for the operation of the project, they are beneficial to both Project Company and Offtaker.

Tolling Contract. In a Tolling Contract the Input Supplier has no commitment to supply at all, and may choose not to do so if the supplies can be used more profitably elsewhere. However, whether supplies are provided or not, an Availability Charge must be paid to the Project Company.

§7.3.2 PHYSICAL DELIVERY RISKS

Title and therefore risk of loss on the input supplies normally passes to the Project Company on delivery to the project site.

If the Input Supplier has to build a physical connection (e.g., a pipeline) to the project site, the Project Company may be required to pay a capacity payment to cover the cost of construction of the pipeline, in a similar way to the Availability Charge under an Offtake Contract (i.e., irrespective of whether it takes the input supplies or not). This payment normally begins on the expected COD, subject to extensions for *force majeure.*

If the connection is not completed on time, the Input Supplier may provide compensation to the Project Company for the extra cost of obtaining supplies elsewhere.

The Input Supplier is normally excused for *force majeure,* which may include problems with third-party connections (e.g., a railway line) used to make deliveries to the project site.

§7.3.3 PRICING BASIS

Where there is an Offtake Contract, the pricing for the input supplies is normally linked to it:

Either the product price under the Offtake Contract is based on the cost of the input supplies (e.g., in the Energy Charge under a PPA); this approach is more likely where the input supplies are a widely traded commodity such as oil;

or the price under the Input Supply Contract is based on the price at which the product is sold under the Offtake Contract. This approach is more likely either where the input supplies are a more specialized commodity such as petrochemicals, or if there is no Offtake Contract and risk is being passed back to the Input Supplier.

If there is no Offtake Contract the input supply price may be linked to the product sale price, based on a negotiated price, or simply based on the open-market price for the product.

Obviously if a Tolling Contract is used there is no price to be paid.

§7.3.4 SECURITY

The Input Supplier may require security from the Project Company for:

Completion of the project. If the Input Supplier incurs costs in building connecting facilities such as a pipeline, the lenders or Sponsors may have to guarantee a penalty payment that enables the Input Supplier to recover these costs if the project is not completed. (Clearly a guarantee from the Project Company would have little value in such circumstances.)

Payment for input supplies. Input supplies are usually sold on credit, with payment being made at, say, monthly intervals in arrears. Again, lenders may be required to guarantee outstanding payments. As an alternative, the Input Supplier may be given security over stocks of input supplies at the plant (if these would normally be sufficient to cover the amounts due), or a first mortgage over the plant itself, ahead of the lenders. Although lenders would not normally allow anyone else to have security ahead of them, this leaves them in the same position as if they had guaranteed the amounts due and so should not be objectionable in principle. This alternative approach also saves the Project Company having to pay the lenders for giving a guarantee.

§7.3.5 FORCE MAJEURE AND CHANGE OF LAW

Force majeure normally excuses the Input Supplier from making deliveries; *force majeure* preventing completion or operation of the project excuses the Project Company from taking them.

A change of law could increase the Input Supplier's cost of fulfilling the contract, either because transportation costs are increased (e.g., because there are stricter rules on how the product is to be transported), or because a change of law (e.g., a new tax) affects the profit margin under the Input Supply Contract. The Project Company can accept these risks if it is able to pass them on to the Offtaker.

§7.3.6 DEFAULT AND TERMINATION

The events which allow the Input Supplier to terminate the Input Supply Contract must be limited or too much uncertainty may be created for the project financing. Typical events of default that could give rise to termination by the Input Supplier are:

- Failure by the Project Company to pay for supplies
- Abandonment of the project, sale of the project assets, or failure to complete the project by an agreed long-stop date (subject to *force majeure* exemptions)
- Insolvency of the Project Company or acceleration of its debt

Termination by the Project Company could be for:

- Failure of the Input Supplier to make deliveries (subject to *force majeure* exemptions)

- Insolvency of the Input Supplier or acceleration of its debt
- Default by a guarantor of the Input Supply Contract

Permanent *force majeure* making continued deliveries impossible also gives rise to a mutual right to terminate the contract.

Rather than termination for failure to make deliveries, and a claim for a loss that may or may not be recovered, the Project Company may wish to enforce specific performance of the contract (i.e., obtain a court order requiring delivery of input supplies as contracted). Whether such a remedy is available varies between different countries. It may also be possible to make provision in the Input Supply Contract for the Input Supplier to be required to obtain supplies from another source.

§7.4 PERMITS AND OTHER RIGHTS

The Permits and other rights required for construction and operation of the project are not separate contracts, but obtaining or providing for these is usually both a key condition precedent to the effectiveness of the Project Contracts and to Financial Close.

Permits divide into two main categories: those required for construction and operation of the project (cf. §7.4.1), and those required for investment in and financing of the Project Company (cf. §7.4.2). In addition, rights of way or easements may be required (cf. §7.4.3), and agreements may be required to use common facilities with another party (cf. §7.4.4).

§7.4.1 PROJECT PERMITS

Permits vary greatly from country to country and from project to project. They may be granted by central government departments or regional or local authorities. If the project has a Concession Agreement or Government Support Agreement, this may automatically grant the project some of the required Permits, or it may give assurances that the government will provide support in obtaining them.

Major projects are likely to require a lot of Permits, and failure to obtain Permits in good time can seriously affect progress. The Sponsors and the Project Company need to ensure that their organization includes people dealing with Permits, in close liaison with local lawyers.

Environmental impact assessment. The first stage in obtaining both construction and operating Permits is often to prepare an environmental impact assessment (EIA) for the project. The EIA examines the environmental impact of the project in a variety of ways such as:

- The effect of construction and operation of the project on the surrounding natural environment (plant and animal habitats, landscape, etc.)
- The effect of construction on any historical remains
- The effect of construction on local communities, including noise, dust, other pollution, and construction traffic
- The level of emissions into the atmosphere caused by operation of the project
- Water abstraction and discharge
- Disposal of waste products (e.g., "tailings" from a mine or ash from a coal-fired power station)
- Long-term effects of the project on local traffic, transportation, and utilities
- Other long-term effects of the project on local communities or the natural environment

As part of this process an environmental audit of the project site is also carried out, which examines the site for potential pollution, taking account of its previous uses. If site pollution is discovered, a program for containing or removing it is required.

Following this assessment, which at a minimum must clearly demonstrate that the project complies with legal requirements on such environmental issues, an environmental clearance may be obtained. Even if this process is not a legal requirement, many lenders, both in the private and bilateral or multilateral sectors, may require an EIA as a condition of providing funding (cf. §8.6).

Construction permits. A wide variety of specific Permits for construction may be required. Responsibility for obtaining such Permits should generally lie with the EPC Contractor, who should be experienced in this area, and should take the risk of delays caused by Permits not being obtained in time. Some Permits may only be issued on application by the Project Company rather than the EPC Contractor, but the EPC Contractor should where possible be responsible for preparing the permit applications on the Project Company's behalf.

Permits may also be needed for the import of equipment for the project and the temporary import of construction equipment.

Operating permits. Permits to operate the project are also likely to be required. These may relate to the operation of particular types of industrial plant, emissions or noise levels from the project, or cover matters such as health and safety in the project. They may also be needed for the import of fuel or raw materials.

It may not be possible to obtain such Permits until the project is complete, because it may be necessary to demonstrate, e.g., the actual emissions, noise levels, etc., of the project.

§7.4.2 INVESTMENT AND FINANCING PERMITS

Specific Permits for the investment in or financing of the Project Company are unlikely to be required in developed countries, but in developing countries investment and exchange controls are likely to be applied to the Project Company.

Investment permits. Permits may be required for foreign investors (including the Sponsors) investing in the Project Company and for remitting dividends paid by the Project Company to investors overseas.

Tax exemptions may also be given (e.g., exempting dividends and interest paid to overseas investors or lenders from withholding tax).

Exchange controls. Countries with exchange control systems restrict the ability of companies to undertake foreign currency exchange and payment transactions. Exchange controls may prevent the Project Company from:

- Having bank accounts in foreign currencies
- Holding bank accounts outside the country
- Borrowing foreign currency or amending the terms of foreign currency loans
- Making payments to suppliers outside the country

In such cases specific approvals are required from the country's central bank or ministry of finance to undertake these transactions where they are required for the project financing.

§7.4.3 RIGHTS OF WAY AND EASEMENTS

In addition to these official Permits, the Project Company may also need to obtain rights of way (e.g., access to the site for construction or operation or to lay a pipeline for delivery of fuel) or easements (e.g., a right to discharge water) from parties owning adjacent land, who may have no other connection with the project.

§7.4.4 SHARED FACILITIES

Some projects may be built in two phases and raise finance separately for each phase (e.g., a process plant or power station with two separate production or power-generation lines). In such cases the construction of the first phase of the project usually includes provision for the common facilities required by both lines such as water intake and outlet.

Similarly, a cogeneration project, in which a power plant sells steam to an industrial user, may also share facilities with the steam buyer, such as a demineralized water supply, water discharge, and other utilities.

In such cases the rights of each party have to be clearly documented, including:

- Access for construction of the new project
- Rights to use the common facilities (including priority of use)
- Obligations to maintain the common facilities
- Provision for the protection of the dependent project if the other project is abandoned or foreclosed

§7.5 GOVERNMENT SUPPORT AGREEMENT

The purpose of a Government Support Agreement is to facilitate the completion and operation of the project by providing government support for any aspect of the project where the parties agree this is required.

This type of Project Contract has a wide variety of names, such as "stability agreement," "implementation agreement," "coordination agreement," "cooperation agreement" or—confusingly—"concession agreement." It is usually supplementary to an Offtake Contract signed with another state entity purchasing the product of the project (e.g., a PPA with the state power company) or to a Concession Agreement that is not signed with the government, but with another Contracting Authority. (If signed with the government, these provisions are included in the Concession Agreement itself.)

In many projects there is no need for a Government Support Agreement—the general law of the country sets up the framework for a project. This would be the case, for example, in a country with a fully privatized electricity sector, where once general permitting conditions are fulfilled there is no need for specific contracts with the public sector regarding a particular power station. Similarly, where a project is based on a license to operate (e.g., a telephone network), no other project-specific contract with the government is required.

But where there is no clear legal framework for the project, as is likely to be the case when particular sectors of the economy are using private-sector finance for the first time, or where there are particular local risks to be considered, as in developing countries, a Support Agreement with the Host Government reduces risk and thus encourages development that would otherwise not take place.

The scope of a Government Support Agreement varies according to the particular project, but some typical provisions may include:

- The Agreement sets the general framework for the project and gives permission for construction and operation of the project on an exclusive basis.
- Guarantees are given of nondiscrimination against the project.
- The financing structure for the Project Company may be specified (e.g., the debt:equity ratio) or the sources or currency of the financing (usually in a country with strict exchange controls or rules on foreign investment).

- The Sponsors may be required to retain their shareholdings for specified periods.
- The Project Company may be given the right (e.g., through a lease) to use the project site, if it is public-sector land or if there are restrictions on foreign ownership of land in the country.
- The Host Government agrees to exempt the Project Company from obtaining Permits required for imports of equipment, construction and operation of the project, or identifies all Permits required and undertakes to ensure that they are granted provided applications are properly submitted (or to provide assistance in this respect), and that they will not be revoked without good cause.
- The Host Government undertakes to ensure that imports of equipment, etc., are cleared promptly through customs.
- The Host Government provides assurances on availability of work permits for expatriate employees of the Project Company, EPC Contractor, and O&M Contractor.
- The Host Government may provide guarantees for the performance of the Input Supplier, the Offtaker or Contracting Authority, or other parties under the Project Contracts, including a guarantee of payment of the Termination Sum under the Project Agreement (cf. §6.8.2).
- Guarantees may be given for the provision of utilities for the project, such as water, telephones, and electricity, and connecting road, rail, or other links.
- Guarantees may be given that port, rail, or other transportation connections will deliver input supplies or take away the product of the project as needed.
- The Host Government (or the country's central bank) undertakes to ensure the availability of foreign exchange for debt service and dividend repatriation.
- The project may be given tax concessions (e.g., exemption from import duties, sales taxes, or value-added taxes, corporate taxes—including taxes levied on the EPC Contractor—or withholding taxes on dividends).
- The Host Government undertakes to provide compensation for expropriation of the project (usually calculated in the same way as default by the Offtaker or Contracting Authority under the Project Agreement—cf. §6.8.2).
- Default under the Government Support Agreement will be treated as a default under the Project Agreement (to allow a claim for the Termination Sum).
- The form of Direct Agreement with the lenders (cf. §7.7) is agreed.
- Disputes will be litigated outside the country, in an agreed jurisdiction or arbitration tribunal (cf. §10.7.1).
- The Host Government waives its right of sovereign immunity in relation to any claims under the Support Agreement.

A contract of this type may obviously be highly political in nature, so the Sponsors need to ensure that the Host Government has followed appropriate constitutional procedures to make it effective.

§7.6 INSURANCE

Insurance requirements in project finance are demanding, and as a result insurance costs are high, but this tends to be a neglected area of project development. This can lead to an underestimation of project costs because all required insurances have not been taken into account or to the financing being held up because the insurances required by the lenders are not in place. At an early stage of the project's development, therefore, the Sponsors need to appoint an insurance broker with specific experience both in insurance for project finance in general, and in insuring major projects in the country concerned, to advise on and eventually place the insurance program.

The broker also plays an important role in communicating information about the project to the insurance company. This is important because insurance is an *uberrimæ fidei* ("of the utmost good faith") contract; if any material information is not disclosed to the insurer there is no obligation to pay under the policy (cf. comments on non-vitiation cover in §7.6.4). The broker must therefore work with the Project Company and the Sponsors to ensure that this does not happen.

Brokers are often paid a percentage of the insurance premiums, but this is obviously not an incentive to keep premiums down, and it is preferable to negotiate a fixed fee for their work.

The insurance is arranged in two phases: first, the insurance covering the whole of the construction period of the project (including start-up and testing), and second, annual renewal of insurances when the project is in operation. It should be noted that the operating phase insurances (other than perhaps the first year) cannot be arranged or their premiums fixed in advance (cf. §8.10.1).

In addition, normal insurances required by law, such as employer's liability, vehicle insurances, etc., have to be taken out by the Project Company or the EPC Contractor, as appropriate.

§7.6.1 CONSTRUCTION PHASE INSURANCES

In construction contracts that are not being project-financed, it is common for the contractor to arrange the main insurances for the construction phase of the project and to include this as part of the contract price. This is logical, because under a standard construction contract the contractor is at risk of loss from insurable events: if part of the project is destroyed in a fire, the contractor is required to replace it, whether it is insured or not.

However, contractor-arranged insurance is not always suitable in project finance for several reasons:

- As will be seen, lenders require Delay in Start-Up insurance, which cannot easily be obtained by the EPC Contractor, who is not at risk of loss in this respect. If the Project Company takes out a separate insurance for this purpose, there is a risk that the two policies will not match properly.

- It is quite common in project finance to arrange insurance for the first year of operation as part of the package of construction phase insurances, to ensure that there are no problems of transition between the two phases; again this could not be done in the name of the EPC Contractor.
- Projects that complete construction in phases (e.g., two production lines in a process plant) have construction and operation insurances in place at the same time; these have to be handled as one package and therefore have to be arranged by the Project Company as the EPC Contractor has no interest in operating insurances.
- Lenders wish to exercise a close control on the terms of the insurance and on any claims, working through the Project Company, rather than leaving this to the EPC Contractor.
- Lenders normally control application of the insurance proceeds.
- There are a number of specific lender requirements on insurance policies that may be difficult to accommodate if the policy is not in the Project Company's name (cf. §7.6.4).

EPC Contractor-sourced insurance may appear cheaper, but this is usually because the coverage is less comprehensive than that required by lenders.

However lender-controlled insurances may cause problems for the EPC Contractor. The EPC Contractor takes the risk of physical loss or damage to the project before completion and is thus responsible for making it good. The EPC Contractor would not be excused for a delay caused by waiting for an insurance claim to be settled, since this delay would not constitute *force majeure,* and may therefore have to order and pay for replacement equipment, even though it is unclear whether the claim will be met in full by the insurance company (the EPC Contractor may have no direct knowledge of the progress of the insurance claim), or the proceeds disbursed by the lenders (rather than used to prepay debt—cf. §7.6.4). This is likely to be an area for delicate tripartite negotiation between the Project Company, EPC Contractor, and lenders.

The main insurances required for the construction phase of a project are:

Construction and erection all risks (CEAR) (also known as Contractor's All Risks (CAR) or Builder's Risk). This covers physical loss or damage to works, materials, and equipment at the project site. Where appropriate cover should include mechanical and electrical breakdown. The level of coverage is normally on a replacement cost basis, including any extra import duties and costs of erection. Insured events include most *force majeure* risks, such as acts of war, fire, and natural disaster, as well as damage caused by defective design, material, or workmanship, or incorrect procedures in start-up and testing.

   The main exception for the requirement for replacement cost coverage is if it is inconceivable that the whole construction site could be destroyed at once (e.g., a road or a long pipeline). In such cases "first loss" coverage may be effected— a level of coverage sufficient to cover the largest possible individual loss which could occur.

Marine cargo. This covers physical loss or damage to equipment in the course of transportation to the project site or in storage prior to delivery. The level of coverage should be sufficient to deal with the largest possible loss in one shipment. The scope of coverage is similar to CEAR insurance.

Third party liability. This is usually bundled up with CEAR and covers all those involved in the project from third party damage claims. As this insurance is relatively inexpensive, the levels of coverage are usually high.

Delay in start-up (DSU) (also known as Advance Loss of Profits [ALOP]). This compensates the Project Company for loss of profit or additional costs (or at least the cost of the debt interest and fixed operating costs, plus any penalties payable for late completion of the project), resulting from a delay in start of operations of the project caused by a loss insured under the CEAR policy. The DSU coverage pays an agreed amount per day of delay, for an agreed maximum period of time. The level of coverage should be sufficient to deal with the longest possible delay caused by loss or damage to a crucial element of the project at the worst possible time. In a power project, for example, coverage for around 18 months of delay is normally required. DSU cover is expensive—roughly speaking it may double the cost of the construction phase insurances, and the scale of coverage can be a matter of considerable dispute between the Sponsors and the lenders.

Marine DSU/ALOP. Marine DSU covers the same scope as DSU in relation to delays caused by loss or damage to equipment being shipped to the project.

Force majeure. The cover provided by *force majeure* insurance is to enable the Project Company to pay its debt service obligations if the project is completed late or advanced following *force majeure* events that do not cause direct damage to the project (which should be covered by DSU) such as:

- Natural *force majeure* events away from the project site, including damage in transit and at a supplier's premises (to the extent this is not covered under the DSU insurance)
- Strikes, etc., but not between the Project Company and its employees
- Any other cause beyond the control of any project participants (e.g. damage affecting third-party connections), but not including a loss caused by financial default or insolvency

   In effect, *force majeure* insurance may be used to cover any significant gaps in the DSU cover.

Insurance may also be available to cover the risk of finding hidden pollution or hazardous waste on the construction site.

The EPC Contractor may take out liquidated damages (or "efficacy") insurance, which covers the liability to pay LDs for delay or poor performance (cf. §7.1.8).

§7.6.2 OPERATING PHASE INSURANCES

In the operating phase, the insurance cover is similar in nature:

All risks. Covers the project against physical damage. The level of coverage is normally the replacement cost of the project or relevant equipment. This coverage may be split into Property (or Material Damage) insurance and Machinery Breakdown (also known as Boiler and Machinery) insurance.

Third party liability. Similar to the coverage during the construction phase.

Business interruption (BI). This is the equivalent of DSU insurance, once the project is operating. Again, the scale of coverage should be sufficient to cover losses (or at least interest, penalties, and fixed operating costs) during the maximum period of interruption that could be caused by having to replace a key element of the project—typically in a process plant project, this is between a year and 18 months.

Force majeure. Similar in scope to the construction phase insurance, covering debt service if the project cannot operate.

Certain categories of project providing services to the public sector on a BTO/DBFO basis (e.g., road and transportation projects) may not take out operating insurances for physical damage through the Project Company. In such cases the public sector has traditionally self-insured (i.e., taken the risks on without any insurances, a reasonable approach given the widespread nature of the risks involved). Therefore the Contracting Authority continues to be responsible for any insurance or for providing the Project Company with compensation for losses that would otherwise be insured.

§7.6.3 DEDUCTIBLES

All these insurances are subject to deductibles (i.e., the loss to be borne by the Project Company before payments are made under the insurance cover). The Project Company may try to make these relatively large, since this cuts the cost of the insurance premiums. The EPC Contractor will try to make the CEAR and Marine Cargo deductibles as low as possible, to limit liability for such uninsured losses. The lenders will also try to keep all deductibles low to reduce their risk.

§7.6.4 LENDER REQUIREMENTS

As the insurance forms an important part of the security package, the detailed terms of the policies and the insurance company's credit standing must be acceptable to the lenders.

There are also a number of specific requirements that lenders require to be included in insurance policies to ensure that they are properly protected (known as "banker's clauses"):

Additional insured. The lenders' agent bank or security trustee is named as an additional insured (or coinsured) party on the policies. (Apart from the Project Company, parties with an interest in the project such as the EPC Contractor, O&M Contractor, and Offtaker may also be named as additional insured.) As an additional insured party, the lenders are treated as if they were separately covered under the insurance policy, but have no obligations under the policy (e.g., to pay premiums).

Severability. The policies are stated to operate as providing separate instances for each of the insured parties.

Changes in and cancellation of the policy. The insurer is required to give the lenders prior notice of any proposed cancellation of or material change proposed in the policies, and agrees that the policies cannot be amended without the lenders' consent.

Nonpayment of premiums. The insurer agrees to give the lenders notice of any nonpayment of a premium. As additional insured, the lenders have the option, but not the obligation, to pay premiums if these are not paid by the Project Company.

Loss payee. The lenders' agent bank or security trustee is named as sole loss payee on policies covering loss or damage (or sole loss payee for amounts above an agreed figure, with smaller amounts payable to the Project Company). (However, payments for third-party liability are made direct to the affected party.) This may also give the lenders the right to take action directly against the insurance company in some jurisdictions, but in any case assignment of the insurance policies forms part of the lenders' security package (cf. §13.7.1).

Waiver of subrogation. The insurer waives the right of subrogation against the lenders; in general insurance law, an insurer who makes payment under a policy claim may be entitled to any share in a later recovery that is made by the lenders, such a repayment to the insurance company is not acceptable to the lenders until the debt is fully repaid.

Nonvitiation. Lenders prefer to have a nonvitiation clause (also known as a breach of provision or breach of warranty clause) included in the insurance policies. This provides that even if another insured party does something to vitiate (i.e., invalidate) the insurances (e.g., failure to disclose material information), this will not affect the coverage provided to the lenders. This can be a very difficult area to negotiate with the insurer, as it may add to their potential liability in a way that is not usual. In fact, in tighter insurance market conditions, it may not be possible to get the insurer to agree, and in such circumstances—if their insurance adviser advises there is no choice—lenders have to live without it.

It is sometimes possible to obtain separate coverage for this risk, and in some jurisdictions it may be dealt with by naming the lenders as additional insured parties and including a severability clause, and thus giving lenders their own direct rights that cannot be affected by the actions of others.

The lenders often wish to have the option of using the proceeds of an insurance claim for physical damage to repay the debt rather than restore the project—the so-called "head for the hills" option. This is unlikely to be realistic, given that even a project on one site (such as a process plant) is unlikely to be a total loss, and it is evident that will not be the case for a project on several sites, or an infrastructure project such as a road: therefore, the insurance claim would normally not be enough to repay all the debt unless it came at a late stage in the project life. Also, the insurance company may require restoration of the project as a condition for paying out under the claim. Similarly, the EPC Contractor or, if there is a Project Agreement, the Offtaker or Contracting Authority, may wish to ensure that insurance proceeds are automatically applied to restoration of the project, rather than used to reduce debt. Nonetheless, the lenders may want to keep the option open, in case the project is no longer economically viable when a claim is made. At the very least the lenders control how the insurance proceeds are disbursed (cf. §13.5.2).

An Offtaker or Contracting Authority will also be concerned that adequate insurance is maintained if this would reduce any Termination Sum payment on termination of the Project Agreement for *force majeure* (cf. §6.8.3).

Any payment covering loss of revenue (i.e., claims on DSU, BI, or *force majeure* policies) is controlled by the lenders in the same way as they control the application of the general revenues of the Project Company (cf. §13.5.1).

§7.6.5 REINSURANCE

Most insurance companies insuring a large project will reinsure some of their liability in the reinsurance market. This is usually of no concern to lenders, as they rely on the primary liability (and credit standing) of the original insurance company.

However, in some countries local law may require that the insurances are all placed with domestic insurance companies. In developing countries these local insurance companies may have neither the credit standing nor the capacity to take on the insurance requirements for a major project.

The local insurance companies therefore normally reinsure the risk on the international market: this reinsurance can provide the route to dealing with investors' and lenders' credit problems with the local insurers, by allowing a "cut-through" to the reinsurance (i.e., the local insurer instructs the reinsurers to pay any claims directly to the Project Company or the lenders), hence reducing the local credit risk issue (although there could still be a problem if the local insurance company, as the person to whom the reinsurance payments are legally due, goes bankrupt).

§7.7 DIRECT AGREEMENTS

The EPC Contractor, O&M Contractor, Offtaker or Contracting Authority, Input Supplier, Host Government (if there is a Government Support Agreement), and other key Project Contract counterparties are all normally required to sign Direct Agreements with the lenders (to which the Project Company may also be a party). These are also known as "acknowledgments and consents," since they acknowledge the position of the lenders, and consent to their taking an assignment of the contracts as security.

Whether Direct Agreements should be classified as Project Contracts or financing documentation is a moot point, but they are usually negotiated at the same time as the Project Contracts, and the form of Direct Agreement is set out as an annex to the relevant Project Contract.

Under these Direct Agreements:

- The lenders' security interests in the underlying Project Contracts are acknowledged.
- If the Project Contract counterpart is making payments, these are to be made to specific bank accounts (over which the lenders have security) or as notified by the lenders.
- The Project Contract counterpart agrees that amendments will not be made to the contract concerned without the lenders' consent.
- The lenders are notified if the Project Company is in default under the underlying contract and have the right to join in any discussions with the contract counterpart at that time.
- The lenders are given "cure periods," (i.e., extra time to take action to remedy the Project Company's default, in addition to that already given to the Project Company) before the contract is terminated. These cure periods are limited in length—perhaps only a week or two—where the Project Company has failed to pay money when due (except under the EPC Contract where a suspension period applies—cf. §7.1.9), but substantially longer for

nonfinancial default (e.g., failure to operate the project to the required minimum performance level) — usually around 6 months—if the lenders are taking active steps to find a solution to the problem.
- The Project Contract counterpart is obliged to continue to perform its obligations during the cure period, so long as payments of money (e.g., for fuel deliveries) during this time are made when due.
- The lenders have the right to "step-in" to the contract. This means that they can appoint a nominee to undertake the Project Company's rights in parallel with the Project Company; the nominee is effectively in charge of the project, but the Project Company remains liable for all the obligations. The period of step-in is at the lenders' discretion, and they can "step-out" again whenever they wish.
- Alternatively, the lenders have the right to "substitution," i.e., appointment of a new obligor in the place of the Project Company, who then ceases to have any further involvement with the project (other than the right to any cash or perhaps a retransfer of the relevant Project Contract, after the loans have been repaid). The technical and financial capacity of the lenders' nominee or substitute obligor may have to be acceptable to the Project Contract counterpart, and any accrued liabilities.
- The lenders themselves will not assume any additional liability as a result of step-in or substitution.
- Neither step-in nor substitution extends the lenders' cure period; they have to take place before the end of the cure period.
- The Project Company undertakes (either in the Direct Agreement itself or in the financing documentation) not to obstruct the lenders' exercise of their step-in and substitution rights provided an event of default under the financing documentation has occurred. (The lenders may wish to step in because there is a default under the financing, even if the Project Contract concerned is not in default.)
- In the case of a Project Agreement with a Termination Sum on Project Company default (cf. §6.8.1), the Offtaker or Contracting Authority may agree that if the lenders enforce their security, the Project Agreement will automatically be terminated, thus ensuring the Termination Sum is paid. (In return, the Offtaker or Contracting Authority may also want the right to terminate the Project Agreement if the lenders cease to make funds available for construction of the project.)
- Additional assurances may also be given to the lenders under a Direct Agreement, e.g., the Host Government may confirm that the lenders will be allowed to remove project assets or proceeds from sale of assets out of the country if they terminate their loan and enforce their security.
- In general, additional provisions may be negotiated through the lenders in a Direct Agreement as an indirect way for the Project Company to improve the terms of the relevant Project Contract, e.g.:

- Extra financial guarantees may be provided by the Host Government for performance of Project Contract counterparties.
- A Host Government may give further assurances on policy matters affecting the project (e.g., privatization of an Offtaker).
- The Project Contract counterpart may also receive some additional assurances or benefits, for example, a right of preemption if the lenders exercise their security.

Some of these provisions may be covered in a Government Support Agreement (cf. §7.5), with the benefit transferred to lenders via a Direct Agreement relating to this Government Support Agreement.

It could be argued that the practical value to the lenders of many of the provisions of Direct Agreements is questionable. (Moreover, third parties, especially in the public sector, are often reluctant to sign such agreements.) The Project Company clearly has little interest in them (unless they indirectly improve the terms of the underlying Project Contracts), since the Direct Agreements effectively cut the Project Company out of the picture once it is in default and create a direct relationship between the lenders and the Project Contract counterparts. In practice, if a project is going wrong, all parties have to sit around the table and try to find a solution, whether there is a Direct Agreement or not. However, from the lenders' point of view probably the most important point is that the real value of their security lies in the Project Contracts, and Direct Agreements may help them to step rapidly into the picture after a Project Company default to preserve these contracts and find another party to take them over (cf. §13.7).

Similarly, the lenders may obtain "collateral warranties" with respect to construction or operation of the project from, e.g., an Owner's Engineer or other person performing a service for the Project Company, under which direct liability is accepted for the performance of this service (to the extent agreed in the contract with the Project Company) *vis-à-vis* the lenders.

Chapter 8

Commercial Risks

§8.1 CATEGORIES OF PROJECT FINANCE RISK

Project finance risks can be divided into three main categories:

Commercial risks (also known as *project risks*) are those inherent in the project itself, or the market in which it operates, as summarized in §8.3 and discussed in this chapter as a whole.

Macro-economic risks (also known as *financial* risks) relate to external economic effects not directly related to the project (i.e., inflation, interest rates, and currency exchange rates); these risks are considered in Chapter 9.

Political risks (also known as *country risks*) relate to the effects of government action or political *force majeure* events such as war and civil disturbance (especially, but not exclusively, where the project involves cross-border financing or investment); these risks are considered in Chapter 10.

§8.2 RISK EVALUATION AND ALLOCATION

Risk evaluation is at the heart of project finance. This is *not* a mathematical process (e.g., using Monte Carlo simulations), although financial modeling comes into the process to assess the financial effect of a limited range of scenarios (cf. §12.10). Project finance risk analysis is based on:

- A due-diligence process intended to ensure that all the necessary information about the project is available
- Identification of risks based on this due diligence

- Allocation of risks (to the extent possible) to appropriate parties to the project through provisions in the Project Contracts
- Quantifying and considering the acceptability of the residual risks that remain with the Project Company, and hence with its lenders

Of course, due diligence and risk assessment are not procedures peculiar to project finance, and all financing involves risk in some way. But the process of contractual risk allocation, and raising finance based on this, are particular characteristics of project finance.

It should be noted that risk assessment by lenders is based as much on the financial impact that a particular risk may have on the project's viability as on the likelihood of it actually happening. As a result, Sponsors may feel that lenders concentrate on risks that are unlikely to arise and therefore of little commercial importance.

Although the process of due diligence and risk evaluation may be thought of as primarily one to be undertaken by lenders, it is evident that if the Sponsors do not go through the same process first, they will not be able to develop a financeable project.

The theoretical principle of risk allocation in project finance is that risks should be borne by those who are best able to control or manage them: for example, the risk of late completion of construction and its financial consequences for the project should ultimately be borne by the EPC Contractor, unless this late completion arises from events, such as *force majeure,* outside the EPC Contractor's control.

In reality, risk allocation is also based on the negotiating power of the different parties, and may in fact take up most of the time spent in negotiating Project Contracts; indeed the price charged under the contract concerned may become overshadowed by issue about which party takes which risks.

However, other parties to Project Contracts have to recognize that the Project Company's ability to absorb risk is limited if it wishes to raise highly leveraged project finance: it is no use allocating risk to a party who cannot sustain the financial consequences if the risk materializes. Similarly, if the Offtaker or Contracting Authority wishes to achieve the lowest possible Tariff, this usually implies that it must absorb a higher level of risk (cf. §2.5.2). A common error in the early development and negotiation of Project Contracts is to leave too much risk with the Project Company, which causes problems later when raising the finance. On the other hand, transfer of all risk away from the Project Company to other parties is not viable; if other parties are asked to assume too much of the risk, they will also expect the appropriate equity return for doing so, with obvious consequences for investors.

Within the financing structure, careful thought also has to be given to appropriate risk sharing between equity and debt. The lenders are not "investors" in the project, although Sponsors often like to use this expression in the heat of negotiation. If the lenders were investors they would get an equity rate of return, but they do not; typically in a successful project, the gross rate of return on the equity is at least twice that on the debt, which reflects the different risks taken by investors and lenders. As the ability of the Project Company itself to absorb equity risk is limited by the low level of its equity, this may mean in some cases transfer of risk from the Project Company to the Sponsors (cf. §8.12).

§8.3 ANALYSIS OF COMMERCIAL RISKS

The main questions considered in the commercial risk analysis process can be summarized as:

- *Commercial viability:* does the project make overall sense? (cf. §8.4)
- *Completion risks:* can the project be completed on time and on budget? (cf. §8.5)
- *Environmental risks:* does the project face any environmental constraints in construction or operation? (cf. §8.6)
- *Operating risks:* is the project capable of operating at the projected performance level and cost? (cf. §8.7)
- *Revenue risks:* will operating revenues be as projected? (cf. §8.8)
- *Input supply risks:* can raw materials or other inputs be obtained at the projected costs? (cf. §8.9)
- *Force majeure risks:* how can the project cope with *force majeure* events? (cf. §8.10)
- *Contract mismatch:* do the Project Contracts fit together properly? (cf. §8.11)
- *Sponsor support:* is there a need for more recourse to the Sponsors? (cf. §8.12)

The due-diligence process therefore examines the risks inherent in the project under these different headings, the extent to which these are covered by contractual arrangements, and whether remaining risks left with the Project Company are reasonable and acceptable to lenders.

One standard approach to this is to produce a "risk matrix" table, which sets out in columns:

- What the risk is
- Whether it is covered in the Project Contracts
- What other mitigation there is for risks not covered contractually (e.g., through guarantees or insurance)
- What impact the risk that then remains would have on the Project Company (and hence effectively the lenders)

A process of "formal" due diligence is also undertaken by the lenders' legal and other professional advisers to consider whether (1) the parties to Project

Contracts have gone through proper procedures to sign these contracts, (2) all necessary legal requirements have been fulfilled to undertake the project, and (3) appropriate tax and accounting assumptions are being used.

It should be noted that the classification of commercial risks set out in the remainder of this chapter is inevitably only a guide to the issues that may have to be considered in any particular case, as each project has its own characteristics.

§8.4 COMMERCIAL VIABILITY

The first step in due diligence for any project is to consider its basic commercial viability (i.e., is there a sound market for the product or service provided by the Project Company?). This initial question has nothing to do with the terms of any contracts signed by the Project Company, although if, e.g., an Offtake Contract has not been signed, the need to consider the commercial viability of the project becomes more obvious. Project finance is a long-term business, and long-term contracts that give an undue advantage to one side are vulnerable; it is impossible to provide in advance for every event that may affect a Project Contract in the future, and an aggrieved party will obviously take advantage of any flaw to get out of an onerous obligation. Therefore the deal underlying any Project Contract should make good long-term commercial sense for both parties.

Questions that may be considered in examining commercial viability include:

- Is there an established market for the project's product or service?
- What competition exists or may exist in this market in the future?
- Is the price at which the product or service is being sold reasonable in relation to the existing market, and does it take adequate account of future competition?
- Can any major structural changes in the market (e.g., deregulation or new technology) be foreseen, and what might the effect of these be?
- Can the prospective end-users of the product or service afford to pay for it?
- Are other players in the same market facing any particular difficulties?
- Are the prices quoted by the EPC Contractor or the fuel or raw material suppliers realistic?
- Is there anything that would prevent the project operating normally when complete (e.g., grid connections for a power station, connecting roads for a bridge) and have arrangements been made to ensure that this is dealt with?

The following are some examples of types of projects that have an apparently sound contractual structure, but which are not commercially viable:

- The EPC Contractor has quoted too low a price, perhaps because of insufficient experience of this sector. An EPC Contractor who finds that there is going to be a loss on the EPC Contract will use every loophole in the contract terms and specifications to claim more money for the job. Such disputes may seriously delay the project and affect its overall viability.

- The cost of the product or service sold under a Project Agreement is not competitive (or is likely to become uncompetitive) with current prices for the same product or service, or too high in relation to the ability of end-users to pay for it. The Offtaker or Contracting Authority, squeezed between the Project Company and the end-users, will inevitably try to find a way out of the contract.
- A power station project depends on the state power company as Power Purchaser connecting the plant to the national grid system; the Power Purchaser is obliged to pay the Availability Charge even if the grid connection is not made. Although this is a reasonable provision for a PPA, a "white elephant" plant is of no use to the Power Purchaser, who will try to find any way to get out of the PPA if the grid connection cannot be funded or completed
- An Input Supplier, relying on the open market to source supplies, faces a large increase in the free-market price for the product concerned, which is not reflected in the long-term sales price in the Input Supply Contract, because the contract price is not linked to the free-market price. Disputes or even default on the Input Supply Contract are highly likely.

§8.5 COMPLETION RISKS

The first detailed due-diligence question is whether the project can be completed on time and on budget—this question obviously mainly revolves around the risks inherent in the construction process.

The key completion risks include:

- Site acquisition and access (cf. §8.5.1)
- Permits (cf. §8.5.2)
- Risks relating to the EPC Contractor (cf. §8.5.3)
- Construction cost overrun (cf. §8.5.4)
- Revenue during construction (cf. §8.5.5)
- Delay in completion (cf. §8.5.6)
- Inadequate performance on completion (cf. §8.5.7)
- Third-party risks (cf. §8.5.8)

The position where there is no final-price date-certain EPC Contract also needs to be considered (cf. §8.5.9).

§8.5.1 SITE ACQUISITION AND ACCESS

Lenders will not normally take on this risk, and therefore only lend when the Project Company has clear title and access to the project site and any additional land needed during construction. This is mainly likely to be a problem in a transport project, e.g., where land has to be acquired for a road or a railway line, and acquisition is not complete at the time construction on one part of the project begins.

It is common for site acquisition to be the responsibility of a Contracting Authority under a Concession Agreement, since this often involves acquiring large areas of land in multiple ownership, for which a public authority's compulsory purchase powers may be needed.

§8.5.2 PERMITS

Lenders generally require construction permits (cf. §7.4.1) to be obtained before any funds are advanced, to ensure that failure to obtain such permits does not delay completion. If, for good reason, such Permits cannot be obtained at this stage, a specific timetable for obtaining them is normally established with the lenders. Where possible lenders prefer the risk of obtaining these later Permits to be placed on the EPC Contractor, who thus becomes responsible for any delay caused by failure to obtain them.

Rights of way, easements, etc. (cf. §7.4.3) may be more difficult where these involve parties not otherwise connected with the project, and the EPC Contractor is unlikely to take the risk of obtaining these; lenders will be uncomfortable if these are not obtained prior to Financial Close.

Investment and financing permits (cf. §7.4.2) must be obtained before the financing can become effective. In some countries the final approval for the financing is not granted by the central bank until after the loan has been signed and registered with them, which means there is an inevitable gap between the loan signing and Financial Close (cf. §13.8).

Final completion of the project may also be dependent on obtaining operating permits that confirm that the project meets emissions or safety requirements. Clearly these cannot be obtained in advance, but obtaining such Permits (or meeting the requirements to obtain them) should where possible be an obligation of the EPC Contractor: if this is made a condition to reaching COD under the EPC Contract, the risk of failure to obtain operating Permits is thus transferred to the EPC Contractor.

A Government Support Agreement (cf. §7.5) can be helpful in reducing the risk of problems with Permits; although it may not eliminate the need for Permits, it can provide a basis for the cooperation of the government in obtaining the permits from ministries and other agencies. The central government may not be willing to take responsibility for ensuring permits are obtained from provincial, state, or local governments, over which it has no control. In projects in developing countries, the Offtaker or Contracting Authority may take the risk of permits not being obtained as required, provided the Project Company can demonstrate that it has applied for them diligently.

§8.5.3 THE EPC CONTRACTOR

Risk analysis of the EPC Contractor takes account of the competence to undertake the work, whether the pricing for the work is appropriate, and the EPC Contractor's overall credit standing. The EPC Contractor's own risk analysis should also be borne in mind.

Competence. The EPC Contractor plays a vital role in most projects, and therefore the first step in risk assessment is to consider whether the EPC Contractor is adequately qualified for this, with sufficient experienced personnel to undertake the job. It is unlikely that finance could be raised for any project where lenders are not convinced that the EPC Contractor has a good record in similar projects.

The right to claim LDs, bonds, and other security provided under the EPC Contract (cf. §7.1.8/§7.1.10) cannot substitute for the competence of the EPC Contractor. Even a termination payment that recovers all the money spent on the EPC Contract will not adequately compensate the Project Company for losses if the project is not built, since the EPC Contract price only covers about 60–75% of typical project costs.

Therefore an EPC Contractor who is not already well-known to the Sponsors is normally required to go through a prequalification process, demonstrating the experience to build the type of project required successfully. This would include providing references for similar projects already built, including, where appropriate, references for the technology being employed in the project. The Lenders' Engineer reviews such references in depth, as well as making checks on the general reputation of the EPC Contractor in the market. Similar references may be required for major subcontractors, and the EPC Contract should provide the Project Company a list of approved subcontractors, or the right to veto them (and may give some rights of approval over the terms of the subcontracts, although subcontract prices are not usually revealed).

If the EPC Contractor is working overseas, experience in the country of the project, and good relationships with strong local subcontractors, are also relevant.

Finally the expertise of the EPC Contractor's key personnel who are actually working on the construction should be examined.

The Owner's Engineer (cf. §7.1.5) and the Project Company's own staff also mitigate this risk by supervising the activities of the EPC Contractor.

Although construction is the EPC Contractor's job, lenders will also wish to ensure that there is adequate supervision of the works, and therefore that the combination of the Project Company's own personnel and the Owner's Engineer have the qualifications and experience for this role.

The EPC Contractor as Sponsor. A Sponsor who is also the EPC Contractor has an obvious conflict of interest between this role and that of an investor in the Project Company (cf. §4.1). The risk of inappropriate contractual arrangements, or a less than rigorous supervision of the EPC Contract, is evident, and lenders therefore have to be satisfied that the EPC relationship is on an arm's-length basis.

This risk may be mitigated in several ways:

- Other Sponsors not involved in the EPC process may specify the work and negotiate the EPC Contract (assuming they have the relevant expertise to do so).
- Supervision of the EPC Contract should be carried out by Project Company personnel who are not connected with the EPC Contractor, with the assistance of an independent Owner's Engineer.
- The EPC Contractor's directors on the Project Company's board should absent themselves from discussions on the EPC Contract.
- The Lenders' Engineer is likely to play a more prominent checking role.

But if the EPC Contractor is a major Sponsor of the project, which is inevitably often the case with infrastructure projects, there is a limit to the extent that the EPC Contractor can be isolated from the Sponsor side of discussions on the EPC Contract. In such cases, the EPC Contractor must at least convince the lenders that the investment and EPC roles are adequately separated internally.

Limited involvement in the contract. An EPC Contractor normally subcontracts a significant part of the contract; for example, a main contractor whose primary business is that of equipment supply will normally subcontract the civil works (charging LDs and taking security from the subcontractors that parallel the terms of the main EPC Contract). This process, however, can be carried too far if the EPC Contractor is not a significant supplier of either equipment or civil works to the project, but just provides an "envelope" for a contract largely carried out by subcontractors. The EPC Contractor may have insufficient experienced personnel "in house" and rely too much on the subcontractors.

In such a situation, the risk of poor overall control of the project may be reduced by requiring the EPC Contractor to work in joint venture with one or more companies that would otherwise have been subcontractors.

EPC Contract price too low or too high. The risk of the EPC Contractor offering too low a price, however attractive this might seem at first sight, has already been mentioned in the general discussion on commercial viability (cf. §8.4). The Owner's Engineer should check the commercial viability of the EPC Contractor's price, which will also be reviewed by the Lenders' Engineer.

Conversely, a price that is too high (even if the higher cost can be covered by project revenues) suggests, at best, that there is not an arm's-length relationship with the EPC Contractor, which is likely to leave the Project Company's lenders in a weak position if something goes wrong, and, at worst, that corruption is involved.

Credit risk. Allocating project risk to the EPC Contractor is not worthwhile if the contractor is not creditworthy. If the EPC Contractor's wider business gets into financial difficulties, the project is likely to suffer. The credit standing of the EPC Contractor therefore needs to be reviewed to assess whether it could cause any risk to the project.

The EPC Contract should also not be excessively large in relation to the EPC Contractor's other business, as otherwise there is a risk that if the Project Contract gets into trouble, the EPC Contractor may not be able to deal with such problems because of their financial effect on the business as a whole. The scale of the EPC Contract should therefore be compared with the EPC Contractor's annual turnover; if it is more than, say, 10% of this figure, the EPC Contract may be too big for the EPC Contractor to handle alone, and a joint-venture approach with a larger contractor may be preferable.

If the EPC Contractor is part of a larger group of companies, guarantees of its obligations by its ultimate parent company may also be necessary to support the credit risk.

The risk of nonpayment of LDs, warranty claims, etc., can be mitigated by bank bonding, but, for the reasons mentioned above, this security is not a substitute for a good general credit standing.

The EPC Contractor's risks. An EPC Contractor might reasonably ask what security is offered that payments will be made by the Project Company. Lenders have first security over the project assets, and therefore these are not available to the EPC Contractor. Neither the Sponsors nor the lenders will normally provide the EPC Contractor with guarantees. (Of course, one of the Sponsors may be the EPC Contractor.)

Normally the EPC Contractor's only security is the existence of the financing arrangements, and the fact that it is seldom in the lenders' interests to cut off funding for construction of the project.

Therefore the EPC Contractor will not normally begin work until (1) all other project and financing contracts are in place, (2) Financial Close has been reached, and (3) when satisfied that sufficient funding has been made available by lenders on terms that should ensure that payments due under the EPC Contract can be made, and that the funding will not be withdrawn by the lenders on an arbitrary basis. (Sometimes the Sponsors may wish the

EPC Contractor to begin work earlier than Financial Close, and therefore provide the EPC Contractor with temporary guarantees against which the work can progress until Financial Close has been reached—cf. §7.1.2.)

The EPC Contractor should also ensure that the EPC Contract payment schedule is linked as closely as possible to its own financial exposure to direct costs and payments to subcontractors and equipment suppliers, so that if the Project Company does collapse the EPC Contractor's losses can be limited.

§8.5.4 CONSTRUCTION COST OVERRUNS

The effects of an overrun in construction costs against the budget on which the funding structure has been based are:

- There may be insufficient funding available to complete the project, thus forcing the Sponsors to invest funds for which they have made no commitment, to avoid a loss of their investment, or putting them at a severe disadvantage (and therefore liable to higher borrowing costs or other disadvantageous changes in loan terms) by having to ask the lenders to advance further funds or to agree to new financing arrangements.
- Even if additional funding is available, the project's cost base, and hence debt service costs, have been increased, with no corresponding increase in revenue: therefore, the investors' return will inevitably be reduced. In the worst case, it could lead to the Sponsors abandoning the project because the increased costs destroy its viability.
- From the lenders' point of view, the increase in debt service costs reduces their cover ratios (cf. §12.9) and thus makes the loan more risky.

The risk analysis therefore needs to consider the main cost headings in the project budget (cf. §12.4.1), how these costs are controlled, and the likelihood of overruns under each heading. In a typical project these cost headings may include:

- EPC Contract
- Development costs
- Mobilization costs
- Insurance premiums
- Other Project Company costs
- Contingency reserve
- Financing costs (cf. §9.2)

To control construction costs a budget is agreed to with lenders, and any actual or projected excesses over the amounts set out in the major cost categories normally need to be approved by them as they occur or are projected, even if there is still enough overall funding to complete the project (cf. §13.3.2). Lenders should be discouraged from trying to set up too detailed a "line-item" control of the budget; most of the construction cost budget is contractually fixed, or represents financing costs, and some flexibility needs to be given to the Project Company to manage remaining minor variations in cost categories, especially if the overall project cost is not significantly affected.

To consider these individual cost items in more detail:

EPC Contract. The EPC Contract is normally by far the largest cost item in the budget—perhaps 60–75% of the total. (The second largest item is usually financing costs.) Therefore it is evident that this is the most important item to control, and the relevance of a fixed-price turnkey contract in this connection is clear. If there is not a fixed-price contract in place, this adds a major dimension of extra risk to the project.

But a so-called fixed-price contract is never 100% fixed, and the risk of the EPC Contractor making claims for additional payments under various contract provisions has to be considered. These claims come under several categories:

- *Changes in the project schedule:* the actual start-up of the EPC Contract may be delayed after signature, perhaps because of difficulties in raising the finance, or satisfying all the lenders' conditions precedent. The EPC Contractor cannot be expected to keep the price fixed indefinitely, and therefore a cut-off date for the fixed price is normally established. Thereafter the EPC Contractor may be willing to agree to a formula for adjusting the final fixed price against CPI or another index after cut-off date; this may be manageable within the financing plan. If no formula is agreed to lenders may be reluctant to continue with work on the financing, as one of the main cost elements is no longer fixed.

- *Site condition:* as set out in §7.1.4, the EPC Contractor will not normally accept extra costs caused by having to remove hidden pollution or hazardous waste on the project site, although the risk of problems with the geology (e.g., affecting piling costs) should be accepted.

  This is often a difficult area of risk transfer in the EPC Contract, because lenders are also often unwilling for the Project Company to accept such risks. A survey of the site can never provide 100% certainty that there is not a problem that has not been picked up by the survey. Similarly, a detailed knowledge of the history of the past usage of the site, while helpful, does not eliminate these risks. The problem is especially acute in "linear" projects (i.e., projects not occupying one site, but being built over a long stretch of land where detailed site investigation may be impossible, such as a road, pipeline or electricity gridline) (cf. §6.5.4).

From the lenders' point of view, the main mitigation of risk is that problems of this nature should be apparent at an early stage of construction, when project costs have probably not yet exceeded the amount of the equity investment; therefore, they can stop advancing funds if any major problems of this nature appear, with their risk covered by the equity.

If there is known to be pollution or hazardous waste on the site this is also likely to be a major issue with lenders, even if removal is budgeted for in the EPC Contract. In some countries (e.g., Canada) lenders have liability for damage caused by pollution from a site over which they take security; in general lenders feel vulnerable, as the parties with "deep pockets," to the problem proving more difficult than expected or to long-term damage caused from site pollution. Insurance may be available to mitigate the risk.

Site risk issues are often difficult to resolve with lenders: where the site is provided by a public authority, there is a case for the Offtaker or Contracting Authority taking responsibility for site condition; alternatively, this is one area where the Sponsors may have to provide limited-recourse support by way of a guarantee to cover extra costs or delays.

- *Owner's risks:* As set out in §7.1.3, the Project Company has responsibilities under the EPC Contract, and if these are not fulfilled, and therefore the EPC Contractor incurs extra costs, a claim can be made for them. The main mitigation here is to ensure that Owner's Risks under the EPC Contract are kept to a minimum. (The same principle applies to delay costs caused by finding fossils or archæological remains on the project site—cf. §7.1.4.)

- *Changes in contract specifications:* all such changes, unless *de minimis* in amount, must be approved by the lenders, who will have to be convinced that there is enough funding available to cover the cost, and that the benefits of the changes (e.g., in reducing operating costs) outweigh their capital costs.

  The EPC Contractor normally carries out detailed design after signature of the EPC Contract, but this should not lead to changes in the EPC Contract price. There remains a high risk, however, in any project where the overall design and specifications are not fully settled in advance in the EPC Contract, which is not likely to be acceptable to lenders.

- *Change of law:* (e.g. requiring lower emissions standards) may add unavoidably to the construction costs of the project; as with any change in specifications, the risk remains with the Project Company as far as the EPC Contractor is concerned (cf. §7.1.4), but may be covered by the Project Agreement (cf. §10.6.1).

- *Spare parts:* If an initial stock of spare parts for the project is required, this may not be included in the EPC price, so the cost of these may be higher than budgeted; however, the amounts should be relatively small.

Development costs. A project's development costs are those incurred by Sponsors before Financial Close, so it might seem that there cannot be an overrun on these costs during the construction period. However, there is often a time gap between when the construction budget is agreed to with the lenders and Financial Close, and during that time there is a risk that legal and similar costs may mount up more than budgeted.

Development costs are normally reimbursed to the Sponsors (if they are not being treated as an initial equity investment) at Financial Close, but if they are finally above budget by that time, lenders may defer reimbursement of the excess until the end of the construction period, at which time reimbursement may be allowed if sufficient funds are then available.

Mobilization and O&M contract costs. Mobilization costs—the costs of training staff to operate the project—are often covered by the EPC Contractor or the O&M Contractor on a fixed-price basis, and therefore should not pose an undue risk. An O&M Contractor who is providing most of the staff will also have mobilization costs, which again should be a fixed-price item.

Insurance premiums. The insurance premiums for the construction period are fixed (and usually paid) at the beginning of the period; therefore, they should not cause any cost overrun, unless there is a gap in time between the final budget and Financial Close. Even in this case, the Project Company's insurance brokers should be able to get good indications of premiums from the market to reduce this risk. Extra insurance premiums will be incurred if there is a delay in completion, as a longer period of cover has to be paid for. There may also be a problem with the premiums for the first year of operation, which may need to be paid just before the end of the construction period, and therefore form part of the construction budget: it is preferable for these to be fixed in advance as part of an insurance package.

Project company costs. These are any remaining categories of costs not covered above, of which the main items are likely to be the costs of the Project Company's offices, office equipment and staff, and continuing payments to advisers such as the Owner's Engineer. The amounts should be relatively small in the context of overall project costs, and it should not be difficult to ensure that such items remain close to budget.

Contingency reserve. However well managed the budget, there is always a risk of unexpected events causing a cost overrun. Despite all the risk mitigations set out above, a contingency reserve covered by matching funding is also required by lenders. As a rough rule of thumb, a contingency of around 10% of the EPC cost, or 7–8% of total project costs, may be needed. The contingency is also intended to cover the effects of delays in the completion of construction, where delay LDs are not payable by the EPC Contractor.

This contingency amount is funded within the total financing package (cf. §13.3.3). Note that such contingency funding is intended to cover cost overruns and the effect of a delay in completion (cf. §8.5.6), not financial risks relating to interest rate and currency exchange rate movements which must be covered in other ways (cf. §9.2 and §9.3).

§8.5.5 REVENUE DURING CONSTRUCTION

In some projects, part of the construction costs may be funded not just by equity and debt financing, but also partially by revenues earned from a part of the project already operating. For example, revenue from an existing toll bridge or tunnel may be paid to a Project Company building a new bridge or tunnel in parallel to expand the traffic capacity. Similarly, a project may be constructed in phases, with revenues from the early phases covering part of the construction costs of the later phases.

Unless this construction phase revenue is very stable in nature, there is an extra dimension of risk that the revenues will not be enough to provide the proportion of the funding required. In such cases projections of revenues during construction have to be conservative, and there may be a need to increase the level of contingency funding to allow for this extra uncertainty.

§8.5.6 DELAY IN COMPLETION

A delay in completion may be caused by:

- Failure of the EPC Contractor to perform under the EPC Contract
- Failure of third parties to provide necessary connections to the project (cf. §8.5.8)
- *Force majeure* and related risks

A delay in completion of the project may have several consequences:

- Financing costs, in particular interest during construction ("IDC") will be higher because the construction debt is outstanding for a longer period: this is, in effect, another form of construction cost overrun.
- Revenues from operating the project will be deferred or lost.
- Penalties may be payable to the Offtaker or Input Supplier.

The effect of delays is thus to increase costs and reduce investor returns and lender cover ratios (as with construction cost overruns).

To consider these delay risks in more detail:

Delay by EPC contractor. A date-certain turnkey EPC Contract is the main protection against the risk of late completion of the project; the EPC Contractor is liable for delay LDs, which should be sufficient to keep the project financially whole, at least for some time (cf. §7.1.8). LDs provide an incentive for the EPC Contractor to take any necessary action to deal with prospective problems. But if the delay extends beyond 6–12 months, it is likely that delay LDs will run out, and the pressure on the EPC Contractor then reduces considerably.

Unless caused by last-minute performance problems, a delay in reaching COD by the EPC Contractor is often quite predictable if detailed programming for the project is in place, as it will become evident that critical-path items (i.e., aspects of the project which, if delayed, will delay the final completion) are falling behind schedule. The Project Company and the Owner's Engineer should be supervising progress sufficiently closely to ensure that they are aware of potential delays in the critical path and assist (or put pressure on) the EPC Contractor to catch up. The Lenders' Engineer also monitors this process.

The EPC Contractor is, however, excused for delay (and hence not liable to pay delay LDs) caused by ground conditions, such as preexisting pollution, or the discovery of fossils or archæological remains, and from failure on the part of the Project Company or third parties (cf. §7.1.6). The only mitigation of this risk from the lenders' point of view is that, as discussed in §8.5.4, such ground conditions are likely to occur at an early stage when project costs are still covered by equity. Similarly *force majeure* events (see below) will excuse the EPC Contractor.

Force majeure **and related risks.** Apart from genuine *force majeure* (i.e., unforeseeable events, for which cf. §8.10), the construction program should contain adequate provision for such events as, e.g., bad weather during the winter, which in most circumstances should not be considered *force majeure.*

Definition of COD. Project completion or COD is a concept that may appear in various different contracts—the EPC Contract, the Project Agreement, the Input Supply Contract, and as a required milestone date in the financing documentation. It is therefore important to ensure that the definitions of COD between all these different contracts fit together from the Project Company's point of view. If the Project Company is subject to penalties for late completion (e.g., in an Offtake Contract), the definition of COD in that contract should be as "loose" as possible so completion can easily be achieved. On the other hand, the Project Company may impose a much higher completion hurdle on the EPC Contractor.

Lenders may be concerned about a rushed completion (i.e., the Offtaker and the Project Company agreeing that the project is complete when problems remain, and allowing the EPC Contractor off the hook too easily: as a result lenders may require that the Project Company cannot agree that COD has taken place until the Lenders' Engineer signs off in agreement. Furthermore, the definition of completion from the lender point of view is likely to be wider than just completion under the EPC Contract (e.g., completion of any third-party connections—cf. §8.5.8).

§8.5.7 INADEQUATE PERFORMANCE ON COMPLETION

Performance risks (e.g., because of problems of poor design or inadequate technology) may affect the ability of the project to perform as expected on completion.

In such circumstances, performance LDs will become payable by the EPC Contractor, which should have originally been calculated as sufficient to cover the NPV of the financial loss from this poor performance for the life of the project (cf. §7.1.8). Performance LDs are normally used to reduce the debt so as to leave the lenders with the same cash flow cover ratios as they would have had if the project had performed as expected. (Any surplus should be paid as a special distribution to investors to compensate them for their reduced equity return.)

But some of the assumptions made during the original LD calculation may also prove incorrect; for example, if the project uses a higher volume of input supplies to operate than originally anticipated, the extra cost of this should be covered by the LDs, but the assumption of the unit cost of the input supplies may itself be proved incorrect by events; if this unit cost turns out to be higher than projected, the LDs will not fully cover the economic loss.

Furthermore, the performance measurements of the project on completion are only a snapshot taken over a limited period of time, and there may still be further variations in performance as time goes on which will not produce further LDs.

Thus the calculation used to fix the performance LDs may be little more than a rough projection, and there is also no opportunity (unless claims can be made under warranty) to go back to the EPC Contractor several years after completion if performance gets worse. The Project Company should be aware of the uncertainty of these assumptions and allow a margin for this in negotiating the LD calculations with the EPC Contractor.

Finally, performance LDs alone may not be sufficient if the project involves new technology: it may be acceptable to lenders for the EPC Contractor to provide higher levels of performance LDs than normal for upgrades of existing technology, but this would not be adequate for something totally new in concept (cf. §8.7.1).

§8.5.8 THIRD-PARTY RISKS

Various risks related to the performance of third parties may also delay completion.

Connections and utilities required for the project. The EPC Contractor may be dependent on third parties, such as a public authority, Input Supplier, or Offtaker, to provide connections to the site that enable the project to be completed. Similarly, such links may be needed before the project can begin operation. For example, a fuel pipeline or water supply may have to be linked to the site, a rail link may be needed to bring in fuel, or a grid connection to export electricity from a power plant, or a connecting road may be needed to enable traffic to use a toll road or bridge. The third party providing the connection may themselves be dependent on others (e.g., for rights of way).

If the third party providing these connections is not otherwise involved with the project, they may have no particular incentive to keep to the project timetable, and the damage to the project caused by late connection may be disproportionate to the cost of the connection. In such cases the Project Company can only assess the degree of risk by looking at the record of the third party in similar situations, and try to control the risk by close coordination with and monitoring of the third party. The EPC Contractor's relationship and experience with such third parties may also be relevant.

If the connections are being provided by a party to a Project Contract, such as a Contracting Authority under a Concession Agreement, an Input Supplier, or an Offtaker, this party should preferably be responsible for the loss or penalties that the project suffers from their delay.

Relocation of utilities. In a similar vein, projects such as construction of a road need to arrange for diversion or relocation of utilities (e.g., a gas, water, or sewage pipeline may need to be moved under the road). The utility concerned will probably have control of this procedure, and their cooperation is needed. Because they have no particular incentive to keep to the project's construction timetable, there is a risk that this could delay progress. This risk may be passed on from the Project Company to the EPC Contractor, as it is a relatively routine requirement in construction.

Protesters. Projects involving the construction of public infrastructure (e.g., a road) may also be the subject of public protest, which may seriously affect the construction schedule. In the worst case this may turn into politically motivated violence (cf. §10.5) rather than just obstruction of the EPC Contractor's work.

In general, if a project involves the construction of public infrastructure, the public sector should take responsibility for delays of this kind, first by providing appropriate police protection for the EPC Contractor to carry out the work, and second by treating delays caused in this way at least as *force majeure,* thus exempting the Project Company from penalties for delay in completion, if not compensating the Project Company for loss of revenue.

Project dependent on another project. The worst kind of third-party risk— often fatal to the development of a project—is where one project finance depends on another. For example, a gas-fired power station may be dependent on delivery of gas through a pipeline that is itself being project financed. If the completion of the pipeline cannot be guaranteed, the power station project will probably not be able to get financing; conversely, if the completion of the power station cannot be guaranteed, the gas pipeline will probably not be able to get financing. Financing the two projects as one may be a way out of this impasse, but the Sponsors of one project may be different from the Sponsors of the other, and each side may have no interest in investing in or guaranteeing the other's project.

§8.5.9 PROJECTS WITHOUT A FIXED-PRICE, DATE-CERTAIN, EPC CONTRACT

The fixed-price, date-certain, turnkey EPC Contract is a major mitigation of risk in project finance. There are some types of project for which such a contract is not available or appropriate, for example:

Mining and other extraction projects. The development of a mine or an oil field tends to suffer from higher than average completion risk because of delays due to bad weather, an inaccessible location, and geological, technical, and labor problems. Even if a fixed-price, date-certain EPC Contract is in place, LDs may be insufficient to cover these risks, and the more common approach is for the Sponsors undertake the construction of the facility themselves, with appropriate subcontractors.

Incomplete design. If the project has not been adequately specified, the EPC Contractor is unlikely to take the risk of providing a fixed price or completion date.

Systems installations. A project may involve installation of a system over a period of time (e.g., a cable TV or mobile phone network) where the speed of installation of the system depends on demand. The lenders may specify that if revenues from customers for the system come in faster their debt can be drawn faster, so construction will speed up, and *vice versa*. Given the uncertainty of the construction timetable, an EPC Contractor cannot easily offer a fixed price, and clearly a fixed completion date is not relevant.

In such cases lenders may require a completion guarantee from the Sponsors to reduce their risks (i.e., the financing becomes limited-recourse rather than nonrecourse—cf. §8.12). If the Sponsors guarantee to complete the project, it necessarily follows that:

- The Sponsors must be responsible for any shortage of funding to complete.
- If the project is not completed, the Sponsors will have to cover the debt service.

Thus, the additional financial liability that Sponsors incur may become very significant in the absence of an EPC Contract.

Furthermore, the definition of "completion" in such cases has to be carefully considered. It usually involves not just physical completion of the project, but a demonstrated ability to operate as projected over a sustained period of time.

§8.6 ENVIRONMENTAL RISKS

The environmental aspects of a project may raise various contractual, legal, and wider political risks. The possibility of preexisting pollution at the site will be an issue under the EPC Contract (cf. §8.5.4), and the EPC Contractor is of course required to construct the project to meet environmental standards on emissions, etc. (cf. §7.1.8).

Even if the Project Company has obtained the necessary Permits to construct and operate the project, it may still remain at risk from changes in law relating to environmental aspects of the project (e.g., emissions) that require extra capital expenditure (cf. §10.6).

Most public-sector lenders, such as the World Bank and European Investment Bank, have their own environmental standards mandated by their members (i.e., state shareholders) and may require these to apply to projects even if local law does not require this. In the worst case this could put the Project Company into default under the financing if it violates these standards, even though it is not breaking the law in the Host Country.

Even if the Project Company is acting within the local law, it may still be at risk on wider political grounds. Public opposition to the project may cause the government to reconsider its obligations under a Project Agreement or Government Support Agreement. Similarly, the lenders themselves may find themselves under attack in their home countries for supporting a project that is perceived to be environmentally damaging; some lenders apply general environmental requirements to all their loans.

Sponsors and lenders cannot rely only on keeping within the law of the Host Country; they need to consider whether any environmental aspects of the project leave them at risk of opposition to construction or operation of the project indirectly discouraging lenders from getting involved with it. An EIA (cf. §7.4.1) is an important part of the due diligence that should reduce any lender concerns.

§8.7 OPERATING RISKS

Once the project has been completed and is demonstrated to be operating to specification, a new risk phase begins, that of long-term operation. Even if the Project Company has hedged many of its risks through a Project Agreement, some level of operating risk is likely to be left with the Project Company, and therefore this aspect of the risks is closely reviewed by lenders.

The key operating risks include:

- Technology (cf. §8.7.1)
- General operation of the project (cf. §8.7.2)
- Operating cost overruns (cf. §8.7.3)
- Availability (cf. §8.7.4)
- Maintenance (cf. §8.7.5)
- Performance degradation (cf. §8.7.6)

§8.7.1 TECHNOLOGY

New technology. Even if the project passes its performance tests (cf. §7.1.6), there may still be concern about the long term risks if it involves new technology.

Lenders are always reluctant to lend against a project that is using new and untried technology, whose performance cannot be checked against existing references. The problem is that the new technology risk is unquantifiable and cannot be covered by performance LDs from the EPC Contractor because they do not cover a future deterioration in performance. In this context, new technology has a wide definition: it includes major improvements to existing technology, for example, a gas turbine for a power plant that is supposed to deliver significantly greater efficiency than the manufacturer's current model. (It is also worth noting that insurance companies charge higher premiums for new technology plants because of the increased uncertainty in their risks.)

If new technology is being used the operating risk can be mitigated in various ways:

- The EPC Contractor may give a long-term performance guarantee, rather than the warranties normally provided, which are limited both in amount and to a term of 2–3 years. The problem with this approach, however, is deciding whether a problem with the plant in several years' time is caused by a defect in design or construction (the EPC Contractor's fault) or in the way it has been operated (the Project Company's fault).
- The Sponsors may provide a long-term performance guarantee, perhaps counterguaranteed by the EPC Contractor or the manufacturer of the plant

In summary, however, project finance is more suitable for established technologies.

Obsolescence. The converse of this is the risk that the technology used in the project may become obsolescent and thus uncompetitive in the market in which the Project Company is operating. This should be considered when reviewing the basic commercial viability of the project (cf. §8.4), but it may be of particular concern in, e.g., projects in the IT sector.

§8.7.2 GENERAL PROJECT OPERATION

If the project is not able to operate as projected due to poor management (e.g., negligent operation, failure to maintain plant, etc.), there is likely to be a loss of revenue or higher operating costs.

An O&M Contract with an experienced operator provides the greatest comfort to lenders in this respect, especially if this is with a Sponsor.

However the O&M Contractor does not guarantee the revenues or costs of the project, and penalties are usually capped at around 1–2 years' fees. The total level of fees paid to an O&M Contractor (and hence the penalties the O&M Contractor would be willing to pay) is small in relation to both the total revenues or the costs (including finance) of projects, and it would not make economic sense for the O&M Contractor to cover the Project Company's loss of revenue by accepting liability to pay penalties many times greater than the fees that could be earned.

The main sanction against a poorly performing O&M Contractor is thus not penalties but the termination of the O&M Contract, which is always available if performance falls below the minimum required standard. In this respect the O&M Contract differs from other major Project Contracts, because replacement of the contractor on other contracts is seldom a realistic possibility.

Coupled with this, however, lenders have a strong preference for O&M Contractors to be investors in the project, because an O&M Contractor who has an equity investment stands to lose more than just the penalties for poor performance.

If the Project Company intends to use its own staff to operate the project (i.e., with no external O&M Contractor), lenders naturally wish to be satisfied that the personnel involved have the requisite experience. Although operating personnel do not have to begin work until the construction process is complete, key personnel have to be in place at the beginning of construction, first to use their expertise to ensure that the design of the project is appropriate from an operating point of view, and second because the lenders wish to be satisfied that the key personnel are there before they start advancing funds.

A Support Services Agreement with one or more of the Sponsors with relevant operating experience to provide the Project Company with back-up technical support, spare parts, etc., is often a lender requirement, even though one might expect that, whether or not there is such an agreement, the Sponsors will provide technical and operating support to protect their investment. Because a Support Services Agreement should not cost anything unless support is actually required, there is no reason for the Project Company not to sign one. Sponsors have to take care, however, that a Support Services Agreement is not used by the lenders as a "back-door" method of making them liable for the project's performance, for example, by insisting on inserting very widely drawn clauses giving the Sponsors liability for negligence under the Support Services Agreement.

§8.7.3 GENERAL OPERATING COST OVERRUNS

The two largest continuing costs for any project are likely to be those for input supplies (if any, for which cf. §8.9), and for debt service, which should, however, be fixed (cf. §9.2). Other costs may be contractually fixed, such as O&M Contract fees.

Lenders will wish to set limits on any variable operating costs that are within the budgetary control of the Project Company in a similar way that they control construction cost budgeting (cf. §8.5.4). It is inappropriate for lenders to restrict the Project Company's ability to fulfill its obligations under its Project Contracts, and therefore such payments (e.g., for fuel) should be outside any budgetary controls.

A standard approach to budgetary controls over items that the Project Company does control (e.g., maintenance—cf. §8.7.5—its own office and personnel costs, capital expenditure after the end of the construction period, etc.) is to agree to a budget for these costs over the life of the financing as part of the Base Case financial projections at Financial Close (cf. §12.5), including provision for adjustment for the general rate of inflation (cf. §12.3.1). The Project Company (or the O&M Contractor, if there is one) then produces an annual operating budget before each operating year, which is automatically approved by the lenders if it is within an agreed-upon margin of tolerance of the original budget (say a 10% variation, depending on how significant these Project Company-controlled budget figures are). If the Project Company wishes to make greater changes in the budget, lender approval is required.

Similarly, a degree of tolerance between the annual budget and actual expenditure may be required so as not to impose unnecessary constraints on the Project Company's day-to-day operations. This actual expenditure is also controlled through the lenders' controls on the application of operating cash flow (cf. §13.5.1).

§8.7.4 PROJECT AVAILABILITY

There will be periods of time when the project is not in operation (i.e., scheduled maintenance periods and unexpected interruptions in operations). Whether the project has an assured revenue through a Project Agreement or relies on selling its project or service into the market, it is evident that if the project is not available to operate it will lose revenue (and may incur penalties—cf. §6.1.7).

Process plant projects require major maintenance of the equipment in the plant, involving a shut down of the whole plant or one part of it (depending on the configuration), at regular intervals that may be annual in some cases, or at much longer intervals in others. Infrastructure projects also require major maintenance (e.g., to replace a road surface or to overhaul a train). Inevitably, there will also be unexpected interruptions in operations caused by some unexpected fault.

Assumptions for these interruptions in availability are built into Base Case projections (cf. §12.5), and allowed for in any Project Agreement. The risks here are that scheduled maintenance may take longer than expected, or that the level of unexpected interruptions will be higher than projected.

The importance of using established technology for the project is again evident; the past record of similar projects should enable the Project Company to produce conservative estimates of scheduled and unscheduled downtime. This is an aspect of project risk where the experience of the operator of the project (whether the Project Company or operating or maintenance contractors) is important to satisfy lenders of the viability of the downtime estimates.

§8.7.5 MAINTENANCE

Compared to most other project operating costs, major maintenance costs are irregular in nature since they are likely to fall outside an annual cycle. Maintenance may be required over a cycle of, say, 5–6 years for a power plant, or 15–20 years for a road.

The main risks related to maintenance are:

- It may take longer than expected (cf. §8.7.4)
- It may cost more then expected
- Insufficient cash flow may be retained to meet maintenance costs
- Higher than expected usage will increase maintenance costs

The longer the maintenance cycle, the greater the risk that the major maintenance costs may be higher than expected. It may be possible for the major maintenance cost risk to be passed on to the O&M Contractor, or to sign an agreement with an equipment supplier to provide maintenance for this equipment on an agreed formula (cf. §7.2.5).

In a long maintenance cycle there is a risk that the Project Company may fall short of cash flow when these costs are to be paid. This is dealt with by the establishment of a Maintenance Reserve Account, in which the Project Company (under the lenders' control) builds up a cash reserve for major maintenance on a level basis during the maintenance cycle period (cf. §13.5.2).

If, however, this cycle is very long—as would be the case in a road project—lenders may agree that the Maintenance Reserve Account only needs to be built up in the latter part of this period.

However, the more a project is used (e.g., by operating a plant or by traffic using a road) the more frequently it is likely to require maintenance. If the Project Company's revenue increases as usage increases, more frequent maintenance may not cause any problems, but this is not always the case. For example, in road projects where "shadow" tolls are being paid, the level of toll per vehicle may decline as usage increases, and perhaps go down to zero above a maximum usage level (cf. §6.2.2), to ensure that the payments the Contracting Authority makes for the road are capped. In such cases, paradoxically, high usage of the project is bad from the lenders' and investors' point of view, since it increases the frequency of maintenance without any corresponding revenue. By definition in such cases the risk is left with the Project Company, and therefore lenders will have to assess the effect of being too successful.

§8.7.6 DEGRADATION

If the project involves a process plant, an allowance has to be made for operating degradation (i.e., the gradual decline in operating efficiency between maintenance of the plant). In a power plant, for example, this will cause a decline in output and increase in heat rate (fuel consumption), which should be largely but not entirely reversed after each major overhaul of the plant. Again assuming the plant is using established technology, it should be possible to assess the degree of this risk and build it into operating and hence financial projections, based on the experience of similar plants elsewhere.

Similarly, the way in which a process plant is used affects degradation and the maintenance cycle. For example, if a power plant is constantly stopping and restarting, or being kept on hot standby by the Power Purchaser, this causes a much more rapid degradation in performance and requirement for maintenance than if it is operating constantly. Therefore the PPA needs to establish a separate category of Tariff costs that take this kind of flexibility of use into account (e.g., if the plant is started up more than a certain number of times in a year, the Power Purchaser will pay so much per start-up—cf. §6.1.5).

§8.8 REVENUE RISKS

The risk that the Project Company may not earn sufficient revenue to service its operating costs and debt and leave an adequate return for investors, is at the heart of project finance.

If the project is producing a product, the risks are whether—assuming it is able to operate as projected—the Project Company can achieve:

(a) The volume of unit sales projected—the *volume* risk
(b) At the projected unit sales price—the *price* risk

These risks may be covered by an Offtake Contract (cf. §8.8.1), a Contract for Differences (cf. §8.8.4), hedging contracts (cf. §8.8.3), or a long-term sales contract (cf. §8.8.5), or the Project Company may take the risk of sales into a competitive market (cf. §8.8.6). To the extent these risks are covered contractually, it is primarily the operating risks (cf. §8.7) that are left with the Project Company.

If the project is providing a service under a Concession Agreement, the risk is whether the Project Company can achieve the volume of usage of the service projected at the toll, fare, or usage charge projected—the *usage* risk. These risks may be covered by the Contracting Authority under the Concession Agreement (cf. §8.8.2), or the Project Company may take the usage or toll risks directly (cf. §8.8.7). Again, to the extent the usage risks are covered contractually, the Project Company is just left with the operating risks.

Finally, the risks assumed by the Offtaker or Contracting Authority also need to be borne in mind (cf. §8.8.8).

§8.8.1 OFFTAKE CONTRACTS

In a take-or-pay Offtake Contract both the volume and price risks are transferred to the Offtaker. In principle, then, no significant revenue risk is left with the Project Company. It follows from this that a project with this type of contract can achieve the highest leverage and hence offer a lower product price.

The main remaining risk for the Project Company with an Offtake Contract is the ability of the Offtaker to pay for the product. The Project Company and its lenders are in fact taking a very long-term credit risk on the Offtaker. Although conventional balance sheet-based corporate credit analysis is the first step in assessing this risk, this alone is not necessarily appropriate to determine whether the Offtaker's credit risk is acceptable. The term of the risk runs well beyond the limits of conventional bank lending to most companies.

The risk assessment here therefore looks back at the fundamental viability of the project (as described in §8.4); if the project makes long-term commercial sense it is likely to survive even if the Offtaker has problems elsewhere. Indeed, one school of thought holds that it is preferable for projects not to have long-term Offtake Contracts because these reduce the need for an assessment of the project's fundamental viability, which is the real security for lenders. Most lenders, however, would rather have an Offtake Contract in the structure if it is available.

A further issue is whether the Offtaker itself—if a private-sector company—is operating in a stable environment or whether its own business may be vulnerable to long-term problems. For example, a project selling power to an industrial plant is obviously taking a risk on the long-term market for the output of that plant.

There may be different long-term credit risk issues if the Offtaker is a public sector entity. In the short term, lenders will take comfort from the public ownership and may assume that the government will provide financial support if needed. If the government owns the Offtaker and regulates its industry, there is a strong case for the Government also guaranteeing the long-term credit risk of the Offtaker (e.g., under a Government Support Agreement), on the grounds that they are best able to control this risk.

There is always a possibility that a government's decision to privatize a public-sector Offtaker (or part of its business) may seriously affect its credit. No government will agree to fetter future governments by contracting not to privatize the Offtaker, but there are various possible approaches to this issue:

- If the Government guarantees the Offtaker this guarantee should not be affected by privatization or any other restructuring of the Offtaker.
- The Government may be required to provide a guarantee on privatization unless the Offtaker meets an agreed credit rating at that time.
- The lenders may take the view that no privatization will be successful unless the privatised company has a strong balance sheet and a sound basis for its business; a state-owned company's real credit standing may therefore get better rather than worse after privatization and so the lenders may not be concerned so long as the project fundamentals are sound.

If the Offtaker is a weaker credit risk, there may be ways of taking security over its own revenues to strengthen the position of the Project Company. For example, the Power Purchaser under a PPA may be a local electricity distribution company; if there is some question about its credit risk, it may be possible for arrangements to be made for the revenues it collects from its customers to be paid into a trust fund or escrow account for the benefit of the Project Company and applied to ensure that payments are made under the PPA.

§8.8.2 CONCESSION AGREEMENTS

In a service-based Concession Agreement, if the Contracting Authority controls the usage of the service provided by the project, directly or indirectly, the Contracting Authority should take this usage risk in the same way as an Offtaker under an Offtake Contract. An obvious example is a privately financed prison. The risk issues in such cases are similar to those in an Offtake Contract.

In cases where the Project Company is taking usage risk, either in projects involving "shadow" tolling or similar arrangements, or in projects where the revenues are directly derived from the public paying tolls or fares, the risk analysis is clearly different (cf. §8.8.7).

§8.8.3 Hedging Contracts

Contracts to hedge the price of a commodity produced by the Project Company are normally concluded with market intermediaries rather than end-users of the product. The risks that remain with the Project Company are:

- Sale of the product: when commodities such as oil are involved there is always a market and therefore this is not a significant risk for the Project Company.
- Credit risk on the intermediary, for example, a commodity trading company
- Generally, as these are standard market instruments, they are not as flexible as, for example, contracts for differences that are individually negotiated.

The main problem with hedging contracts of this type is that the term available in the commodity markets may be limited, and therefore the later years of the project may be left exposed to market price movements.

One type of hedging arrangement can be undertaken directly with lenders, namely, commodity-denominated loans. Gold loans, for example, have been used to finance gold mine projects. In this structure of financing, the lenders lend gold rather than a currency to the Project Company; the latter then sells the gold and uses the proceeds to finance the mine development; the gold produced is then used to repay the gold loan.

The disadvantage of any form of product price hedging for the Sponsors is that the Project Company may have to undertake the hedging at a time of low commodity prices (this is when lenders will be most anxious about the project economics) and then not benefit from later price rises.

§8.8.4 Contracts for Differences

Contracts for Differences are commonly used in the electricity industry. Because such contracts are primarily used because power cannot be sold directly to the end-user, the risks involved are very similar to those of an Offtake Contract.

The main additional risk that the Project Company may still be taking under such an agreement is that it has to sell the power produced to the grid or electricity pool system. This is less of a problem so long as the pool works on a marginal pricing basis (i.e., the price paid by the pool is equal to the highest price bid at which enough electricity is supplied by all bidders to meet demand). In such cases the Project Company merely has to bid a low price to ensure that its power is sold at the price paid to the pool as a whole. If the pool works on the basis of only paying the price bid by each bidder, the bidding risk will probably have to be passed to the counterpart under the CfD, because they will wish to control more closely the price that is being bid by the Project Company to ensure they do not have to pay further amounts to the Project Company to compensate for too low a bid price.

§8.8.5 Long-Term Sales Contracts

A long-term sales contract removes the volume risk from the Project Company, but leaves it with the price risk. Such a contract may be appropriate if:

- The product produced by the project is a commodity that is not sold in widely traded markets and requires a sales organization to sell the product (as is the case with petrochemical products, for example);
- If the end-user is willing to contract for the product on a long term basis, but wishes to index the price to a commodity market (e.g., in long-term contracts for the sale of LNG, where is price is often linked to that of oil).

In such cases, lenders will wish to ensure that there is a clearly defined pricing basis for the product, so that the extent of the price risk can be measured. It is clearly preferable for pricing to be based on some widely traded index such as oil prices, since price projections are easier for such commodity markets. However it is apparent that the risk for the Project Company remains much higher than under the other offtake arrangements described above, and therefore the leverage that can be achieved for projects where the price risk is being taken by the Project Company is lower.

If a Project Company takes the price risk, the lenders' main concern is the extent of cash flow cover for the debt (cf. §12.9); obviously the higher the cover the less the risk of loss caused by fluctuations in the market price for the project's product. The extent of this risk can also be measured by looking at the product price required to enable the Project Company to break even (i.e., a combination of a unit price and unit sales just sufficient to cover the Project Company's operating costs and debt service, but providing no return to shareholders). This break-even price should be low in relation to historical and projected prices, and take account of likely price volatility.

§8.8.6 Price and Volume Risk

Adding the volume risk to the price risk (i.e., if the Project Company has not got a long-term sales contract of any kind) can be acceptable to lenders where the product concerned is a commodity that is widely traded in a market.

The two main types of projects in which lenders have traditionally been willing to lend to Project Companies taking the price risk (and volume risk, if necessary) on their products are natural resources projects, and, more recently, "merchant" power projects in the electricity market.

Natural resources projects. The volume risk is not significant in hydrocarbon and minerals projects because the product concerned can easily be sold on widely traded commodity markets.

The price risk is obviously very significant, however, and lenders take a cautious attitude in this respect. Commodity prices are affected by the economic cycles: lenders therefore base their projections for the Project Company and hence the viability of the project on the lower range of historic prices for the commodity over a long period of time. Factors that might lead to a growth in supply need to be considered (e.g., opening of new mines elsewhere or developments of new mining technology) as well as anything that could lead to a drop in demand in future (e.g., because another commodity can be substituted, such as plastic bottles instead of aluminum cans).

Lenders and their advisers also look at the cost competitiveness of the project in the market as a whole and would normally expect the project to be able to produce at a cost placing it in the lowest quartile of world production costs for the product, based on the assumption that if 75% of the world's production is being sold below cost, this is not a sustainable position over the long term. Even then, unless some form of commodity price hedging is in place, the leverage of the project will be relatively low (i.e., lenders require high debt cover ratios).

Merchant power plant projects. More recently, with the development in a number of countries such as the United Kingdom, Australia, and the United States (in certain states) of market trading in electricity, lenders have provided financing for merchant power plants that do not have long-term power purchase agreements.

Again the volume risk is relatively small, since the existence of a pool or similar market trading system should ensure that power produced can be sold at a market price, so long as transmission or other constraints do not inhibit this.

Price risk is much more difficult to assess; these markets generally do not have long enough trading data to assess clearly the factors affecting electricity prices, and in some cases (such as the U.K.) a few large generators have been able to manipulate market prices, thus making past prices meaningless as a basis for future projections. Although demand for electricity is relatively stable, unlike the markets for oil and minerals, it is difficult to predict the future supply of electricity to a market, since this is affected by investors' decisions on whether to keep older more inefficient plant in existence, and new investors' changing perceptions of whether it is worthwhile to build new plant. Most lender risk analyses therefore concentrates on the cost competitiveness of the Project Company's plant and hence its break even unit price by comparison with other plants, which is a factor of:

- Capital cost (i.e., the EPC price)
- Funding structure (more debt and a longer term make the project's unit prices more competitive—cf. §2.5.2)

- Efficiency (i.e., output and fuel consumption)
- Fuel cost

If a project is cost competitive against others in the market, the presumption is often made by lenders that it is unlikely to have to operate at a loss for a sustained period of time, and therefore although it may have temporary problems, in the medium term it should make enough money to service its debt. This, however, may not adequately address issues of over capacity from construction of too much new plant with a similar cost base. It also does not address the effect of a change in the costs of different types of fuel (e.g., coal *vs* gas) causing a major change in the cost base between different types of plants, or a drop in the price of fuel making a long-term input fuel supply contract uncompetitive compared to other plants using short-term contracts (or *vice versa* if the project is using short-term fuel supply contracts).

Although lending to merchant power projects has greatly expanded over the last few years, it is still considered high risk, and hence a low leverage is applied. In fact, the ratings agencies have not given investment-grade ratings (cf. §5.2.1) to merchant plant projects unless the risk for bondholders is significantly reduced by structures such as:

- Hedging arrangements or a Contract for Differences (perhaps not for all the plant's output or the full term of the loan, but covering a significant proportion of both)
- Signing a PPA with an "anchor tenant" (e.g., a large industrial plant), which will purchase a significant proportion of the plant's output
- The fuel supplier taking on some of the risks by:
  - Indexing the cost of the fuel to the market price of the electricity, so reducing the price risk, or
  - Subordinating fuel payments to the lenders, so if there is a shortage of cash flow because of adverse market conditions the lenders get paid ahead of the fuel supplier, or
  - A Tolling Contract (cf. §7.3.1), whereby the fuel supplier pays the plant to process its fuel into electricity, and takes upon itself the risk of selling that electricity
- Financing a mixed portfolio of plants rather than an individual plant, thus spreading the risk.

There is an obvious relationship between this spectrum of risk and the amount of debt that can be raised against a project; at one end of the scale a full Contract for Differences or a Tolling Contract gives much the same protection to lenders as a PPA, and so the amount of debt raised (i.e., the debt:equity ratio) will be similar, whereas at the other end of the scale the pure market risk of selling into a power pool will greatly reduce the proportion of debt to equity in the project.

§8.8.7 USAGE RISK

In a Concession Agreement, transfer of usage risk from the Contracting Authority to the Project Company is appropriate in projects where the Project Company can predict usage, and to some extent influence it by the cost or quality of its service. Projects with usage risk divide into two main categories (cf. §6.2.2):

- Real toll-based projects, in which the Project Company's revenues are derived from the general public paying tolls, fares, mobile phone charges, or a similar payment for usage.
- Shadow toll-based projects, in which the end-user (usually the general public) does not pay directly for the service, but payments are made by the Contracting Authority to the Project Company based on the general public's usage of the services provided.

In the former case public use of the project is affected by the cost of the service, while in the latter case it is not.

Real toll-based projects. Finance can only be raised for a transportation project with real tolls where there is a clearly established demand. For example, a project may consist of building a tolled bridge alongside an existing one to add capacity: the established traffic flows make projections of future toll revenues relatively easy. The risk assessment is more difficult if, for example, a toll road is to be built near to other roads with no toll. Similarly, a transportation project may have competing transport modes. In these cases, however, if the current demand is clearly demonstrated by congestion on the roads, or in trains, and the cost of tolls or fares is reasonable in relation to the cost of existing transport modes, lenders are willing to take the usage risk.

If the project involves provision of a new service to the public, such as cable TV, mobile phones, or internet access, demand cannot normally be established until the system is able to offer the service. In this type of project lenders minimize their risk by requiring a relative high level of equity (typically 50% of project costs). The usual approach is to establish the initial usage, ideally by the first stage of development of the project being funded by equity rather than debt; once an initial level of penetration into the market, and revenues from usage, has been established part of the debt is advanced for further expansion of the network, and releases of debt continue in this way as successive penetration, usage and revenue targets are met. A more liberal approach is for lenders to lend based on the progress of similar projects elsewhere, and their rate of growth in usage and revenues.

Shadow tolling. Shadow tolls and similar structures are typically used either where it is not feasible to collect real tolls or fares because the Project Company is not providing a stand-alone project but rather a part of, say, a larger road or rail system, or where the level of usage is too low to justify charging the public directly.

In such cases the risk profile usually lies between full usage risk and the service-based Concession Agreement referred to in §8.8.2. Payments are made for usage, but a large proportion of the payments (sufficient to cover operating costs and debt service) are likely to be based on relatively low levels of usage. As a result, shadow toll projects typically are able to secure high leverage.

Usage projections for transportation projects are based on complex financial modeling by the Project Company's traffic consultants, which is reviewed by the lenders' traffic advisers. Modelling of usage is based on projections that take into account factors such as:

- Overall population growth, distribution, and movement
- General and local economic activity
- Land use around the area of the project
- Travel at different times of the day or different seasons
- Distribution of travel (i.e., the split between local and long-distance travel)
- Origins and destinations of trips
- Split between commercial and private traffic (the former being more willing to pay tolls)
- Split between modes of travel such as bus, car, or train

These and other factors combine to produce a model of current traffic patterns, which it should be possible to validate by using it to project traffic growth from a date in the past up to the present and comparing the results with the actual growth figures.

Future projections of traffic growth for project finance purposes are based on macroeconomic factors such as growth in the national and regional economy leading to growth in private and commercial vehicle ownership, and generally do not take into account extra traffic that may be created by the construction of the project itself.

Any project involving usage risk on public infrastructure also has to take into account the effect of government policies on this usage. These policies may be local to the project (e.g., competition from untolled roads or construction of other roads that take traffic from a toll road) or national, but affect the project (e.g., an increase in fuel prices that reduces road traffic volume in general). Lenders often require some protection against risks of this type to be built into the Concession Agreement.

§8.8.8 Risks for the Offtaker or Contracting Authority

The Offtaker or Contracting Authority is of course taking the risk that the Project Company may not succeed in constructing and operating the project as expected, and as a result a public service may not be provided, or the Offtaker or Contracting Authority has to buy the product or service more expensively from elsewhere. The Sponsors will not provide any support in this respect, as any such guarantees would destroy the nonrecourse structure of the project finance. The Offtaker or Contracting Authority can take various steps to mitigate this risk by ensuring that:

- The project has credible Sponsors.
- The project is technically sound.
- The other major Project Contracts are to be signed with appropriate parties. While the Offtaker or Contracting Authority should not normally get involved in negotiating the contracts (cf. §6.4), it may be prudent to ensure that there are reasonable levels of LDs (cf. §7.1.5) and bonding (cf §7.1.10).
- As far as the information to do so is available, the project is financially sound, with appropriate costings, and reasonable returns for the Sponsors. The Offtaker or Contracting Authority should perform a financial analysis on the project even if the full data are not available from the Sponsors.
- The lenders are experienced in project finance and have carried out a sound and independent due diligence.
- Payments on termination (cf. §6.8.1) are structured to ensure that the Offtaker or Contracting Authority does not pay out the full cost of a poorly performing project, and is able to deduct extra costs to bring the project up to the required standard.

An irregular Tariff structure may produce a particular risk for the Offtaker or Contracting Authority: as the Tariff in a Project Agreement reflects the debt that the Project Company has raised, the Tariff level may drop sharply in the later years of the contract, reflecting the repayment of the debt. Sponsors will also "front load" the Tariff to recover their equity return faster, if at all possible. This leaves the Offtaker or Contracting Authority potentially exposed to the Project Company having a much lower interest in the operation of the project in the later years of the Project Agreement. Apart from trying to ensure the Tariff gives the Project Company an equal incentive to perform over the life of the project, the Offtaker or Contracting Authority may be able to take security over the project assets for performance penalties (cf. §6.1.7) after the debt has been repaid to give some extra protection.

§8.9 INPUT SUPPLY RISKS

In a process plant project, a reliable supply of fuel or other raw materials, on an appropriate pricing basis, is essential. Lenders are unlikely to accept the Project Company taking an open risk on the availability of its main fuel or raw material supplies. Unless it can be clearly shown that the fuel or raw material concerned is a widely available commodity, a long-term Input Supply Contract is required, even if the project has not got an Offtake Contract (e.g., in the case of a merchant power plant project).

Similarly, some form of hedging or other protection is needed against the risk that the price of the fuel or raw material increases so much that the project becomes unable to operate. This can be achieved by:

- Passing the risk through to the Offtaker (e.g., through an Energy Charge in a PPA (cf. §6.1.6 and §7.3.3)
- Linking the price paid to the Input Supplier to the market price for the project's product (cf. §7.3.3)
- Long-term hedging of supply requirements in the commodity market (cf. §6.1.1)

The risks involved in Input Supply Contracts are further discussed in §8.9.1, and the acceptability of doing without them in §8.9.2.

Certain other inputs may be free, but still represent a risk for the Project Company, for example, water for a hydroelectric power project, or wind for a wind power project (cf. §8.9.3). Similarly, the "reserve risk" has to be assessed for projects extracting oil, gas, or minerals (i.e., the risk of whether the oil or gas field or mine has the volume of reserves projected — cf. §8.9.4). Risks involved in the supply of other utilities are discussed in §8.9.5.

§8.9.1 INPUT SUPPLY CONTRACTS

An Input Supply Contract provides the Project Company with defined volumes of fuel or other raw materials on an agreed-upon cost basis. The contract therefore should eliminate supply or price risks for the Project Company, but there remain some risk issues that require examination in the due-diligence process:

Credit of supplier. As with Offtake Contracts, the credit risk of the supplier has to be considered, not just in the context of a corporate credit analysis, but also taking into account the place of the supply arrangements in the supplier's business. The supplier's experience, ability, and resources to manage its side of the project must also be considered.

Issues of direct or indirect political risk on the supplier may arise in some markets (e.g., the European gas market, where a significant proportion of the supply is from one supplier in Russia).

Source of supply. If the inputs are traded commodities such as oil, the Project Company does not normally need to be concerned where the supplier is securing them. If the Input Supplier is a major oil or gas company, they are normally willing to take the input supply risk. If, however, the inputs are being supplied from, say, a particular oil or gas field, the issue is who will take the reserve risk (cf. §8.9.4). If the risk is taken by the Project Company, this may fall into the trap similar to that of one project being dependent on another to succeed (cf. §8.5.8). However, lenders are willing to take this risk if it is clear that the reserves are well in excess of what is required for the project.

Viability of pricing. The pricing basis for the supply must, as with all Project Contracts, be viable for both sides. The price must be one at which the Input Supplier can continue to make a reasonable return. The price paid by the Project Company should also be reasonable in relationship to the market into which it is selling its product (even if the price risk is being taken by the Offtaker), for similar reasons of commercial viability.

Quantity and timing of supply, The quantity and timing of supply must match the needs of the project, with some flexibility to allow, for example, for delays in completion of construction of the project.

Quality of supply. Obviously most Input Supply Contracts place the risk of the quality of the product on the supplier, but there are some exceptions to this, e.g., in a waste-burning project (e.g., a waste-to-energy power or district heating plant) where the plant may have to accept and burn whatever waste is delivered. (Indeed, in this type of project the Project Company is paid for disposing of the input supply, rather than paying the Input Supplier.)

Take-or-pay risk. Lenders are unlikely to accept the Project Company entering into a Take-or-Pay Contract for input supplies unless:

- The Project Company has passed this risk onto the Offtaker under the Project Agreement, or
- The Project Company can easily dispose of any surplus, without taking an undue sale price risk, or
- The contract is structured on a take-or-pay basis for a quantity reasonably smaller than the project's expected needs and take-and-pay for the balance of the expected needs.

Effect of failure to supply. If the Input Supplier fails to supply, the Project Company may lose revenue, incur extra cost by securing supplies from elsewhere, or incur penalties from an Offtaker (unless the Offtaker takes this risk). If the Input Supplier is under the same ownership as the Offtaker (e.g., both owned by the government) it or the Offtaker may compensate for this loss of revenue, but otherwise the Input Supplier is not normally willing to compensate for any more than the cost of obtaining alternative sources of supply if possible, (i.e., not the Project Company's loss of revenue).

This may be dealt with by:

- Storage of supplies at the project site, or the use of an alternative back-up supply (e.g., diesel oil in lieu of a supply of natural gas to a power station); these approaches normally cover 30–60 days' interruption of supply, but are unlikely to provide a long-term substitute
- A provision in the Offtake Contract that if the Project Company cannot operate because of nondelivery of input supplies it remains "available" for the purposes of the Offtake Contract, and therefore can continue to earn its Availability Charge, although the Project Company may have an obligation under the Offtake Contract to operate with reserve stocks (to an agreed extent), or obtain alternative input supplies where this is possible
- *Force majeure* insurance where physical damage to the connections is involved (cf. §7.6.2)

Failure to complete concessions. Similarly, the Project Company may suffer loss of revenues or have to pay penalties to its Offtaker for its inability to start operations if connections being constructed by the Input Supplier (e.g., a gas pipeline) are not completed in time, but again the Input Supplier is unlikely to agree to a compensating penalty payment on an adequate scale, unless the Input Supplier is under common ownership with the Offtaker. This may be treated as *force majeure* under the Offtake Contract, thus extending its start date so the Project Company at least does not suffer penalties for the late start-up, or again be covered by *force majeure* insurance.

Third-party delivery risks. A further problem arises if delivery is not through the Input Supplier's own facilities, but by road, rail, or through a port for which the Input Supplier has neither control nor responsibility. The Input Supplier could reasonably claim that if the national rail system does not deliver on time, or the nearby port is not able to berth or unload ships carrying input supplies, this is *force majeure* for which the Input Supplier should not be responsible.

The third party providing transport is very unlikely to accept liability for the consequences of the failure to supply; lenders therefore have to be shown that this party has a good record and experience in delivering similar supplies in the area in order to be convinced that they should allow the Project Company to accept the risk. If the Project Company or the lenders are uneasy about the capacity or capability of the delivery system, and if adequate guarantees for this are not available, this may be a major obstacle to the project finance. This kind of risk may be covered in a Government Support Agreement (cf. §7.5).

The Input Supplier may rely on being able to bring the product through another country (e.g., in a pipeline). The risk of interruption of this supply—

perhaps for political reasons—needs to be considered, as does allocation of liability for this risk.

Risk for the Input Supplier. Mitigation of risks from the Input Supplier's point of view is discussed in §7.3.4.

§8.9.2 WHEN IS AN INPUT SUPPLY CONTRACT NOT NEEDED?

In some circumstances, lenders will accept that a Project Company requiring fuel or raw material inputs does not need to rely on an Input Supply Contract, if the project is using supplies of a commodity that is easily available and can be transported to the project site without special arrangements. This would be the case for, say, a coal-fired power plant, situated close to good transportation connections, which can buy its coal from the international markets. (The plant would also store sufficient quantities of coal on site to guard against temporary interruptions in supply.)

Similarly, a wood-chip burning power plant situated in the middle of an area with an active forest products industry may not need a long-term contract for wood-chip supplies, since these are a waste product of the local industry with limited other uses. If in the longer term the local wood industry declines, the plant may be in danger, but in that case a long-term supply contract would not provide the lenders with much real security, since the supplier will probably default anyway.

§8.9.3 WATER AND WIND

Many process plant projects depend on significant quantities of water from rivers, lakes, or canals, as do hydroelectric power plants and, of course, water-supply projects. The availability of this water may vary significantly during the year or from year to year. To enable them to accept this kind of water risk, lenders need to be provided with long-term statistics demonstrating the volume, quality, and reliability of the water supply.

The same principle applies to projects using wind for power generation: the Sponsors need to provide statistics on wind volume, direction, and so on, at the project site location over a number of years as a basis for the projected assumptions in this respect.

§8.9.4 MINERAL RESERVES

Both in a project that involves the extraction and sale of natural resources, and in a project that depends on the supply of natural resources from a specific source as an input fuel or raw material, there is a risk that these natural resources may not be extracted as expected.

Lenders commonly ask their advisers to classify the estimated hydrocarbons or minerals reserves in the ground into "proven" reserves, which also have to be economically recoverable—further classified into "P90" and "P50" (i.e., reserves that have a 90% possibility of recovery, and those that have a 50% possibility)—and "possible" reserves. Lending is only against proven reserves, and primarily against the P90 reserves, taking into account the geology of the project and hence the difficulty of extraction.

Lenders also only take into account a proportion of the proven reserves, and require a reserve "tail" (cf. §12.9.5), i.e., lenders usually do not lend to the end of expected life of the reserves, but to a date on which 25–30% of the original proven reserves are expected to be left. This allows for difficulty in recovering reserves as they become more depleted and the eventual costs of closing down the project.

§8.9.5 OTHER UTILITIES

The Project Company needs to demonstrate that it has a reliable supply of any general utilities needed for the project, such as electricity, telephone, water, and sewerage.

§8.9.6 WASTE DISPOSAL

Disposal of waste products such as ash or mineral "tailings" is obviously an environmental issue (cf. §7.4.1), but may also be a financial and contractual one. If it is necessary to dispose of such waste products off-site, the Project Company must normally have long-term contracts in place for this purpose.

§8.10 *FORCE MAJEURE*

Force majeure (cf. §6.6) can be a temporary problem, leading to a delay in completion of the project, or an interruption in its ability to operate, or in the worst case can prevent the completion of the plant or its operation permanently. (There is clearly also a gray area where "temporary" slips into "permanent"; in general, if the effects of the temporary *force majeure* event last for more than a year they must be considered permanent.)

Force majeure is a difficult area in negotiating Project Contracts:

- By definition *force majeure* is nobody's fault, but someone has to suffer the consequences.

- The effects of *force majeure* on the different Project Contracts overlap, and so the provisions of the contracts need to be coordinated in this respect.
- Lenders are concerned if *force majeure* risks left with the Project Company could affect its ability to service the debt.

Insurance covers most but not all of the problem, and a way of allocating any residual *force majeure* risks between parties, none of whom is at fault, has to be found.

§8.10.1 *Force Majeure* and Insurance

The purpose of insurance is to cover the Project Company against unpredictable losses, and so it might be thought that the Project Company and its lenders should therefore not be at risk from *force majeure* events. There may be gaps, however, between the scope of insurance coverage (cf. §7.6) and the potential for *force majeure* losses.

First of all, insurance generally only covers loss caused by physical damage to the project (the cost of repair or replacement), or economic loss deriving from this (delay in start-up of the project or loss of revenue), caused by the same physical damage. Thus a *force majeure* event such as a national strike preventing completion or operation of the plant would not be covered by standard DSU or BI insurance. *Force majeure* insurance may be available to cover this type of risk, but issues of cost or scope of the cover may arise.

Second, political *force majeure* events (discussed in Chapter 10) cannot be covered by general insurance unless physical damage (e.g., from war) is involved, and in some cases (e.g., coverage for terrorism) the cover may be theoretically available but at a cost that is commercially unattractive.

Third, certain risks of physical damage cannot be covered by insurance:

- All insurance policies have deductibles (i.e., limits below which the loss must be suffered by the insured party rather than the insurance company). The higher the deductible the lower the insurance premiums will be. The Project Company may wish to reduce costs by increasing deductibles, whereas the EPC Contractor (in relation to construction insurances) and the lenders prefer to have a fuller coverage.
- Certain risks, such as damage caused by a nuclear explosion, cannot be insured. Lenders accept these standard exclusions.

Finally, changes in the insurance market may leave the project exposed to uninsured *force majeure*. This relates to insurance during the operating period (construction phase insurances are fixed at Financial Close). An estimate for cost of this insurance is agreed to with lenders in advance as part of the operating cost budget, but market fluctuations may affect the actual costs considerably. The lenders will generally wish the agreed-upon levels and terms of insurance coverage to be obtained even at a higher cost, but there may come a point when the insurance market has changed so much as to make this commercially unattractive, and, e.g., deductibles have to be higher than originally expected.

In the worst case, actual availability of the required insurance may be a problem, perhaps because the insurance market has had a recent poor claims record in the industry or with the equipment concerned.

Availability and cost of operating insurances is an open risk for lenders and investors; it is not possible to obtain long-term operating insurance coverage at the beginning of the construction period (although coverage for the first year of operation may be possible). Lenders have generally been willing to allow the Project Company to assume this risk without requiring Sponsor support. However, in some Project Agreements, especially in developing countries, the Offtaker or Contracting Authority takes the risk of availability of insurance at reasonable cost; if the insurance is not available and the project cannot be completed or operate because of temporary *force majeure,* the Offtaker or Contracting Authority will still pay the Availability or Unitary Charge and provide funding for repair.

Therefore while the financing documentation may set out detailed provisions for what the Project Company is obliged to do in respect to operating insurances, such provisions must be qualified by a "market out" provision: if the insurances are not available, or not available at reasonable cost, the Project Company must be permitted to take out the insurances on the best basis reasonable available on the market.

Thus even though the Project Company is required, both by Project Contracts and by lenders, to cover *force majeure* risks through insurance as far as possible, the risks to the Project Company of additional costs or loss of revenue caused by a *force majeure* event cannot be completely mitigated in this way.

It is therefore relevant to look at how *force majeure* events are dealt with in the Project Contracts. Two categories of *force majeure* events need to be examined: a *force majeure* event that causes a delay in completion or temporary unavailability of the project for operation (cf. §8.10.2), and an event that destroys the project or otherwise makes it permanently impossible for it to continue in operation (cf. §8.10.3).

§8.10.2 TEMPORARY *FORCE MAJEURE*

The general principle is that the party suffering temporary *force majeure* is relieved from performance and penalties (hence such temporary *force majeure* events are also known as "relief events"), and given time to sort the situation out, but is not relieved from the obligation to make any contractual payments and must cover any costs incurred (e.g., for repair) as a result of the *force majeure.* Not surprisingly, however, lenders do not always fully accept the logic of this as far as the Project Company's risks are concerned. In general the Project Company (encouraged by its lenders) will obviously try to limit the list of *force majeure* events if these excuse any project counterparts, but extend the list if it is excused.

It is also important to ensure that the definitions of *force majeure* in different Project Contracts are both comprehensive and consistent with each other (cf. §8.11).

- **Force majeure** **causing a delay in completion.** Physical damage to the project site or equipment in the course of delivery that delays completion should be covered by the CEAR or Marine Cargo insurances, and loss of revenue by the DSU or Marine DSU insurances (cf. §7.6.1), unless the event concerned falls outside the scope of coverage. Obviously, if insurance payments are made to the Project Company it should not receive any windfall payments or relief under the Project Contracts.

  It should be noted that one of the main purposes of the contingency reserve included in the project budget (cf. §8.5.4) is to cover the possibility of a *force majeure* delay in completion or additional cost for which insurance is not available.

  The effects of this *force majeure* have to be tracked through the various Project Contracts.
  - *EPC Contract: Force majeure* events relieve the EPC Contractor from liability for LDs for delay in completion of construction (cf. §7.1.7), but do not create any right to additional payments. However, the EPC Contractor may try to get some events designated as Owner's Risks (cf. §7.1.3) rather than *force majeure,* e.g., strikes at the project site or at a supplier's factory; this is not usually acceptable to a Project Company — only general (national) strikes should be included — but may be agreed to if it can be reflected in the Project Agreement (so avoiding penalties for late completion of the project) or Input Supply Contract (so avoiding fuel or other input supplies having to be paid for before they are needed).
  - *Project Agreement:* This same delay from *force majeure* affecting the EPC Contractor should also relieve the Project Company of any penalties for delay in reaching COD, but because the project is not available it does not usually receive any revenue; *force majeure* that prevents the Offtaker or Contracting Authority completing any necessary connections to the project site does not generally relieve them from having to paying the Availability or Unitary Charge following the general principle set out above.
  - *Input Supply Agreement:* Following the same general principle, if *force majeure* prevents the completion of the project, the Project Company should still have to make any minimum payments required under the

Input Supply Contract; however, this risk may remain with the Input Supplier, or be passed on to the Offtaker under the Offtake Contract; if *force majeure* prevents the Input Supplier from completing its connections to the project site, the Input Supplier should not have to pay any penalties for this, but again the risk may be passed on to the Offtaker who thus has to start paying the Availability Charge. (It may also be feasible for the Project Company to store back-up supplies of fuel or raw materials, and so use these to start operation.)

Temporary *force majeure* causing an interruption in availability. As with delay in completion, the effect of a *force majeure* event affecting project availability has to be tracked through the various Project Contracts:

- *Project Agreement:* The Project Company is relieved from penalties but does not receive the Availability or Unitary Charge payment; on the other hand, the Offtaker or Contracting Authority must continue to make Availability or Unitary Charge payments if *force majeure* eventsaffect its ability to continue taking the Project Company's product or service.
- *Input Supply Contract: Force majeure* generally does not excuse the Project Company for paying for input supplies, but the risk may be passed on to the Offtaker under the Project Agreement; *force majeure* will excuse the Input Supplier from making deliveries, but again the effect of this may be passed on under the Project Agreement.

A Debt Service Reserve Account (cf. §13.5.2) provides some protection against a temporary interruption of revenue not covered by insurance.

In projects in developing countries the political *force majeure* risk (cf. §10.5) is usually passed on to the Offtaker.

§8.10.3 PERMANENT *FORCE MAJEURE*

If a *force majeure* event makes it permanently impossible to complete construction or continue operation of the project it must clearly lead to the termination of a Project Agreement. The meaning of "permanently" needs to be agreed to: a period of around a year may be normal.

If the Project Agreement is terminated the question of a Termination Sum arises on a BOOT/BOT/BTO contract (cf. §6.8.3). On a BOO contract the risk normally remains with the Project Company, with insurance therefore the only mitigation.

§8.11 CONTRACT MISMATCH

When the due-diligence process is being undertaken, it is easy to get bogged down in the details of individual Project Contracts, and as a result miss risks that may arise from incompatible provisions in different Project Contracts. Each Project Contract is not self-contained, but affects the others, and the contracting structure of the project must be reviewed as a whole.

Examples of areas where contract mismatches may arise are:

- Differences between COD under the EPC Contract and under the Project Agreement (cf. §8.5.6)
- Differences between the first date for deliveries under the Input Supply Contract and under the Offtake Contract
- A different procedure for fixing the cost of a variation in the project requested under the Project Agreement by the Offtaker or Contracting Authority, and for fixing the cost of the same variation in the EPC Contract, so that the cost of the variation payable to the EPC Contractor may not be fully passed through to the Offtaker or Contracting Authority
- A similar issue arises with extra costs caused by a change of law (cf. §10.6.1)
- Differences in the pricing formula for fuel or other input supplies between the Input Supply and Offtake Contracts
- Timing differences between revenue receipts, payment for input supplies, and loan payments
- Different definitions of *force majeure* (cf. §8.10)

§8.12 RECOURSE TO THE SPONSORS

Lenders are unlikely to spend time on detailed due-diligence work on the project if the parties behind it are not credible. A project that appears entirely commercially viable will still probably not find financing without appropriate Sponsors, with arm's-length relationships with the Project Company (cf. §4.1).

Similarly, lenders wish to see Sponsors earning an adequate rate of return on their investment, to encourage their continuing commitment to and involvement in the project. If the Sponsors appear to be only earning a low rate of return, this may also suggest that they are compensating themselves in another way (at the expense of the lenders' cash flow cover)—e.g., by a high-cost EPC Contract if the EPC Contractor is a Sponsor, or by the provision of O&M or other services to the Project Company.

Finally, if a commercial risk involved in the project is not adequately mitigated by other means, the Sponsors may have to step in to fill this gap. "Comfort letters" are sometimes offered to lenders as a risk mitigation in place of formal guarantees; for example, a Sponsor may state that it owns the shares in the Project Company, that it presently intends to maintain this ownership and keep the Project Company in a sound financial condition, and that it provides management support. Such undertakings seldom have effective legal force, and while helpful in some circumstances are unlikely to eliminate risks that are otherwise unacceptable.

The only financial obligation that Sponsors have in all project financings is to subscribe their equity share in the Project Company (i.e., the lenders provide a loan to the Project Company with no guarantee of repayment from the Sponsors, thus the loan is nonrecourse to the Sponsors).

While in principle Sponsors do not provide loan guarantees to the Project Company's lenders, limited guarantees may sometimes be provided to cover a risk that proves to be unacceptable to lenders. Examples of such limited-recourse guarantees are:

- *Contingent equity commitment:* The Sponsors agree to inject a specific additional amount as equity into the Project Company to meet specified cash flow requirements.
- *Cost overrun guarantee:* The Sponsors agree to inject additional equity up to a certain limit to cover any cost overruns during construction (or operating cost overruns).
- *Completion guarantee:* The Sponsors undertake to inject extra funding if necessary to ensure that construction of the project is completed by a certain date, thus taking on the risk that more funding for construction or initial debt payments may be required (cf. §8.5.9).
- *Financial completion guarantee:* The Sponsors provide a guarantee not only that the project will be physically completed, but that it will achieve a minimum level of operating revenues or cash flow.
- *Input supply undertaking:* The Sponsors agree to secure supplies of the fuel or raw material required for the project, at a fixed or maximum price, if these cannot be obtained elsewhere.
- *Payment subordination:* If a Sponsor is a supplier of fuel or raw material to the project, payments for these supplies are deferred in favor of paying the lenders if the Project Company is short of cash.
- *Performance guarantee:* The Sponsors agree to provide additional funding for debt service if the cash flow is reduced by the project not operating to a minimum performance standard.
- *Product price guarantee:* The Sponsors guarantee to make up any deficit if the product produced by the Project Company sells below an agreed-upon floor price, or to buy the product at the floor price.
- *Clawback guarantee:* The Sponsors agree to make up any deficiency in the Project Company's cash flow for debt service, to the extent they have received distributions from the Project Company (cf. §13.5.5).
- *Interest guarantee:* The Sponsors agree to pay the interest on the loan if the Project Company cannot do so (in practical terms this is very close to a full guarantee of the loan; if it is not paid back the Sponsors will have to keep paying interest indefinitely).
- *Cash deficiency guarantee:* The Sponsors agree to make up any debt service

that cannot be paid because of a lack of cash in the Project Company (this is, of course, virtually a full financial guarantee).

- *Shortfall guarantee:* A guarantee to pay any sums remaining due to lenders after termination of the loan and realization of other security.

If Sponsors have contractual relationships with the Project Company other than their obligation to invest their equity, nonrecourse project finance is more likely to be diluted into limited-recourse; for example, a Sponsor acting as a fuel supplier is likely to have to take liability for the financial consequences if the fuel is not delivered.

Even if limited-recourse financial support is not being provided, Sponsors may agree to provide technical support through a Support Services Agreement (cf. §8.7.2).

Chapter 9

Macroeconomic Risks

External macroeconomic risks (also known as financial risks), namely inflation (§9.1), and interest rate (§9.2) and currency exchange rate movements (§9.3), do not relate to the project in particular, but to the economic environment in which it operates. These risks need to be analyzed and mitigated in the same way as the more direct commercial risks discussed in the previous chapter.

§9.1 INFLATION

Depending on its timing, inflation may be either a risk or a benefit to the Project Company.

During the construction period, if inflation leads to higher project costs than projected, a cost overrun results, with the consequences set out in §8.5.4. Most of the construction costs should not be vulnerable to inflation-based increases; the EPC Contract price, financing costs, and most advisers' costs should all be fixed. In preparing the construction cost budget, however, an allowance has to be made for inflation over the construction period in costs that are not fixed, such as the Project Company's general personnel costs, and purchase of any items (such as spare parts) not included in the scope of the EPC Contract.

During the operating period, if inflation leads to higher operating costs than projected, the level of lenders' cover ratios, and the return for investors, may be reduced. If the Project Company has a long-term Project Agreement under which revenues are received on the basis of an agreed Tariff, some elements of the Tariff may be indexed against inflation (cf. §6.1.6), thus substantially reducing any inflation risk mismatch between costs and revenues. (Equally, sales prices in a

183

competitive market should also reflect inflation.) In fact, if revenues and operating costs are both indexed against inflation to the same extent, the Project Company may actually be better off in real terms. This is illustrated by Table 9.1, which assumes a 500 loan repaid in 5 equal annual installments, at an interest rate of 10%. The revenues and expenditure are not affected by inflation in Case (A), whereas in Case (B) they are both inflated at 5% *p.a.* The difference in net cash flow arises because one of the main operating costs is debt service, which is not directly subject to inflation (so long as it is at a fixed interest rate—cf. §12.3.3).

Investors may wish to look at the "real" return on their equity investment (i.e., deducting the element of the return that is due to inflation). In the context of leveraged project finance, however, this may give a false result because of the effect of debt service0 just discussed. Table 9.1(A) ignores inflation and shows a total cash flow to the investor of 350. But as Table 9.1(B) shows, if the inflated cash flow to the investor shown is itself deflated by the rate of inflation, the return of 455 shown in the table reduces to 385 (i.e., higher than the apparent "real" return of 350, which results from ignoring inflation). (And cf. §12.7.8 for the effect of inflation on tax payments, which also illustrates that the effect of inflation on project cash flows cannot be eliminated by using "real" calculations.)

In summary, inflation can be a friend or a foe to the Project Company in the long term—the financial model should be used to check whether a high rate of inflation is an optimistic or a conservative assumption and this risk reviewed accordingly.

Table 9.1
Effect of Inflation on Project Cash Flow

	Year					
	1	2	3	4	5	Total
(A) 0% inflation						
Revenues	1000	1000	1000	1000	1000	5000
Expenditure	−800	−800	−800	−800	−800	−4000
Debt interest	−50	−40	−30	−20	−10	−150
Debt repayment	−100	−100	−100	−100	−100	−500
Net cash flow	**50**	**60**	**70**	**80**	**90**	**350**
(B) 5% inflation						
Revenues	1000	1050	1103	1158	1216	5526
Expenditure	−800	−840	−882	−926	−972	−4421
Debt interest	−50	−40	−30	−20	−10	−150
Debt repayment	−100	−100	−100	−100	−100	−500
Net cash flow	**50**	**70**	**91**	**112**	**133**	**455**
Net cash flow deflated at 5% *p.a.*	**48**	**63**	**78**	**92**	**104**	**385**

§9.1.1 Inflation-Indexed Financing

In some markets (e.g., the U.K.) it is possible to issue bonds where the coupon (interest rate) is $X\%$ + CPI (i.e., the total interest paid is linked to the rate of inflation). This is especially appropriate where the Project Company has a long-term Project Agreement where most of the revenue is inflation-linked. Inflation-linked financing is beneficial in a low inflation environment, since it ensures a lower cost of debt if a lower rate of inflation reduces the growth in revenues.

§9.2 INTEREST RATE RISKS

If the project is being financed with fixed-rate bonds or loans from lenders providing fixed-rate funding, then, in principle, the Project Company has no interest rate risk.

In many markets, however, bank lenders do not provide long-term loans at fixed rates because their deposit base is short-term, and fixed-rate long-term funding is either unavailable or uneconomic. The base interest rate on project finance loans is thus often adjusted at intervals (say six monthly) to the then current wholesale market rate at which the lenders raise their funding, and is therefore on a "floating" (variable) rate rather than fixed-rate basis. In the international market, the most important floating rate benchmark is the London interbank offered rate (LIBOR), in which interest rates are quoted by banks for borrowing from and lending to each other in all the major international currencies. Banks basing their lending on LIBOR quote the interest rate for the financing as a margin over the LIBOR rate, with the base interest rate usually refixed against the then current LIBOR rate every 3 or 6 months. (These are known as "rate fixing dates" or "interest dates.")

Interest is not paid in cash on the financing until the project is in operation. During the construction period the accrued interest is normally capitalized (i.e., added to the loan amount) or paid by making a new drawing on the loan. Thus interest during construction (IDC) becomes part of the project's capital budget, and if the interest rate for the IDC is not fixed, and is eventually higher than originally projected, this is a construction cost overrun (cf. §8.5.4). Lenders do not normally allow the general construction cost contingency to be used to cover this risk, as it is primarily intended to cover overruns in the "hard" costs (mainly the EPC Contract), or the effect of a delay causing higher total interest costs.

The same applies to the interest rate during the operating period, where a higher interest rate leads to a lower project cash flow, and hence reduction in cover ratios for the lenders and lower returns for investors.

At the time of arranging the financing, the Sponsors may take the view that it is more likely that interest rates will go down than up; therefore, they prefer to finance on a floating interest rate basis for the time being. This is unlikely to be acceptable to lenders, who will not support the Project Company taking unnecessary financial risks, however small these risks may appear at the time.

There is also an argument that if a project's revenue is inflation-linked, the interest rate on its financing should also be based on short-term interest rates, which tend to move with inflation (cf. §12.3.3). Again, this view has not received much support among project finance lenders.

Interest rate hedging arrangements therefore need to be put in place to mitigate the interest rate risk when floating rate loans are used. The commonest type of hedging used in project finance is interest rate swaps (cf. §9.2.1); to a lesser extent interest rate caps, collars, and other instruments are used (cf. §9.2.2); 100% of the risk may not need to be covered (cf. §9.2.3). The Project Company may also have to cover other funding costs incurred by lenders (cf. §9.2.4) and arrange for hedging of the funds drawn down under a bond and not yet used for the project (cf. §9.2.5). Sponsors may face particular problems with interest rate movements prior to Financial Close (cf. §9.2.6).

§9.2.1 INTEREST RATE SWAPS

Under an interest rate swap agreement (also known as a "coupon swap") one party exchanges an obligation for payment of interest on a floating rate basis to payment at a fixed rate, and the other party does the opposite. Banks in the capital markets run large books of such interest rate swaps.

In a project financing, a Project Company that has an obligation to pay interest at a floating rate under its loan agrees to pay its counterpart (a bank or banks—the "swap provider") the difference between the floating rate and the agreed-upon fixed rate if the floating rate is below this fixed rate, or will be paid by the swap provider if the floating rate is above the fixed rate.

Calculation of interest swap payments. The calculation of the net payment amounts between the Project Company and the swap provider is based on the "notional principal amount" for each period (i.e., the amount of the loan on which the interest is being calculated), although in a swap agreement neither side lends the other any money but simply pays over the difference in the two interest rates.

Table 9.2 shows how an interest rate swap between 6-month LIBOR and a fixed rate might work in practice, assuming that the Project Company borrows 1000 (i.e., this is the notional principal amount), at LIBOR refixed 6-monthly, swaps this floating interest rate against a fixed rate of 6%, and repays the loan in one installment at the end of 6 years:

Table 9.2

Interest Rate Swap

			6 Month Period					
			1	2	3	4	5	6
(a)	Notional principal amount		1000	1000	1000	1000	1000	1000
(b)	LIBOR		4%	5%	6%	7%	8%	9%
(c)	Swap fixed rate		6%	6%	6%	6%	6%	6%
(d)	LIBOR interest	[(a) × (b)]	20	25	30	35	40	45
(e)	Fixed-rate interest	[(a) × (c)]	30	30	30	30	30	30
(f)	Difference	[(d) − (e)]	−10	−5	0	5	10	15
Project Company position								
	Interest on loan	[= (d)]	20	25	30	35	40	45
	Swap payment / (receipt)	[= −(f)]	10	5	0	−5	−10	−15
	Net interest cost	[= (e)]	30	30	30	30	30	30
Swap provider position								
	Interest on notional principal	[= (e)]	30	30	30	30	30	30
	Swap payment / (receipt)	[= (f)]	−10	−5	0	5	10	15
	Net interest cost	[= (d)]	20	25	30	35	40	45

Thus the Project Company has turned its floating rate LIBOR interest payments into a fixed rate of 6%, and the swap provider has done the reverse.

Interest swap breakage costs and credit risk. Although neither side of the swap arrangement is lending the other any money, each side is taking an credit risk on the transaction. If the Project Company defaults on its debt, the swap arrangement has to be canceled ("unwound" or "broken"). The swap provider unwinds the swap by entering into another swap for the balance of the term (i.e., another party takes over the obligations of the Project Company). But if long-term fixed interest rates have gone down since the swap was originally signed, the new counterpart will not be willing to pay the same high rate of fixed interest as the Project Company. The difference between the original fixed rate and the new fixed rate represents a loss to the original swap provider. This is known as the "unwind" or "breakage" cost.

Of course if, when the default takes place, the long-term fixed rate for the remainder of the swap term is higher than the original rate, there is no breakage cost to the swap provider; on the contrary, there is a profit due to the Project Company.

For example, if a swap with a notional principal of 1000 is provided for 15 years, at a fixed rate of 10%, after 2 years the Project Company defaults, and the swap provider is only able to redeploy the swap at 8%, the latter's breakage cost can be calculated as shown in Table 9.3.

The swap provider's loss on termination is therefore not the same as the notional principal amount, but amounts to 20 *p.a.* for the remaining 13 years. The

Table 9.3

Calculation of Swap Breakage Cost

	Year												
	3	4	5	6	7	8	9	10	11	12	13	14	15
Fixed-rate payment													
Original amount	100	100	100	100	100	100	100	100	100	100	100	100	100
Revised amount	80	80	80	80	80	80	80	80	80	80	80	80	80
Swap provider's loss:	20	20	20	20	20	20	20	20	20	20	20	20	20
NPV[a] of loss (@ 8% discount rate) = 158													

[a]For NPV calculations see §12.8.1.

NPV of this cash flow is the swap breakage cost—in this case this is 15.8% of the notional principal amount.

Table 9.4 sets out the swap breakage costs for a typical project loan cash flow, calculated year by year during the loan, assuming:

- Loan of 1200
- Repaid in 12 annual installments of 100
- Original fixed rate of 10%
- Reinvestment rate of 8% after default by the Project Company

Thus if the Project Company goes into default just after the time the loan and swap are signed, and long-term interest rates have also gone down from 10% to 8% at that time, the loss to the swap provider is 111. If the default occurs at the end of Year 1 the loss is 97, at the end of Year 2, 82, and so on. Of course if the reinvestment rate is higher than 10%, there is a profit—which benefits the Project Company—rather than a loss on the breakage. The calculation of the profit or loss on a swap if it is unwound at any point is known as "mark-to-market"; a swap that shows a profit on being unwound is said to be "in the money," and one which shows a loss is "out of the money."

Table 9.4

Swap Breakage Costs over Time

	Year												
	0	1	2	3	4	5	6	7	8	9	10	11	12
Notional principal	1200	1100	1000	900	800	700	600	500	400	300	200	100	0
Fixed-rate payment													
Original amount		120	110	100	90	80	70	60	50	40	30	20	10
Reinvestment		96	88	80	72	64	56	48	40	32	24	16	8
Loss		24	22	20	18	16	14	12	10	8	6	4	2
NPV of loss	111	97	82	69	56	45	34	25	17	11	5	2	

This potential loss is the credit risk that the swap provider is taking on the Project Company, but unlike the credit risk of a loan, this is not a fixed figure, but depends on:

- The remaining length of the swap
- The way market rates have changed, when the default takes place
- Whether the original swap is at a historically high or low rate (if at a low rate, the likelihood of a breakage cost is less because long-term rates are less likely to go even lower, and vice versa)

A swap provider entering into a swap with the Project Company therefore has to make an initial assessment of the level of the credit risk, which cannot be more than an educated guess at that stage. Very roughly speaking (as there are many variables), for a 15-year interest swap based on an amortizing loan repayment schedule like that in Table 9.4 (which is typical of project finance), banks might assume an initial credit risk of 15–20% of the maximum notional principal amount.

For the swap provider, arranging a matching swap in the market is far easier than raising long-term fixed rate funding and on-lending this to the Project Company, since its own counterparts take a much lower credit risk in providing a swap than making a long-term loan, whereas the bank providing a swap to the Project Company has easy access to short-term floating rate funding and assumes this will always be renewed (but cf. §9.2.4).

Breakage cost on fixed-rate loans. A lender providing a fixed-rate loan or bond also has a breakage cost if the Project Company defaults, for exactly the same reason as the swap provider: if the rate at which the fixed rate funds can be re-lent has gone down when the Project Company defaults, the fixed rate lender makes a loss. However in some markets the breakage cost on early termination of a bond issue can be substantially higher than the breakage cost for an interest rate swap:

- When a loan is repaid early for whatever reason, a lender usually loses the future profit margin, (although a small prepayment fee may be charged). The purpose of the breakage calculation is just to avoid the lender's making a loss in this situation; however, bond holders may require payment of the NPV of some or all of their future profit margin.
- The breakage calculation for a bond may be one way—i.e., if interest rates have gone down the bond holder is compensated by the borrower, but if they have gone up the bond holder does not pay over this profit to the Project Company.

A floating rate lender also may have a small breakage cost if the Project Company defaults between the two interest rate fixing dates.

How interest swap rates are determined. The swap market works on the basis of "bullet" repayments of notional principal—i.e., the type of loan repayment schedule shown in Table 9.3, which assumes none of the notional principal of 1000 is repaid until the end of the 6-year schedule shown. However, a project finance loan cash flow, and hence notional principal repayment, is like that set out in Table 9.4, i.e., repayment in installments over a period of time (known as an "amortising swap"). The way the market deals with this is to quote a weighted average rate for a series of swaps covering each repayment date, and thus on the schedule in Table 9.4 the swap provider would quote the weighted rate for the swaps based on 100 notional principal repaid after 1 year, 100 after 2 years, 100 after 3 years, and so on.

The swap quotation also has to take into account that the notional principal is not drawn all at once; most projects have a drawing period of 2–3 years or so during construction, so are quoted swap rates in advance for an increasing notional principal amount during the construction/drawing period (this is known as a "accreting swap")

The fixed rate quoted by the swap provider is based on three elements:

- *Government bond rates for the relevant period in the relevant currency:* These provide the "base rate" for the swap; for example, a swap in US$ for 7 years would be based on the current yield of a U.S. Treasury bond for the same period.
- *The swap market premium:* This reflects supply and demand in the swap market and also in the fixed-rate corporate bond market, since corporate bond issuers can arbitrage between the fixed-rate market and the floating rate market with a swap. (Swap market rates—i.e., the total of the government bond rate and the swap market premium—are quoted in the financial press and on dealing screens.)
- *A charge for the credit risk of the Project Company:* If the swap provider assumes that the level of risk is, say, 15% of the initial notional principal amount, and the credit margin on the loan to the Project Company is, say, 1.5%, then the credit risk premium on the swap rate should be 15% of 1.5% (i.e., 0.225% *p.a.*).

Swap structures. The simplest way for the Project Company to cover its interest rate risk through a swap is to have its syndicate of banks providing the floating rate loan also provide the swap *pro rata* to their share of the loan; however, the problems with this are:

- The final syndication of the loan to banks may not be completed until after Financial Close (cf. §5.1.8), and swap arrangements have to be concluded at or shortly after Financial Close, in order to fix the project's interest costs.
- Some of the syndicate banks may be less competitive than others in their swap pricing, and the Project Company may end up having to pay the swap rate of the most expensive bank.

- It leaves the syndicate banks with no competition, and therefore the Project Company may not get the best rates for the swap.

It is not normally possible for the Project Company to go directly to other banks in the market and ask them to quote for the swap, because a bank not already involved in lending is unlikely to want to spend the time bringing in its project finance department to analyze the risk involved.

If there are several banks in a lending syndicate, they can be asked to compete with each other for the swap business, rather than each bank providing a swap to cover its share of the loan. (Each bank in the syndicate may then provide a *pro rata* guarantee for the swap to the swap provider, or the latter may be willing to take the whole of the risk on its own books.) But if there are only one or two banks in the syndicate, which may be the case if the loan has been underwritten but not syndicated before Financial Close, competition in this way may not work.

A structure that gives the Project Company access to the best market rates is for one or more of the banks in the lending syndicate to act as a "fronting bank." The Project Company goes into the swap market for quotations, based on the swap provider entering into a swap with the fronting bank; the Project Company then enters into an identical "back-to-back" swap with the fronting bank. (The fronting bank itself can still quote in competition for the market swap.) The fronting bank charges the credit risk premium discussed above or is counter-guaranteed by the syndicate banks and charges a smaller premium reflecting this.

Rollover risk. The notional principal schedule used as a basis for the swap is based on estimates of when drawings on the loan will be made during construction, and when loan repayments will be made (beginning when the project is completed). Inevitably these estimates will prove incorrect; e.g., a delay in the construction program affects the timing of drawings, or the final completion of the project is delayed, which also delays the repayment schedule, as this is normally calculated from the completion date.

If the shift in timing is a relatively short period of a month or so, this does not matter, and the swap can be left to run on the original schedule (assuming that the Project Company will have funds available to make any net payment that is due) since any extra loss in a one-month period is likely to be compensated by a profit in another. If a significant shift in the schedule takes place—say 6 months—because of a delay in completion of the project, it is preferable to "roll over" the swap (i.e., terminate the original swap and enter into a new one on the new schedule). Any breakage cost on termination would be largely matched by the benefit of a lower long-term fixed rate, and any profit would compensate for a higher fixed rate.

However the Project Company may face some difficulty with the swap provider:

- The swap provider may no longer wish to provide the swap and try to use the rollover request as a way of getting out of it.
- If there is no competition on the rate for the rollover, the Project Company could pay too much for the rollover swap.

If the fronting bank structure described above has been used, rollover of the swap should be less of an issue; in other cases it may be possible to agree to a competitive approach in advance. If not the Project Company (and its lenders) may just have to take this risk as one of the inevitable adverse consequences of a delay in completion.

A similar issue arises if the loan amount is increased (e.g., by drawing on contingent funding because of a delay in completion), and the swap needs to be increased correspondingly.

Documentation. Interest rate swaps are documented in a standard form, based on documentation produced by ISDA (International Swap and Derivatives Association), and on which there is limited room for negotiation. This is necessary because swap dealers want to be able to trade their entire swap book on the basis of standard terms.

For the intercreditor relationship between swap providers and other lenders, cf. §13.13.1.

§9.2.2 INTEREST RATE CAPS AND OTHER INSTRUMENTS

Interest rate caps may provide a short-term solution to interest rate hedging, for example, if a floating rate loan during the construction period is to be refinanced by a fixed rate loan on completion of the project. They have the advantage that the provider does not take a credit risk on the Project Company, and so can be obtained from any provider in the market, but the disadvantage is that there is an up-front fee payable that adds to the project's development costs. They are therefore seldom used for long-term hedging.

Under an interest rate cap, the cap provider agrees to pay the Project Company if floating interest rates go above a certain level. For example, the current floating rate may be 5%, and the cap rate set at 7%. So long as the floating rate remains below 7% the Project Company just pays the floating rate. If the floating rate goes above 7%, the cap provider pays the Project Company the difference between the two in the same way as in an interest rate swap. For budget purposes the Project Company can thus assume an interest cost of 7% fixed, and insofar as the floating rate cost comes out below this level, this is a bonus.

Other more sophisticated instruments may be useful for some projects; a "swaption" (or "contingent swap") is the right to enter into a swap at a future date, which may give some flexibility in timing. "Collar" arrangements combine an interest rate cap with a floor rate (i.e., the maximum rate is fixed with a cap as above, while if the floating rate goes below a floor rate of say 3% the Project Company pays the difference to the provider). Interest rate collars may be done at no cost (i.e., without a front-end fee), because the cost of the cap is offset by the fee received from selling the floor rate. (However the taker of the floor rate has a credit risk on the Project Company, albeit usually a lower level of risk than that for an interest rate swap provider.)

§9.2.3 SCALE AND TIMING OF INTEREST RATE HEDGING

Lenders normally accept that the Project Company does not have to hedge 100% of its interest rate risk. First, some flexibility needs to be left for the draw-down and repayment timing differences mentioned above; second, the interest rate risk on contingent funding, which may never be drawn at all, need not be hedged at the beginning of construction. The Project Company may agree with the lenders that initially it should hedge not less than 90% of its interest rate risk, ignoring contingent funding. Subject to the rollover risk point discussed previously, finance documentation can be left sufficiently flexible for a higher level of interest rate hedging to be added later if contingent finance is drawn or if the Project Company wants to increase the hedging percentage.

The hedging transaction is normally carried out at or shortly after Financial Close, to ensure the budget costs are fixed as quickly as possible. A window of up to a month after Financial Close may be left for concluding the swap, to ensure that the Project Company does not have to go into the swap market on a bad day.

§9.2.4 ADDITIONAL COSTS

Lenders are also exposed to the possibility of additional funding costs, which would erode their interest margin, arising from:

- An increased requirement from their central bank for liquidity reserves against long-term lending, or for increased capital to support such lending (known as "MLRs," i.e., minimum liquidity requirements, or "MLAs," i.e., minimum liquid asset requirements—not to be confused with the different meaning of MLAs in §11.6); obviously this relates only to commercial banks.
- Withholding taxes on interest payments from the Project Company that the lenders may not be able to offset against their other tax liabilities

These risks are not peculiar to the project finance market, and the extra costs involved are always borne by the borrower; however, interest payments should only be increased to cover the banks actually affected, not the whole syndicate. In the case of withholding taxes, the Project Company must "gross up" its interest payments (i.e., increase them by an amount sufficient to produce the amount of net interest payment to the lenders after deduction of tax). A lender may agree that if it can offset this amount of tax against its other tax liabilities in due course, the withholding will be refunded to the borrower. However, lenders are not prepared to get into debates about how they manage their tax affairs, and therefore any refund relies entirely on a lender's good faith.

The Project Company also takes the risk, where the borrowing is on a floating rate basis, that the lenders may not be able to renew their short-term funding due to disruption in the market—this could mean that if, say, LIBOR is no longer quoted and another pricing basis has to be used, or if the lenders cannot fund at all, that the loan must be repaid. If one or two lenders get into trouble because of their own rather than general market problems, these provisions do not apply.

In practice, these provisions (other than that relating to withholding tax) have not had to be applied in recent years.

§9.2.5 REDEPOSIT RISK

As mentioned in §5.3, one of the disadvantages of bonds compared to loans is that the funding cannot be drawn in pieces as and when required, but must all be drawn at once, and any funding temporarily surplus to requirements is kept on deposit until needed. The interest earned on this deposit is itself a source of funds for construction of the project, but the deposit is likely to be at a floating rate. This exposes the Project Company to a short-term interest rate risk during the construction period, until the financing has all been spent on project costs, because if the rate of interest earned on these redeposited funds is lower than projected, the Project Company may be short of funds to complete the project.

This can also be dealt with by taking out a swap, but this time the other way round; the Project Company agrees to receive a fixed rate of interest in return for paying the same floating rate as it is receiving on the deposit. Alternatively, a bank may offer a fixed rate for the deposit and carry out the swap internally; this is known as a "guaranteed investment contract" ("GIC").

§9.2.6 INTEREST RATE HEDGING BEFORE FINANCIAL CLOSE

A particular problem for Sponsors is how to deal with interest rate risk during the development period of the project. The Sponsors may have originally put in a bid for a project with a Project Agreement with a Tariff or Unitary Charge covering debt service on a fixed basis, thus leaving the Project Company rather than the Offtaker or Contracting Authority with the interest rate risk, and there may be a substantial period of time between the original bid and Financial Close. If interest rates go up before Financial Close has been reached and no interest rate hedging is in place, the investors' returns, and the financing as a whole, may be jeopardized.

One answer to this problem is for the Sponsors to take up the long-term interest rate hedging arrangements themselves in advance of Financial Close, and then transfer the hedging to the Project Company at Financial Close—but they are then taking on an extra risk if the project, for whatever reason, does not reach Financial Close. If long-term interest rates go down, there will be a loss in unwinding a long-term interest rate swap, because the swap provider now has an obligation at a high long-term rate that cannot be written off elsewhere except at a loss. (Of course the reverse is true if rates go up. The calculation is also affected by the difference between short-term and long-term interest rates, as this difference has to be covered before Financial Close (i.e., if short-term rates are lower than long-term rates, the Sponsors will be out of pocket before Financial Close and *vice versa*). Sponsors therefore need to be confident that Financial Close can be reached, and realistic about the schedule for doing so, before taking on interest rate hedging in this way. Similarly, a swaption (cf. §9.2.2) can be used, but may involve a cost that will be lost if the bid does not succeed.

In some cases the Offtaker or Contracting Authority may be willing to take the risk (or benefit) of any adjustments to interest rates between agreement on terms with the Sponsors and the hedging finally being undertaken at Financial Close and adjust the Tariff or Unitary Charge accordingly. If so, the Offtaker or Contracting Authority will wish to control the process of fixing the interest rate in due course.

§9.3 EXCHANGE RATE RISKS

Currency exchange rate risks may exist during both the construction and operating phases of the financing.

During the construction phase, if costs are in one currency and funding in another, the Project Company is exposed to the risk that the currency in which the costs are being incurred may appreciate. For example, if the EPC Contract costs $100, and €100 of funding for this has been arranged when the €:$ exchange rate is 1.00:1.00, and the Euro subsequently depreciates to €1.20:$1.00, the funding is then only enough to pay for $83.3 (€100 ÷ 1.20) of EPC costs, and in effect the project has a construction cost overrun (or a funding deficit) of $16.7.

During the operating phase, if the Project Company's revenues are in one currency and its financing or other costs are in another, movements in the exchange rate will affect its net revenues, and hence ability to repay debt. Ideally, finance should be arranged in the local currency, hence eliminating such long-term currency risks, but in practice this may not be possible in developing countries where the domestic financial markets are not able to provide project finance (cf. §3.1.2).

As with interest rate risks, lenders will not accept the Project Company taking exchange rate risks in its financing, however much of a "safe bet" this may appear to be. Lenders wish such risks to be minimized or eliminated wherever possible.

Note that the complete inability to exchange or transfer currency out of the country is treated as a political risk (cf. §10.3).

§9.3.1 Hedging of Currency Risks

It is theoretically possible for forward foreign exchange contracts to be used to cover exchange risks: in this type of contract a Project Company that had construction costs in € but funding in $ could agree at Financial Close to sell $ and buy € on the estimated loan drawdown dates, thus fixing the exchange rate at which the € costs are being funded in $.

Similarly a Project Company that had costs and revenues in $ but funding in € could agree

- To sell $ and buy € on the estimated loan drawdown dates
- To sell the same amount of € and buy $ on the estimated loan repayment dates, which would fix the exchange rate at which the loan is being repaid.

In practice, however, market-based hedging of exchange rate risks is generally not used in project finance, apart from adjusting small and temporary exchange rate differences that may arise, because the credit risk involved for banks is significantly greater than for an interest swap: a movement on the exchange rate of 20% increases loan principal payments and hence the level of risk by 20%, whereas a movement in the interest rate of 20% affects the interest payment only, and (assuming an interest rate of 10%) equates only to an additional 2% *p.a.* of the (declining) loan principal outstandings. Furthermore, the techniques described below generally enable the Project Company to cover its foreign exchange risk without any need for such market-based hedging.

There thus are two interlinked approaches to dealing with the issue:

Construction period. For construction cost exchange rate risks, either the costs have to be redesignated into the currency of the funding or the funding currency has to be changed, whichever is easier and is also in line with the approach to long-term (operating period) exchange rate risk discussed below.

The largest item of construction costs is likely to be the EPC Contract; if the EPC Contractor can be persuaded to fix the price in the currency of the funding, most of the problem disappears, as the next largest cost during construction is likely to be the financing (IDC and fees), which will automatically be in the funding currency.

However this transfers the foreign exchange exposure to the EPC Contractor, who may be reluctant to quote a price in another currency without a cost base in that currency. The EPC Contractor could cover this exposure with forward foreign exchange cover as above, but the EPC Contractor may not be prepared to quote a price in this way at the time of bidding for the EPC Contract, since there is no certainty of being awarded the contract or of the schedule for construction and thus payment. If the EPC Contractor takes out forward exchange cover and is not awarded the contract or the timing changes, this could result in a heavy loss.

In such cases the EPC Contractor may be prepared to quote the initial price in the home currency, but enter into forward exchange contracts with the Project Company at Financial Close (i.e., when the EPC Contract is signed and financed, and so the schedule for construction and payment is then fixed), so hedging the payments under the EPC Contract (probably on a back-to-back basis with the EPC Contractor's bankers). This, of course, leaves the Sponsors and the Project Company with this risk until Financial Close.

Operating period. During the operating period, revenues should be in the same currency as expenses and debt service costs. The currency of the revenues therefore dictates the currency of the financing, or *vice versa:*

- If revenues are earned in a currency in which financing can be provided (e.g., $ or €), the financing should be in that currency.
- If funding for a project in a developing country can only be arranged in $, then any payments from an Offtaker or Contracting Authority under a Project Agreement must also be in $, or paid in local currency but indexed against $ (cf. §6.1.6, but also cf. §9.3.5).
- If the project is producing a commodity whose price is $-based (e.g., oil), then funding should be in $ (cf. §10.3.1).

Similarly, continuing operating costs need to match the revenue currency as far as possible. On some projects local operating costs (offices, staff) may not be incurred in the revenue currency, but the degree of risk here is usually not significant.

It follows from this that if the funding has to be in, say, $ to match revenues, the construction costs, especially the EPC Contract, also have to be in this currency. As discussed in §12.7.7, an inherent exchange rate risk related to the tax position may also remain.

§9.3.2 FINANCE IN MORE THAN ONE CURRENCY

If the funding for debt or equity is being provided in more than one currency (and the currencies concerned are not each provided *pro rata* by debt and equity), the exchange rate between these currencies shortly before signing of the financing should be used to fix the relationship between the currencies for the debt:equity calculation (cf. §13.1.4). If this is not done, it is impossible to provide the correct amounts of funding in advance, as illustrated by in Table 9.5.

The Table shows that if the Project Company is required to maintain a debt:equity ratio of no more than 80:20, and if the exchange rate at COD is used, the project will be in default. There is no way of foreseeing in advance what the exchange

Table 9.5

Debt : Equity Ratio and Changing Exchange Rates

	At financial close	At COD
	£1 = €1.3	£1 = €1.5
Equity	€200	€200
Debt	£615	£615
Debt in € equivalent	€800	€923
Debt:equity ratio	80 : 20	92 : 20

rate will be: no form of hedging is appropriate because the mixed currencies of funding will have been used to reflect the Project Company's costs and revenues as discussed above, and hedging back into, say, £ will undo this.

The problem can also be avoided by arranging for both equity and debt to be contributed *pro rata* between £ and € (i.e., 80 of £ to each 20 of £ in the case above), with the amounts in each currency fixed at the exchange rates at Financial Close. This gives the result shown in Table 9.6.

Table 9.6

Mixed Funding and Debt : Equity Ratio

	At financial close (£1 = €1.3)			At COD (£1 = €1.5)		
	€	£	€ equivalent	€	£	€ equivalent
Debt	€640	£208	€800	€640	£208	€952
Equity	€160	£52	€200	€160	£52	€238
Debt:equity ratio			80:20			80:20

§9.3.3 CONVERSION OF LOCAL CURRENCY REVENUES

Although a Project Company's exposure to foreign currency debt may be hedged by indexing its local currency revenues under a Project Agreement to the foreign currency concerned, this may not provide complete hedging because of timing differences on conversion:

Gap between billing and payment. There is inevitably a gap between the time the Project Company calculates the amount due from the Offtaker or Contracting Authority, including currency indexation, and the time payment of the bill is made (perhaps a month or more). The Project Company is thus exposed to further exchange rate movements in that time, although obviously the risk is limited as only one month's payments are involved at any one time. The risk can be covered by short-term hedging in the local financial market if this is possible, or by adjusting the next month's bill to reflect the actual indexed rate at the time the previous month's bill was paid.

Timing of currency conversions. Host Country exchange control regulations may specify that local currency can only be changed into foreign currency when the payment is due to be made. If revenues indexed to foreign currency that are intended for foreign currency costs, debt service or dividends cannot be converted until payment of these is due, an unacceptably long period of risk may result (up to six months for the typical half-yearly debt service and dividend payments). If forward exchange cover is not available in the local market (or credit risks in this market are not acceptable to the lenders, which is quite likely), the Host Country's central bank or ministry of finance has to be persuaded to allow a more liberal interpretation of the rules to allow immediate conversion.

§9.3.4 FIXING OF SECURITY IN LOCAL CURRENCY

When the lenders register their mortgage (or other security) over the Project Company's assets in the Host Country, local law may require that the amount of the mortgage be fixed, and stated in local currency even if the debt is in foreign currency. This leaves the lenders exposed if the local currency depreciates, and the Project Company has other junior or unsecured creditors, who may have a *pari passu* claim for any amounts not covered by the mortgage. It may be possible to register the mortgage for an amount larger than the loan at the current exchange rate, to leave room for maneuvre, but if not the increase in the loan amount in local currency terms will have to added to the mortgage at intervals (which besides being cumbersome and involving the Project Company in extra costs, may not be wholly secure against other lenders for a period of time).

§9.3.5 CATASTROPHIC DEVALUATION

The currency hedging techniques described in §9.3.1 enable the Project Company to deal with the risk of normal market movements in exchange rates, but if economic mismanagement in the Host Country leads to a major currency devaluation, these techniques are liable to break down. An Offtaker or Contracting Authority who is taking the exchange rate risk by indexing the Tariff or Unitary Charge payments against a foreign currency (cf. §6.1.6) probably cannot pass on the greatly increased cost of this indexation after a major devaluation to the local end-users of the product, and if the Offtaker's or Contracting Authority's exchange risk has been hedged in the local banking system, these banks probably cannot sustain the losses involved.

The effect of this was seen, for example, in the Asian crisis of 1997, and in Turkey in 2001, where Power Purchasers under long-term PPAs had linked Tariff payments to foreign currencies. When the Power Purchasers' home currencies suffered huge devaluations, they had an obligation under the PPA to increase the Tariff payments accordingly. However, it was simply not economically or politically realistic for the tariff to their own end-users of electricity to be increased immediately to a similar extent, to enable the required payments to be made to foreign lenders and investors. Thus in practice the protection supposedly given by currency indexation in the Tariff did not work and the PPAs of course fell into default.

"Catastrophic devaluation" (i.e., a sudden major devaluation of the local currency) is now recognized as one of the most serious risk in providing project finance in foreign currencies to developing countries, where the project is not a natural generator of foreign exchange revenues.

Paradoxically, there is an argument that in this situation it is better for the Project Company's revenues to be derived from a Tariff or Unitary Charge indexed not to a foreign currency, but to local inflation. Therefore, if a product such as electricity suddenly becomes cheaper for the end-user after a devaluation (when measured in foreign currency), this will only be a temporary phenomenon—in due course the rate of inflation will increase correspondingly. So a devaluation of 40% should lead to an increase in inflation of 40%, and a Tariff or Unitary Charge based on local inflation will thus increase by 40% to compensate for the devaluation.

This approach is likely to be politically far more acceptable in the Host Country, and hence more sustainable during an economic crisis. The main problem, however, even in a completely free market without Host Government interference with prices, is that it takes time for the adjustment in prices to take place; in the meantime the Project Company with a Tariff or Unitary Charge based on inflation may not have enough revenues to cover its debt service.

In 2001 the first facility to deal with the problem of catastrophic devaluation was provided by OPIC (cf. §11.5.2) to a power project in Brazil. This is not insurance, but a revolving liquidity facility, to cover the time lapse between a major devaluation and the subsequent increase in inflation that should, over time, be sufficient to compensate the Project Company (with a Tariff based on local inflation) for the effect of the devaluation on its ability to service foreign currency debt. OPIC agreed to provide additional subordinated debt to the Project Company equal to a maximum of 10% of the Project Company's $ bond issue if, as a consequence of a devaluation, the Project Company cannot generate sufficient foreign currency to sustain its debt service payments. This amount was sufficient to cover, on average, the additional payments in local currency resulting from a devaluation of 90% in any one year, well above even the worst historical experience. (However, OPIC will not "lend into a default"—if even after drawing the OPIC loan the Project Company cannot service its senior debt, the OPIC loan will not be disbursed.) Repayment of any OPIC loan will be made on a subordinated basis (cf. §13.13.5), but with a *pari-passu* claim on security. This facility was a key element in securing an investment grade rating for the project bond. It remains to be seen how widely this type of facility—essentially an untied standby loan—will be available from ECAs, IFIs, or other sources, and how widely it will be accepted in the financing market as adequately dealing with this major issue.

Chapter 10

Political Risks

§10.1 PROJECTS AND POLITICS

Governments play a very important role in project finance. Projects financed in this way are often major long-term investments, for which a political will and sustained political support are needed. They may also form part of a government policy of privatization or the provision of public infrastructure through PPPs, whose success or failure may have considerable political consequences.

In fact, few major projects can be structured and financed without political backing. Political support from a high level is often necessary to enable a project to be completed successfully; for example, if a PPA is being negotiated with the state-owned power company, the latter's management may consider that such a contract is not in their interests, and it would be better if they developed the power station themselves as they have done in the past. Thus the Power Purchaser has no incentive to negotiate constructively. The only way to break this impasse is for the Power Purchaser to be given a strong direction from the Host Government that they must not take this attitude.

Once the project is operating, continued political support is needed. The project will be weakened if it becomes a political football because it provides a handle for the opposition to attack the government, or for a new government to try to undo the deal agreed by the previous government, e.g., because it did not go through a transparent (competitive) public procurement process (cf. §4.6) or it produces very high returns for the investors (cf. §6.9.3), and so is open to charges, at best, of having been favored unfairly, or, at worst, of corruption. Once a project is complete it cannot be taken out of the country again, and the Project Company's position inevitably becomes weaker than it was when the Host Government first wanted to attract the investment.

So just as a project has to be commercially viable (cf. §8.4), it must also be politically viable. The fundamental issue is whether the project is beneficial to the country; if it is not beneficial, e.g., because the cost of its product or service is out of line with local costs, investors and lenders cannot just rely on Project Contracts and ignore this political aspect. And a high rate of return, which is meant to compensate for risk, may paradoxically increase the risk if it becomes politically unacceptable.

The project also has to be set up in a way that leaves the Host Government in a position to make future changes in the market in which it operates. For example, if the state-owned power distributor is to sign a long term PPA, the Host Government will have to consider whether this contract could be an impediment to a future privatization of the electricity industry, and if so how it can be structured to leave future flexibility in this respect.

More specifically, the Project Company may be subject to political risks relating to the project's presence in a particular country and its relationship with the Host Government, rather than to the commercial and financial risk aspects of the project covered in Chapter 8 and Chapter 9. These risks are discussed in detail in this chapter.

§10.2 CLASSIFICATION OF POLITICAL RISK

Political risks fall into three main categories:

Investment risks. The standard "investment" risks are:
- currency convertibility and transfer (cf. §10.3)
- expropriation of the project by the state (cf. §10.4)
- political violence (i.e., war and civil disturbance—also known as political *force majeure*) (cf. §10.5)

Investors and lenders into the country where the project is situated (the Host Country) are likely to be concerned about these issues if the project is located in a developing country that is politically unstable or has a lower credit rating.

These risks may be passed on by the Project Company to the Host Government under a Project Agreement or Government Support Agreement, by requiring the Offtaker or Contracting Authority (guaranteed by the Host Government) or the Host Government itself to compensate the Project Company for losses caused by them. However when the time comes the Host Government may simply be unwilling or unable to fulfill this obligation, and some form of political risk coverage (cf. Chapter 11) may be required.

Change of law risks. Changes in the law, either because of new legislation or changes in regulations under existing laws, may have a serious effect on the viability of the project (cf. §10.6). These risks exist whether or not funding for the project is raised overseas, and may affect a project in both developed and developing countries. Again they may be passed on under the Project Agreement to the Offtaker or Contracting Authority, or under a Government Support Agreement to the Host Government.

Quasi-political risks. This category includes issues such as contract disputes, which may have a political or commercial background; it illustrates that the dividing line between commercial risks and political risks is not a precise one (cf. §10.7).

It might be thought that incorporating the Project Company outside the Host Country could mitigate some of these political risks, but this is seldom a workable solution. The project itself obviously cannot leave the country, and most of the risks relate to the project itself rather than its ownership. Furthermore, investment laws of the Host Country may not allow the project to be owned by a foreign company, and even if they do the activities of the foreign company inside the Host Country in running the project are subject to the same laws and risks as a domestic company. Using an overseas governing law or jurisdiction for Project Contracts may provide some protection however (cf. §10.7.1).

Political risk insurance or guarantees for lenders (or, in some cases, direct loans for the Project Company) are available from a variety of bilateral and multilateral entities and private-sector insurers (cf. Chapter 11).

§10.3 CURRENCY CONVERTIBILITY AND TRANSFER

It is often not possible to raise funding in the currency of the Host Country in developing countries (cf. §3.1.2). Therefore, although a Project Company's revenues are normally earned in the currency of the Host Country, they may be indexed to a foreign currency under a Project Agreement (cf. §9.3.1) in order for these revenues to be used to repay offshore lenders and provide a return to investors in foreign currencies. Two processes have to be carried out for these purposes: sufficient revenues have to be converted into the foreign currency amounts required by lenders and investors, and these foreign currency amounts have to be transferred out of the Host Country to lenders and investors. (Foreign currency may also be required to pay for fuel or other operating costs.)

If a project is able to rely on the free international financial markets that exist in developed countries, the only real currency risk is that of an adverse movement of the exchange rate between the domestic and foreign currencies (i.e., devaluation of the local currency, discussed in §9.3). However, if a developing country gets into economic difficulties and so runs short of foreign currency reserves, it may totally forbid either the conversion of local currency amounts to foreign currencies or the transmission of these foreign currencies out of the country. In effect, at this point the Host Country has defaulted on its foreign currency debt. One of the standard provisions of a Government Support Agreement (cf. §7.5) is a Host Government or central bank guarantee of foreign exchange availability and transfer, but if the Host Country has no foreign exchange reserves this guarantee will be of little value.

Apart from complete unavailability of foreign currency, the worst problem of this nature likely to be faced by a project in a developing country is a catastrophic devaluation of the Host Country's currency. A Host Government guarantee of an Offtaker's or Contracting Authority's payment liabilities may also be of limited value in this situation (cf. §9.3.5).

Lenders assess the degree of these risks by examining the macroeconomic position, balance of payments, and foreign debt levels of the Host Country. If the country has a well-managed and sound economy, then lenders may find the risk acceptable, but if not mitigation of these risks is required.

Apart from political risk guarantees or insurance (cf. Chapter 11), there are some other possible ways of mitigating the risks (but seldom entirely eliminating them):

- Enclave projects (cf. §10.3.1)
- Countertrade (cf. §10.3.2)
- Use of offshore accounts (cf. §10.3.3)

§10.3.1 ENCLAVE PROJECTS

If a project's revenues are paid in foreign currencies from a source outside the Host Country, in principle the project can thus be insulated against both currency exchange and transfer risks. Because the foreign currency never arrives in the country, it cannot be restricted from leaving it, and the foreign currency revenues can be retained to service debt raised outside the country. This may be a feasible approach if the project involves production of a commodity for export, for example, oil, gas, or minerals, or the sale of electricity across a border.

Lenders find generally enclave projects in developing countries more attractive than those that do not generate their own foreign currency earnings from outside the Host Country. As the term implies, they are relatively isolated from what lenders consider to be the main risk of lending to developing countries—that of failure to pay foreign currency debt—and this approach can mean that a developing country may be able to raise foreign currency for development of its resources that would not be otherwise possible. In a similar way, the bond rating agencies may give a higher rating to a bond issued by an enclave project than to the sovereign debt of the country in which the project is located. The World Bank's Enclave Guarantee is another example of this approach (cf. §11.6.1).

Typical factors that would create a feasible enclave project are:

- Importance of the sale of the commodity to the country's economy and balance of payments
- A limited market for the commodity inside the country (so it is unlikely to be diverted for domestic use)
- An infrastructure oriented towards exports (pipelines, ports, etc.), again to avoid diversion
- Sales through a third party with a good credit standing, located outside the jurisdiction or control of the Host Country
- Direct payment of revenues to an SPV or escrow account outside the Host Country
- Difficulty of diverting payments elsewhere

The issue with enclave projects from the Host Country point of view is that they lose control over what may be their most important export earnings, and so are less able to manage their foreign currency reserves and balance of payments situation in the way they consider appropriate, which they may consider a form of economic colonialism. Enclave projects, however, are a way of raising development finance on more attractive terms for a project in a country with a poor credit rating.

§10.3.2 COUNTERTRADE

The Project Company could enter into an arrangement under which it barters its product or services in exchange for a commodity that can then be exported and produce foreign currency, thus creating an enclave project in two stages. However this is a complex approach that is unlikely to be viable for most projects.

§10.3.3 USE OF OFFSHORE RESERVE ACCOUNTS

Even if the Project Company's revenues are not being generated in foreign currencies and held outside the Host Country, the currency exchange and transfer risk can be mitigated for a limited period by the use of offshore Reserve Accounts. As described in §13.5.2, lenders normally require a Debt Service Reserve Account (DSRA) to be built up so that these funds can be used to deal with temporary problems in debt payments. If the DSRA is maintained in foreign currency outside the Host Country, it can also be used to cover temporary problems in obtaining foreign currency for debt service. Other Reserve Accounts to accumulate cash for specific purposes can also be set up offshore.

Lenders therefore prefer overseas Reserve Accounts for projects in countries with poor credit ratings, but this may be difficult in countries with strict exchange controls, where domestic companies are not allowed to have such accounts (cf. §7.4.2).

§10.4 EXPROPRIATION

A government always has the power and right to take over privately owned assets temporarily where this is necessary for reasons of national security (for example, states requisition ships and aircraft in time of war). Many countries have also legislation that gives powers to take over or direct the actions of privately controlled utilities, or divert oil or other fuel supplies, to maintain essential services. Any investor or lender takes this risk, and in any case the government usually provides compensation for such actions.

Expropriation goes beyond this; it is the seizure by the Host Government of the Project Company or its physical or financial assets without payment of just compensation (which is illegal under international law). This is a risk that concerns lenders and investors involved in projects in less politically stable countries. It is greatest in high-profile projects that might otherwise be in public ownership, such as power plants or transportation projects, or projects related to a country's natural resources, such as oil or minerals (where such expropriations have been common in the past, but less so in recent times). Technically the Host Government does not even need to deprive the Project Company of its assets or the investors of their shares; for example, it could pass a law giving it the right to appoint a majority of the directors of the Project Company and so gain control in that way.

Expropriation of private assets for political reasons does not just affect cross-border investors and lenders, but is primarily considered to be a cross-border risk affecting loans to developing countries.

A Project Agreement or Government Support Agreement should treat expropriation as a default by the Offtaker or Contracting Authority, and therefore provide for compensation (through a Termination Sum) accordingly. Expropriation is defined as widely as possible to include not just taking over the assets of the project, but also actions that give the Host Government control of the Project Company. This may provide some deterrent to the Host Government acting arbitrarily against the project. However, it does not deal with the issue of "creeping expropriation" discussed in §10.7.3.

It should be noted that there can be an overlap between expropriation and the currency conversion and transfer risk discussed above, because the reason for the Project Company being unable to convert or transfer its revenues in the host currency may be that its bank accounts have been expropriated (or frozen) by the Host Government.

§10.5 WAR AND CIVIL DISTURBANCE

Investors and lenders have to face the risk of internal political instability, including civil unrest, sabotage or terrorism, or a war against the Host Country causing physical damage to the project, or preventing its operation, and so causing additional capital costs or a loss of revenue. (These risks are collectively described as "political *force majeure*" or "political violence.")

There is also the possibility of a blockade or other sanctions against the Host Country that do not cause physical damage to the project, but prevent its completion because equipment cannot be imported, or prevent its operation because its products cannot be exported or its input supplies imported. A war outside the Host Country may have a similar effect.

Physical damage and consequent loss of revenue caused by this type of political *force majeure* may be covered by insurance; in the absence of this, a Project Agreement or Government Support Agreement may provide for compensation to the Project Company, but there is an obvious risk that when the time comes the Offtaker, Contracting Authority, or Host Government may not be able to fulfil this obligation. Again, therefore, mitigation in the form of political risk guarantees or insurance may be required by lenders.

§10.6 CHANGE OF LAW

The political risks discussed so far (currency exchange, expropriation, and political violence) are risks that mainly cause concern in developing countries. The risk of a change of law, however, is of a much wider application and needs to be considered for any project, wherever it is located.

The Project Company must operate in a stable legal and regulatory environment—this requires:

- General legislation that allows for private ownership of the project and adequately protects private investment
- A clear legal and regulatory framework for the project's operation
- Consistency of legal and regulatory policies
- Straightforward procedures for obtaining construction, operation, and financing Permits (cf. §7.4)
- The ability for the lenders to take and enforce security (cf. §13.7)

This may not be wholly feasible if the type of project is new to the country concerned; in such cases, especially in developing countries, a Government Support Agreement (cf. §7.5) may be required. But, however stable the legal framework is, the risk of a change of law affecting the project cannot be eliminated.

Changes in law may take place through new legislation, new regulations under existing laws, or new interpretations of the law by courts. They can affect the Project Company in a variety of ways, which range from legitimate exercise of a state's right to a "creeping expropriation" of the project (cf. §10.7.3), e.g.:

- Imposition of new environmental requirements under which the project has to incur the cost of investing in new equipment, or is prevented from using the planned fuel or other raw materials
- Imposition of price controls on the Project Company's products or services
- Removal of price controls on input supplies
- Increases in import duties or imposition of import controls on equipment for the project during construction, or on fuel or raw materials required during operation
- Increases in general corporate or other tax rates, so reducing the Project Company's net income
- Imposition of special taxes or levies on the Project Company or the industry in which it operates
- Imposition of or increases in withholding taxes on dividend payments to investors (which reduces their return), or interest payments to lenders (the cost of which usually has to be borne by the Project Company)
- Deregulation or privatization of a previously regulated or state-owned sector, increasing competition or risk for the Project Company
- Changes in employment, health and safety rules or other operating requirements that require more personnel to be employed to run the project, or otherwise increase operating costs
- Amendment or withdrawal of the Project Company's or its contractors' construction or operating Permits
- Invalidation of Project Contracts

A Project Agreement or Government Support Agreement may have a nondiscrimination clause, under which the Host Government agrees not to pass any legislation or otherwise take action that specifically discriminates against the Project Company. However, such action is rare, and normally the risk is that general legislation or other government action may have a particular effect on the Project Company's costs, ability to operate, or the validity of its contracts. Unlike expropriation, this is not usually an illegal act on the part of the Host Government.

As already said, this is not an issue that relates only to developing countries. One of the most serious risks in this category is that of regulatory control of prices charged by the Project Company, which is a particular concern for project companies operating in developed countries where sales are into a competitive but regulated market—as may be the case with utilities such as electricity—rather than under a Project Agreement. This can work in different ways; the government or an industry regulator may cap prices which have been pushed up by shortages of supply, or fail to allow increases in prices that are needed because of increased costs. Even if the Project Company has the right to increase prices under a Project

Agreement, it may not always be able to do so: there have been cases of toll road and bridge projects where a campaign against the tolls by users has resulted in the government's preventing the Project Company from charging what it was entitled to do.

§10.6.1 CHANGE OF LAW RISK IN PROJECT CONTRACTS

The general principle is that the person paying for the product or service under a Project Contract should take the risk—and thus pay for—a change of law. The argument for this is that a change in the law affecting the industry in which the Project Company operates will affect the industry as a whole, and any extra costs will normally be passed on by the industry to the end-users of the product or service provided; therefore an Offtaker or Contracting Authority who does not cover this cost will be earning a windfall profit at the expense of the Project Company.

Also, if the project counterpart concerned is a public-sector body, it is evidently in a better position to assess and control this risk—directly or indirectly—than the Project Company.

Thus under the EPC Contract, the Project Company is responsible for paying for any extra cost that the EPC Contractor faces from having to modify the specifications of the project to comply with changes in the law (e.g., additional equipment to reduce emissions), and cannot penalize the EPC Contractor for delays caused by having to make these modifications. This risk should then be passed by the Project Company to the Offtaker under an Offtake Contract, who should again be responsible for extra costs or loss of revenue caused by the change of law. In cases where the Project Company provides services directly to the public, as under a toll contract, there should be a right to pass such costs through directly to the tolls.

While this position is generally accepted where the changes in law are specific to the industry concerned, if the change is of a more general nature there is less of a market consensus on how this should be treated. The argument against passing this risk on in such cases is that a change of law that is not related to the particular industry but is general in nature is part of the normal risk of doing business in the country. A typical case of such a general change is that of changes in general taxes (e.g., changes in company tax rates, the introduction of new taxes, a change in the tax depreciation rates on investments, or changes in withholding taxes on interest to lenders or dividends to the investors). (It is generally accepted that a change in taxes that specifically affects the industry—e.g., taxes on emissions—should be compensated.)

In Project Agreements the market practice tends to vary between developing countries, where any change in taxes is treated as a change of law and compensated accordingly, and developed countries, where the risk of a change in general taxes tends to remain with the Project Company. In EPC Contracts (whatever the location of the project), the EPC Contractor generally bears the risk of changes in taxes on its own business (i.e., direct corporate taxes), but not in indirect taxes such as VAT or in import duties. Similarly, an Input Supply Contract normally passes on the costs of any extra taxes directly levied on the product being supplied.

An adverse decision by a court affecting the Project Company's costs, rights, or revenues may lie outside the protection that the Project Company can get from passing the change of law risk under a Project Agreement. It can be argued that the court decision does not change the law, but only correctly interprets the law as it stands, and indeed most courts would present their decision in this way. Including "changes in the interpretation of the law" in the contractual definition of change of law may provide some protection in this respect (but cf. §10.7.1).

§10.6.2 Funding the Costs of a Change of Law

If the Project Company is able to pass on the costs of a change of law under a Project Agreement (whether incurred directly or via, say, the EPC Contractor) the question arises of how any Tariff adjustment or compensation is calculated. If the Project Company is directly compensated for additional operating costs as they arise, this should not cause too much difficulty. But if a large additional capital cost is incurred, how will this be financed? Because this cost will not have been included in the original financing plan for the project, the Project Company has no immediate funds available to pay for it.

The normal approach to dealing with such additional capital costs is that, if possible, the Project Company raises additional funding and is compensated by an adjustment in the Tariff, or if this cannot be done, the Offtaker or Contracting Authority must pay the cost directly.

Raising new funding may face various difficulties. First, if the existing lenders are not willing to provide the funding, they may also not be willing to allow new lenders to do so, as this may create intercreditor problems (cf. §13.13). In any case, any such changes in project specifications or additional funding will require lender approval, which may put the Project Company at a disadvantage in any other negotiations with the lenders at the time.

Second, if a future Tariff is to be adjusted for a present cost, more complex issues arise. The financial model for the project (cf. Chapter 12) may be used to calculate the Tariff increase needed to preserve the cover for the lenders' debt, and to maintain the investors' return, but there are potential problems with this:

- The model may not be adequately designed to carry out this calculation, as it will be difficult to provide for all possible permutations of events in advance, and there may be disagreement about how the calculation is to be done in practice.
- The Project Company may not wish the Offtaker or Contracting Authority to

have access to the financial model as it gives details of the operating costs and profit.

It may be appropriate to ask a third-party arbiter (such as the firm of accountants that acted as the Model Auditor for the lenders) to agree to such calculations. For more minor capital costs, it may be sufficient to agree that they will be repaid in the Tariff on an annuity basis at an agreed interest rate over the balance of the term of the Project Agreement (but cf. §8.11).

Most of the political risk insurers discussed in Chapter 11 do not directly cover change of law risk, but will provide cover indirectly for the Host Government defaulting on an obligation to compensate the Project Company for the costs incurred as a result of changes in law.

§10.7 QUASI-POLITICAL RISKS

The categories of what might constitute political risk are, however, even wider than those set out above, because the boundaries between political and commercial risks cannot be easily defined. This is relevant to obtaining political risk cover through insurance or guarantees (cf. Chapter 11); if the boundaries of risk cannot be defined, the cover cannot be obtained.

Issues that arise in this context are:

- Breach of contract and court decisions (cf. §10.7.1)
- Subsovereign risks (cf. §10.7.2)
- Creeping expropriation (cf. §10.7.3)

§10.7.1 BREACH OF CONTRACT AND COURT DECISIONS

Breach of contract (also called "contract repudiation" in this context) is the failure by a public-sector Offtaker, Contracting Authority, or other Project Contract counterpart to fulfill its obligations under the relevant Project Contract (e.g., as an Input Supplier or Offtaker) or by a Host Government to fulfill its obligations to compensate for this under a Government Support Agreement.

Clearly a distinction should be made between a genuine commercial dispute about contract terms or liability, and a refusal on the part of the Host Government or its agencies to honor their obligations, the former being a commercial and the latter a political risk.

But even if the reasons given for the breach are spurious, and an attempt to hide the fact that the contract is actually being repudiated, the only objective way to determine who is in the right is to resort to a court, and if the Host Country's court system is unused to dealing with disputes of this type, or subject to political pressures, the judgement on an action brought by the Project Company against the Host Government or other public-sector counterpart may not be on objective legal grounds.

Where there is concern about the possibility of arbitrary behavior by the Host Government or its courts, some protection may be obtained by specifying that Project Contracts are to be governed by the law of a country other than the Host Country, and that disputes about the contracts are to be litigated or arbitrated in a forum outside the Host Country (i.e., both the governing law and the jurisdiction are outside the Host Country). The forum used may be the courts of another country or a national or international arbitration tribunal. These provisions are fairly standard in Project Contracts signed in developing countries.

Apart from giving protection against arbitrary decisions in the local courts, this approach also means that the Host Country cannot easily change the law to affect the Project Contracts themselves. The issue is especially acute for Government Support Agreements, or Concession Agreements with the government, where the government obviously has an ability to change the law to its own direct benefit.

But the approach may run into opposition with the Host Government, and can easily be translated into a claim that the Project Company is acting like a 19th-century great power, securing extraterritorial rights in the Host Country.

It also may not prevent action being taken in a court in the Host Country on a claim that the Project Agreement or other Project Contract is not valid under the laws of that country (e.g., as to ownership or control of public infrastructure), and therefore, for example, payments should not be made by parties in the Host Country to the Project Company. Such cases may be brought by individuals, organizations, or other parties with a genuine interest in the matter, but they may also be brought by a "front man" for the Host Government itself if it is trying to evade its liabilities (or by opponents of the government for political reasons).

Alternatively, local courts may prevent the Project Company from using international arbitration even if this is a term of the Project Agreement or other Project Contract, on the grounds that the relevant contract provisions are not valid under local law.

Even if the Project Contracts remain governed by local law and jurisdiction, it is standard practice for financing contracts (other than security documentation—cf. §13.7.1) to be governed by the law and jurisdiction of a developed country if the borrower is located in a developing country. (English or New York law are recognized as the most creditor-friendly.) This also ensures, for example, that a change of law preventing payment of loans in foreign currency would not prevent lenders from maintaining their claim for such payment.

Another minor issue that may arise in this context is the language in which Project Contracts and financing documentation are to be prepared. Generally, a Project Company seeking financing from the international market should try to ensure Project Contracts are prepared in English, as this will make it easier to access the widest range of potential lenders; Project Contracts or financing documentation governed by English or New York law should also preferably be drafted in English.

§10.7.2 "Sub-sovereign" (or "Sub-state") Risks

Political risk has been analyzed as if it always a risk on the central government of a country; however, the risks on a Project Contract, and of political action, may not just lie with the central government. A regional government or local municipality may have the right to pass its own legislation and raise its own taxes, and contract as Offtaker or Contracting Authority under a Project Agreement. If it gets into financial difficulty, the central government may have no obligation (or political will) to support it, nor have agreed to do so under a Government Support Agreement, and municipal bankruptcies are of course not unknown.

Other project counterparts, whether established under special legislation or general company law, come into a similar category. The state electricity utility may have been established by the Host Government under such a special law, and its board may all be appointed by the government, but the government does not necessarily have any liability for its obligations under a PPA unless this is specifically agreed to in a Government Support Agreement. And it is evident that the government does not automatically have any liability for a limited company that happens to be owned by the state.

The behavior of such obligors under Project Contracts may be more difficult to predict than that of the government, because such obligors may be less concerned with overall considerations on the credit-worthiness of the country, or its attractiveness to foreign investors, compared to their own local problems.

Lenders therefore make a careful distinction between the sovereign risk of a country (i.e., a risk carrying the "full faith and credit" of the country) that may be acceptable, and public-sector risks below this level—known as "sub-sovereign" risks, which may not. Political risk guarantees or insurance may be available for sovereign risks, but not necessarily for subsovereign risks.

§10.7.3 Creeping Expropriation

A government has many ways to take action against a Project Company without specifically repudiating contractual obligations. State agencies can be slow and obstructive in issuing Permits, imports or exports can be held up at the docks, the Project Company can be accused of tax offenses and subjected to lengthy investigations, Project Company personnel can be accused of criminal offenses such as corruption or harassed in other ways, and so on. The cumulative effect of such actions may be to deprive the Project Company or its investors of the real benefit of the project, even though each action, taken by itself, would not have this result. This is a "creeping expropriation" of the project—very difficult to define in advance, or to recognize until it has actually taken place, although some potential issues (such as Permits) may be addressed in a Government Support Agreement.

A complex project must rely on the good faith and fairness of the state, but the government may use political pressure in bad faith and unfairly as a way of obtaining commercial concessions from the Project Company, or even taking the project over. There is no clear boundary between a legitimate use of state power (cf. §10.6) and deliberate harassment of the project. Moreover, it may be difficult to prove that the project would not have defaulted on its debt or failed to pay dividends to the investors if these acts of creeping expropriation had not taken place, and hence to make a claim on any political risk cover. Creeping expropriation has been recognized in the last few years as one of the most difficult problems in political risk insurance, and political risk insurers are still struggling to draw precise boundaries for this risk, as discussed in the following chapter.

Chapter 11

Political Risk Guarantees, Insurance, and Finance

§11.1 MITIGATION OF POLITICAL RISKS

If a project's political risks are not sufficiently mitigated in the ways described in Chapter 10 to satisfy private-sector lenders, the Project Company may be able to obtain:

- Guarantees or insurance for political risks ("political risk cover"), thus leaving private-sector lenders with only the commercial risks on the project (e.g., project completion)
- Guarantees or insurance that cover all risks, both political and commercial, thus leaving lenders to provide finance with no risk on the project itself ("full cover")
- Direct loans to the Project Company from public-sector (national or multilateral) lenders that are prepared to accept political risks not acceptable to private-sector lenders; such entities may also accept the commercial risks involved in the project and thus take the full risk on the project, or require these to be wholly or partially covered by commercial bank guarantees.

Similarly, political risk cover may be obtained by investors (but obviously not cover for commercial risks).

The main sources of political risk cover, full cover, or direct loans are: [1]

- Export credits (i.e., guarantees or insurance to lenders or direct loans to the Project Company) tied to export sales to the Project Company (cf. §11.3),

---

[1] Information and data on the ECAs, IFIs, and other organizations discussed in this chapter can generally be found on their websites, links to which are maintained at www.yescombe.com.

provided by individual countries' export credit agencies or export–import banks (ECAs) (cf. §11.2); information on some of the major ECAs is set out in §11.5

- "Untied" financing, guarantee/insurance or investment programs (i.e., not linked to exports), provided by ECAs or other bilateral institutions (cf. §11.4)
- Loans, guarantees, or investment insurance from international financing institutions (IFIs) such as the World Bank (cf. §11.6)
- The private insurance market (cf. §11.7)

A significant proportion of project financings in developing countries make use of these techniques. It should be noted that if ECAs or IFIs provide direct loans rather than just guarantee or insure private-sector lenders these direct loans are not included in the market statistics set out in Chapters 2 and 3.

§11.2 EXPORT CREDIT AGENCIES

If the Project Company is in a developing country and imports equipment for the project, ECAs can provide political risk cover, full cover, or direct loans. If political risk or full cover is provided, ECAs can also provide funding support through interest subsidies to commercial banks. Thus either by direct loans or through interest rate subsidies, ECAs may enable the exporter to offer competitive fixed-rate finance. ECAs also provide investment insurance (against political risks) for equity investors.

ECAs are either public-sector institutions in their respective countries, established to provide support for the exports of that country, or private-sector companies that act as a channel for government support for exports from the country concerned. In a similar way, investment insurance is provided to nationals of an ECA's country. ECAs may also support loan packages that include exports from other countries, depending on arrangements between individual ECAs. In the European Union, for example, ECAs from one E.U. country will cover exports from other E.U. countries up to 30% of the contract value.

Most major ECAs have also now signed cooperation agreements with each other, to deal with the common situation where exports from more than more country, and hence more than one ECA, are involved in a project. A typical structure in this situation is for a "lead" ECA to be designated, usually the ECA for the lead contractor for the project, and for all the cover or finance to be provided by this ECA. Any other ECA(s) involved then reinsure their share of the risk. Thus the Project Company has only to deal with one set of ECA documentation and payments.

All major ECAs (as well as OPIC—cf. §11.5.2, MIGA—cf. §11.6.4, and some private-sector insurers—cf. §11.7) are members of the Berne Union (International Union of Credit and Investment Insurers), which promotes international coordination and exchange of information in the sector.

Business undertaken by members of the Berne Union in recent years has been as follows:

Table 11.1

Business Undertaken by Berne Union Members

($ billions)	1995	1996	1997	1998	1999	2000
Export credits	398	407	349	373	465	491
of which: medium / long term[a]	87	79	64	61	62	71
Outstanding exposure at year end	570	561	469	482	446	453
Investment insurance	10	15	9	12	14	13
Outstanding exposure	36	43	40	43	61	57

[a]Project finance is included in this category.
Source: *Berne Union Yearbook, 2002*

The use of export credits declined in the 1990s as lenders were increasingly willing to assume risk in developing countries without this cover, and investment insurance followed a similar trend, but this trend reversed after the Asian crisis of 1997, in which significant losses were made by uninsured investors and lenders.

Berne Union members' outstanding exposure of $516 billion of export credits (short and medium/long term) at the end of 1999 represented about a quarter of developing countries' $2200 billion of debt.

As the figures indicate, a large proportion of ECA business is for short-term trade finance; this aspect of ECA business is increasingly being privatized (i.e., carried out without public-sector support) and of course has no relevance to project finance.

Project finance is a relatively new area of business for ECAs; their finance for major projects had traditionally been in the form of buyer credits to large utilities in the country concerned, often secured by a Host Government guarantee. They have now had to adopt new financing products, as such major projects have been increasingly financed in the private sector rather than by the Host Government. ECAs have only a small number of staff working on project finance: a number of ECAs therefore use outside financial advisors to help them assess project finance risks.

§11.3 EXPORT CREDITS

Export credits used in project finance are normally buyer credits (i.e., direct loans provided to the importer by the exporter's bank or the ECA itself) rather than supplier credits (i.e., loans provided by the exporter to the importer, with finance from the exporter's bank or ECA). Therefore, formally speaking, ECAs deal with the exporter or the exporter's bank rather than the Project Company, although Sponsors of major projects usually have their own direct discussions with ECAs.

§11.3.1 EXPORT CREDIT STRUCTURES

ECA *financial* support for exports (i.e., offering finance at low rates) is provided in two different ways:

Direct loans. Some countries, such as the United States, Canada, and Japan, have Export–Import Banks that can lend directly to the Project Company in a similar way to a private-sector commercial bank, but at low fixed interest rates.

Interest rate subsidies. Other countries, such as France (COFACE), Italy (SACE), and the United Kingdom (ECGD), rely on the commercial banking market to fund export credits, but provide an interest rate subsidy. In effect, the ECA enters into an interest rate swap agreement with the commercial banks (cf. §9.2.1), enabling them to provide the Project Company with a low fixed rate of interest. (In some countries the interest rate support is provided by a different body than the provider of the export credit insurance— cf. §11.5.)

Similarly, ECA *credit* support for exports (i.e., assumption of political and other risks) is also provided in two different ways:

Direct loans. If the ECA provides a direct loan it takes the whole credit risk of the project on to its own books, although in some cases a commercial bank guarantee is needed (e.g., for the completion risk).

Credit insurance. Other ECAs insure or guarantee loans made by private-sector banks (i.e., provide full cover) or specific risks under the loans, such as political risks (i.e., provide political risk cover). ECA-covered loans are attractive to commercial banks because their banking regulatory authorities normally allow them to allocate less of their own capital to support such loans.

In most cases where the ECAs insure loans, an insurance payment is triggered only if the covered risks lead to a default in payment by the Project Company (i.e., these are payment guarantees not performance guarantees). Many ECAs do not then repay the commercial banks' loan immediately, but only according to its original repayment schedule (with interest).

Some countries, such as the United Kingdom, are now advocating abolition of financial support (i.e., low-rate loans or subsidized interest rates) for exports, with the aim of restricting ECAs to providing "pure cover" (i.e., credit insurance for exports, but with finance at market interest rates).

§11.3.2 THE OECD CONSENSUS

A decision by an ECA to provide support for exports to a particular country is partly based on the creditworthiness of the country concerned, but also on political factors.

The detailed terms on which ECAs provide support for export credits (whether direct loans, interest rate subsidies, or credit insurance for lenders) are governed by an international agreement under the ægis of the Organisation for Economic Cooperation and Development (OECD). The Arrangement on Guidelines for Officially Supported Export Credits dates from 1978, and is subscribed to by Australia, Canada, the European Union, Japan, Korea, New Zealand, Norway, Switzerland, and the United States (i.e., most major exporters). This "OECD Consensus" ensures the operation of an orderly export credit market and seeks to prevent countries from competing to offer the most favorable financing terms for exports. Competition between ECAs is therefore limited to the amount of credit support available (i.e., how much credit risk they wish to assume for a particular project in a particular country). The OECD Consensus has no legal force as such, although its provisions are given legal effect in some areas (e.g., the European Union).

The main provisions of the OECD Consensus are:

- 85% of the export contract value can be financed (including up to 15% to cover local costs in the Host Country), thus a cash down payment of 15% of the contract value is required.
- The maximum repayment term (from final delivery, i.e., COD in the case of most project financings) is 8½ years for Category I countries (GNP per capita above $5,445 based on 1997 World Bank data), and 10 years for Category II (all others). Most project finance with export credits is likely to be to Category II countries; there is a special régime for power plant, which may be financed for up to 12 years.
- Repayments are to be made in equal principal installments at least semi-annually, beginning not later than 6 months from completion of performance tests under the EPC Contract
- A temporary arrangement initially agreed to in 1998 allows more flexibility on project finance: the repayment term and schedule can differ from that set out above provided that
  either the average life of the debt (cf. §13.2.2) does not exceed 5½ years, and the ECA is providing support for a minority of the financing (in which case there is full flexibility on the repayment schedule)
  or the average life does not exceed 7¼ years provided that:
  - The first loan repayment is made within 2 years
  - The maximum repayment term does not exceed 14 years
  - The borrower is not in a high-income OECD country

In either case, no one principal repayment is to exceed 25% of the loan amount. (These provisions thus allow for longer-term financing and annuity repayments, which are more suitable for project finance—cf. §13.2.)

- Interest (either on direct loans or via interest rate subsidies) is charged at minimum fixed rates of 1% over the cost of the equivalent long-term government bonds in the currency concerned: these rates, known as "CIRR" rates (Commercial Interest Reference Rates) are the same for any one currency irrespective of where the credit is provided (e.g,. a $ interest rate is the same whether the credit is supported by an ECA in the United States or Europe); the rates are recalculated once a month, and the interest rate charged on a particular project is fixed based on the CIRR rate in the month the ECA makes an offer of finance. (If the loan repayment term exceeds 12 years under the temporary arrangements set out above, the CIRR rate is increased by 0.2%.)
- Following agreement on the "Knaepen Package" in 1997, the ECAs participating in the OECD Consensus have also based the risk premiums charged for each country on a commonly agreed minimum formula since 1999

It should also be noted that the OECD Consensus has provisions on the use of tied aid funds (i.e., linked to the purchase of goods or services from the donor country), which limit their use to poorer countries and projects that are not otherwise financially viable.

§11.3.3 ASSUMPTION OF RISKS AND SCOPE OF COVER

ECAs may not be willing to assume the full risk of a project (i.e., by providing full cover or direct loans without any commercial bank guarantees). Policies between ECAs differ considerably in this respect (these issues do not form part of the OECD consensus), and ECAs also work in other different ways:

Risk percentage. Some ECAs providing guarantees or insurance have a policy of not covering more than, say, 95% of whatever risk they are assuming, leaving 5% with the lenders (thus they would cover 95% of 85% of the cost of the equipment being exported, after allowing for a 15% down payment), on the grounds that this will help to ensure that the lenders look after the ECAs' interests in the project, rather than relying on the insurance and not pursuing claims with any vigor. Others cover 100% of the relevant risk.

Completion risk. Some ECAs will not take the completion risk on the project, on the grounds that this risk is mainly within the control of the exporter (i.e., the EPC Contractor), and they are not in business to take a risk on the exporter's performance. They thus require commercial banks to take this risk and only guarantee the political risk of the project during the construction period. In cases where an ECA would normally provide a direct loan, commercial banks may be required to provide the loan for the construction period (again with political risk cover only during this period), which is then refinanced by the ECA on completion of construction.

Commercial risk. Some ECAs are not willing to take the continuing commercial risks of the project even when it is operating, and only provide political risk cover throughout the project's life. Others cover the whole of the lenders' risk on the project (i.e., provide full cover); others might cover 95% of the political risk and 80% of the commercial risk. There is a general trend towards providing full cover because of the difficulty of distinguishing between political risk and commercial risk (cf. §10.7). An ECA providing a direct loan obviously takes the full commercial and political risks of the project, although in some cases a completion guarantee from commercial banks is required.

Political risk. Where coverage is being provided for political risk only (with funding by commercial banks), ECAs' policies on what is meant by political risk also differ:

- All ECAs provide coverage for the standard investment risks, i.e., currency availability and transfer (cf. §10.3), expropriation (cf. §10.4), and political violence (cf. §10.5), although the precise scope of the cover may vary between ECAs.
- Some ECAs do not provide coverage for creeping expropriation (cf. §10.7.3).
- The effects of a change of law (cf. §10.6) are normally only covered indirectly (i.e., if provisions for compensation for change of law are included in the relevant Project Contract and breach of this contract is covered).
- Some ECAs provide coverage for breach of contract (cf. §10.7.1), if the Host Government has direct contractual liabilities (e.g., under a Government Support Agreement) or provides guarantees for liabilities under a Project Contract, provided nonpayment leads to a default under the loan; this is known as "extended political risk" coverage.
- Whether or not the risk of breach of contract by a sub-sovereign risk (cf. §10.7.2) can be covered is very much a case-by-case question.

Direct agreements. Some ECAs may require to sign a Direct Agreement with the Host Government under which the latter accepts liability for any payments made to lenders by the ECA in cases where the Offtaker or Contracting Authority is a public-sector body or gives some weaker assurances to the ECA in this respect; others do not consider this as appropriate, because project finance is regarded as being in the private sector.

Finance of premiums. ECA insurance premiums (i.e., the payments for an ECA assuming full cover or political risk cover) can be substantial, as they are generally paid at Financial Close, but cover the risk for the whole life of the financing (i.e., the premium is the NPV of an annual fee charged for insuring the debt). The level of premium varies according to the risk of the country and the nature of the coverage provided, but on a typical project financing for a developing country may reach or exceed 10% of the amount covered.

Some ECAs include their premium within the costs for which they will provide coverage or finance, but others will not.

Interest during construction. Similarly, some ECAs will cover and finance IDC, but others will not.

Environmental issues. While not directly a financing issue, there are differences between ECAs on environmental standards; in particular, a minority of ECAs, led by U.S. Exim, require an EIA for projects they finance, while the majority do not unless the Host Country's law requires it.

Eligibility. Similarly, eligibility for ECA coverage differs from country to country, though again this issue is not limited only to project finance. Some ECAs providing guarantees or insurance will only do so for banks incorporated and resident in the ECA's country; others will do so for any bank doing business in the country (i.e., including branches of foreign banks); others will do so for any bank wherever located.

Documentation. The nature of the documentation required varies considerably between ECAs, although this is becoming less of a problem thanks to the cooperation agreements mentioned in §11.2.

§11.3.4 CASH COLLATERALIZATION

As mentioned above, some ECAs do not fully cover the amount of risk they are insuring; for example, if 85% of the contract value is being financed by a commercial bank with coverage from an ECA, the insurance may only extend to 95% of this 85%, thus leaving the commercial bank uncovered for 5% of its exposure, or 4.25% of the contract cost. Even this small level of exposure in a difficult country may not be acceptable to the commercial bank.

One approach to this problem is for the Project Company to place cash to this extent in a collateral account, as security for the commercial bank's uncovered exposure. This is likely to be an issue with the ECA concerned; their policy is usually that under their right of subrogation the commercial bank must be at exactly the same risk for their 5% exposure as the ECA is for its 95%, and any security must be shared on a 5:95 ratio. The ECA will therefore demand 95% of the proceeds of the cash collateral account on a default.

§11.3.5 BENEFIT OF ECA SUPPORT

With the need to keep within the structure of the OECD Consensus rules, the complexity always caused by having another party to the financing, and the relatively high initial premiums charged by ECAs (in lieu of a loan margin), it generally only becomes attractive to use ECA support if commercial lenders are not willing to provide finance to the country or project concerned without it.

Another key point is that ECAs primarily support exports of equipment, not the whole of the amount payable under an EPC Contract: power or infrastructure projects incur substantial costs under their EPC Contracts for civil engineering work (normally carried out by local subcontractors, with no export element involved), which ECAs can only support under the OECD Consensus to the limited extent of 15% of the total contract value. These costs may be partly covered by the investors' equity contribution, but if a project has a sizable civil engineering component (e.g., a road or a hydroelectric power plant), export credits alone will not usually provide enough funding.

The CIRR interest rate charged on export credits is generally attractive if available, because it is a subsidized fixed rate; moreover, this rate is fixed when the credit is approved, well before the financing is complete, which is very helpful for a project's financial planning, as it eliminates the problem of interest rate movement before Financial Close (cf. §9.2.4.).

ECA involvement may also provide a degree of intangible political support for the project that could help the investors as well as the lenders, but this alone is seldom a reason for choosing to use ECA coverage.

Set out in §11.5 are some examples of the ways in which individual ECAs provide support for project finance. Although there are differences in the mechanisms used, all the OECD member countries' ECAs provide a similar range of support, subject to the points set out in §11.3.3.

§11.4 UNTIED COVER AND FINANCING

Untied loans or guarantees/insurance cover (i.e., not linked to an export of equipment from the country concerned) are also provided by ECAs. Investment cover (for political risks only) is provided to both investors (cf. §11.4.1) and lenders. In 2000 members of the Berne Union (including MIGA—cf. §11.6.4) provided $13 billion of investment insurance, in addition to export credits.

The use of investment insurance for lenders is becoming a more important product for ECAs, especially in project finance. It is usually dependent on a Sponsor from the ECA's country being involved in the Project Company. Such cover, or the untied loans that are also available from some ECAs, may sometimes fill gaps in the financing package (e.g., caused by export credits only supporting exports of equipment and not civil works). The loans and loan guarantees provided by OPIC (cf. §11.5.2) are an example of this type of program.

Provision of untied loans and political risk guarantees by ECAs for projects with no connection with the country providing this support are less common, but important programs of this nature are provided by JBIC and NEXI in Japan (cf. §11.5.4).

This type of coverage is not governed by the OECD Consensus.

Many countries also have separate Development Financing Institutions (DFIs) that can provide limited amounts in equity or untied loans (cf. §11.4.2).

§11.4.1 POLITICAL RISK INSURANCE FOR EQUITY INVESTMENT

Investors in Project Companies do not necessarily make use of political risk insurance (from ECAs, IFIs, or the private sector) even if their lenders require it on the debt side. The theoretical argument for this is that their investment in the Project Company is well known, and part of their ordinary business, and the risk involved is therefore reflected in their share price. Another similar argument is that if they are not comfortable doing business in the country concerned they should not hide behind insurance, but should not do business there at all. However the high-profile political nature of many project finance investments may make such insurance prudent (cf. §10.1).

There is a particular difficulty with political risk insurance for equity investment in a Project Company. An insurer or guarantor who makes payment under a claim normally has the right to take over the assets that were insured or guaranteed (i.e., a loan or an equity investment), although ECAs usually require the commercial bank lenders to continue to attempt to recover the loan on their behalf, as do private insurers. ECAs will thus only pay claims against political risk insurance on equity if the investors' interests in the shares are assigned over to the insurer. This is known as the right of subrogation, and may cause a major problem for investors insuring their equity, as it may indirectly lead to their losing the benefit of the insurance.

Assignment of the investors' shareholding in the Project Company is a standard part of the lenders' security (cf. §13.7) to enable them to control the Project Company more easily after a default. This causes two levels of problem if the investors have insured their equity against political risk, and a political risk-based loss occurs:

- If the loan is not fully repaid after a default, the lenders will be disinclined to release their security over the shares to allow the investors to hand them to their insurer in return for a payment under their political risk cover; they will argue that lenders should be repaid before investors and therefore the proceeds of the insurance on the equity should be paid to the lenders. But from the point of view of the investors in the Project Company, if the lenders are paid the proceeds of insurance on the equity, this may make the investors' political risk insurance pointless.

- Even if the lenders concede the point, the problem may remain if there are different political risk insurers of equity and debt, since the insurer covering the debt will want to take over the lenders' security, including the pledge of the shares in the Project Company, and recover any value that can be derived from disposal of this equity, which again means that the insurer covering the investors will not be prepared to pay out.

From the point of view of the insurers, the problem is a somewhat theoretical one, since once a Project Company is in default it is unlikely that much value will be recovered on the equity, and the chances of recovering this before the debt has been repaid are very low. Nonetheless it has proved a major obstacle to financing on some projects. Even U.S. Exim and OPIC—both owned by the U.S. government—could not agree on this issue until 1999, at which time they signed a joint claims agreement, under which they agreed that they would postpone debate and work together on recoveries and worry about how to divide any proceeds afterwards. This works because both are part of the U.S. Federal budget, so the only issue is which pocket the recoveries go into, but no such agreements are in place between other agencies.

This issue appears to be less of a problem for private sector insurers (cf. §11.7), who may be willing to accept a subordinated position to the lenders (i.e., they can only recover any payments for the equity if lenders have been repaid).

§11.4.2 DEVELOPMENT FINANCE INSTITUTIONS

Apart from untied loans and political risk guarantees from ECAs, many countries have DFIs that can provide limited amounts of untied loans and/or direct equity investment for projects in developing countries, such as:

France: PROPARCO—Société de Promotion et de Participation pour la Coopération Economique, owned 71% by Agence Française de Développement (AFD), and the remainder by private shareholders, provides equity and debt for projects in developing countries, which do not have to include a French partner.

Germany: DEG—Deutsche Investitions und Entwicklungsgesellschaft (DEF

——German Investment and Development Company) is a state-owned body
that provides long-term debt and equity for projects.

Italy: Simest (cf. §11.5.7) provides loans and equity investment.

Netherlands: FMO—Nederlandse Financierings-Maatschappij voor Ontwik-
kelingslanden (Netherlands Investment Bank for Developing Countries),
which is 51% owned by the Dutch state and the balance by the leading Dutch
banks and a variety of private sector investors, provides loans and equity.
Projects do not have to have a Dutch shareholding.

Sweden: Swedfund International AB is owned by the Swedish government
and provides equity or loans to joint-venture projects, which must include
a Swedish partner.

United Kingdom: CDC Capital Partners, formerly the state-owned Commonwealth Development Corporation, converted in 2000 into a government-
owned company into which private-sector shareholders are to be introduced.
CDC formerly provided debt and equity for projects in developing countries,
but now concentrates on equity investment, which do not have to be in projects with other British partners. This change in status has rather eroded its
development finance role.

Abu Dhabi: Abu Dhabi Fund for Development, a public autonomous institution, provides direct loans, grants, and equity for projects in Arab, African,
Asian, and other developing countries. The loans extended are of 7–25 years
at concessionary interest rates.

Kuwait: Kuwait Fund for Arab Economic Development operates in a similar
way to the Abu Dhabi fund.

Saudi Arabia: Saudi Fund for Development provides soft loans and guarantees
for projects in developing countries.

IFIs (discussed in §11.6) are nonetheless the main source of such financing as far
as the project finance market is concerned.

§11.5 ECA STRUCTURES AND PRODUCTS

Set out in this section are examples of the range of products, coverage, and direct
loans offered by or through ECAs and related institutions in several countries,
namely the United States (§11.5.1 and §11.5.2), Canada (§11.5.3), Japan (§11.5.4),
France (§11.5.5), Germany (§11.5.6), and the United Kingdom (§11.5.7). Together
these examples provide a good cross-section of the various different approaches
used. Despite differences in structure, the combination of market forces and the
OECD Consensus ensures that the end results are fairly similar, although as summarized in §11.3.3 there are some differences in risk assumption in the project
finance field.

§11.5.1 UNITED STATES (U.S. EXIM)

U.S. exports are covered by Export–Import Bank of the United States (U.S. Exim), which was established in 1934, and set up a project finance division in 1994. U.S. Exim provides long-term loans (typically for up to 55% of project cost) or guarantees to commercial banks, to the maximum OECD Consensus level. Support is provided on the standard OECD Consensus terms, the lesser of 85% of the contract price or 100% of the U.S. content. So long as U.S. exports are involved, U.S. Exim will provide support to non-U.S. banks (unlike OPIC—cf. §11.5.2).

Before completion, U.S. Exim has not generally assumed commercial risks (i.e., the risk of completion), and therefore if funding is provided by commercial banks, U.S. Exim provides them with a political risk guarantee, or if U.S. Exim is providing the funding, this is done against a commercial bank completion guarantee. Finance is provided for the risk premium and IDC. After completion, funding is generally provided by U.S. Exim, assuming the full (political and commercial) risks of the project, or full or political risk-only coverage can be given to commercial bank lenders.

Political risks covered are currency convertibility and transfer, expropriation, including creeping expropriation, and political violence (resulting either in physical damage to the project or loss of revenue). Nonpayment because of contract disputes or repudiation is not covered; this is less of a problem than it might seem if U.S. Exim is providing finance postcompletion: nonpayment by the Host Government before then can only occur if the Project Company terminates its contract and calls on the Host Government guarantee, and the range of defaults that might cause this (before the Project Company is due to begin operations or earn any revenue) is limited.

Changes are, however, taking place in the scope and nature of U.S. Exim coverage for project finance:

- In certain types of project (e.g., power generation projects) where the completion risk is perceived to be limited, U.S. Exim began in 2000 to assume this risk and therefore provide full coverage or funding from the beginning of the project.
- There is a trend away from political risk only coverage, because of the difficulty of drawing dividing lines between political and commercial risk (cf. §10.7).
- Political risk coverage for bond issues is now also possible, although it has not been used.
- U.S. Exim may provide coverage for local costs in the Host Country's currency, within OECD Consensus rules.

Other major ECAs are also gradually extending their coverage in similar ways. U.S. Exim may require to sign a bilateral agreement (known as a Project Incentive Agreement) with the Host Government, which gives them recourse to the host government if a default occurs as a result of political risks: this is dealt with on a case-by-case basis.

U.S. Exim provides a useful checklist of its criteria for assessing projects, which may be compared with the risks analyzed in Chapters 8, 9, and 10:

General project

- The project should have long-term contracts from credit-worthy entities for the purchase of the project's output and the purchase of the project's major project inputs, such as fuel, raw materials, and operations and maintenance. Such contracts should extend beyond the term of the requested financing. In sectors such as telecommunications and petrochemicals, if long-term contracts are not available, projects are reviewed on a case-by-case basis, looking for an economically compelling business rationale.
- The project should contain an appropriate allocation of risk to the parties best suited to manage those risks. Sensitivity analysis should result in a sufficient debt service cover ratio to ensure uninterrupted debt servicing for the term of the debt.
- Total project cost should be comparable to projects of similar type and size for a particular market.
- Product unit pricing and costs should reflect market-based pricing.
- Devaluation (exchange rate) risk needs to be substantially mitigated through revenues denominated in hard currencies, revenue adjustment formula based on changing currency relationships, or other structural mechanisms.

Participants

- Project Sponsors, Offtakers, contractors, operators, and suppliers must be able to demonstrate the technical, managerial and financial capabilities to perform their respective obligations in the project.

Technical

- Project technology must be proven and reliable, and licensing arrangements must be contractually secured for a period extending beyond the term of the financing.
- A technical feasibility study or sufficient detailed engineering information needs to be provided to demonstrate technical feasibility of the project.

Host country

- Host Government commitment to proceeding with the project needs to be demonstrated.
- Legal and regulatory analysis needs to demonstrate that the country conditions and the project structure are sufficient to support long-term debt exposure for the project through enforceable contractual relationships.

U.S. Exim uses external financial advisors (at the Sponsors' expense) to review the risks in a project financing.

As to the scale of U.S. Exim's operations in project finance, between 1995 and 2000, a total of $8 billion in project finance support was approved, for 35 different projects, the largest sectors being power and hydrocarbons.

§11.5.2 UNITED STATES (OPIC)

Overseas Private Investment Corporation (OPIC) is a United States government agency, founded in 1971 to take over the political risk insurance responsibilities of the U.S. Agency for International Development (U.S. AID), itself the successor in this respect to the post-World War II Marshall Plan, which provided the first insurance for political risks. OPIC (and AID before it) has a good track record of payment of most of the political risk claims submitted. Given this long history, the OPIC approach to political risk insurance has been used as a model by later entrants into the market; the use of OPIC political risk cover, and the direct loans that OPIC can also provide, have become more common in the project finance market.

OPIC can insure up to $250 million per project, covering 90% on equity investments and 100% on loans, for up to 20 years. (There is no requirement to insure both equity and debt, although this can be done.) OPIC can also provide direct loans on similar terms. For equity investments, OPIC typically issues insurance commitments equal to 270% of the initial investment, 90% representing the original investment and 180% to cover loss of future earnings. If a claim arises on a loan insurance, OPIC may choose not to repay the loan immediately, but to make payments on the original debt service schedule.

In 2000 OPIC's outstanding guarantee commitments amounted to $6.6 billion, of which $3.6 billion related to project finance (note that these are gross figures, including future interest liabilities, and that "project finance" is "financing of projects" in this context), and OPIC had a further $240 million in loan commitments.

The eligibility criteria for OPIC support are:

- It is provided to U.S. investors or lenders (i.e., U.S. entities owned at least 50% by U.S. citizens, or foreign companies controlled 100% by such entities, or 95% by U.S. citizens).
- The investment or loan relates to project companies overseas where a majority of the equity or the day-to-day management remains in private hands, and 25% of the equity is owned by U.S. investors.
- Total OPIC support cannot exceed 50% of the cost of a new project or 75% on an expansion of an existing project.
- Applicants have to demonstrate that the insurance required cannot be provided by the private sector.

OPIC does not require the investment or loan to be used to cover export of equipment from the United States, although generally equipment imported from industrialized countries would not be covered (since export credit coverage should be available). OPIC is not constrained by the OECD Consensus.

The risks covered are the "standard" investment risks (currency convertibility and transfer, expropriation, and political violence), as well as creeping expropriation and nonpayment due to breach of contract.

The U.S. and Host Governments sign bilateral agreements covering OPIC programs, and the Host Government has to approve any insurance issued by OPIC.

In 2000 OPIC began to provide political risk insurance for bond investors, who traditionally have not been covered by ECAs (whose products are generally structured to support commercial bank loans), although U.S. Exim and other ECAs are changing their stance on this issue. However this insurance only covers currency convertibility and transfer.

For OPIC's facility to cover catastrophic currency devaluation, cf. §9.3.5.

§11.5.3 CANADA (EDC)

Export Development Corporation (EDC), established in 1944, is a government-owned institution that both provides direct loans for export credits on the CIRR basis, and also provides export credit guarantees for commercial banks (inside or outside Canada), or bond issues. EDC also supports projects which bring indirect benefits to Canada (e.g., research and development activities).

EDC's project finance department was established in 1995. EDC covers up to 90% of political and commercial risks (but does not cover IDC). Political risk coverage is provided for the standard investment risks. EDC also provides investment insurance against the standard investment risks.

In 2000, EDC provided finance or coverage of C$45 billion, about 10% Canada's exports.

§11.5.4 JAPAN (NEXI/JBIC)

Export credit insurance was formerly provided by the Export-Import Insurance Division of the Ministry of International Trade and Industry (EID/MITI), established in 1950. In 1993, EID/MITI were one of the first ECAs to provide coverage for project finance transactions, and had a specialized project finance department since 1995. In 2001 the Ministry of Economy, Trade and Industry (METI) replaced MITI, and MITI's export credit and investment insurance responsibilities were transferred to Nippon Export and Investment Insurance (NEXI), an autonomous agency that provides export credit and investment insurance. 95% of NEXI's liabilities are reinsured by METI. (Total medium/long-term export credit insurance commitments in 2000 were $2.1 billion.)

NEXI insures up to 80% of lenders' commercial risks (after completion) and up to 97.5% of political risks. Political risk coverage is provided for currency convertibility and transfer, war, revolution, and civil war, and "any other occurrences arising outside Japan which cannot be imputed to the insured party or the borrower," which covers matters such as expropriation. NEXI also provides investment insurance ($687 million in 2000).

NEXI also provides lenders with untied political risk guarantees as part of Japan's aid program ($1.8 billion in 2000, a substantial portion of which related to oil projects in Brazil).

CIRR-based funding for exports may be provided by the state-owned Japan Bank for International Cooperation (JBIC), usually cofinancing with commercial banks. JBIC was formed in 1999 from a merger of Export-Import Bank of Japan (JEXIM) and Japan's Overseas Economic Co-operation Fund (OECF). JEXIM had established a project finance department in 1996.

JBIC also provides untied funding under two main programs: overseas investment credits, which require a Japanese involvement in ownership and management of the Project Company, and untied direct loans as part of Japan's aid program.

§11.5.5 FRANCE (COFACE)

Compagnie Française d'Assurance pour le Commerce Extérieur (COFACE), established in 1946 and owned by the private sector (its shares are quoted on the Paris stock exchange), acts on behalf of the French government in providing export credit insurance. It established a project finance department in 1995. Coverage is provided to commercial banks in France. Both commercial (postcompletion) and political risks (for the standard investment risks) can be covered, up to 95% of the insured risk. The COFACE-covered loan cannot exceed 50% of the total project costs. COFACE also provides investment insurance.

By 2000, COFACE had covered 26 project financings, for a total of $2.7 billion.

CIRR interest subsidies are provided by Natexis Banque (formerly Banque Française du Commerce Extérieur) on behalf of the French Treasury.

§11.5.6 GERMANY (HERMES/KFW)

Hermes Kreditversicherungs A.G. (Hermes), now majority owned by Allianz A.G., administers the German government's export credit insurance scheme. It established a project finance department in 1988. Both commercial and political risks can be covered, on a flexible basis up to 95% of the insured risk. Investment insurance is provided via PwC Deutsche Revision A.G. (in consortium with Hermes) also covering 95% of the risk. In 2000 Hermes handled €19.5 billion of export credit cover, of which €8.8 billion was for medium and long-term business, including €1.4 billion for project finance transactions (mainly power generation projects). (For comparison, Hermes handled €2.1 billion of cover for exports of Airbus aircraft in the same year.)

Kreditanstalt für Wiederaufbau (KfW), a state-owned development bank founded in 1948, provides direct loans for export credits, cofinancing with German commercial banks, and administers the CIRR interest subsidies on behalf of the German government. KfW also provides untied loans to projects with German investors, or related to the acquisition of raw materials for Germany. Out of the total of €36 billion of loans and guarantees provided by KfW in 2000, €11 billion was for export and project finance overseas, and €1.5 billion for loans to developing countries.

§11.5.7 ITALY (ISACE/SIMEST)

Istituto per i Servizi Assicurativi e il Credito all'Esportazione (ISACE) an autonomous state-owned agency established in 1999, took over responsibility for export credit insurance from Sezione Speciale per l'Assicurazione del Credito all'Esportazione (SACE), a department of the Italian Treasury, established in 1977. SACE's first project finance cover was provided in 1994. 95% cover can be provided to commercial banks inside or outside Italy for both commercial and political risks: ISACE requires that investors take at least 30% of the risk in a project, and at least 35% of the cost is covered by other commercial bank loans (i.e., ISACE does not cover more than 35% of the total project cost). The cost of ISACE's insurance premium cannot be included in its cover or the subsidized financing, and breach of contract is not covered.

Società Italiana per le Imprese all'Estero (Simest), a state-controlled company with private-sector shareholders established in 1991, provides commercial banks with CIRR interest subsidies (a role that it took over from Mediocredito Centrale in 1999). Simest also provides untied loans to and takes equity interests in projects that are controlled by Italian investors.

§11.5.8 UNITED KINGDOM (ECGD)

The Export Credits Guarantee Department (ECGD), which was established in 1920, is a department of the U.K. Treasury, and provides both guarantee cover and interest subsidies for U.K. exports of capital goods and projects, within the OECD Consensus, for any bank doing business in the U.K. Short-term trade finance has been privatized (i.e., covered by private sector insurers), since 1991, although the ECGD continues to provide some reinsurance facilities for such business. (The

U.K. government is advocating withdrawal of state support for short-term trade business by all ECAs.)

In 2000/1, ECGD covered £3.7 billion in buyer credits (plus £1.5 billion in supplier credits), issuing 199 guarantees. Eight of these guarantees totalled £3.0 billion (a substantial proportion of which related to aircraft). Up to 100% of the risk amount is covered.

As for project finance, although ECGD does not use any precise formula to define what are acceptable projects, it offers some general guidelines:

- International commercial bank finance should be provided on the same security as that offered on the ECGD-backed finance.
- The individual performance and financial obligations of all the parties to the project, including the Host Government, the Sponsors, contractors, suppliers, operators and buyers of the product involved must be regarded as acceptable.
- Independent appraisal of the validity of the assumptions in the feasibility study must confirm a reasonable assurance of timely payment of amounts due to the lenders.

Other factors that ECGD would regard as helpful include the following:

- IFIs (such as IFC) supporting the lending on the same security;
- The project is given an investment grade rating by Standard & Poor's, Moodys, or other acceptable rating agency.

ECGD provides cover for political risks, defined as:

- War, civil war, rebellion
- Prevention of, or delay in, the payment of external debt by the Host Government or by that of a third country through which payment must be made
- Cancellation or nonrenewal of an export licence
- Expropriation where the Host Government is not a shareholder in the project
- Failure by a Host Government to honor written obligations towards the project, provided such failure causes a loan default and is not itself brought about by any action or inaction of one or more of the other parties in the project

Alternatively, ECGD is also willing to assume full cover (including completion). In this case ECGD also requires:

- Part of the project to be financed without ECGD support by other acceptable financiers, including some international commercial banks, with no better security than is available to ECGD. (Commercial bank lending from local banks in the Host Country may be an important part of the financing, but will not normally suffice alone);
- ECGD participation to be restricted to loans representing no more than 40%

of the total project capital requirements of both loan and equity. In addition, all lending covered by ECAs should not normally exceed 60% of total project capital costs;
• At least 25% of the project funding as equity and/or subordinated debt.

ECGD also provides political risk insurance on similar terms for overseas investments, as well as for bank loans to overseas projects with a British sponsor. This investment insurance can be provided on an annual basis rather than for the life of the project, so enabling the investor who has become comfortable with the country concerned to drop the insurance cover and save costs. In 2000, £312 million of cover was provided.

§11.6 INTERNATIONAL FINANCING INSTITUTIONS (IFIS)[2]

IFIs are also known as Multilateral Lending Agencies (MLAs) or Multilateral Development Banks (MDBs). The IFIs discussed in this section consist of the World Bank (cf. §11.6.1) and its affiliates IFC (cf. §11.6.2), IDA (cf. §11.6.3), and MIGA (cf. §11.6.4), and the regional development banks: Asian Development Bank (cf. §11.6.5), African Development Bank (cf. §11.6.6), Inter-American Development Bank (cf. §11.6.7), and European Bank for Reconstruction and Development (cf. §11.6.8), as well as European Investment Bank (cf. §11.6.9), Nordic Investment Bank (cf. §11.6.10), and Islamic Development Bank (cf. §11.6.11). All are owned by governments—the World Bank by governments around the world, and the other IFIs by governments in their respective regions as well as from other developed countries.

IFIs can play an important part not just as direct lenders to projects, but also in mobilizing private sector funding for projects in developing countries. Private-sector lenders are more comfortable about lending to developing countries under the sponsorship of or in parallel with an IFI because of the IFI's general involvement in the economy of the Host Country, the importance of its general lending programs to the economy, and its ability to access the host government at the highest level should the project run into political difficulties (although the degree of their influence in these respects differs widely between different countries). This gives the Project Company the protection of an IFI "umbrella," which can also of course benefit investors.

An important factor in encouraging private-sector lenders to participate in IFI-arranged financings is the "preferred creditor" status that arises from the practice

---

[2]Cf. International Finance Corporation: *The Private Sector Lending Activities of International Financing Institutions* (IFC, Washington, 1999).

of providing a preference to IFIs when resources for repaying external creditors are limited, and not involving IFI loans in country debt reschedulings. This status was established to reduce the risk to IFIs (and their shareholders) due to their special role within the international financial community. It is important to note that this preferred creditor status exists by custom and not by law, but it has been honored in practice where countries have run into debt problems.

The IFIs have also developed a variety of guarantee instruments for political risk that have further encouraged private-sector lenders' involvement in developing countries' projects in recent years.

IFIs pay more attention than private sector-lenders to examining whether the project to be financed is appropriate in the wider economic context of the Host Country. This can be a double-edged sword, however, as some Host Governments resent attempts by IFIs to use lending to a particular project as a means of promoting a wider politico-economic agenda. Similarly, if a project gets into trouble, an IFI may have a more long term agenda in dealing with the problem that may not be relevant for a lender or investor who is simply trying to get the loan repaid or recover the equity.

§11.6.1 THE WORLD BANK

The International Bank for Reconstruction and Development (IBRD), normally known as the World Bank, was founded in 1944, and is an international organization owned by most world governments. Its affiliates IFC, IDA, and MIGA (discussed below) have been added to the World Bank Group since its original foundation. Its lending mandate is to provide credit to governments (originally for reconstruction in Europe after the Second World War, and, from the 1960s, for developing countries), and therefore its immediate relevance to project finance, which is always a private-sector activity, might appear limited; however, the increased importance of private-sector funding for infrastructure in developing countries has inevitably led to some change of emphasis in the World Bank's approach.[3]

Direct Loans. The World Bank first encouraged private-sector bank involvement in its activities through cofinancing operations, also known as B Loans. Under this structure the private-sector bank lends in parallel with the World Bank (which is providing the A loan in this context), and benefits from the preferred creditor status of World Bank loans. This is of limited relevance in the project finance context, because these loans still have to be to the public sector, but as will be seen, the same structure has been used extensively by the World Bank's affiliate IFC and other regional IFIs.

[3]Cf. Philippe Benoit: *Project Finance at the World Bank: An Overview of Policies and Instruments* (World Bank, Washington, 1996).

The only way in which the World Bank itself can provide loans to private-sector projects is by using the Host Government as an intermediary. This can be done by the World Bank's providing funding to the host government, and the latter lending it directly to the Project Company, or, more commonly, via a local development bank or agency. Alternatively, the World Bank can lend directly to the Project Company under a guarantee of the Host Government.

A Project Company must follow World Bank procurement rules in purchasing equipment or services to be funded in this way, unless these rules were followed by the Offtaker or Contracting Authority in selecting the Project Company itself (cf. §4.6.4). These rules are set out in the World Bank's international competitive bidding (ICB) procedures.

As with all its lending, the World Bank tries to encourage provision of parallel facilities by other IFIs, ECAs, and DFIs, and is the "lender of last resort" among IFIs, including the other members of the World Bank group.

Total World Bank loan commitments in 2000/1 were $11 billion, less than half the levels of 1998/9 because of falling demand from the "crisis" borrowers of previous years—Argentina, Brazil, Indonesia, Korea, Russia, and Thailand.

Partial Risk Guarantee. However, the use of direct loans is no longer the World Bank's preferred approach to supporting private-sector project finance. The instrument now offered is the World Bank Partial Risk Guarantee (previously known as the ECO [expanded cofinancing] Guarantee), which was first used for project finance in 1994.

This is a political risk guarantee that can be provided to lenders to a Project Company. It is not linked to the export of goods from any country, nor does the Project Company have to follow World Bank procurement rules (though procurement should be "economic and efficient"). It is available in any countries eligible for World Bank loans, which excludes the poorest countries, who obtain funding from IDA (other than the Enclave Guarantee discussed below). Up to 100% of the debt can be covered.

The Partial Risk Guarantee covers the standard investment risks of foreign currency convertibility and transfer and expropriation, but not political violence or war risks. Creeping expropriation is also not covered. The Guarantee also provides direct coverage for changes in law and for breach of contract; therefore, political risks not covered directly can be covered indirectly by imposing a contractual obligation in a Government Support Agreement.

As with export credits, this is a guarantee of payment, not a guarantee of performance; therefore, any event giving rise to a claim has to lead to a default on the project finance itself, not just, for example, cause a loss to the

Project Company that may affect its investors but does not put its financing in default.

In all cases the Host Government has to counterindemnify the World Bank for any calls under its guarantee, which means that it cannot be used for subsovereign risks; in other words, all the obligations guaranteed have to be direct obligations of the host government or obligations of an Offtaker or Contracting Authority guaranteed by the Host Government.

The Partial Risk Guarantee is intended as a last resort and is thus available only to projects where (a) private-sector financing is not available, and (b) sufficient funding cannot be obtained via IFC or with MIGA support (see below). As with direct loans, the World Bank also tries to act as a catalyst to mobilize funding or guarantee support from other multilateral and bilateral development agencies. Unlike other IFIs, there is no upper limit on the amount of a World Bank Partial Risk Guarantee, other than general prudence and limits on its overall exposure to the country concerned.

However, although the Partial Risk Guarantee appears to be a useful and flexible instrument for project finance in developing countries, it has actually been used less than might have been expected. Since 1994 it has only been used in less than 10 individual project financings. One reason for this is the requirement for a Host Government counterguarantee, which eliminates many projects from its scope; another is the need for the project to fit in with the requirements of the World Bank's general policy towards the country or the particular sector. Also the World Bank Group's general emphasis is on providing support for projects via IFC or MIGA where possible; therefore, the Partial Risk Guarantee is best applied in large and complex projects where both the political and financial support of the World Bank is essential to secure the total financing package.

Partial Credit Guarantee. The World Bank can provide a guarantee for part of the loan provided by private-sector lenders; the main use of this has been to cover the later repayments of a loan if the lenders are not willing to lend for the required term. It can also be used to cover a "bullet" maturity (i.e., a large final repayment that the Project Company intends to refinance in due course). Obviously, in such cases this represents a full guarantee rather than political risk cover only. Its use in project finance has so far been limited.

Enclave Guarantee. The World Bank also provides Enclave Guarantees (i.e., guarantees for export-based "enclave" projects—cf. §10.3.1) in IDA countries. Here there is no Project Agreement involving the Host Government, since the project is based on sale of a commodity internationally. The scope of the guarantee is therefore limited to expropriation, changes in law, war and civil strife, and also excludes currency convertibility and transfer risks, since these should not arise as revenues are earned offshore.

§11.6.2 INTERNATIONAL FINANCE CORPORATION (IFC)

IFC, established in 1956, is the private-sector financing affiliate of the World Bank, and is therefore the only member of the World Bank group that does not need direct host government involvement in projects as a basis for its financing.[4]

Loan program. IFC can invest or lend up to $100 million per project, with a limit of 25% of project cost (50% for expansion of an existing project). Loan maturities can be up to 20 years. IFC loans are based on market pricing (i.e., with no element of subsidy), and IFC does not accept direct Host Government guarantees.

Apart from its own direct loans, IFC has an active B Loan program, under which it brings in parallel private-sector financing for projects. This B Loan program dates back to 1957 and follows similar principles to that of the World Bank: IFC sells participations in B Loans (which carry full market rates of interest reflecting the risk) to commercial banks, but continues to act as the lender of record, to administer the loans, and to hold security. Thus it is not possible for a borrower to pay IFC but default on the B Loan, since all payments are divided *pro rata* between the A and the B Loan in a transaction, and so a default on a B Loan is a default on IFC's loan.

Although there is no formal guarantee for political risk, the preferred creditor status accorded to IFIs applies to IFC B Loans, and most bank supervisory authorities do not require banks to make loan provisions against IFC B Loans merely because the country is in default on its general debt. (Of course the loan can still go into default if the project is not successful.)

IFC has been a major lender to private-sector borrowers in developing countries. In March 2000 there were some $8.25 billion in outstanding and committed IFC B Loans, lent by some 225 financial institutions, and $10 billion in IFC's own loans. (These figures include all types of IFC lending, much of which would not be classified as project finance.)

It is perhaps worth noting that there is a potential conflict of interest between IFC's role as a manager of other banks' B Loans, and as an equity investor in the same projects, as well as with IFC's role as part of the World Bank Group, and therefore concerned with wider development policies that may conflict with the investors of a particular project.

Equity Investment. IFC can also take minority equity investments (normally 5–15% and a maximum of 35%) in project companies; IFC does not take an active role in company management and is considered a passive investor. To

---

[4]Cf. International Finance Corporation: *Project Finance in Developing Countries* (IFC, Washington, 1999).

meet national ownership requirements, IFC shareholdings can, in some cases, be treated as domestic capital or "local" shares. IFC usually maintains equity investments for a period of 8–15 years and is considered a long-term investor. IFC's preferred objective is to sell its shares through the domestic stock market.

IFC's equity investment has been the subject of some controversy, as IFC may insist on purchasing equity at par—i.e., neither paying a premium to the Sponsors to cover their initial risks (cf. §12.2.2) nor covering any development costs itself.

Derivative products (hedging). Since 1990, IFC has been offering currency and interest rate swaps, options, forward exchange contracts, and other derivative products to its borrowers to allow them to better manage their financial risks. Because of the credit problems discussed in Chapter 9, project companies in developing countries cannot easily access directly the markets for such risk-management products. IFC seeks to bridge this gap by providing this market access by intermediating the purchase of hedging instruments, mobilizing the participation of commercial banks in such transactions on a risk-sharing basis, and promoting the development of local capital markets by bringing these techniques to local financial institutions.

Guarantees. IFC offers Partial Credit Guarantees similar to those of the World Bank, which cover all credit risks during a specified portion of the loan term and can thus be used to extend the repayment term of loans offered by the private sector.

§11.6.3 INTERNATIONAL DEVELOPMENT ASSOCIATION (IDA)

IDA, established in 1960, is the World Bank affiliate providing development finance on concessionary terms (35–40-year loans, with no interest but a service charge of 0.75% p.a.) for the poorest countries, which cannot qualify for World Bank loans. IDA can provide indirect loans for projects in a similar way to the World Bank, and has also begun its own guarantee program (for projects where World Bank Enclave Guarantees cannot be used). Total IDA lending in 2000/1 was $6.8 billion.

IDA is also working on a facility to provide protection to investors for currency convertibility (covering both dividend and operating costs in foreign currency) in cases where other investment insurance is not available.

Funds available to IDA are limited by comparison with other World Bank group members: the current limit for guarantees is $300 million in total.

§11.6.4 MULTILATERAL INVESTMENT GUARANTEE AGENCY (MIGA)

Another World Bank affiliate, MIGA, was established in 1988 to encourage private-sector investment in developing countries by providing cover to lenders and investors against political risks. It is intended as the primary World Bank group vehicle for political risk guarantees (and was clearly modeled on OPIC—cf. §11.5.2). In 2000/1 $2 billion of political risk coverage was provided to 66 different projects in 28 countries. (Again this coverage was provided to a much wider range of investments than just those in Project Companies.)

The parameters of MIGA coverage are:

- Both equity and debt can be covered (MIGA previously required equity to be covered if debt was to be covered, but this is no longer required in some circumstances).
- MIGA covers 95% of the scheduled payments of loan interest and principal, or of the equity risk.
- Up to $200 million can be insured in any one project, and up to $420 million per Host Country.
- MIGA can normally provide coverage for 15 years, and for 20 years where justified.
- MIGA operates a Co-operative Underwriting Programme (CUP) with private-sector insurers, which is based on the principle of the World Bank and IFC's "B" Loans (i.e., MIGA acts as a front for private-sector participation in its risks); using these reinsurance arrangements, MIGA can cover up to $200 million in any one project.
- The premiums are in the range 0.50–1.75% p.a. on the amounts insured.
- The beneficiary has the option to cancel the coverage after 3 years.

MIGA guarantees cover:

- *Currency convertibility and transfer:* on receipt of the blocked local currency from an investor, MIGA pays compensation in the guaranteed currency; cover includes excessive delays in making transfers.
- *Expropriation, including creeping expropriation:* bona fide, nondiscriminatory measures by the Host Government in the exercise of legitimate regulatory authority are not covered. For total expropriation of equity investments, MIGA pays the net book value of the insured investment. For expropriation of funds, MIGA pays the insured portion of the blocked funds. For loans and loan guarantees, MIGA insures the outstanding principal and any accrued and unpaid interest.
- *Civil disturbance, sabotage, terrorism and war:* this covers not only the cost of physical damage to the project, but also extends to events that, for

a period of one year, result in an interruption of project operations essential to overall financial viability; at that point, MIGA will pay the book value of the total insured equity investment. For loan guarantees, MIGA pays the insured portion of the principal and interest payments in default as a result of business interruption caused by covered events.

- *Breach of contract by the host government* after a dispute resolution mechanism (court action or arbitration) has led to an award for the Project Company; however, if after a specified period of time, payment has not been received or if the dispute-resolution mechanism fails to function because of actions taken by the Host Government, MIGA will pay compensation. MIGA may make a provisional payment pending the outcome of the dispute-resolution mechanism. This is a fairly new area of coverage for MIGA, which was added to its portfolio in 1999.

As with the World Bank, MIGA does not cover sub-sovereign risks and only provides coverage under an agreement with the Host Government.

In keeping with MIGA's objective of promoting economic growth and development, investment projects must be financially and economically viable, environmentally sound, and consistent with the labor standards and other development objectives of the Host Country. As with the World Bank Partial Risk Guarantees, therefore, the ability to offer coverage may be hampered by policy issues that do not relate to the particular project, but rather the country or sector in general, as well as the requirement for a Host Government counterguarantee.

Note that among the World Bank Group, and the older regional IFIs (ADB, AfDB, IADB), only MIGA provides political risk coverage for investments.

§11.6.5 ASIAN DEVELOPMENT BANK (ADB)

ADB was established in 1966 as a regional IFI. Total loan commitments in 2000 were $5.9 billion.

ADB began private-sector operations in 1983 and can lend directly to private-sector projects, invest equity, or provide loan guarantees. Its total exposure to any one project cannot exceed the lower of 25% of the project cost or $50 million (50% or $150 million where guarantees are provided), and it cannot invest more than 25% of the equity. Loans are provided in US$, ¥, and Swiss Francs, for up to 15 years. Four private-sector loan commitments were made in 2000, totaling $156 million. ADB also has a B Loan program, which it calls CFS (Complementary Financing Schemes) loans, two of which were provided to projects in 2000.

ADB's loan guarantee program is similar to that of the World Bank: two types of guarantee are provided for private-sector projects:

Political Risk Guarantee. ADB's first political risk guarantees were issued in 2000 (two of them for project financings, totalling $122 million). Coverage is available for expropriation, currency convertibility or transfer, political violence and breach of contract, for loan terms of up to 15 years. The guarantee is, however, only issued for projects in which ADB also has a direct loan or equity involvement, and the maximum limit is reduced to the extent of such involvement. A Host Government counterguarantee may be required.

Partial Credit Guarantee. Similar to the Partial Credit Guarantee provided by the World Bank, this can cover all events for a specific portion of the debt service, or the principal and/or interest for debt maturities that would be difficult to obtain from commercial lenders. One partial risk guarantee for $120 million was issued in 2000 for an electricity grid project in India. Coverage can be provided to domestic banks in the Host Country's currency, so enabling long-term funding without exchange risks, which might not otherwise be available, to be raised by the Project Company.

§11.6.6 AFRICAN DEVELOPMENT BANK (AFDB)

AfDB was established in 1963. Total financing commitments (loans, equity investments, and grants) in 2000 were $2.6 billion.

AfDB does not offer a political risk guarantee program: loans can be made to project companies, but only for a maximum amount of $15 million.

§11.6.7 INTER-AMERICAN DEVELOPMENT BANK (IADB)

IADB was established in 1959, and is thus the oldest of the regional IFIs, covering Latin America and the Caribbean. IADB is the main source of IFI credit in the region, with total new loan commitments in 2000 of $5.3 billion.

IADB's Private Sector Department was established in 1994. IADB provides direct loans to private-sector borrowers in $, and brings in private-sector participation in these loans through a B Loan structure, in a similar way to IFC. IADB itself can provide up to $75 million or 25% of total project cost in an A Loan, with maturities up to 20 years.

In 1996, IADB established a program of providing political risk guarantees in favor of commercial bank lenders and bond issues. Coverage is provided for currency convertibility and transfer, expropriation, and breach of contract. In this case, up to the lesser of $150 million or 50% of project cost can be provided.

In 2000 11 loans and 2 guarantee commitments, totalling $512 million, were provided for private-sector projects, and a further $851 million was provided by private-sector lenders in B Loans. IADB estimates that each $1 of its support brings in $5 from other sources, and that the total private-sector infrastructure investment generated by its support therefore amounted to $3 billion.

IADB has an affiliate, Inter-American Investment Corporation, which invests equity in projects.

§11.6.8 EUROPEAN BANK FOR RECONSTRUCTION AND DEVELOPMENT (EBRD)

EBRD—generally known as the European Bank—was formed in 1991 and operates in 26 countries in Central and Eastern Europe and the CIS. The European Bank promotes private-sector activity, the strengthening of financial institutions and legal systems, and the development of the infrastructure needed to support the private sector. Total financing commitments in 2000 were €2.7 billion, of which private sector loans were €1.3 billion and equity investments €0.6 billion.

The European Bank's private-sector activities resemble those of IFC; it provides both equity and debt as well as guarantees, encouraging cofinancing (through syndicated loans similar to IFC's B Loan system) and foreign direct investment from the private and public sectors, and helps to mobilize domestic capital. For private-sector projects, the European Bank is normally prepared to provide, in the form of debt or equity, up to 35% of the long-term capital requirements of a single project or company. Its guarantee program is flexible, with various types available, ranging from all-risk to risk-specific contingent guarantees, but the program has been little used to date. In project finance the European Bank has been active, *inter alia,* in the telecommunications, electricity, petrochemicals, and infrastructure fields.

§11.6.9 EUROPEAN INVESTMENT BANK (EIB)

EIB was created in 1958 as an autonomous body within the European Union to finance capital investment furthering European integration by promoting EU economic policies. Its capital is provided by the member countries of the EU, but only 7.5% of this is paid in, the rest being available if required for debt payments. Like other IFIs, EIB raises its funding on the capital markets, and with its ownership and capital structure it benefits from an AAA rating.

EIB has two main areas of activity:

Inside the European Union. Inside the EU EIB financing is available for projects which:
- Strengthen economic and social cohesion, and foster the economic advancement of the less favored regions
- Improve infrastructure and services in the health and education sectors
- Develop transport, telecommunications, and energy transfer infrastructure networks with an EU dimension

- Preserve the natural and urban environment, notably by drawing on renewable energy
- Secure the energy supply base by more rational use, harnessing of indigenous resources, and import diversification

These definitions are sufficiently wide to cover a large sector of the European project finance market, and EIB is a major lender in this sector. Loans are provided for up to 50% of the project costs, for periods of up to 12 years for industrial projects, and 20 years for infrastructure projects. Repayment schedules are flexible. €31 billion of loans were provided in 2001 (not just for project finance of course).

EIB does usually not take completion risk on projects (but see the Structured Finance Facility described below). EIB will only take operating risks on a fairly conservative basis, and not immediately on completion of the project, but based on its initial performance. For example, in a power project, EIB may be willing to assume operating risks on a gradual basis over the first 2 years of operation assuming the project meets specified debt cover ratios, and in a road project much more slowly than this (e.g., in a 25+ year loan, it may assume 50% of the operating / revenue risk after year 8 and the rest after year 15).

EIB therefore requires commercial bank guarantees for its loans until it is "on risk;" the amount of these guarantees covers not only the loan outstanding, but also 6 months' interest and an allowance for the breakage cost (cf. §9.2.1) if its loan is repaid early. Guarantees must be issued by "qualifying banks," usually based on minimum credit ratings; if a bank's credit rating is lowered, EIB may require the guarantee to be cash collateralized.

In some circumstances EIB may take political risk (insofar as this is relevant in European Union countries). For example, if completion of a bridge project depends on connecting roads being built by the Host Government, EIB may not require the commercial banks to guarantee this aspect of the completion risk.

Despite the fact that it is usually provided with guarantees covering most of its risk, EIB carries out a detailed examination of the technical viability and wider economic benefits of the project. Projects have to meet EU environmental standards and follow EU procurement rules (under which invitations to bid must be published in the *Official Journal of the European Communities* [OJEC], and a transparent procurement procedure adopted). Finance can be provided both in Euros and other major currencies.

Unlike the other IFIs discussed in this section, EIB does not have a concept of additionality (i.e., only acting as lender of last resort for projects that the private-sector cannot finance). In fact, EIB has often refinanced loans made by commercial banks some time after Financial Close, because its own procedures can be too slow to enable EIB to provide finance at the same speed as the private sector.

EIB can provide funding on a fixed or floating rate interest basis, the fixed-rate option being that usually adopted in project finance. This provides the Project Company with the main benefit of EIB financing—its low cost. EIB does not charge arrangement fees or a commercial loan margin, only a small administrative fee to cover its costs. Given its AAA rating, it raises funds in the bond market at low fixed rates and passes this benefit on to the Project Company. Therefore, even allowing for the cost of the commercial bank guarantees that EIB requires, the overall cost of the financing is likely to be lower for the Project Company than borrowing from the commercial bank market directly.

In effect, as a public-sector body of the European Union, the EIB provides low-cost public-sector finance for projects while these still retain the benefits of private-sector management and control (cf. §3.6).

Outside the European Union. Outside the European Union, EIB lends on the basis of "mandates" decided by the EU, which fix the amounts it can lend in various areas. These mandates cover:

- Countries that are candidates for EU membership (to whom €2.7 billion was lent in 2001)
- Various Mediterranean countries outside the EU (Euro-Mediterranean Partnership Countries), various developing countries elsewhere, and the Western Balkans (loans of €2.9 billion in 2001).

EIB takes political risk on such loans outside the EU, requiring full bank guarantees for commercial risks. The definition of political risks in this context is a narrow one, confined to the standard investment risks of currency convertibility and transfer, expropriation (not creeping expropriation), and political violence. Sub-sovereign risks are not acceptable without a Host Government guarantee, and EIB does not take breach of contract risk. As a result, EIB funding outside the EU is generally only useful either if there is direct Host Government involvement in the project (either by way of providing a guarantee for the substate risks, or by the Host Government borrowing the EIB funding and on-lending it to the Project Company), or if commercial banks are happy to take the substate risks and commercial risks, including disputes on the Project Contracts. If so, there is again likely to be a cost benefit in using EIB finance.

As with other IFIs, there is also a "comfort factor" in EIB involvement in a project finance, based on the assumption that they are better able than commercial lenders (or investors) to put political pressure on a Host Government that takes unfair action against a Project Company.

Other activities. EIB set up the European Investment Fund (EIF) in 1994 in partnership with private sector financial institutions. The objectives of EIF include support of the development of trans-European networks in the areas of transport, telecommunications and energy infrastructure. Loan guarantees or equity investments up to 50% of project costs (but not exceeding €176 million) can be provided. Activities are focused primarily in the European Union. In project finance, EIF often joins bank syndicates which are providing commercial guarantees to EIB.

In 2000, EIB established a Structured Finance Facility (SFF), under which it will take a variety of project risks through providing:

• Senior loans and guarantees under which it will assume pre-completion and early operating risks;
• Mezzanine finance and guarantees ranking ahead of shareholder equity or subordinated debt;
• Project-related derivatives (hedging).

Total reserves of €750 million have been set aside for a 3-year program, with the aim of adding value for priority projects by complementing commercial banks and capital markets. These operations will be undertaken chiefly in the countries of the EU, but also in nonmember countries.

§11.6.10 NORDIC INVESTMENT BANK (NIB)

NIB was founded by the countries in the Nordic region to promote regional co-operation. NIB now finances projects both within the Nordic region and elsewhere in the world where the project has a Nordic connection (e.g., in ownership of the Project Company). A high proportion of its financing outside Nordic countries has been provided in Asia.

NIB operates in a similar way to EIB, but on a smaller scale, and offers the benefit of long-term low-cost fixed rate funding to projects. Its approach to risk is similar to that of EIB. Loan commitments in 2000 were €1 billion.

§11.6.11 ISLAMIC DEVELOPMENT BANK (IDB)

IDB was established in 1974. It provides financing on an Islamic basis (i.e., without charging interest), but sharing in the profitability of the project in other ways, namely:

• Islamic lease (*ijara*)—basically similar to leasing elsewhere in the world (i.e., allowing use of equipment for a period of time against fixed rental payments) (cf. §3.4)
• Installment sale (*murabaha*), with a "mark up" on the price that provides the profit margin
• *Istisna'a*—basically similar to *murabaha,* but based on the sale of an item yet to be manufactured.

These various modes of financing, also provided by other private-sector Islamic banks and Islamic finance departments of international banks, can be provided as part of a project finance package, in parallel with banks lending on a conventional basis.

IDB financing is provided for up to 12 years, at fixed or floating rates of mark-up, and for a maximum of 20 million "Islamic dinars" (an artificial unit equal to one Special Drawing Right [SDR] of the IMF, i.e., approximately $25 million).

§11.7 PRIVATE-SECTOR INSURANCE

Until recently the private-sector insurance market played little role in the political risk field. The coverage offered was limited in amount, scope, and term. This situation has changed rapidly, not least because of cooperation with the public sector, such as through MIGA's CUP program or coinsurance with OPIC. Major insurers in the market include AIG, Chubb, Lloyds, Swiss Re, and Zurich-American; overall, more than 20 insurance companies offer political risk coverage of up to $150 million per project, in some cases for terms of up to 15 years. The nature of the coverage reflects that offered by that of ECAs to both investors and lenders. Private-sector insurers may, like some ECAs, require the investor to retain, say, 10% of the insured risk.

The private sector may also offer "bridging" cover, if it would take too much time until the necessary procedures for ECAs or IFIs to provide coverage have been completed; if the ECA or IFI coverage is never provided, the private-sector coverage continues.

It should be noted that whereas public-sector insurers of political risk, whether of equity or debt, generally require that their presence in the transaction is publicly known (and often require the Host Government to counterindemnify them), private insurers may make it a condition of their insurance's validity that its existence is not revealed, so as avoid any party behaving badly in the knowledge that insurers will pick up the loss.

Chapter 12

Financial Modeling and Evaluation

This chapter reviews the main building blocks of information and assumptions used for projections that are assembled to create inputs for a project financial model (cf. §12.1, §12.3–§12.6), the basic structure of, and outputs produced by, the model (cf. §12.2), and how the project and the financial model are affected by accounting and taxation issues (cf. §12.7).

The chapter also covers how the financial model is used by investors to evaluate their returns (cf. §12.8) and by lenders to calculate the level of cover for their loans (cf. §12.9) and to create a Base Case (cf. §12.10) and sensitivity calculations (cf. §12.11).

The ways in which investors establish their return requirements, and how these may change over time, or because of the effect of a later sale of the investment or restructuring of the debt, are also considered (cf. §12.12).

An adequate financial model is an essential tool for financial evaluation of the project. It serves several purposes:

- *Pre-Financial Close*
  - Initial evaluation and reevaluation of the project's financial aspects and returns for the Sponsors during the development phase
  - Formulating the financial provisions of the Project Contracts (including use as a bidding model to calculate a Tariff if the Sponsors have to bid for the project, checking LD calculations, etc.)
  - Structuring the finance and reviewing the benefits to the Sponsors of different financial terms
  - As part of the lenders' due-diligence process
  - Quantifying critical issues in the finance negotiations
  - Providing the Base Case (cf. §12.10)

- *Post-Financial Close*
  - As a budgeting tool
  - As a basis for lenders to review the changing long-term prospects for the project and thus their continuing exposure .

The financial model covers the whole of the Project Company's operations, not just the project, and thus takes into account, for example, tax and accounting issues that may affect the final cash flow of the Project Company.

Although separate and parallel financial models may be developed by the Sponsors and the lenders, as discussed in §5.1.6 it is often more efficient for a single model to be developed jointly. This may mean that the Sponsors develop the model initially and then work on it jointly with the lenders, depending on the timing of the lenders' involvement in the project. The Sponsors may then use the model to calculate their own returns, taking into account the ownership structure of the Project Company, the results of which are not of concern to the lenders.

§12.1 MODEL INPUTS

The input assumptions for the financial model for the Project Company can be classified into five main areas:

- Macroeconomic assumptions (cf.§12.3)
- Project costs and funding structure (cf.§12.4)
- Operating revenues and costs (cf.§12.5)
- Loan drawings and debt service (cf.§12.6)
- Taxation and accounting (cf.§12.7)

These inputs need to take account of the terms of the Project Contracts, including expected and required completion of construction, timing of payments or receipts, and calculation of penalties or bonuses.

The basis for the inputs must be clearly documented; the standard way of doing this is for an "assumptions book" to be compiled. This takes each line of the financial model and sets out the source for the input or calculation of that line, with copies of the documentation to back this up.

These input assumptions are used to calculate projections of the project's cash flow (cf.§12.2, §12.10), which serves as a basis for calculations of investors' returns (cf.§12.8) and lenders' debt cover ratios (cf.§12.9). The model must be able to calculate a reasonable range of sensitivity scenarios (cf.§12.11).

The inputs are usually entered in separate input sheets (e.g., one for specific assumptions such as project costs, and one for long-term macroeconomic and operating assumptions that cover the life of the project). Inputs should not be scattered throughout the model, as someone not familiar with it will find it much harder to understand what is going on.

To calculate the investors' returns correctly the financial model should cover the whole period from when the initial development costs on the project are incurred to the end of the project life, although for the purposes of the lenders the model is only needed from Financial Close, with past expenditure on project development being "day 0" figures. The project life is either the term of the Project Agreement or the expected economic life of the project if it is not operating with such a contract. A residual value of zero, with the whole of the Sponsors' equity having been repaid by the end of the project life, is normally assumed unless there is good reason to the contrary.

The model is usually prepared on the basis of 6-month periods. During construction, where this may not be detailed enough (e.g., including interest calculations, the precise timing of payments to the EPC Contractor, etc.), separate projections may be made on a monthly basis and consolidated in the main model.

§12.2 MODEL OUTPUTS

The model outputs are a series of calculations:

- Construction phase costs
- Drawdown of equity
- Drawdown and repayment of debt
- Interest calculations
- Operating revenues and costs
- Tax
- Profit and loss account (income statement)
- Balance sheet
- Cash flow (source and use of funds)
- Lenders' cover ratios (cf. §12.9) and investors' returns (cf. §12.8)

A summary sheet usually sets out the key results on one page, such as:

- Summary of project costs and funding
- Cash flow summary
- Lenders' cover ratios
- Investors' returns

§12.3 MACROECONOMIC ASSUMPTIONS

Macroeconomic input assumptions are those that are not directly related to the project, but that affect its financial results. Such assumptions may include:

- Inflation (cf. §12.3.1)
- Commodity prices (cf. §12.3.2)

- Interest rates (cf. §12.3.3)
- Exchange rates (cf. §12.3.4)
- Economic growth (cf. §12.3.5)

Ideally, macroeconomic assumptions for modeling projections should be taken from an objective source unconnected with the Sponsors; for example, most major banks produce general economic research with generic projections that can be used for this purpose.

§12.3.1 INFLATION

Inflation should be taken into account in the financial model, as it may be misleading to draw up projections on a "real" basis (cf. §9.1).

Different indices may need to be used as a basis for projections of inflation in different types of revenue or cost, for example:

- Consumer price inflation (CPI) in the Host Country for general operating costs
- Indices of employment costs in the country of suppliers or providers of services to the project, in relation to these costs
- Industrial price inflation for the cost of spare parts
- Specific price indices for commodities produced by or purchased by the project (supply and demand in the commodity's own market may affect its price more than general inflation)

Care should be taken to ensure that an artificial result is not produced by using higher inflation rates for revenues than for costs.

If the Project Company has a Project Agreement in which revenues are indexed against inflation (cf. §6.1.6), the financial model should also reflect this.

§12.3.2 COMMODITY PRICES

It is usually inappropriate to treat commodity prices in the same way as inflation (i.e., to assume that they will keep going up). The vulnerability of the project to cyclical movements in commodity prices, which are normal for most commodities, needs to be examined in the financial modeling.

One of the key problems of project finance is that projects are often developed when commodity prices are high, and assume that these high prices will continue, underestimating the effect of the development of the project itself, and others like it, on the market for the commodity. (Or conversely, if a project is developed using a commodity as a fuel or raw material when it is at a low price, it is assuming that this low price will continue.)

Commodity price movements may be very violent on a short-term basis, whereas project finance is inevitably a long-term business; therefore, it must be demonstrated that the project is robust enough to deal with significant fluctuations in commodity prices (cf §8.8.6).

§12.3.3 INTEREST RATES

If the interest rate on the debt is to be fixed throughout the term of the debt (cf. §9.1) the assumption for this rate should be used for projections. However, even in such cases, another floating (short term) interest rate will probably have to be projected for earnings on surplus funds held by the Project Company as security for lenders or prior to distribution to investors (cf. §13.5.2).

There are two approaches to projecting short term interest rates: either (a) an assumption can be made as to the rate itself, or (b) "real" interest rates (i.e., the interest rate after allowing for inflation) can be used for this purpose, and the actual interest rate is determined by the assumed CPI rate. In the latter case, as shown in Table 12.1, if a real interest rate of, say, 4% is used, the projected nominal interest rate is the real interest rate adjusted for the rate of inflation using the "Fisher formula:"

Table 12.1

Interest Rate Projections

	Year 1	Year 2	Year 3
(a) Projected real interest	4.00%	4.00%	4.00%
(b) Real inflation rate	5.00%	4.00%	3.00%
Nominal interest rate $[(1 + (a)) \times (1 + (b)) - 1]$:	9.20%	8.16%	7.12%

§12.3.4 EXCHANGE RATES AND CURRENCY OF THE MODEL

If a Project Company raises debt and equity funding in its Host Country's currency, and all its construction and operating costs and revenues are in that currency, the question of exchange rates becomes irrelevant.

If this is not the case, the financial model should still be prepared in the Host Country's currency, with the ability to make assumptions about long-term exchange rate movements between this currency and other currencies used for the costs or funding of the project. Overseas investors and lenders may feel it preferable to have the model in their home currency, but this is likely to give inaccurate or misleading results (e.g., because of the effect of exchange rate movements on tax payments—cf. §12.7.7, and because some costs will inevitably be in the Host

Country's currency). It is not difficult for the model to generate reports that translate the results of projections in the Host Country's currency to the relevant foreign currency, thus maintaining the accuracy of the calculations, but presenting the results in a more convenient form.

There are two approaches to projecting exchange rates between currencies, similar to those for projecting interest rates: either (a) specific assumptions can be made as to the future exchange rates, or (b) purchasing power parity rates can be used. The latter calculation takes the difference in projected inflation rates between the two currencies and adjusts the exchange rate accordingly, based on the assumption that the future exchange rate between the two currencies will move in line with their inflation differential (see Table 12.2. In year 1, with a difference between the two inflation rates of 6% in favor of Currency B, Currency A depreciates against Currency B by 6%, and so on.

§12.3.5 GDP and Traffic Growth

Infrastructure projects may be affected by the general growth rate of the economy, which translates itself into traffic for the project (cf. §8.8.7). For example, there has been a fairly consistent ratio between the rate of long-term growth in air travel and GDP, with air travel's growth at twice that of GDP. Thus assumptions in the GDP growth rate are crucial for an airport-related project. A similar situation is likely to apply for a project involving road traffic or other forms of transportation.

§12.4 PROJECT COSTS AND FUNDING

The next stage in the detailed modeling process is the preparation of a budget for the construction costs from the Project Company's point of view and determining how these are to be funded.

Table 12.2

Purchasing Power Parity

	Now	Year 1	Year 2	Year 3
Projected inflation rates				
Currency A		9%	10%	9%
Currency B		3%	4%	3%
Projected exchange rates				
Currency A / Currency B	10.00	10.60	11.24	11.80

§12.4.1 PROJECT COSTS

The project cost budget takes into account costs incurred since the beginning of the project development and covers the period until the project is complete and ready to operate. A typical budget for a process plant or infrastructure project (cf. §8.5.4) is likely to include:

- **Development costs.** These are the costs incurred by the Sponsors (and charged on to the Project Company), or by the Project Company itself, in the period prior to Financial Close. Sponsors need to agree among themselves to a methodology for allocating their own costs to the project, including staff overheads and travel costs, which are likely to be significant over a long development period. Costs of the Sponsors' or Project Company's advisers also need to be taken into account.
- **Development fees.** Project economics may allow one or more Sponsors to take out an initial fee from the Project Company for developing the project, and thus realize an upfront profit (cf. §12.12.2). This figure may fluctuate (or be eliminated entirely) as the financial evaluation of the project develops.
- **Project Company costs.** These include costs after Financial Close such as:
  - Personnel costs
  - Office and equipment
  - Costs for Permits and licences
  - Owner's Engineer costs (for construction supervision)
  - Training and mobilization costs (including any payments to the O&M Contractor)
- **EPC Contract price.** (cf. §7.1.4).
- **Construction phase insurance.** (cf. §7.6.1).
- **Start-up costs.** These are costs for any fuel or raw materials used by the EPC Contractor during the testing and start-up of the project, before final completion; in some projects it may also be possible to earn some revenue from the project's output during this period to offset these costs.
- **Initial spares.** These are costs for initial stocks of spare parts (if these are not included in the EPC Contract).
- **Working capital.** The working capital required for operation of the project is the amount of money required to cover the time difference over the Project Company's invoicing cycle between payment of operating costs and receipt of revenues in cash. In effect it is the short-term (usually 30–60-day) cash flow cycle of the project, which cannot be calculated directly in a financial model that runs for six monthly periods during the operating phase of the project.

The initial working capital requirement can be calculated as the costs that the Project Company has to incur until it receives its first revenues. These costs may include:

- Initial inventories of fuel or other raw materials
- Office and personnel costs
- The first operating insurance premium
- Any timing differences between payments for input supplies and product outputs

   Thereafter changes in the amount of working capital required are usually a product of major movements in sales or purchases of input supplies, which should be reflected in the general cash flow.

- **Taxes.** These include taxes payable on the various project costs, such as VAT or sales taxes.
- **Financing costs.** These include:
  - Loan arrangement and underwriting fees
  - Loan or security registration costs
  - Costs of lenders' advisers (both before and after Financial Close)
  - Interest during construction (IDC)
  - Commitment fees
  - Loan agency fees
- **Funding of Reserve Accounts.** See §13.5.2 for a discussion of whether Reserve Accounts should be funded as part of project costs.
- **Contingency.** The contingency (cf. §8.5.4) needs to be added to the project costs.

§12.4.2 PROJECT FUNDING

Based on the cost plan, the funding plan is drawn up to cover the total amount of funding required, divided into debt and equity (cf. Chapter 13 for particular issues that need to be considered in this respect, including the calculation of how much debt can be raised).

If particular funding is only available for particular purposes (e.g., an ECA-insured loan that can only be used to pay for an export contract with the ECA's country) the calculations need to take this into account. Thus if project costs of 100 include equipment of 70 under the export contract, a financing plan that uses ECA funding for 80 and other financing for 20 is not going to work.

The Project Company should not use a short-term loan to finance working capital; this is a permanent requirement, which should be covered by the long-term project finance. However it may be useful to have part of the project finance in the form of a revolving credit for working capital (i.e., allowing the Project Company to repay some of the financing when it has surplus cash, and reborrow it again when cash is short). This may reduce the required level of Sponsors' equity and thus also be advantageous for this reason.

Separate short-term funding may be required for VAT or other taxes payable during construction that are recovered from offsetting against taxes on revenues once operations begin.

§12.5 OPERATING REVENUES AND COSTS

Taking a process plant as an example, the main elements of operating cash flow may include:

- Operating revenues from sales of products

minus

- Cost of fuel or raw materials
- The Project Company's own operating costs (personnel, office, etc.) (cf. §8.7.3)
- Maintenance costs
- O&M Contract costs
- Insurance (cf. §7.6.2)

The first stage in projecting the operating revenues, and the cost of fuel or raw materials, in the model is to identify the key operating assumptions—e.g., for a process plant:

- What is the initial output?
- How does this output change over time?
- How much time is needed for maintenance?
- How much time should also be allowed for unexpected downtime?
- What is the rate of consumption of fuel or raw materials?
- How does this consumption change over time?

The revenues from sales and the costs of fuel or raw materials are the product of:

- These operating assumptions
- The terms of any Project Agreements, such as an Input Supply Contract or Off-take Contract
- Assumptions about market prices in the absence of such contracts

The projections also have to take into account.

§12.6 LOAN DRAWINGS AND DEBT SERVICE

During the construction period the model takes into account:

- The required ratio between equity and debt (cf. §13.1)
- The priority of drawing between equity and debt (cf. §13.3.1)
- Any limitations on the use of debt (e.g., ECA loans to be used only for

exported equipment, or costs in one currency to be funded by loans in that currency)

and having done so calculates:

- A drawdown schedule for both equity and debt;

Drawings on the debt give rise to interest payments (IDC), which also need to be funded.

During the operating period the model takes into account:

- Priorities for allocation of net operating cash flow (cf. §13.5.1)
- Allocation of cash for debt repayment (cf. §13.2.4)
- Calculation of interest payments, allowing for hedging contracts (cf. §9.2)

§12.7 ACCOUNTING AND TAXATION ISSUES

Although the decision to invest in a project should be based primarily on cash flow evaluation (cf. §12.8), the accounting results are important to the Sponsors, who will not wish to show an accounting loss from investment in a Project Company affiliate. In fact, a Sponsor may choose to fund a project in a less than theoretically ideal way (e.g., through leasing—cf. §3.4) if this produces a better reported profit.

Thus although a financial model for a project financing is concerned with cash flows rather than accounting results, it is usually necessary to add accounting sheets to the model (i.e., profit and loss accounts [income statements] and balance sheets for each calculation period).

Apart from the need to check the effect on a Sponsor's reported earnings, there are a number of reasons why accounting results are needed in the financial model for the Project Company:

- Tax payments are based on accounting results rather than cash flow (cf. §12.7.1).
- The accounting results affect a company's ability to pay dividends (cf. §12.7.2) and could affect its ability to keep trading (cf. §12.7.3).
- Adding a balance sheet is a good way of checking for errors in the model: if the balance sheet does not balance, there is a mistake somewhere.

§12.7.1 CAPITALIZATION AND DEPRECIATION OF PROJECT COSTS

The most important difference between accounting and cash flow calculations on a project relate to the capitalization and later depreciation of the project costs.

If the Project Company had to charge off the costs of the project as they were incurred, the result would be an enormous loss in the construction phase of the project, followed by enormous profits in the operating phase. This obviously does not represent the real situation of the project.

In most countries, the project's capital costs are capitalized (i.e., added to the asset side of the balance sheet), instead of being written off immediately. "Cost" in this context includes not only the EPC construction cost (or the "hard" cost) but also the "soft" costs incurred until the project is in operation, (i.e., development and financing costs [including IDC], payments to advisers, etc.).

Thereafter, the capitalized cost is depreciated (written down) against revenues. A standard straight-line accounting depreciation of a project might allow the Project Company to write off the project asset, over, say, a 20-year life. Thus the depreciation on a project costing 1000 would be 5% of its original cost (or 50) *p.a.* If this depreciation is offset against taxable income, assuming a tax rate of 50%, the depreciation allowance will reduce the tax by 25 *p.a.* for 20 years.

The Project Company may benefit from greater initial tax deferrals because its investment in fixed assets is eligible for an accelerated tax-depreciation allowance. If, for example, the tax depreciation allowance on the project cost is 25% of the declining balance — a pattern of "accelerated" depreciation allowances that is a typical investment incentive — this means that the depreciation allowance on an investment of 1000 is:

Year 1: 25% of cost   250
Year 2: 25% of (cost *minus* Year 1 depreciation)   188, or 438 in total
Year 3: 25% of (cost *minus* depreciation from Year 1 to Year 2) = 141, or 578 in total
Year 4: 25% of (cost *minus* depreciation from Year 1 to Year 3) = 105, or 684 in total
Year 5: 25% of (cost *minus* depreciation from Year 1 to Year 4) = 79, or 763 in total
. . . etc.

Thus over the first 5 years more than 75% of the project costs can be written off against tax, compared to 25% on the 20-year straight-line depreciation schedule mentioned above. In the later years of the project, tax payments in a case like this where there has been accelerated depreciation increase as the cost of the project has already been written off against tax, and so by the end of 20 years the total reduction in tax through the depreciation allowance (at a 50% tax rate) will be the same (i.e., 500).

Another common type of tax depreciation is that of "double depreciation"—if the normal rate of depreciation for an asset is, say, 10% *p.a.* straight line, double depreciation allows depreciation at the rate of 20% *p.a.* for say the first 3 years, and then 10% *p.a.* thereafter. Thus, to compare with the declining balance method set out above, by the end of year 5, on this basis 80% of the cost would have been written off against tax.

In some countries (e.g., the U.S. and U.K.) depreciation is dealt with in different ways for accounting and tax purposes: for accounting purposes, the project asset is depreciated over its useful life, thus spreading the cost of the asset against the earnings it generates and increasing the reported profits in the early years of the project, whereas for tax purposes accelerated depreciation is used. The difference between the two is taken directly to (or later deducted from) a tax reserve on the liability side of the balance sheet. In other countries (e.g., France and Germany), the accounting and tax depreciation must be the same.

Different depreciation rates may apply to different parts of the project (e.g., buildings and equipment). In such cases the EPC Contractor will have to break up the lump-sum EPC Contract price into these components for tax-classification purposes (cf. §7.1.4).

§12.7.2 THE DIVIDEND TRAP

The "equity" provided by the Sponsors may not be in the form of ordinary share capital. For tax and accounting reasons, it is often preferable for the Sponsors to provide part of this equity in the form of subordinated debt. One reason is that interest on shareholder subordinated debt may be tax-deductible, unlike dividends on ordinary shares.

Another reason that shareholder equity is often provided as a combination of share capital and shareholder subordinated loans (which leave lenders in exactly the same risk position, provided the investors' rights are completely subordinated in payment and ability to accelerate, etc. to those of the lenders—cf. §13.13.5) is the possibility of falling into what is known as the "dividend trap," whereby the Project Company has cash flow but cannot pay a dividend to the investors because of a negative balance on its profit & loss account, as illustrated by the Table 12.3.

The assumptions for the calculations are:

- Project cost is 1500, funded 1200 by debt and 300 by equity.
- Income and expenditure are constant at 475 and 175 *p.a.*, respectively.
- The tax depreciation allowance on the project cost is 25% of the declining balance (see above).
- Accounting depreciation is the same as tax depreciation.
- The tax rate is 30%.
- If the Project Company makes a tax loss, a tax credit of 30% of the loss is carried forward, and applied against future taxes payable.
- Loan principal repayments are 200 *p.a.*
- The figures run for 6 years to illustrate the point, although the project life is longer than this.

Table 12.3

The Dividend Trap

		Year 1	Year 2	Year 3	Year 4	Year 5	Year 6	Total
(a)	Revenues	475	475	475	475	475	475	2375
(b)	Expenditure (including interest)	−175	−175	−175	−175	−175	−175	−875
(c)	Tax depreciation	−375	−281	−211	−158	−119	−89	−1144
(d)	**Taxable income / loss** [(a) + (b) + (c)]	**−75**	**19**	**89**	**142**	**181**	**211**	**567**
(e)	Tax credit / due [(−d) × 30%]	23	−6	−27	−43	−54	−63	
(f)	Tax credit used		6	17	0	0	0	
	Tax credit carried forward	23	17	0	0	0	0	
(g)	Tax payable [(e) + (f)]			−10	−43	−54	−63	−170
(h)	**Net income** [(d) − (g)]	**−75**	**19**	**79**	**99**	**127**	**148**	**397**
(i)	Loan repayments	−200	−200	−200	−200	−200	−200	−1200
(j)	Dividend paid			−23	−99	−127	−148	−397
(k)	**Cash flow** [(h) − (c) + (i) + (j)]	**100**	**100**	**67**	**−42**	**−81**	**−111**	**33**
	Cash balance	**100**	**200**	**267**	**225**	**144**	**33**	
(l)	**Opening P&L account**	0	−75	−56	0	0	0	
	Closing P&L account [(l) + (h) + (j)]	**−75**	**−56**	**0**	**0**	**0**	**0**	**0**

The calculations show that the Project Company has a positive cash flow available for payments to investors from Year 1, but it would still not be able to pay a dividend, because its balance sheet shows a negative balance of 75 in the profit and loss account, caused by the accelerated tax depreciation, which creates an accounting loss in Year 1. Not until Year 3 is this negative balance eliminated, so the Project Company would not be able to pay dividends until then. Even by Year 6 the cash surplus has not been fully paid out to the investors, and the considerable delay in receiving these payments will substantially reduce their rate of return.

In effect, the dividend trap in this case is a function of the difference between tax depreciation and debt principal repayment; if the former is much greater than the latter a trap develops, which disappears as the situation is reversed. (This is clearly less of an issue in countries where the accounting depreciation does not have to mirror the tax depreciation.)

If the investors' equity is partly paid in as subordinated debt, with the balance in share capital, payments to the investors in the early years when dividends cannot be paid can be made as repayments of subordinated debt. It should thus be possible for the Project Company to pay out the whole of the surplus cash balance.

A further point about these figures is that a portion of the benefit of the accelerated depreciation is in effect being wasted—tax credits of 23 in Year 1 cannot be fully offset against taxes payable until Year 3. In such a case the Project Company may consider:

- Not taking advantage of the accelerated depreciation allowance in full (i.e., writing off the cost of the project against tax at a slower rate), which many countries will allow, and thus not creating a negative profit, so also enabling earlier payment of dividends, or

- Using tax-based leasing (cf. §3.3) and passing on the allowances to a leasing company that can make immediate use of them and pass on the benefit to the Project Company through a lower funding cost.

The other advantage of mainly using shareholder subordinated debt rather than share capital to finance the Project Company's equity requirement is that it is much easier to return these funds to investors if a refinancing takes place and the senior debt is increased, or in the later years of the project when the investors may wish to have their equity investment gradually paid back.

§12.7.3 NEGATIVE EQUITY

But the Project Company has to ensure that by avoiding the Scylla (rock) of the dividend trap it does not fall into the Charybdis (hard place) of wiping out the whole of its equity. If a large part of the Project Company's funding is through subordinated debt, and the company makes large accounting losses in its early years, the end result may be to eliminate its equity completely. In most countries a company with negative equity (i.e., its share capital is less than the negative balance on the profit and loss account) has to cease trading and go into liquidation.

In the case in Table 12.3, if the 1500 of project cost is funded with 20% equity (i.e., 300), of which 267 is subordinated debt and thus 33 is share capital, the subordinated debt could be repaid first, and hence repayments of 267 of subordinated debt would be made over the first 3 years, with dividend payments beginning thereafter. The Project Company has made an accounting loss of 75 in Year 1 (even ignoring any interest on the subordinated debt), which is already greater than this share capital of 33, and so this split between share capital and subordinated debt is not feasible. (In this case the Project Company probably has to look at the possibility of a slower rate of tax depreciation.)

A similar result could arise even with straight-line tax depreciation, but a lower level of profitability in the early years of the project (e.g., from high interest charges, including the subordinated debt).

Therefore, because of the low level of equity inherent in project finance, the accounting results of the Project Company in the financial model need to be carefully checked to ensure that even if cash flow is available, (a) it can legally be paid over out to the investors, and (b) the Project Company maintains a positive equity.

§12.7.4 TIMING OF TAX PAYMENTS

Corporate tax payments are often paid in arrears, which means that there is a gap between the time the tax payment accrues and the time it is paid. The financial model must therefore show the tax calculation, in the profit and loss statement, and the actual payments, in the cash flow calculations, at these different times.

§12.7.5 VALUE-ADDED TAX

In some countries (e.g., in the European Union), VAT will be payable by the Project Company on the construction cost of the project, but the amount paid can in due course be offset by VAT chargeable on sales by the Project Company once it begins operations. The lenders often provide a separate VAT loan to deal with this short-term financing requirement.

§12.7.6 WITHHOLDING TAX

The Project Company may be required to deduct local income taxes on payments of interest to lenders outside the country or on payment of dividends to overseas investors. Although lenders may be able to offset this deduction against other income, they generally require the Project Company to bear this cost (cf. §9.2.4): for this reason it may be preferable to use lenders inside the country, if possible, rather than overseas.

Investors may or may not be able to offset the withholding tax on their dividends against taxes on other income, but if it cannot be offset the deduction should be taken into account in calculating their return on the investment in the project, even though it does not appear in the Project Company's accounts or cash flow.

§12.7.7 EXCHANGE RATES AND TAX

If the Project Company has debt in a foreign currency, exchange rate movements against the Host Country's currency affect tax payments and hence the investors' return on the project, even if revenues and operating costs are all indexed against the foreign currency.

This can be seen in Table 12.4, which again illustrates why the financial model has to be calculated in the Host Country's currency and not in the overseas investors' and lenders' currency.

These calculations look at the return to a $-based investor in a Project Company based in Europe, with its accounts and tax calculations in €. Two calculations are shown: one based on a financial model in $, the other on a financial model in €. The assumptions in the calculations are:

- All project costs, revenues, and expenses (including debt interest and principal repayments) are either denominated in or indexed against $, so that the project theoretically has no exchange exposure.

- The initial €/$ exchange rate is €1.10 = $1.00.
- € depreciates against $ by 5% *p.a.* for the beginning of the project.
- Project cost is $1000, which equates to €1100 at the time the expenditure is incurred.
- The tax depreciation allowance on the project cost is 10% *p.a.* on a straight-line basis.
- The tax rate is 50%.

As can be seen, when the depreciating exchange rate is taken into account, the total tax deduction for depreciation in $ terms is not $150, as would appear in a $-based model, but $130. Hence a $-based model would not properly reflect this and would overstate the cash flow of the model.

Therefore, in a project with foreign currency funding, even if this is fully hedged, the effect of a variety of exchange rate movements—both up and down in the rate and at different stages of the project—should be checked.

§12.7.8 INFLATION AND TAX

Apart from the general effect of inflation on project cash flows (cf. §9.1), for much the same reasons as those set out in §12.7.7, a project that operates in an environment of high inflation, and whose revenues and costs are all fully indexed against inflation, will still not produce a return which increases fully with inflation, because the tax depreciation of the project cost is based on the original uninflated cost. (In some countries the cost of the project on the company's balance sheet can also be revalued against the inflation index before calculating the tax depreciation allowance.)

Table 12.4

Exchange Rates and Tax

		Year 0	Year 1	Year 2	Year 3	Year 4	Year 5	Total
$ calculation								
(a) Initial cost		$1000						
(b) Depreciation	[(a) × 10%]		$100	$100	$100	$100	$100	$500
(c) Tax deduction	[(b) × 30%]		$30	$30	$30	$30	$30	$150
€ calculation								
(d) Initial cost		€1100						
(e) Depreciation	[(d) × 10%]		€110	€110	€110	€110	€110	€550
(f) Tax deduction	[(e) × 30%]		€33	€33	€33	€33	€33	€165
(g) Exchange rate		€1.10	€1.16	€1.21	€1.27	€1.34	€1.40	
(h) Value of depreciation in $	[(e) ÷ (g)]		$95	$91	$86	$82	$78	$433
(j) Value of tax deduction in $	[(f) ÷ (g)]		$29	$27	$26	$25	$24	$130

Again this illustrates the importance of calculations based on "nominal" not "real" figures in a project finance cash flow (cf. §9.1) (i.e., taking the effect of various inflation scenarios into account).

§12.8 EQUITY RETURNS

The standard measurements of return on equity for investors in a project are calculated on a cash flow basis, taking into account:

- **The timing of the cash investment.** As discussed in §13.3, there may be a considerable gap between the time the equity is committed and the time it is actually invested in cash. Rightly or wrongly, most investors assess their return based on this cash investment, not on the funds they have at risk but have not yet invested in cash.
- **The timing of dividend payments.** Similarly, it is not when the Project Company generates cash that matters, but when that cash is paid out to investors as distributions (i.e., dividends or interest and repayments on investors' subordinated debt): there may be a considerable gap between these two points (e.g., because the lenders may require cash to be held back in Reserve Accounts with dividend payments twice a year, based on the half-yearly cash flow results—cf. §13.5.3).

In order to measure the return to investors from cash flows occurring at different times it is necessary to reduce these to a common basis through discounted cash flow calculations. Two interrelated measures are commonly used: the net present value (NPV—cf. §12.8.1) of a cash flow, and the internal rate of return (IRR—cf. §12.8.2), both of which are measures of the value of a future cash flow adjusted for the time value of money. However these measures have to be used with care (cf. §12.8.3), and they may also be misleading if significant amounts of the investment are not drawn in cash (cf. §12.8.4).

And as noted in §12.7, companies also inevitably look at how their investment in a project will appear in their published accounts as well as these cash flow-based calculations.

§12.8.1 NET PRESENT VALUE

The NPV is the value today of a sum of money due in the future, taking account of the cost of money, known as the discount rate. The formula for an NPV calculation is:

$$\frac{C}{(1 + i)^n}$$

where C is the future cash sum, i is the interest or discount rate, and n is the number of periods. (The discount rate may be an annual, or, say, semi-annual rate corresponding to the period.)

Thus if the discount rate or cost of money is 10% *p.a.,* and a sum of 1000 is due in a year's time, the NPV of that sum is:

$$\frac{1000}{(1 + 0.10)}$$

or 909.1. To turn the calculation the other way round, if 909.1 is invested for a year at 10%, 1000 (i.e., 909.1 $\times$ 1.10) will be repaid at the end of the year. Similarly, the NPV of a sum of 1000 due in two years' time, at a discount rate of 10% *p.a.* calculated semiannually (i.e., 5% per half year) is:

$$\frac{1000}{(1 + 0.05)^4}$$

or 822.7.

The NPV of a cash flow calculates the present value of a series of future cash sums. It is calculated as:

$$\sum_n \frac{C^n}{(1 + i)^n}$$

i.e., the sum of the net cash flow for each future period (usually semiannually in project finance calculations), each period's cash flow being discounted to its NPV at the discount rate. (There is no need to use formulae or books of tables to work out NPV calculations—this can easily be done using financial calculators or spread-sheet software.)

The use of NPV calculations can be illustrated by the two contrasting investment cash flows set out in Table 12.5. Both have an initial investment of 1000, and cash flows over 5 years of 1350, producing a return (net of the initial investment) of 350. The cash flow for each annual period has been discounted to its NPV at 10% *p.a.* Year 0 is the first day of the project, when the investment is made; the remaining cash flows take place at annual intervals thereafter.

It will be seen that although the undiscounted cash flows are the same, the NPV of Investment A is 49 (i.e., discounted cash flows from years 1–5 of 1049, less the original investment of 1000), whereas that of Investment B is −2.

The discount rate used by the investor in the equity of a Project Company is the required minimum rate of return on the investment, which is usually derived from the investor's cost of capital (cf. §12.12.1). If the NPV using this discount rate is a positive figure, the investment has met the minimum requirements; if not, the in-

Table 12.5

NPV Calculation

(a) Year	(b) Discount factor $[(1 + 0.1)^{(a)}]$	Investment A		Investment B	
		(c) Cash flow	NPV $[(c) \div (b)]$	(d) Cash flow	NPV $[(d) \div (b)]$
0	1.0000	−1000	−1000	−1000	−1000
1	1.1000	340	309	200	182
2	1.2100	305	252	235	194
3	1.3310	270	203	270	203
4	1.4641	235	161	305	208
5	1.6105	200	124	340	211
Total		**350**	**49**	**350**	**−2**

vestment should not be made. In Table 12.5, if 10% is the investor's required minimum rate of return, it is evident that Investment A meets the minimum requirements as the result is positive, but not Investment B. An NPV calculation may also be used to calculate which is the better of two projects with different cash flows (but cf. §12.8.3)—clearly in the case above Investment A is the better project. These differences in the NPV calculations illustrate the importance to investors of the timing of cash flows.

As will be seen (cf. §12.9), NPV calculations are also used by lenders in calculating debt cover ratios.

§12.8.2 INTERNAL RATE OF RETURN

The IRR measures the return on the investment over its life. It is the discount rate at which the NPV of the cash flow is zero. Thus in the examples in Table 12.5, the IRR of Investment A is 12.08% and Investment B is 9.94%, so again showing that Investment A is the better of the two; the calculation can be checked by discounting the two cash flows at these respective rates (Table 12.6). Some caution must be exercised with IRR calculations; they are not suitable where a cash flow flips between negative and positive in different periods, as the same calculation may then give more than one different answer.

Apart from the IRR on the equity investment in the Project Company, a Project IRR can also be calculated, based on the cash flow of the project before debt service and equity returns, measured as a return on the cash investment required (whether debt or equity). This is sometimes done at the early stage of development of a project to check its robustness without taking account of its particular financing structure. Otherwise, it has limited relevance in the project finance context,

Table 12.6

IRR Calculation

	Investment A		Investment B	
End year	Cash flow	NPV @12.08%	Cash flow	NPV @9.94%
0	−1000	−1000	−1000	−1000
1	340	303	200	182
2	305	243	235	194
3	270	192	270	203
4	235	149	305	209
5	200	113	340	212
Total	**350**	**0**	**350**	**0**

where one of the main points of gearing the project with debt is to improve the equity return, and so a measurement of the return on the project without gearing serves a limited purpose. It may still be used by investors who have a portfolio of balance sheet-financed and project-financed projects, to compare one project with another. It may also be used in Termination Sum calculations since it is equal to the blended costs of the debt service and the equity returns on the project. (cf. §6.8.1).

§12.8.3 USING NPV AND IRR CALCULATIONS FOR INVESTMENT DECISIONS

When looking at whether to invest in individual projects, and how changing assumptions affect their return, most investors look at both IRR and NPV calculations. These measures have to be used with some caution, and an understanding is necessary of how the calculations work. This can be illustrated by the two cash flows in Table 12.7. It is evident that Investment D gives a better return, and the NPV calculation supports this, but the IRRs of the two investments are the same. This is because the standard IRR calculation assumes that cash taken out of the project is reinvested at the IRR rate until the end of the calculation period. (Thus, as shown in the third column of Table 12.7, if the cash flow in years 1–4 is reinvested at 15% *p.a.*, the total amounts to 2011 at the end of year 5.) Clearly some account should be taken of Investment C generating cash more quickly, but the assumption that this cash can be reinvested at 15% is probably not correct, or at least double-counts the return on another investment at that rate. Thus an IRR calculation overvalues early cash flows; longer the cash flow period, the more the IRR is exaggerated by using a high reinvestment rate.

Table 12.7
IRR and Differing Cash Flows

Year	Investment C Cash flow	Investment D Cash flow	Investment C Annual cash flow reinvested @ 15% to year 5
0	−1000	−1000	
1	298	0	522
2	298	0	454
3	298	0	395
4	298	0	343
5	298	2011	298
Total	**492**	**1011**	**2011**
NPV @ 12%	75	141	
IRR	**15%**	**15%**	

There are two ways of dealing with this type of distortion:

- **Modified IRR (MIRR).** The MIRR calculation assumes a lower reinvestment rate (e.g., the investor's cost of capital, as assumed for an NPV calculation, instead of the IRR rate) for cash taken out of the project. This is a better representation of the real world. In the examples in Table 12.8, if the reinvestment rate is taken as 12% (i.e., the cost of capital used for the NPV calculation), the MIRR of Investment C reduces to 13.6%, while that of Investment D of course remains unchanged.
- **Payback period.** An alternative approach is to ignore the reinvestment issue in looking at IRR calculations but require that any investment also has a maximum payback period (i.e., the length of time that it takes to recover the original cash investment). This to a certain extent balances the exaggerating effect of IRR calculations on longer term cash flows but it is a crude measure—in particular it does not take account of returns after the end of the payback period. None the less, it still provides a useful check. The payback period for Investment C is less than 4 years, and that for Investment D is the full 5 years. Thus besides requiring a minimum IRR level, investors also often require a maximum payback period of not more than a certain number of years as one of the criteria for making a new investment.

Again, when comparing two different projects, account has to be taken of their relative sizes. This is illustrated in Table 12.8. Investment F has a higher NPV than Investment E, but this is merely because of its larger size. As is apparent from the IRR calculation, Investment E is the better investment; the incremental 1000 invested in Investment F compared to Investment E gives a much poorer return.

Table 12.8

NPV and Different-Sized Projects

	Investment E	Investment F
Original investment	1000	2000
Return after 1 year	1400	2600
IRR	40%	30%
NPV @ 12%	250	321

§12.8.4 NONCASH INVESTMENT

Another factor that also significantly affects the IRR or NPV calculation is the timing of actual payment to the Project Company of the equity in cash (cf. §13.3).

Furthermore, if the investors provide a standby commitment to invest equity only if the Project Company's cash flow is inadequate, this is not reflected in a IRR calculation (cf. §13.3.3).

In summary, an IRR or NPV calculation reflects the return on a cash investment, not the return on any amount that the investors have at risk but which has not yet been drawn in cash. Therefore, if the Project Company has substantial amounts of undrawn equity, an IRR or NPV calculation may be misleading for the investors.

A way of bringing undrawn equity into the calculations is to assume for IRR calculation purposes that it is drawn on day 1 of the project, and earns a cash return equivalent to the investors' cost of capital (i.e., the NPV discount rate) until it is in fact drawn by the Project Company. This more accurately measures the return on the investor's real risk.

§12.9 DEBT COVER RATIOS

The level of debt that can be raised for a project is based primarily on its projected ability to pay interest and repay loan principal installments as they fall due, with a comfortable margin of safety. To assess this margin of safety, lenders calculate cover ratios, namely:

- Annual debt service cover ratio (ADSCR) (cf. §12.9.1)
- Loan life cover ratio (LLCR) (cf. §12.9.2)
- The averages of the ADSCR and LLCR over the term of the debt (cf. §12.9.3)
- The project life cover ratio (PLCR) (cf. §12.9.4), or the Reserve Cover Ratio for a natural resources project (cf. §12.9.5)

Calculations of these ratios for a typical project are set out in §12.9.6.

It should be noted that none of these cover ratios can be calculated for a period before the Project Company begins operating, as they all deal with the relationship between *operating* cash flow and the level of debt or debt service requirements.

§12.9.1 ANNUAL DEBT SERVICE COVER RATIO

The ADSCR assesses the Project Company's ability to service its debt from its annual cash flow, and is calculated as:

- *Operating cash flow* of the project over the year—i.e., operating revenues less operating expenses—taking account of any Maintenance Reserve Account or similar Reserve Accounts covering anything other than debt service (cf. §13.5.2), and ignoring any noncash items such as depreciation. This may look similar to the EBITDA (earnings before interest, depreciation, and tax) measure used in corporate financing, but should be based on cash flow rather than accounting results.

divided by

- *Debt service* of the project over the year—i.e., interest payments and principal repayments, ignoring transfers to or from Reserve Accounts for debt service.

Thus if operating cash flow for the year is 120, interest payments are 55, and loan repayments are 45, the ADSCR would be 1.2:1 (120 ÷ (55 + 45)).

The ADSCR is usually calculated semiannually, on a rolling annual basis. The ratio can obviously only be calculated when the project has been in operation for a year, although because it may affect the ability to pay dividends (cf. §13.5.3), it may be calculated for the previous 6 months only for the first period after the project begins operation.

In their initial Base Case projections (cf. §12.10), the lenders look at the projected ADSCR for each period throughout the term of the loan and check that this does not fall below their required minimum at any time. The actual ADSCRs are reviewed (and projections may be recalculated) once the project is in operation (cf. §13.5.3).

The minimum ADSCR requirement obviously varies between projects, but very approximate levels for standard projects could be:

- 1.2:1 for an infrastructure project with a Project Agreement with no usage risk (e.g., a public hospital or prison)
- 1.3:1 for a power or process plant project with an Offtake Contract
- 1.4:1 for an infrastructure project with usage risk (e.g., a toll road or mass transit project)

- 1.5:1 for a natural resources project
- 2.0:1 for a merchant power plant project with no Offtake Contract or price hedging

Higher cover levels would be required for a project with nonstandard risks, or located in a country with a poor credit risk.

It should be noted that, unlike in corporate loans, the cash flow cover ratio for annual interest (as opposed to total debt service) is not generally considered a significant measurement. This is because corporate loans are often renewed from year to year, whereas project finance loans have to be repaid because the project has a finite life; therefore, the Project Company must be able to reduce its debt each year as scheduled, and payment of interest alone is generally not adequate.

§12.9.2 LOAN LIFE COVER RATIO

The LLCR is based on a similar calculation, but taken over the whole term of the loan:

- *Projected operating cash flow* (calculated as for the ADSCR), from the date on which the project is projected to begin operations, to the date on which the loan is repaid, discounted to its NPV at the same interest rate as that assumed for the debt (taking account of any interest swap or other hedging)

  divided by

- *Debt outstanding* on the calculation date, less the balance of debt-related Reserve Accounts

The minimum initial LLCR requirement in Base Case projections for "standard" projects is around 10% higher than the figures shown above for minimum ADSCR.

Apart from the initial LLCR on project completion, the LLCR may be recalculated throughout the rest of the project life, comparing the projected operating cash flow for the remainder of the loan terms with the remaining loan outstanding on the calculation date.

LLCR is a useful measure for the initial assessment of a project's ability to service its debt as a whole and for continuing to look at it over its remaining life, but clearly it is not so useful if there are likely to be significant cash flow fluctuations from year to year. ADSCR is thus a more significant measure of a Project Company's ability to service its debt as it falls due.

§12.9.3 AVERAGE ADSCR AND LLCR

If the projected ADSCR from year to year is at the same level, the average ADSCR will be the same as the LLCR. However, if the ADSCR is higher in the earlier years, the average ADSCR will be higher than the LLCR, and *vice versa*. Therefore, average ADSCR is sometimes given more weight by lenders than LLCR as a long-term measure of coverage; if so, the minimum requirements are likely to be similar to those for LLCR.

The average LLCR (i.e., recalculating the LLCR every 6 months for the remainder of the loan, and then taking the average of these figures) is also used as a measure by some lenders, although its usefulness is perhaps questionable.

§12.9.4 PROJECT LIFE COVER RATIO

Another point that lenders check is whether the project has capacity to make repayments after the original final maturity of the debt, in case there have been difficulties in repaying all of the debt in time. This extra debt service capacity is known as the "tail," and lenders normally expect at least a year or two of cash flow cover in this way. The tail can be based on:

- The general ability of the Project Company to keep operating and so generating cash after the loan term (in any case the technical life of the project should be significantly longer than the loan term)
- The existence of Input Supply and Offtake Contracts, or a Concession Agreement, which specifically ensure that the Project Company will continue to operate

The value to lenders of the tail can be calculated using the PLCR; here the net cash flow before debt service for the whole life of the project (not just the term of the debt as for the LLCR) is discounted to its NPV, and this figure is divided by the debt outstanding. Obviously the PLCR will be higher than the LLCR; lenders may wish to see it around 15–20% higher than the minimum ADSCR.

§12.9.5 RESERVE COVER RATIO

In natural resources projects, the PLCR (here usually known as the reserve cover ratio) is of more importance, because of the specific requirement in such projects for a reserve tail (i.e., proven reserves of the commodity concerned that remain to be extracted over a period after the loan term—cf. §8.9.4).

The standard rule of thumb is that the reserve cover ratio should be 2:1, based on the lenders' conservative projection of commodity prices, and obviously not less than 1:1 in a downside price projection.

§12.9.6 CALCULATING COVER RATIOS

Table 12.9 sets out cover ratio calculations for a typical project, with:

- An even annual cash flow before debt service of 220
- 1000 loan, repaid in equal annual principal installments over 10 years
- Interest rate on the loan of 10% *p.a.* (= NPV discount rate)

If it is assumed that the project generates 200 *p.a.* of cash for a further 3 years after the end of the loan (i.e., years 11–13), the NPV of the total 12 year cash flow is 1499, and so the initial PLCR is 1.50:1 (1499 ÷ 1000).

One issue in calculation of these ratios is whether tax payments should be deducted from the net cash flow before debt service, especially when calculating the ADSCR, since a variation in interest payments also affects the tax payments. It may be prudent to do this if there are wide variations in taxes paid between one year and another (for example, because of the effect of accelerated tax depreciation allowances), which should be taken into account. The argument against this is that taxes are only paid after deductions for interest costs, which are not included in the operating cash flow figure; also, significant fluctuations in tax between one year and the next can be dealt with by placing cash in a Tax Reserve Account (cf. §13.5.2). However, so long as the inclusion or exclusion of taxes is taken into account when deciding what the ratio level should be, the choice of approach is not too important.

It should be noted that "accounting" ratios such as the current or liquid ratio are generally not used in project finance (short-term liquidity is dealt with through the establishment of Reserve Accounts). Similarly, when the debt:equity ratio is used to calculate the required level of equity investment in the Project Company (cf. §13.1.4), this calculation is based on cash injections rather than what appears on the balance sheet.

Table 12.9
Cover Ratio Calculations

Year:		0	1	2	3	4	5	6	7	8	9	10
(a) Operating cash flow			220	220	220	220	220	220	220	220	220	220
(b) NPV of operating cash flow		1352	1267	1174	1071	958	834	697	547	382	200	
(c) Loan repayments			100	100	100	100	100	100	100	100	100	100
(d) Loan outstanding (year end)		1000	900	800	700	600	500	400	300	200	100	0
(e) Interest payments			100	90	80	70	60	50	40	30	20	10
(f) Total debt service	(c) + (e)		200	190	180	170	160	150	140	130	120	110
ADSCR	(a) ÷ (f)		1.10	1.16	1.22	1.29	1.38	1.47	1.57	1.69	1.83	2.00
Average ADSCR			1.47	1.51	1.56	1.60	1.66	1.71	1.77	1.84	1.92	
LLCR	(b) ÷ (d)	1.35	1.41	1.47	1.53	1.60	1.67	1.74	1.82	1.91	2.00	
Average LLCR		1.65	1.68	1.72	1.75	1.79	1.83	1.87	1.91	1.95	2.00	

§12.10 THE BASE CASE AND CHANGES IN ASSUMPTIONS

Once the lenders and Sponsors agree that the financial model's structure and calculation formulae reflect the project and its contracts correctly, the basic input assumptions are settled, and the financial structure and terms (cf. Chapter 13) are agreed to and also incorporated in the model, the final run of the model on this basis is known as the "Base Case" or "banking case." This final calculation usually takes place just before signing or Financial Close, to enable the lenders to check that, using fully up-to-date assumptions and the final versions of the Project Contracts, the project still provides them with adequate coverage for their loan.

But the project does not stand still thereafter, and lenders continue to review their exposure. As will be seen, adverse changes in ADSCR or LLCR in the future may affect the ability of the Project Company to pay dividends to the investors (cf. §13.5.3), or even put the Project Company into default on the loan (cf. §13.11). However, if a new projection is to be calculated once the project is under way, someone has to decide how the input assumptions previously used should be changed. If the Project Company is left to decide the assumptions, the lenders may not agree and *vice versa*.

There is no simple answer to this problem, but as far as possible it is usually best to use objective rather than subjective sources for revising projections where this is possible, e.g.:

- Macroeconomic assumptions (including commodity prices) can be based on an economic review published by one of the lenders or another outside source, so long as this is a general publication, not specific to the project.
- Changes in operating or revenue assumptions should generally be based on the actual performance of the Project Company.
- Lenders usually have the greatest weight in the final decision on the assumption changes, but where possible investors should ensure that these decisions are based on and are required to follow specific advice from the Lenders' Engineer, market, insurance, or other advisers, who should have expertise on the issues involved, rather than leaving it to an arbitrary decision by the lenders.

§12.11 SENSITIVITY ANALYSIS

The financial model also needs to be sufficiently flexible to allow both investors and lenders to calculate a series of "sensitivities" (also known as "cases") showing the effects of variations in the key input assumptions in the Base Case when initially reviewing the project. Such sensitivities may include calculating the effect on cover ratios and returns of:

- Construction cost overrun (usually based on a full drawing of the contingency funding)
- Payment of the LDs under the EPC Contract to cover delays or failure of the project to perform as specified
- Delay in completion (say for 6 months) without LDs from the EPC Contractor
- Reduction in performance without LDs from the EPC Contractor
- Higher downtime or lower availability
- Reduced volume of sales or usage of the project
- Reduced sale prices
- Breakeven sales prices
- Higher input costs
- Higher operating costs
- Higher interest rates (where these are not yet fixed)
- Exchange rate movements

In summary, the sensitivities look at the financial effect of the commercial and financial risk aspects of the project not working out as originally expected.

Lenders also usually run a "combined downside case" to check the effects of several adverse things happening at once (e.g., 3 months' delay in completion, a 10% drop in sale prices, and 10% more downtime). This calculation of several different things happening at once is also called "scenario analysis."

§12.12 INVESTORS' ANALYSIS

Investors usually aim at a minimum level of equity IRR (cf. §12.12.1), which may vary according to when they come into the project (cf. §12.12.2). A resale of equity when the project is complete and operating successfully may give the original investors an opportunity for a quicker realization of value in their investment (cf. §12.12.3); similarly, the investors' return may be significantly improved by a debt refinancing at this stage (cf. §12.12.4).

§12.12.1 Investors' Returns

Investors usually have "hurdle rates" for the IRR on their equity (equity IRR), above which an investment is acceptable, and below which it is not. The hurdle rates are generally fixed based on:

- The investor's cost of capital (based on the investor's own mixture of equity and debt), which is also used as the discount rate for an NPV calculation on the investment
- The additional return over cost of capital required for particular types of risk (e.g., type of project, location, extent to which risks are hedged by Project

Agreements, extent to which the investment adds to or diminishes the spread of risk in the investor's portfolio, etc.)

Setting a required return for the risk based on the Project Company's equity IRR may be circular in nature, because the equity IRR is dependent on the level of gearing, which is itself dependent on the risk: but it is common practice nonetheless.

Equity IRRs in projects with moderate risk, such as a power project with a PPA, or an infrastructure project with limited usage risk, tend to be in the range of 12–20% (pretax, and as a nominal basis, i.e., including inflation in the cash flow projections). This is relatively low compared to returns on other types of new equity investment, reflecting the lower level of risk: in fact, the returns obtained are akin to a return on subordinated or mezzanine debt rather than a true "equity" return. Market rates for equity IRRs have developed in industries where projects are frequently put out to investors for bidding by governments or Offtakers (cf. §4.6), such as power generation and public infrastructure.

Investors may require their investment to show a positive NPV, and to achieve a minimum payback period (cf. §12.8.3) in addition to meeting an IRR hurdle.

§12.12.2 TIMING OF EQUITY COMMITMENT

The return required by investors also varies depending on when they come into the project. Investors come in to projects at different stages and with different investment strategies. Any project has various different levels of risk over time:

Stage	Risk level
• Development / bidding stage (i.e., pre-Financial Close)	High risk
• Construction / operation start-up	Medium risk
• Long-term operation:	Low risk*
	*How low the risk is depends on factors such as:
	• The extent to which commercial risks are covered by Project Agreements, *or*
	• The stability of traffic or demand in a usage-based project

If the project develops successfully, the equity IRR required by new investors therefore declines as it passes through these various stages.

A Sponsor developing a project who brings in another Sponsor to commit the required balance of the equity shortly before Financial Close expects to be compensated for having assumed the highest risk. This can be achieved by requiring the new Sponsor to pay a premium for its shares (a higher price per share than that paid by the original Sponsor), or crediting the original Sponsor with a notional high rate of interest on cash already spent on the project, which is taken into account when calculating each Sponsor's share of development costs, and allocating shares based on this.

As an alternative to selling equity at a premium, the original Sponsor may take money out of the project by charging the Project Company a development fee, which is usually payable at Financial Close. This is in effect an early return on investment, which, since it is funded as part of the project development costs, is partly financed by the lenders. A development fee can thus be used as an alternative way for one Sponsor to compensate another for taking the development risk. Development fees may be contentious with lenders, but can be acceptable, provided that the original Sponsor's real cash investment has not been effectively reduced to an unacceptably low level by doing this, and obviously also provided that the project can support the corresponding increase in debt.

§12.12.3 EFFECT OF EQUITY RESALE

Another investor may not be willing or able to sustain the high level of costs and risks in the development and construction stages of the project, but may buy shares in the Project Company from the original investors when the project is completed and operating smoothly, at a higher price that reflects the lower equity IRR now acceptable because of the reduction in risk.

A sale of part or all of their equity investment when the project is complete and operating successfully is likely to offer Sponsors and other original investors a chance for a significant improvement in their originally projected return. Indeed, to achieve their return objectives, some investors such as project finance investment funds may depend on a profitable sale of their equity at this stage of the project's life.

The benefit of such a sale is illustrated by Table 12.10. This relates a project with:

- Project cost: 570
- Construction period: 2 years, with ½ of the cost paid on day 1, and the balance at the end of each following year
- Funding: 85% debt to 15% equity, drawn down *pro rata* during the construction period
- Net revenues: 70 *p.a.* before debt service, over a 20-year project life.
- Debt service: debt is repaid on an annuity basis (cf. §13.2.3) over the first 15 years of operation (i.e., to year 17 of the project), at an interest rate of 7% *p.a.* (N.B. IDC is added to the debt and financed as part of project costs)

(N.B. The effects of tax are ignored. Figures are rounded to whole numbers.)

As can be seen in Table 12.10, (1) the original investor's equity IRR was 18%; (2) shows the effect of a sale of the equity at the end of the second year of operation to a buyer who is willing to accept a lower IRR of 15%, reflecting the lower risk of an established project. Purchasing the Project Company's equity for 130

Table 12.10

Effect of Equity Resale

Year:	Construction			Operation								
	0	1	2	3	4	5	...	17	18	19	...	22
(1) Initial project finance												
(a) Project cost (including IDC)	−190	−190	−190									
(b) Net Revenues				70	70	70	...	70	70	70	...	70
(c) Debt drawings / payments	162	162	162	−53	−53	−53	...	−53				
Net cash flow [(a) + (b) + (c)]	−29	−29	−29	17	17	17	...	17	70	70	...	70
Equity IRR = 18%												
(2) Sale at the end of year 2 of operation (year 4 of project)												
(i) Position of the original investor												
Project cash flow	−29	−29	−29	17	17							
Sale					130							
Net cash flow	−29	−29	−29	17	147							
Equity IRR = 25%												
(ii) Position of the new investor												
Purchase					−130							
Project cash flow						17	...	17	70	70	...	70
Net cash flow					−130	17	...	17	70	70	...	70
Equity IRR = 15%												

produces this 15% IRR for the buyer; this sale increases the original investor's IRR to 25% and gives a profiit of 43 on the original equity investment of 87. (Of course although the original investor's IRR has considerably improved, the benefit of future returns from the project has been lost.)

This type of early "windfall" profit for the investors may raise issues with an Off-taker or Contracting Authority under a Project Agreement (cf. §6.9.2), and sale of equity by the Sponsors at this stage may still be subject to lenders' consent (cf. §4.1).

§12.12.4 BENEFIT OF REFINANCING

Table 12.11 is based on the same project as Table 12.10, but considers the benefit of a refinancing of the debt 2 years into operation (year 4 of the project). The refinancing adds two years on to the final maturity of the loan, and also increases the loan outstanding at the end of year 4 by 125.

The refinancing is based on the assumption that at this stage of the project the lenders are comfortable both with lending for a further 2 years of the project life, and with a lower future ADSCR (and LLCR) of 1.25 (as well as the PLCR reducing to 1.38, compared to 1.53 at the end of year 2). As a result of this the investors recover an extra 125 of cash flow in year 4—thus recovering all of their original

Table 12.11

Effect of Refinancing

Year:	Construction			Operation								
	0	1	2	3	4	5	...	17	18	19	...	22
(1) Initial project finance												
(a) Project cost (including IDC)	−190	−190	−190									
(b) Net revenues				70	70	70	...	70	70	70	...	70
(c) Debt drawings	162	162	162									
(d) Debt repayments					−19	−21	−22	...	−50			
(e) Year-end debt outstanding	162	323	485	465	445	423	...	0				
[(e){previous year} + (c) + (d)]												
(f) Interest payments [(e) @ 7%]				−34	−33	−31	...	−3				
(g) Debt service [(d) + (f)]				−53	−53	−53	...	−53				
(h) Net cash flow	−29	−29	−29	17	17	17	...	17	70	70	...	70
[(a) + (b) + (c) + (g)]												
ADSCR [(b) ÷ (g)]				1.32	1.32	1.32	...	1.32			...	
PLCR* [NPV(b) ÷ 465	1.53											
*end year 2												
Equity IRR = 18%												
(2) Refinancing												
(a) Project cost	−190	−190	−190									
(b) Net Revenues				70	70	70	...	70	70	70	...	70
(c) Debt drawings	162	162	162	65								
(d) Debt repayments				−19	−21	−20	...	−46	−49	52	...	
(e) Year-end debtoutstanding	162	323	485	465	510	489	...	101	52	0	...	
[(e){previous year} + (c) + (d)]												
(f) Interest payments [(e) @ 7%)]				−34	−33	−36	...	−10	−7	−4	...	
(g) Debt service [(d) + (f)]				−53	−53	−56	...	−56	−56	−56	...	
(h) Net cash flow	−29	−29	−29	17	82	14	...	14	14	14	...	70
[(a) + (b) + (c) + (g)]												
ADSCR [(b) ÷ (g)]				1.32	1.32	1.25	...	1.25	1.25	1.25	...	
PLCR* [NPV(b) ÷ 510]	1.38											
*end year 4												
Equity IRR = 24%												

equity investment by that date—and their overall IRR increases to 24%. (These calculations do not take into account the fees and legal and other costs of the refinancing itself, which may be 1–1.5% of the refinanced amount.)

Again, however, refinancing may raise issues with an Offtaker or Contracting Authority under a Project Agreement (cf. §6.9.1), and provision also has to be made in the loan documentation to allow the refinancing to take place (cf. §13.6.3).

Chapter 13

Financial Structuring and Documentation

This chapter examines some of the main financial structuring issues likely to arise once the commercial fundamentals and risks of the project, and the cash flow that results from these, have been reviewed as set out in previous chapters.

The main elements in the financing negotiations between the Project Company and its lenders are likely to include:

- The debt:equity ratio (cf. §13.1)
- The term (length) of the debt and its repayment schedule (cf. §13.2)
- The drawdown schedule for debt and equity (cf. §13.3)
- The interest rate and fees to be charged by lenders (cf. §13.4)
- Lenders' control of the Project Company's cash flow (cf. §13.5)
- Provisions for prepayment (cf. §13.6)
- Lenders' security (cf. §13.7)
- Conditions precedent to Financial Close and drawings on the debt (cf. §13.8)
- Representations and warranties to be given by the Project Company (cf. §13.9)
- Covenants or undertakings by the Project Company (cf. §13.10)
- Events of default (cf. §13.11)
- Voting and enforcement on default (cf. §13.12)
- Intercreditor arrangements (where more than one lending group is involved) (cf. §13.13)

As discussed in §5.1.7, these conditions are set out first in a term sheet with the lenders (or an investment bank—cf. §5.2.1) and then in a loan agreement and associated security documentation.

There is no merit in innovation for the sake of it in project finance. As is evident, this is a highly complex form of financing, and innovative financing structures may just add to the time and cost of putting the deal together, or be too rigid if something goes wrong, or add extra risks that cannot be foreseen at the beginning. The financial structure should therefore be kept as simple as possible; for example, several different sources of debt should not be used if sufficient finance can be raised from one source, as it is far quicker and easier to deal with one group of lenders (e.g. avoiding intercreditor problems). As far as possible, financing should also be kept sufficiently flexible to accommodate changes in the project over time.

It is also easy for both Sponsors and lenders to get so carried away by the detail of structuring and negotiating the deal that the big picture of what really matters gets buried. For example, lenders often fall into the trap of imposing unnecessary controls over the Project Company's activities, or an overelaborate system of information flow about the project, which both hinder the Project Company from doing its job of running the project efficiently, and burden the lenders with information they do not read or with the task of taking decisions that are a waste of their time.

§13.1 DEBT:EQUITY RATIO

As already discussed, a high ratio of debt is the essence of project finance. Within prudent limits, therefore, Sponsors wish to limit the amount of equity they invest in a project, to improve their own return, and thus to raise the maximum level of debt.

Once the maximum level of debt a project can raise has been determined, the difference between this figure and project costs in principle determines the amount of equity acquired (although some of the gap may be filled with mezzanine debt (cf. §3.3) or public-sector grants.

§13.1.1 LEVEL OF DEBT

Two factors determine the level of debt that can be raised for a project:

Lender's cash flow cover requirements. There is obviously a fundamental difference between a project with a Project Agreement that provides reasonable certainty of revenues and hence cash flow cover for debt service and a project such as a merchant power plant selling into a competitive and comparatively unpredictable market with no form of hedging of the revenue risks; it is evident that the latter type of project cannot raise the same level of debt as the former.

Similarly, a project in a high-risk country cannot raise as much debt as the same project in a low-risk country, because the lenders will consider the cash flow less certain, even if it is contracted through a Project Agreement.

The certainty of the cash flow affects the level of cash flow cover (ADSCRs, LLCR, PLCR) that the lenders wish to have: the less certain the lenders consider the cash flow to be, the higher the cover ratio they will require (cf. §12.9.1).

Lenders' views on leverage. Lenders also have views about the debt:equity ratio that is appropriate for particular types of project, e.g.:

- 90:10 for an infrastructure project with a Project Agreement with no usage risk (e.g., a public hospital or prison)
- 85:15 for a power or process plant project with an Offtake Contract
- 80:20 for an infrastructure project with usage risk (e.g., a toll road or mass transit project)
- 70:30 for a natural resources project
- 50:50 for a merchant power plant project with no Offtake Contract or price hedging

§13.1.2 Effect of Cover Ratio Requirements

Balancing the two requirements of debt cover ratios and leverage, however, is not always simple, as Table 13.1 illustrates. This table is based on a project with the following assumptions:

- Project cost: 1000
- Debt interest rate: 7% *p.a.*
- Debt repayment schedule: annuity repayment (cf. §13.2.3) over 15 years
- Required equity IRR: 16% *p.a.* (earned on an annuity basis over a project life of 15 years)

In Case (1) in the table, the lenders require a debt:equity ratio of 80:20, whereas in Case (2) a more liberal requirement of 90:10 has been agreed. Following the simplified example set out in §2.5.2, it might be expected that the higher leverage should lead to a lower Tariff, but this may not be the case.

In Case (1), with a debt:equity ratio of 80:20; the revenue of 122 (88 for debt service and 34 to cover the investors' return) provides an ADSCR of 1.39:1, and therefore unless the lenders require a cover ratio higher than this, there is more revenue than required to provide the minimum ADSCR and to give the investors their required return. This suggests that the leverage should be increased.

If the debt:equity ratio is increased to 90:10, however, it can be seen that the revenue required to cover debt service plus the equity return produces an ADSCR of only 1.17:1, which is insufficient to provide the levels of cover ratios that lenders would normally require, and therefore an increase in the Tariff is required.

This leads to the paradoxical result that a Project Company may have to reduce its leverage to produce a more competitive Tariff for its product or service, even if

Table 13.1

Relationship between Leverage and Cover Ratio

(1)	**Debt:equity ratio of 80:20**				
	(a) Annual debt service		88	88	88
	(b) Annual return on equity		34	34	34
	(c) Total revenue (e.g., fixed tariff) required to cover debt service				
	+ equity return	[(a) + (b)]	122	122	122
	(d) Actual ADSCR	[(c) ÷ (a)]	1.39:1	1.39:1	1.39:1
	(e) Minimum ADSCR required by lenders		1.20:1	1.30:1	1.40:1
	(f) Revenue required for lenders' minimum ADSCR [(a) × (e)]		105	114	123
	Excess revenue above that required for minimum ADSCR				
	[If [(c) > (f), (c) − (f)]		*17*	*8*	n/a
	Additional revenue required to achieve minimum ADSCR				
	[If [(f) > (c), (f) − (c)]		n/a	n/a	*1*
(2)	**Debt:equity ratio of 90:10**				
	(a) Annual debt service		99	99	99
	(b) Annual return on equity		17	17	17
	(c) Total revenue (e.g., fixed tariff) required to cover debt service				
	+ equity return	[(a) + (b)]	116	116	116
	(d) Actual ADSCR	[(c) ÷ (a)]	1.17:1	1.17:1	1.17:1
	(e) Minimum ADSCR required by lenders		1.20:1	1.30:1	1.40:1
	(f) Revenue required for ADSCR	[(a) × (e)]	119	128	138
	Excess revenue above that required for minimum ADSCR				
	[If (c) > (f), (c) − (f)]		n/a	n/a	n/a
	Additional revenue required to achieve minimum ADSCR				
	[If (f) > (c), (f) − (c)]		*3*	*13*	*22*

lenders are happy with a higher leverage. In this case, if the lenders require an ADSCR of 1.3:1, the tariff with leverage of 90:10 must be 128 *p.a.,* whereas that with leverage of 80:20 is 122. In fact the best balance between revenue and ADSCR is achieved with a leverage of 84:16, which produces a tariff of 120.

§13.1.3 PROJECTS WITHOUT EQUITY

If a project has a high degree of certainty in its cash flow (thanks to a Project Agreement that transfers the price and demand risks) and high ADSCRs and LLCR, arithmetically it might need no equity at all and still have enough cash flow to support 100% debt financing. Generally however, lenders wish the Sponsors to be at risk with a reasonable amount of equity in the project, and again given the requirement for cover ratios there must always be surplus cash flow above that required for debt service, that must be used somehow. Some projects have been financed with "pinpoint" equity (i.e., a nominal amount of equity), but these are exceptional. They usually arise when an existing cash flow is being fed into a new project—e.g., construction of a new bridge alongside an existing one, where the Project Company has the benefit of already established cash flow from traffic tolls on the old bridge. In effect, the existing cash flow is the equity in the project. In such cases the surplus cash required for the cover ratios may be used for debt pre-payment, with the project being transferred back to the public sector when the debt has all been paid off, but this still means that a higher tariff is required in the early years of the project's operation to provide the required cover ratios.

There is probably more scope than has been used in the project finance market so far, however, for the use of "contingent" equity, that leaves investors with the same equity risk but is not drawn unless needed to support the cash flow (cf. §13.3.3).

§13.1.4 CALCULATION OF DEBT:EQUITY RATIO

The point at which the Project Company is normally required to demonstrate that it has met the required debt:equity ratio (assuming that debt and equity are not being drawn down *pro rata*—cf. §13.3.1) is the later of COD, or the date on which no further drawings can be made on the debt (which may be up to 6 months after COD).

The calculation is based on the cash injections of debt and equity, not whatever appears on the balance sheet, and if more than one currency is being used for funding, the calculation should be based on the exchange rate between these currencies at Financial Close (cf. §9.3.2).

§13.2 DEBT SERVICE

Debt service (i.e., loan interest payments and principal repayments) is one of the biggest factors in the financing structure that influences an investor's rate of return.

The faster investors in a Project Company are paid dividends, the better their rate of return. Investors therefore do not wish cash flow from operation of the project to be devoted to repayments to lenders at the expense of these dividends. Lenders, on the other hand, generally wish to be repaid as rapidly as possible. Striking a reasonable balance between these conflicting demands is an important part of the loan negotiations.

The issues that come up in negotiating the debt repayment schedule are:

- The term of the financing (cf. §13.2.1)
- The average life of the financing (cf. §13.2.2)
- The repayment profile (cf. §13.2.3)
- Flexibility in repayment (cf. §13.2.4)

§13.2.1 TERM OF FINANCING

In general, project finance loans and bonds are much longer in term (repayment-period) than normal bank loans; a power project may have a 2- to 3-year drawdown period during construction, and then 15 years of repayment, giving a total term of 17–18 years; an infrastructure project finance may be for 25 years or more. (But cf. §13.6.3 on the use of the shorter "mini-perm.") Financing for natural resources and telecommunications projects is usually much shorter in term, taking account of the shorter life cycle of such projects.

The overall term of the financing depends mainly on the long-term certainty of the cash flow of the project, taking into account the need for a cash flow "tail" (cf. §6.3 and §12.9.4): thus a Project Company with a 20-year Project Agreement may aim to raise debt for 18–19 years.

The cover ratios are of course affected by the debt service schedule; the shorter the term the higher the debt service payments, and the lower the ADSCRs and LLCR will become, and so if the debt is made too short-term it cannot be supported by the cash flow.

Another factor that may affect the financing term is the location of the project; if it is in a high-risk country, the term of the financing will be less than the same project in a low-risk country.

The notional term of the financing may be lengthened by the use of a "cash sweep" arrangement (cf. §13.5.4).

§13.2.2 AVERAGE LIFE

Apart from the overall term of the loan, lenders also look at the repayment schedule to assess how rapidly their risk reduces over the term. There is obviously a considerable difference in risk between a loan of 1000 repaid in 100 installments over 10 years, and a loan of 1000 repaid in one bullet installment at the end of 10 years. This is measured by looking at the loan's average life, which is used by lenders in a similar way to the payback period calculation by investors (cf. §12.8.3) (i.e., a check to ensure that the repayment schedule is not overextended).

The average life of a loan is the average number of years (or shorter periods, e.g., 6 months) that the principal is outstanding. This is calculated by taking the loan principal outstanding for each year, adding these together, and then dividing by the original loan amount. Thus if a loan of 4 is repaid over 4 years in annual installments of 1, the average life is 2.75 years ([4 + 3 + 2 + 1] ÷ 4). Table 13.2 illustrates how this works on a variety of loan repayment schedules.

However this calculation is not as simple as it might seem in a project finance context, as project finance loans are drawn down over a period of time—in such a case what is the "original" loan amount?

There are three ways of dealing with this:

Table 13.2

Calculation of Average Life

End	Loan outstanding		
	Loan A	Loan B	Loan C
Year 0	1000	1000	1000
Year 1	900	1000	1000
Year 2	800	1000	1000
Year 3	700	1000	1000
Year 4	600	857	1000
Year 5	500	714	1000
Year 6	400	571	1000
Year 7	300	428	1000
Year 8	200	285	1000
Year 9	100	142	500
Year 10	0	0	0
Total of loan outstandings for each year:	5500	6997	9950
Average life (years):	**5.5**	**6.997**	**9.95**
[Total of loan outstandings ÷ loan amount (1000)]			

- Add the whole drawdown period onto the calculation of the average life of the repayment period, the argument for this being that the lenders are on risk for the whole of their loan during the drawdown period. This would have the effect of increasing the average lives in Table 13.2 by a further two years.
- Ignore the drawdown period and look only at the average life of the repayment (which is how ECAs calculate it under the OECD Consensus—cf. §11.3.2)
- Make the denominator of the calculation the peak loan principal outstanding (though this becomes rather problematical if the loan principal outstandings revolve, i.e., go up and down because they are being drawn, repaid from some other cash flow source, and then drawn again). Thus in Table 13.2, if it is assumed that the loan is drawn over a 2-year construction period in three installments, ⅓ at the beginning, and ⅓ at the end of each of the two following years, and the various repayment schedules remain the same, the results are as in Table 13.3 (i.e., in this case the average lives have all increased by 1 year, which is logical given that the loan is being drawn down evenly over a 2 year period).

§13.2.3 REPAYMENT SCHEDULE

Loan repayments usually begin around 6 months after the construction of the project is complete, and are usually made at 6 monthly intervals. Where bond financing is used, a sinking fund may be built up to repay the whole amount of

Table 13.3

Average Life Calculation with Construction Period

End	Loan outstanding		
	Loan A	Loan B	Loan C
Year 0	333	333	333
Year 1	667	667	667
Year 2	1000	1000	1000
Year 3	900	1000	1000
Year 4	800	1000	1000
Year 5	700	1000	1000
Year 6	600	857	1000
Year 7	500	714	1000
Year 8	400	571	1000
Year 9	300	428	1000
Year 10	200	285	1000
Year 11	100	142	950
Year 12	0	0	0
Total of loan outstandings for each year:	6500	7997	10950
Average life (years):	**6.5**	**7.997**	**10.95**
[Total loan outstandings ÷ maximum loan amount (1000)]			

the bond on its final maturity rather than making repayments in installments, but this obviously adds to the financing cost and is not common in the project finance bond market. Hence project finance bonds are amortized (repaid) in a similar way to loans.

As to the repayment structure, it might be thought that the fairest way to deal with lenders, assuming the project's cash flow is reasonably even over time, would be to repay the financing in equal installments (e.g., if the debt is 1,000, and it is being repaid over 10 years, repayments would be 100 *p.a.* as for Loan A in Table 13.3). In fact, this repayment structure, although not uncommon, is disadvantageous to the investors in the Project Company, as far more of the cash flow is being paid out to the lenders in the early years of the loan when the interest payments are added on. It also leaves the project with lower ADSCRs in the early years, just at the time when project cash flow is more likely to be affected by start-up problems. A fairer approach is to use an annuity repayment structure, which keeps principal and interest payments level throughout the loan term.

This can be illustrated by the simplified examples in Table 13.4 and Table 13.5, which have the following common assumptions:

- Project cost: 1250
- Debt:equity ratio: 8:20
- Loan amount: 1000

- Repayment: 10 years, annually in arrears
- Interest rate: 10% *p.a.*
- Equity amount: 250
- Cash flow before debt service and dividend payments: 220 *p.a.*
- Cash flow after debt service is all paid out as dividends to investors
- Residual value of the project: nil
- Investors' NPV discount rate (cost of capital): 12%
- Investors' reinvestment rate (for MIRR calculation): 12% *p.a.*

An immediate and obvious problem with the level principal payment structure is that the annual debt service in year 1 (200) is almost double that of year 10 (110), and correspondingly the ADSCR is 1.10:1 (too low for comfort) in year 1, and 2.00:1 (much higher than needed) in year 10.

Investors' dividends, on the other hand, are heavily back-ended, with dividends increasing by 5½ times between year 1 and year 10; it takes nearly 6 years to pay back the original investment.

The benefits from the change in repayment to an annuity structure are self-evident: the ADSCR is a comfortable 1.35:1 throughout, thanks to the level debt service payments, the same as the LLCR.

The dividends are also level throughout, and although the total dividends received by the investors over the life of project reduce from 650 to 573 (because more interest is being paid to lenders), the investors' IRR improves from 16.6% to

Table 13.4
Effect of Level Principal Payments

Year		0	1	2	3	4	5	6	7	8	9	10
(a) Project cash flow			220	220	220	220	220	220	220	220	220	220
Lenders' viewpoint												
(b) Loan repayments			100	100	100	100	100	100	100	100	100	100
(c) Loan outstanding (year end)	1000	900	800	700	600	500	400	300	200	100	0
(d) Interest payments			100	90	80	70	60	50	40	30	20	10
(e) Total debt service [(b) + (d)]			200	190	180	170	160	150	140	130	120	110
ADSCR [(a) ÷ (e)]			1.10	1.16	1.22	1.29	1.38	1.47	1.57	1.69	1.83	2.00
Average ADSCR			1.47	1.51	1.56	1.60	1.66	1.71	1.77	1.84	1.92	
LLCR [NPV(a) ÷ (c)] 1.35			1.41	1.47	1.53	1.60	1.67	1.74	1.82	1.91	2.00	
Average life of loan 5½ *years*												
Investors' viewpoint:												
Equity investment:	250											
Dividends [(a) − (e)]			20	30	40	50	60	70	80	90	100	110
NPV of investment	66											
IRR	*16.6%*											
MIRR	*14.6%*											
Payback period	*c. 6 years*											

Table 13.5

Effect of Annuity Repayments

Year:	0	1	2	3	4	5	6	7	8	9	10
(a) Project cash flow		220	220	220	220	220	220	220	220	220	220
Lenders' viewpoint											
(b) Loan repayments		63	69	76	84	92	101	111	122	134	148
(c) Loan outstanding (year end)	1000	937	868	792	709	617	516	405	282	148	0
(d) Interest payments		100	94	87	79	71	62	52	40	28	15
(e) Total debt service [(b) + (d)]		163	163	163	163	163	163	163	163	163	163
ADSCR [(a) ÷ (e)]		*1.35*	*1.35*	*1.35*	*1.35*	*1.35*	*1.35*	*1.35*	*1.35*	*1.35*	*1.35*
Average ADSCR		*1.35*	*1.35*	*1.35*	*1.35*	*1.35*	*1.35*	*1.35*	*1.35*	*1.35*	
LLCR [NPV(a) ÷ (c)]	*1.35*	*1.35*	*1.35*	*1.35*	*1.35*	*1.35*	*1.35*	*1.35*	*1.35*	*1.35*	
Average life of loan *6¼ years*											
Investors' viewpoint											
Equity investment:	250										
Dividends [(a) − (e)]		57	57	57	57	57	57	57	57	57	57
NPV of investment	*74*										
IRR	*18.8%*										
MIRR	*14.9%*										
Payback period	*4½ years*										

18.8%; however, the improvement in MIRR (a fairer reflection of the picture) is more limited, from 14.6% to 14.9%. The payback period reduces significantly, to within 4½ years.

The repayment structure is relatively more important to the investors than the interest rate on the debt. If, in this example, the lenders offered to reduce their interest rate by 0.25% in return for a level principal payment structure instead of an annuity repayment, the IRR benefit of this to the investors would be 0.6%, whereas the annuity repayment structure is worth an extra 2.2%. Similarly, it is likely to be worth paying a higher rate of interest to obtain longer term financing, if there is sufficient cash flow "tail" to allow this.

However, an annuity repayment structure considerably increases the debt service payments and so reduces the ADSCR in the later years of the project. It also increases the average life of the lenders' risk: in Table 13.4, it is 5½ years, whereas in Table 13.5 it is just over 6¼ years.

If there is more uncertainty about the later cash flows from the project, lenders may look for higher cover ratios and a shorter average life than can be achieved with an annuity repayment. A compromise between level principal payments and annuity repayments may need to be agreed to in such cases.

On the other hand, if the project is projected to produce higher cash flows in the later years, a repayment schedule with loan installments being paid even more slowly than an annuity structure but with adequate annual cover ratios could be feasible, although lenders resist too much back-ending of repayments and hence an unduly long average life for their loan.

If irregular cash flows are projected, the loan repayments can also be structured on an irregular schedule such that the same level of ADSCRs are maintained throughout the loan term (this is known as a "sculptured" repayment schedule). This may be necessary, for example, if after-tax cash flows in later years decrease because deferred taxes start becoming payable if the Project Company has benefited from accelerated tax depreciation on its assets in the early years of operation.

These considerations are not only relevant to the investors: the debt repayment structure clearly affects the cost of the Project Company's products or services and may be a crucial factor if Sponsors are in a competitive bidding situation for a prospective project.

§13.1.4 FLEXIBLE REPAYMENT

To provide the Project Company with some room to maneuver if a temporary cash flow problem occurs (especially when the project is just beginning operations), lenders may agree to a "target" repayment structure. Two repayment schedules are agreed to: one is the level that the lenders actually wish to achieve if the project operates as expected (i.e., the target repayments), and one is the minimum level of repayment required to avoid a default by the Project Company. For example, if the target loan repayments for a 1000 10-year loan are 20 equal semiannual installments, the minimum schedule could be calculated as in Table 13.6.

If the Project Company has cash flow available, it must make a repayment sufficient to bring the loan outstanding down to the target schedule, but if not, it must at least achieve the minimum schedule. As can be seen in Table 13.6, the two schedules differ by one loan repayment (50) to begin with, this loan repayment being spread over the remaining 19 payments in the minimum schedule. The loan outstanding in each schedule becomes closer and closer as time goes on so that final repayment is achieved at the same time on both schedules; thus at the end of the first 6 months the whole 50 of repayment can be deferred, while only 2.6 of the penultimate repayment can be deferred. This gives the Project Company 6 months' room to maneuver at the beginning of the project's operation, when things are likely to go wrong because of so-called teething troubles.

§13.3 DRAWDOWN OF DEBT AND EQUITY

§13.3.1 PRIORITY OF DRAWING

Once the debt:equity ratio has been agreed to with the lenders, the question arises about which is to be spent first, debt or equity? Sponsors often prefer to delay putting their cash equity into the project, since the later they invest their

Table 13.6

Target and Minimum Repayments

Repayment no	Target repayments		Minimum repayments		Difference
	Repayment	Loan outstanding	Repayment	Loan outstanding	
0	—	1000	—	1000	0.0
1	50	950	—	1000.0	50.0
2	50	900	52.6	947.4	47.4
3	50	850	52.6	894.7	44.7
4	50	800	52.6	842.1	42.1
5	50	750	52.6	789.5	39.5
. . . etc.					
18	50	100	52.6	105.3	5.3
19	50	50	52.6	52.6	2.6
20	50	0	52.6	0.0	0.0

money, the higher their IRR (because the period of time between investment and return is shorter).

For example, in the annuity repayment structure financing in Table 13.5, it is assumed that the equity is invested at the end of the construction period, with loan repayments and dividends beginning one year later. In fact, the IRR would only have been as high as the 19% shown in the table if an equity bridge loan (see below) had been used, as otherwise the equity would have to have been invested to cover project costs before the end of the construction period. If, on the other hand, the equity is assumed to be invested 50% at the start of a 2-year construction period, and 50% one year into construction, the investors' IRR reduces from 19% to 14%.

Lenders would obviously prefer the equity to be invested first, or *pro rata* with the debt, but will not normally object to the debt being put in first so long as the Sponsors are legally committed to invest the equity (and will do so immediately if the project goes into default). Bank guarantees or letters of credit may need to be provided as security for this uncalled equity. Thus the investors' risk is the same whether the equity is invested early or late, but nonetheless many investors evaluate their returns—rightly or wrongly—based on the timing of cash investments (cf. §12.8.4).

If pre-Financial Close development costs are included as part of the project costs (cf. §12.4.1), these can be treated as part of an initial equity investment, or refinanced by debt if equity is being injected last.

For investors who want to squeeze the maximum IRR benefit out of the timing of their cash equity investment, an equity bridge loan can be provided by the lenders. This is a loan to the Project Company for the amount of the equity, normally secured by corporate guarantees from the Sponsors. This loan is used to cover the equity share of the project costs, and at the end of the construction period the real equity is finally paid in and used to repay the bridge facility. (This structure can also be continued into the operating period of the project—cf. §13.3.3.)

The only disadvantage of not contributing the equity before debt is that project costs are increased because of the need to fund IDC. If there is any difficulty in raising the marginal amount of debt funding required for this (e.g., because the total funding available is limited, or because only tied funding that does not fund IDC is available), the Sponsors may have to go first.

Certain types of projects do require equity to be invested before any debt is advanced:

- If equity is to be obtained from a public issue of shares, lenders would also not consider it prudent to rely on a future public issue, even if this is underwritten, because such underwriting commitments are likely to have unacceptable qualifications (e.g., a provision that the underwriting can fall away in certain market conditions).
- In a project where revenue is being built up gradually as investment is being made in the system (e.g., a mobile phone network), lenders set targets for how much of the system has to be built out with equity funding, and what minimum revenue levels have to be achieved, before any part of the debt is advanced. This approach is suitable when the project does not consist of building one plant, but is a continuous process of investment.

§13.3.2 PROCEDURE FOR DRAWING

The procedure for drawing on the loan usually involves the Project Company presenting a formal drawing request several days in advance of the date on which funds are required (there is usually only one drawing a month).

The drawing request:

- Attaches a payment request from the EPC Contractor, certified by the Lenders' Engineer
- Summarizes the purpose for which other funds are required
- Sets out how these costs are to be funded (i.e., by equity or debt, and if there are several loans, which one is to be drawn)
- If tied funding from ECAs or other sources is being used, provides the certification on the origins of the equipment or services required for this
- Compares the monthly and cumulative project costs with the construction budget (cf. §12.4.1)
- Demonstrates that enough funds remain available to complete the project
- Demonstrates compliance with any other conditions precedent to drawings (cf. §13.8)

Both equity investment and loan drawings are paid into a Disbursement Account in the Project Company's name over which the lenders have a security interest (or they are paid directly to the beneficiaries, especially the EPC Contractor—cf. §7.1.4). Lenders may control all payments from the Disbursement Account, or allow the Project Company to make the payments for the purposes set out in its drawing requests, only taking control of payments if there is a default. (The latter is a more practical procedure; if a drawing request procedure as set out above is being used, there is no need for lenders to do anything other than monitor payments out of the Disbursement Account.)

§13.3.3 CONTINGENCY FUNDING

The Project Company needs to have contingency funding available to cover any unexpected extra project costs during the construction period (cf. §8.5.4). This is normally provided as additional equity and debt, usually in the same ratio as the base equity and debt. Contingency funding, if required, is drawn after the Base Case equity and debt is fully drawn.

Sponsors normally have no liability to invest any further funds in addition to the contingent equity if the project gets into trouble; that is what nonrecourse funding to the Project Company implies.

Contingent debt and equity funding usually remains available for drawing only until shortly after completion of construction of the project. Contingent risks during operations are covered by Reserve Accounts (cf. §13.5.2).

Taking the principle of an equity bridge loan (cf. §13.3.1) further, funding beyond the construction period can continue to be provided only as debt, with the base equity committed purely on a contingent basis (i.e., to be drawn if required). Such a use of contingent equity:

- Reduces the Project Company's cost of funding, assuming that investors are willing to accept a lower level of IRR or NPV than they would have obtained from a cash investment of equity
- Avoids the need for the Project Company to be capitalized with equity at a level to meet the worst conceivable scenario—which may never occur—and so again makes its financial cost base more competitive

This approach has only been used in a limited way in the project finance market to date. It should be noted that IRR and NPV calculations are not appropriate for investors in this scenario as they do not take account of amounts that are at risk but not drawn in cash (cf. §12.8.4), and the cover ratio problem discussed in §13.1.2 would apply in such cases.

Similarly, contingent subordinated debt may be provided by a third party to meet a particular risk that may never arise (e.g., as OPIC has done to meet the risk of catastrophic currency devaluation) (cf. §9.3.5).

§13.4 INTEREST RATE AND FEES

Apart from the lenders advisors' fees (and the costs of the rating agency if the debt is rated), the main financing costs payable by the Project Company are:

- If the loan is on a floating interest rate basis, the base interest rate (e.g., LIBOR) plus the interest margin, together with net payments under an interest rate swap (cf. §9.2.1)
- If the loan (or bond) is on a fixed rate basis, the interest rate
- Advisory, arranging and underwriting fees
- Commitment fees
- Agency and security trustee fees

International project finance loans at a floating rate based on LIBOR typically have interest margins in the range of 1–2% over LIBOR. Pricing is usually higher until completion of construction, reflecting the higher risk of this stage of the project, then drops down, and then gradually climbs back again over time. (Thus in a project with a loan covering a 2-year construction and 15-year operation period, the margin might be 1.25% for years 1–2, 1.1% for years 3–7, 1.2% for years 8–13, and 1.3% for years 14–17.)

Commercial bank lenders also require standard "market disruption" and "increased costs" provisions in their long-term floating rate loans; these provide that if the cost base (e.g., LIBOR) is no longer available in the market, or does not represent their true cost of funds, or a change of law or regulation has increased the costs of funding the loan, the full cost is passed on to the borrower (cf. §9.2.4).

If fixed-rate lending is being provided by an ECA or IFI on a subsidized or noncommercial basis, the rate will probably reflect the cost of funds for a AAA borrower plus a small margin (say $\frac{1}{8}$% *p.a.*). The rates for other types of fixed-rate lending, including bonds, are based on similar factors to those that affect the pricing of interest rate swaps. Bond pricing is usually quoted as a margin over the rate for a government bond with a similar maturity to the average life of the debt.

Arranging and underwriting fees charged by bank Lead Managers are derived from several factors:

- The size and complexity of the financing
- The time and work involved in structuring the financing
- The risk that a success-based fee may not be earned because the project does not go ahead
- The bank's overall return targets for work of this kind (bearing competitive pressure in mind), taking into account both the fees earned and the return on the loan balance that it keeps on its own books
- The length of time the underwriting bank has to carry the syndication risk—

for a variety of reasons there can often be a considerable time lag between the signing of loan documentation and hence underwriting, and syndication to other participating banks in the project finance market.

- The proportion of the fee that has to be reallowed to subunderwriting or participating banks to induce them to join the syndication (which is itself a function of the time the participating bank spends reviewing it, the overall return the market requires for the risk, taking interest margin and fees together into account, and perhaps competition from other transactions in the market at the same time)

Roughly speaking, the overall level of fees may vary between 1–2% of the loan amount with the level of arranging and underwriting fee at about the same percentage as the interest margin. If the arranging bank is also acting as Financial Adviser, this may increase the fees by around 0.5–1%.

The considerations affecting bond arranging and underwriting fees are much the same, except that the investment bank underwriting the transaction does not intend to retain the bonds in its own portfolio and therefore does not take this into account in assessing return; also, the period of risk on the bond underwriting may be much shorter than for a bank syndication. Bond underwriting fees are therefore around two thirds of those for comparable loans.

Commitment fees are paid on the available but undrawn portion of the debt during the construction period (i.e., so long as drawings may be made on the loan). In project finance loans commitment fees are usually between 0.5% *p.a.* to half the interest margin. As most project finance loans are drawn very slowly (taking 2–3 years in most cases) banks need the commitment fee to give them a reasonable rate of return on their risk during the construction of the project. (Commitment fees do not apply to bonds or a loan drawn immediately after it is signed.)

Finally there are the agency fees payable to the agent bank or security trustee (cf. §5.1.9). The time that a bank has to spend on agency work can be quite considerable, and it is in the Project Company's interests to ensure that a reasonable annual agency fee covers this work adequately, but this fee should be based on a fair assessment of costs, not a major source of extra profit for the agent.

§13.5 CONTROL OF CASH FLOW

Just as during the construction period of the project the lenders only allow drawings to be made and costs to be paid when they are satisfied that these are for the budgeted and approved purposes (cf. §13.3.2), similarly, during the operating period, the lenders normally control the application of the cash flow of the project by controlling the way in which the cash is used. These controls include:

- an order of priorities in applying cash, known as the "cascade" (cf. §13.5.1)
- requirements for the Project Company to establish reserve (or escrow) accounts (cf. §13.5.2)

- control on distributions of cash to investors (cf. §13.5.3)
- in some cases, cash sweep (cf. §13.5.4) or cash clawback requirements (cf. §13.5.5)

§13.5.1 THE CASH FLOW CASCADE

The controls for application of cash earned by the Project Company from its revenues are set out in a cash flow cascade (or "waterfall,") setting out the order of priorities for the use of this cash. A typical order of priorities is:

1: Payment of fuel or raw material and operating costs, including the O&M Contract (based on the agreed budgetary procedures—cf. §8.7.3) and taxes (i.e., all the costs the Project Company needs to pay to continue operating the project).
2: Fees and expenses due to the agent bank, security trustee, etc.
3: Interest on the debt and any swap or other hedging payments[1]
4: Debt repayments (to the "target" schedule if there is one—cf. §13.2.4)[1]
5: Payments to the Debt Service Reserve Account, and other Reserve Accounts (cf. §13.5.2)
6: Distributions to investors (cf. §13.5.3)
7: Cash sweep, if any (cf. §13.5.4)

Once all the funds required for the first category have been paid, remaining cash available is moved down to the second, and so on (like water flowing down a series of pools—hence the names for this system of cash flow allocation). It follows that if there is insufficient cash to pay the first 5 items, no cash is distributed to the investors. Items 6 and 7 are usually only paid half-yearly, during a limited time window after calculations of the Project Company's results and hence the lenders' cover ratios for the previous six months.

Revenues can flow into the cascade in two ways:

- Lenders may require the Project Company to segregate funds for the first category of costs in a separate Operating Account under the Project Company's day-to-day control, leaving the other funds in a Revenue Account under the joint control of the agent bank or security trustee and the Project Company until the other cascade payments need to be made.
- Alternatively, all revenues may flow into one account, from which the cascade payments are made by the Project Company when required.

The latter is obviously preferable for the Project Company and generally more

---

[1] These may be accumulated on a month-by-month basis in a Debt Payment Reserve Account (see below).

practical for day-to-day operations, but the lenders have to be comfortable with trusting the Project Company not to misapply revenues on a short-term basis.

It should be noted that this cascade arrangement is largely dormant during the construction of the project, when funds from equity and debt are paid into the Disbursement Account (cf. §13.3.2).

§13.5.2 RESERVE ACCOUNTS

Lenders require the Project Company to establish separate Reserve Accounts (also known as "control" or "escrow" accounts) into which various sums of money are held. Although these are in the Project Company's name, withdrawal of funds from these requires the consent of the agent bank or security trustee, and the balances in these Reserve Accounts form part of the lenders' security.

The Reserve Accounts provide security against short-term cash flow problems and are also established if funds need to be set aside for major expenditure in future. They also segregate funds such as insurance proceeds, which are to be used for a particular purpose. (Some of the Reserve Accounts may come higher up the cash flow cascade than shown above, depending on lenders' views of the key priorities for cash allocation.)

Insofar as Reserve Accounts are built up, the investors' return decreases, as they prevent or delay distribution of net cash flow. Assuming that the Reserve Accounts are being established anyway, the Sponsors' main concern will be that the Project Company should not be left in the position of having insufficient cash to carry on its normal business, while other cash is trapped in Reserve Accounts.

Some of the standard Reserve Accounts are:

Debt Service Reserve Account (DSRA). This account contains sufficient funds to pay the next debt service (principal and interest) installment, usually six months' worth of debt service. If the Project Company cannot pay some or all of the debt service from its normal cash flow (or a Debt Payment Reserve Account, if any), funds are taken out of this account to do so.

The DSRA has to be established at the beginning of the operating period. There are two ways of doing this:
- Including the DSRA as part of the construction cost budget for the project
- Funding the DSRA from operating cash flow under the cascade (which means that it is not filled up at COD, but as cash flow comes in from initial operations)

The first approach is preferable from the investors' point of view, because most of the funds required for the DSRA are funded by the lenders (i.e., *pro rata* to the debt portion of the debt : equity ratio). It also has the benefit from the lenders' point of view that they know that the DSRA is funded as soon as the project begins operation. As a halfway house between these two alternative approaches, the Project Company may be allowed to draw funds for the DSRA at COD from the contingency fund, so long as the unused funding at that time is not needed for any other purpose.

To improve their IRR the Sponsors may provide the lenders with a bank L/C or, if acceptable, corporate guarantees, for the amount of the DSRA, which avoids this cash being trapped in the Project Company.

Some lenders may accept the provision of an Interest Reserve Account only (i.e., with a balance equal to the next interest payment due), coupled with the establishment of a Debt Payment Reserve Account.

Debt Payment Reserve Account. This account may be used to accumulate funds on a month-by-month basis to pay the next installment of principal and interest, instead of leaving the funds in the Project Company's operating account (usually if the Project Company's revenues flow into one account, instead of being split into Operating and Revenue Accounts as described in §13.5.1). If so, the account is emptied at the end of each payment period to pay the interest and principal installment then due.

Maintenance Reserve Account. If a project has a major maintenance cycle (e.g., the plant has to be maintained every 5 years, with most of the maintenance costs thus being incurred every 5 years rather than annually), these payments are "smoothed out" by placing one-fifth of the estimated maintenance costs in the Maintenance Reserve Account every year, and then drawing on the account to pay for the maintenance in year 5 (cf. §8.7.5).

Tax and other "smoothing" Reserve Accounts. If the Project Company incurs a significant tax liability in one year, but does not have to pay the tax until a later year, a Tax Reserve Account is normally established to set aside the cash for this purpose. Other "smoothing" Reserve Accounts of this nature may be established to cover significant deferred liabilities or irregular costs.

Insurance Proceeds Account. A separate Reserve Account may be established into which the proceeds of insurance claims are paid, and from which amounts are paid under the lenders' control for restoration of the project or reduction of the debt (cf. §7.6.4). Similar accounts may be used for other types of compensation received by the Project Company, such as LDs. In these accounts, where money has been received for a specific purpose, the cash does not flow through the cascade, but directly into the account.

Reserve Accounts and Cover Ratio Calculations. In calculating the ADSCR (cf. §12.9.1) and LLCR (cf. §12.9.2), payments to Reserve Accounts other than for debt service are treated as a deduction from the operating cash flow in the period concerned, and drawings from such accounts (e.g., to pay maintenance costs) are added back to the cash flow (and hence offset the actual expenditure). Payments to and from the DSRA are ignored in the ADSCR calculation (which is intended to show the Project Company's ability to service its debt on a regular basis without using reserves).

The balance on the DSRA is normally deducted from the debt outstanding in calculating the LLCR (cf. §12.9.2), on the basis that this cash could be used for immediate repayment of the loan.

The Project Company may argue that balances on other Reserve Accounts such as that for maintenance should also be deducted in the LLCR calculation for the same reason; lenders may, however, point out that this cash is not intended for debt reduction.

Interest earned on Reserve Accounts is normally added to the operating income when calculating cover ratios, unless the balance of the Reserve Account concerned is below the minimum required (which would mean that the interest earned cannot be taken out of the Reserve Account).

§13.5.3 Controls on Distributions to Investors

The investors come at the bottom of the cash flow cascade; once operating costs, and all the lenders' repayment and Reserve Account requirements have been met, in principle distributions to investors can be made. (In this context, distributions includes interest or repayments on the investors' subordinated debt, as well as payment of dividends or any repayment of equity.) If the Project Company cannot immediately pay these amounts over to the investors (e.g., because there may be a delay before the annual general meeting can be held and a dividend declared), they are paid into a Shareholder Distribution Account in the name of the Project Company (which should be outside the lenders' security package).

But it is seldom quite as simple as seeing if there is any cash left over and paying it to the investors: there are other hurdles to jump.

The Project Company obviously has to demonstrate that sufficient cash will remain or be generated in the future to repay debt after the distributions have been made. This is dealt with by establishing "dividend stop" or "lock-up" ratios; for example, if the Base Case projected average ADSCR was 1.35:1, distributions cannot be made if the previous year's actual ADSCR is lower than, say, 1.2:1. The calculation of whether there is sufficient cash to make distributions is usually carried out once every six months (and hence distributions are only made every six months). If cash flow cannot be distributed because dividend stop ratio requirements are not met, any cash available may be used to reduce the debt or held in a special Reserve Account, until the cover ratio calculations again fall on the right side of the line after allowing for the debt reduction or funds held in the special Reserve Account.

An issue in calculating the dividend stop ratio is whether "forward-looking" ratios (i.e., the projected ADSCR for the next year or the LLCR or average ADSCR as projected for the rest of the loan) should be also used for this purpose. Once the project is operating, the best way of projecting how it will operate in the future is to look at how it has actually operated in the past, but in that case the actual ADSCRs achieved are what should mainly concern lenders. Especially in a project with a regular assured cash flow under a Project Agreement, it is difficult to conceive why the projections of cash flow for the next year should be much lower than those for the last year (predictable fluctuations, e.g., maintenance, should be dealt with using Reserve Accounts). Therefore, although beloved by lenders, forward looking ratios are largely a waste of time in this situation, and doing away with them also eliminated the problem of deciding what assumptions should be used in the financial projections for this purpose (cf. §12.10). If a Project Company is selling a commodity into the open market or taking full usage risk in a transportation project, there is more of a case for forward-looking ratios.

The Project Company will have to fulfill further requirements before making distributions, in particular no event of default (cf. §13.11) should have occurred under the Project Contracts or the financing documentation.

§13.5.4 CASH SWEEP

In some projects a cash sweep may apply; after an agreed-upon level of distribution to the investors, the balance of the cash flow is used to prepay the debt or split between prepayment and a further distribution to the investors. Thus if the project performs according to the agreed Base Case, the investors will receive the Base Case return, but cash flow from the project above this level is split between investors and debt repayment.

This approach is normally used if there are likely to be substantial fluctuations in cash flow (e.g., because of commodity price movements), and the lenders wish to ensure that some of the surplus cash generated in good times is used to reduce debt and so provide a buffer against a downturn.

A cash sweep is also very useful as part of a package of measures dealing with problems that lenders might otherwise have with the total length of the financing, or because they are concerned about the "tail" risk (cf. §12.9.4 / §12.9.5). In such cases most or all of the cash flow generated after debt service is not distributed to the investors, but is used for debt prepayment, or placed in a Reserve Account.

For example, suppose the lenders have been asked to provide a 16-year loan, but really only feel comfortable with a 15-year loan, because the Offtake Contract only runs for 16 years and so a 16-year loan would have no contract tail. In such a case a 16-year loan repayment schedule is agreed to, but a partial cash sweep may be applied from, say, year 12, such that a large enough cash reserve is built up to pay off the balance of the loan at the end of year 15. This reserve could be released by the lenders to the investors if the Project Company manages to extend the Project Agreement beyond 16 years or if cover ratios at a higher level are achieved during the final years (say an ADSCR of 1.5 : 1 instead of 1.3 : 1), so ensuring there is plenty of cash to cover the final loan installments.

Similarly, the lenders may not want to lend for more than, say, 12 years in the country where the project is located, whereas the Project Company needs a 15-year repayment to make the project viable. In this case, the Project Company may agree to a cash sweep from, say, year 10 of a 12-year loan, whose repayment schedule is based on that of a 15-year loan with a "balloon" payment of the outstanding balance after 12 years. This is, in the expectation that when the time comes the lenders will be prepared to waive the cash sweep requirement and lend for a longer term. In such cases the interest margin may also increase sharply from year 10, to encourage refinancing if agreement is not reached with the original lender.

It might seem that the Project Company could achieve the same result by just borrowing the funds for the period the lenders are actually prepared to lend for (15 years in the first case or 12 in the second). However, in this case the repayment schedules are unlikely to be as attractive; the lenders would require a higher level of repayments in the early years of the loan, instead of relying on the cash sweep at the end.

In some projects it may be known that costs have to be incurred a long time in future, which are too substantial to be covered by setting aside spare cash in a Maintenance Reserve Account. For example, a road project may require a major resurfacing of the road after 15 years, and the cost of this is to be covered by tolls or Tariff payments over the following 15 years. The initial loan may run for 20 – 25 years (i.e., past the date when additional funding will obviously be needed). It is likely to be very difficult to fix the costs of the major works 15 years in advance, and raising debt that would not be used for 15 years is virtually impossible. Again, the solution may again be a cash sweep arrangement beginning several years before the date for the major works, to encourage the Sponsors to refinance the loan and raise the additional debt required when it becomes feasible at that time.

§13.5.5 Cash Clawback

If there is some uncertainty about future costs (e.g., a major maintenance) or revenues, lenders may still be prepared to allow investors to take cash distributions out of the Project Company, provided a clawback undertaking is given. Under such an undertaking, the Sponsors agree that if the possible future cash flow problem develops, they will repay or lend to the Project Company up to the amount they have received in dividends or other distributions over a set period of time.

In a similar way, investors can offer a guarantee or bank L/C for the amount that would otherwise have been placed in a Reserve Account, in return for the lenders allowing this cash to be distributed.

§13.6 DEBT PREPAYMENTS AND REFINANCING

A cash sweep is a form of mandatory (compulsory) prepayment of the loan by the Project Company. Other mandatory prepayments are normally required:

- If the Project Company realizes cash from the sale of assets (unless the cash is used to replace the asset)
- If performance LDs are received from the EPC Contractor (prepayment is made to the extent necessary to maintain the lenders' cover ratios; any surplus LDs flow into the cash flow cascade—note that delay LDs flow straight into the cascade)
- If insurance proceeds are not applied to the restoration of the project

In these cases the cash is applied directly to prepayment rather than passed through the cascade.

A mandatory prepayment of the loan is required if it becomes illegal for the lenders to continue with it; this is usually meant to cover the possibility of international sanctions against the country in which the Project Company is located. (The obligation may be limited to prepayment insofar as the Project Company has available cash flow.)

The Project Company may also wish to reduce or prepay part or all of the loan voluntarily:

- The total funding raised may not all be needed (cf. §13.6.1).
- Cash distribution restrictions imposed by the lenders or for other reasons may make it cost effective for the investors to prepay part of the (expensive) debt rather than have funds trapped in the Project Company, which raises the issue of which loan installments such prepayments should be applied against (cf. §13.6.2).
- The Project Company may wish to prepay the whole loan and refinance it on more attractive terms elsewhere (cf. §13.6.3).

§13.6.1 LOAN COMMITMENT REDUCTION

As construction of the project progresses, the Project Company may consider that it will not need all the funding raised for the project (including the contingency funding), and it could save commitment fees by reducing the committed amount of the debt, perhaps also reducing its investors' risks (and increasing their return) by reducing the committed equity *pro rata*.

In principle, lenders should not object to this, so long as the Project Company can demonstrate that after the reduction there will be enough funds to complete the project as scheduled, with an adequate remaining safety margin. It is therefore unlikely that lenders would allow reduction in committed funding until quite a late stage in the construction of the project.

§13.6.2 PARTIAL PREPAYMENT

Bank lenders should normally accept prepayment of part of the loan once the project is in operation: the only exception to this may be with a public-sector lender, for whom unexpected payment of part of the loan causes problems with the internal bureaucracy. Breakage costs need to be covered. Partial prepayment is not normally allowed in bond issues.

The main question with a partial prepayment (whether voluntary or mandatory) is, against which future loan payment installments should it be applied? If, for example, a prepayment of 120 is made on a loan of 500 due to be repaid in five future annual installments, the prepayment could be applied in any of the ways shown in Table 13.7.

Provided that surplus cash flow can be distributed, application of prepayments in order of maturity is most beneficial to investors, since this releases the cash for future distributions more quickly. This approach is the fairest if the Project Company has made a free choice to prepay the loan because of temporary constraints on distributions to investors. Lenders, on the other hand, may wish to reduce the average life of their loan, and hence their risk on the project, by applying prepayments in inverse order of maturity. Some types of prepayment must be applied *pro rata* if they are going to work (e.g., the EPC Contractor's performance LDs are applied *pro rata* to all installments, to maintain the lender's ADSCRs at an even level). It may therefore be necessary to specify different applications of partial prepayments depending on the circumstances in which they are made.

§13.6.3 REFINANCING

Prepayment of the whole of the debt before it reaches its final maturity, to allow for a refinancing, is very common in project finance (cf. §6.9.1) because it can considerably improve the original investors' return (cf. §12.12.4). Therefore, just as investors may have a strategy for realizing value by sale of part of their equity when the project moves to a lower level of risk (e.g., on completion—cf. §12.12.3), so the Project Company should consider a strategy for refinancing even before the original loan is signed.

Table 13.7

Order of Prepayment

		Remaining loan payment installments after prepayment in:		
	Original schedule	– order of maturity	– inverse order of maturity	– *pro rata*
Year 1	100	—	100	76
2	100	80	100	76
3	100	100	100	76
4	100	100	80	76
5	100	100	—	76
Total	500	380	380	380

In most project financings bank lenders are generally prepared to accept a refinancing at any stage, but they may require a refinancing fee (typically 0.5–1.0% of the amount refinanced) if it occurs during construction and perhaps in the first year or two of operation. It should be noted that although bank lenders are flexible on prepayment, bond investors are generally not, or at least any prepayment of a bond is only likely to be allowed on payment of a more substantial penalty (cf. §9.2.1). ECAs that charge an upfront premium covering their risk over the whole life of the financing (cf. §11.3.3) were traditionally unwilling to refund any of this premium when the debt was repaid early by a refinancing, but this approach is now changing.

A more complex situation arises if the Project Company wishes to partially refinance a loan with a another loan or a bond, as this raises intercreditor issues (cf. §13.13), or, for example, to introduce European Investment Bank funding where commercial bank lenders would be asked to convert part of their loan into a guarantee for commercial risks (cf. §11.6.9). If provision is not made for this in advance, the original lenders will be able to hold the Project Company to ransom (i.e., extract additional fees or unfair improvements in their own lending terms) in return for their agreement to add new debt.

It might reasonably be asked why it is necessary to arrange such long-term loans if refinancing, especially after completion of the project, is so common. The answer is that in some markets it is not necessary; in the United States, for example, banks will provide short-term construction loans, which are taken out by long-term permanent loans or bond issues, on completion. The initial loan is usually arranged to mature 2–3 years after completion of construction (making it what is known as a "mini-perm") to allow flexibility of timing for the refinancing, the refinancing in such cases often being with a bond issue. In a mini-perm, any principal repayments after completion of construction are based on, say, a 15-year schedule, but cut off after 3–5 years, so giving rise to a residual (or "balloon") repayment of the balance of the loan. Some 85% of project financings in the United

States in 2000 were structured as 3–5-year mini-perms. This approach is, however, only viable in a sophisticated financing market, where banks are happy that there is no significant refinancing risk and the project can accommodate or hedge the risk of higher interest rates at the time of the refinancing, which is more difficult for a highly-leveraged financing. (It also reflects an unwillingness in the U.S. banking market to offer much longer term loans.)

In many otherwise sophisticated markets, banks are still unwilling to accept the refinancing risk for a loan with a balloon maturity. Given the extensive experience of refinancing in project finance translations, this generally unsophisticated approach is surprising. Logically, either the project will go well, in which case it will be refinanced, or it will go badly, in which case repayments will not be made, but in either case few long-term project finance loans run for the whole of the original loan term. (This issue may be partly dealt with by a cash sweep arrangement—cf. §13.5.4.)

The other party who may have a view on refinancing is an Offtaker or Contracting Authority under a Project Agreement (cf. §6.9.1).

§13.7 SECURITY

As already discussed (cf. §2.2), lenders do not expect to be able to get their money back by selling the Project Company's assets, as in most project financings only the cash flow of a successful continuing operation will provide this repayment. Foreclosure on project assets is seldom a solution to a problem with the project; however, security over the project as a whole remains important:

- To ensure the lenders are involved at an early stage if the project begins to go wrong
- To ensure that third parties (such as unsecured creditors) do not gain any prior or *pari passu* rights over the project assets
- To ensure that project assets are not disposed of without the lenders' agreement
- Generally, to enable the lenders to encourage cooperation by the Project Company if it gets into trouble

The lenders' security normally has four layers:

- Control of cash flow (cf. §13.5)
- The ability to step-in to the project under Direct Agreements (cf. §7.7)
- Mortgages and assignments of the Project Company's assets and contracts (cf. §13.7.1)
- Security over the Project Company's shares (cf. §13.7.2)

§13.7.1 MORTGAGES AND CONTRACT ASSIGNMENTS

There is seldom any substantial disagreement between Sponsors and lenders about the latter's right to take security over all physical assets, contractual rights, and guarantees, which the Project Company has. The security package therefore includes:

- Mortgages or charges over the project site, buildings, and equipment
- Assignment of Project Contracts, including advisory contracts with parties such as the Owner's Engineer, and any bonds or guarantees for these contracts
- Assignment of Permits and licenses
- Charges over project bank accounts, including Reserve Accounts, with dual signatures from the Project Company and the agent bank or security trustee required where lender approval is needed to transfer funds from an account
- Undertaking by the Offtaker or Contracting Authority, if any, to make payments only to the Reserve Accounts (if this is not covered in a Direct Agreement)
- Assignment of insurance policies (cf. §7.6.4)
- Assignment of the Project Company's right to receive any payment due to it if the interest swap is unwound (cf. §9.2.1)
- Assignment of the Project Company's right to receive payments of equity from the Sponsors

Problems may arise however if third-party cooperation is needed to create or make this security effective:

- If the project is on a BOT/BTO basis (i.e., the Project Company does not own the project land and buildings, and any right to use them terminates if the Project Agreement is terminated), then the lenders clearly cannot take a mortgage over them and must rely primarily on contract assignments.
- Consent to assignments by the other parties to Project Contracts may not be forthcoming. (If possible, this should be covered by ensuring there are appropriate provisions in the original contract documentation for Direct Agreements.)
- It may not be possible to assign Permits or licenses as security; some countries may not allow some types of Permits or licenses to be assigned because they are granted to a specific permit or license holder (Direct Agreements may provide some support in such cases).

Since the Project Company's assets are in the Host Country, the security over them usually has to be governed by local law and jurisdiction (unlike the situation that may apply to the Project Contracts or financing documentation, cf. §10.7.1). In developed countries this approach does not normally cause any difficulties, although good local legal advisers are of course necessary. However, in some developing countries the lenders may not be able to achieve an ideal security position:

- The local law may prevent foreigners from owning land, and so the lenders cannot take over the Project Company's rights in this respect.
- High levels of stamp duty or similar *ad valorem* taxes may be charged on registration of lenders' loans or security, adding significantly to the financing costs payable by the Project Company.
- There may be preferential creditors (such as tax payments) that automatically rank ahead of the lenders' security.
- Lenders may only be able to register security over assets that already exist, not those that will be acquired or constructed in future.
- Lenders may only be able to register their security for a fixed amount, leaving a risk that the total amount payable on default may be higher when interest, breakage costs, and enforcement costs are included.
- Lenders may only be able to register their security in the local currency, with the risk the lenders may become undersecured if the local currency depreciates against the currency in which they are lending (cf. §9.3.4).
- The procedures for enforcing security may be too cumbersome for lenders who want to be able to take over control of the project quickly; in particular, lenders may be required to sell the assets in a public auction or after a court action rather than take over their control and operation through an administrator or receiver.
- Exchange controls may hinder the lenders from removing enforcement proceeds from the country.

Security may have to be taken in several different jurisdictions apart from that of the Host Country; if Reserve Accounts are held offshore (cf. §10.3.3), then the security must be registered under the law of the country where they are held; the same applies if the shares of an offshore holding company are pledged to the lenders.

In common law countries such as England and Australia, it is possible to have a "floating charge" over the Project Company's assets. This does not require registration of security against each specific asset and contract but nonetheless gives security over all of them, which crystallizes when enforcement proceedings are taken.

If for some reason the lenders cannot be granted a security over project assets, the Project Company must give a "negative pledge" undertaking (i.e., not to pledge the assets concerned to anyone else). This is obviously of limited value compared to a proper security interest and is only acceptable to lenders if the Project Company does not own the physical assets because it is operating under a BOT/BTO contract.

§13.7.2 SECURITY OVER PROJECT COMPANY SHARES

Lenders normally take security over the Sponsors' shares in the Project Company. This is to enable the lenders to step in more quickly to take over management of the Project Company than may be achieved by taking action under mortgages or contract assignments. There may be some difficulties with this:

- A Sponsor's corporate lenders may impose negative pledge provisions, under which the Sponsor is not to give security over its assets to any third party. This may prevent a pledge being given over the Project Company's shares.
- As discussed above, cumbersome court procedures may make enforcement of a pledge over the shares too slow.
- There is a potential problem if the Sponsors wish to take out political risk insurance to protect their investment (cf. §11.4.1).

As for the former problem, it may be necessary for the Sponsor to negotiate a waiver of this provision in the case of its Project Company shares. There are various possible ways of dealing with the second problem:

- Lenders take security over the shares of an offshore holding company, owned by the investors, and in a more creditor-friendly jurisdiction, which owns the shares in the Project Company, thus enabling the lenders to take control of the Project Company quickly through taking control of its only shareholder. (Care needs to be taken that there are no other creditors of the Project Company who could interfere with this process, and that the intermediate holding company has no debt, even to its own shareholders, or these creditors will have first call on its assets, i.e., the Project Company's shares, at the expense of the Project Company's lenders.)
- Lenders take a call option over the Project Company's shares (i.e., the Sponsors agree to sell the shares to the lenders for a nominal sum if the loan goes into default).
- Sponsors give the lenders a "golden share" that allows them to appoint directors if the loan is in default.

The latter two approaches may cause regulatory difficulties for banks and may create legal liabilities if the lenders become directly involved in management of the Project Company.

Lenders will also wish to ensure that the Project Company is not affected by financial difficulties or even bankruptcy of a Sponsor or another investor (i.e., it is "bankruptcy remote"). For example, if a Sponsor is made bankrupt this should not result in its Project Company subsidiary or affiliate being made bankrupt as well, or remove the benefit of a pledge of the Project Company's shares. Depending on the location of the project and Project Company, it may be necessary to insert an intermediary company between the Sponsor(s) and the Project Company to reduce this risk.

§13.8 FINANCIAL CLOSE—CONDITIONS PRECEDENT

Signature of the financing documentation alone does not mean that the lenders will start advancing funds to the Project Company. In order to draw down any debt at all, the project must first reach Financial Close. This is the date at which all Project Contracts and financing documentation have been signed, and the conditions precedent to the effectiveness of the lenders' commitments have been satisfied or waived. The conditions precedent are effectively a checklist of documents the lenders require as the basis for their financing; when these are provided the lenders are obliged to advance funds. (This does not mean that lenders have no obligations before that date; for example, if the financing documentation requires the lenders to keep information about the project confidential, this is effective on signing.)

The list of conditions precedent documentation for a project finance can be of immense length, often running into several hundred documents and certificates. Typical requirements by lenders (all of which must be satisfactory to them in form and content) include:

- Corporate documentation
  - Corporate documentation, board resolutions, etc., for the Project Company
  - Similar corporate documentation for any other parties to Project Contracts or financing documentation, and providers of guarantees, bonding, or other security
  - Signed copies of the Shareholder Agreement(s) relating to the Project Company (cf. §4.5.2)
- Project documentation
  - Evidence of title to (or right to use) the project site
  - Signed copies of all the Project Contracts and evidence that all their conditions precedent have been fulfilled and that they are in full force and effect
  - Contract guarantees, bonds, or other security
  - Signed Direct Agreements (cf. §7.7)
  - Permits for the financing, construction, and operation of the project (cf. 7.4)
  - NTP given to the EPC Contractor (cf. §7.1.2)
  - Arrangements for construction of third party facilities and connections (cf. §8.5.8)

- Financing documentation
  - Signature of all financing documentation:
    - Bank loan agreement, agency agreement
    - Bond terms and conditions and trust deed
    - Fee letters, covering payment of arranging and underwriting fees
    - Any Sponsor Support Services Agreements or other guarantees (cf. 8.11)
  - Security documentation (cf. §13.7)
  - Registration of security
- Financial due diligence
  - Evidence that all investor funding (equity or subordinated debt) has been paid or committed and any security for this is in place
  - Evidence that any other parallel financing arrangements are in place and effective
  - Evidence that interest swap or other hedging arrangements are in place (cf. §9.2), if these have to be concluded immediately at Financial Close
  - Evidence that the Reserve Accounts and other banking arrangements are in place
  - Evidence that the required insurance is in place (cf. §7.6.1)
  - Up-to-date financial statements for relevant parties
  - Final reports from the Lenders' Engineer, insurance advisers, and any other advisers (cf. 5.4)
  - The financial model (cf. §5.1.6)
  - Model Auditor's report (including report on tax aspects of the project)
  - Final construction and funding budget and drawdown schedule (cf. §12.4)
  - Base Case projections (cf. §12.10)
- Legal due diligence
  - Legal opinions from lenders' lawyers (and in some jurisdictions also from borrowers' lawyers)
  - Confirmation that no event of default (cf. §13.11) has occurred
  - The Project Company is not the subject of any litigation

Some of these conditions precedent are circular in nature (e.g., the right to issue a notice to proceed to the EPC Contractor may be dependent on Financial Close having been reached, and Financial Close cannot be reached until the NTP has been issued). In such cases the legal advisers to the various parties arrange a simultaneous closing of the documentation.

The period between the signature of loan documentation and finally achieving Financial Close can become very lengthy. It is the Sponsors' responsibility to manage this process effectively, preferably by gathering as much of the condition precedent documentation as possible in advance of the loan signing, to ensure the minimum delay before Financial Close. Agreeing to conditions precedent documentation before signing the financing also ensures that there are no unexpected surprises from issues raised by lenders after the loan has been signed.

There may be further conditions precedent to each individual drawing of the debt (cf. §13.3.2), in particular:

- Confirmation by the Project Company and the Lenders' Engineer that the amounts payable to the EPC Contractor are properly due and that the construction remains on schedule
- That other amounts to be paid from the drawing are within the agreed construction budget (cf. §8.5.4)
- That enough funds remain to complete construction
- That continuing representations and warranties (cf. §13.9) remain correct
- That no change of law has taken place (cf. §10.6)
- That no event of default or potential event of default has occurred (cf. §13.11)

Lenders may also require that no material adverse change (MAC) to the project should have occurred after the financial documentation was signed, as a condition precedent both to Financial Close and subsequent drawings of the debt (this is known as a MAC clause). The problem with this kind of vague general provision is the Project Company may be left vulnerable to an arbitrary decision by the lenders to stop funding the project. Careful legal drafting is needed to ensure that if a MAC clause is inserted it is reasonably objective and limited in nature (cf. 13.11).

§13.9 REPRESENTATIONS AND WARRANTIES

The facts that form the basis of the lenders' provision of the project finance are set out and confirmed in representations and warranties given by the Project Company in the financing documentation. As these are the basis for the financing, if any of the representations and warranties are later found to be incorrect this will create an event of default (cf. §13.11).

In effect, the representations and warranties are a check list of the key elements that lenders need to review in their due diligence to confirm that they are satisfied with the risks of the financing. (The Project Contracts also have extensive representations and warranties, e.g. from the EPC Contractor, which the lenders also review.) Typical representation and warranties provisions in the finance documentation are that the Project Company:

- Is duly incorporated and has the power and has taken all necessary corporate actions to undertake the project and the financing

- Is owned by the Sponsors in the proportions approved by the lenders
- Has no business, assets, or subsidiaries, nor any contractual obligations, except those relating to the project (all of which have been disclosed to the lenders)
- Has the capacity to enter into the various Project Contracts and other agreements, and that all these are legally valid and in effect, with no defaults outstanding; no event of *force majeure* has occurred affecting the Project Company or any Project Contracts
- Has title to its property and all rights required to construct and operate the project
- Has obtained all licenses and Permits required for the project and these are still valid
- Is in compliance with the law in all respects and has paid all taxes due
- Has not made, nor have the Sponsors nor any other party made, any corrupt payment (this is of particular concern under the U.S. Foreign Corrupt Practices Act of 1977, often referred to as FCPA, and in other countries with similar legislation)
- Is not in breach of any existing agreements
- Is not insolvent, and there is no litigation outstanding or threatened against it
- Has no other debt, and the lenders have a valid prior charge over the Project Company's assets through their security arrangements; there are no other security claims on project assets.
- Has provided complete and accurate information on the project in an information memorandum (cf. §5.1.8), or by other means. The Project Company should only take responsibility for information that it provides directly, and not, e.g., summaries of the Project Contracts prepared by the Lead Manager(s) and their lawyers. (This provision can be a problem if the loan is underwritten by banks who will syndicate it with an information memorandum later; the undertaking may then have to apply to an information memorandum to be issued in the future, which the Project Company has not yet seen: this can be dealt with by giving the Project Company some degree of control over the parts of the information memorandum for which it is takes responsibility.)
- Has provided complete and accurate financial statements, and no significant changes have occurred since the date of the statements
- Has prepared budgets and projections in good faith using reasonable assumptions
- Believes that completion of the project will take place by the agreed date

Insofar as any of these statements are not correct when the representation is to be made, or the Project Company cannot fully subscribe to them, it must notify the lenders accordingly, and the latter may decide to waive the requirement (temporarily or permanently). If requirements are to be fulfilled later (e.g., obtaining an operating permit), this may be covered in the covenants (cf. §13.10).

For its own protection, the Project Company may wish to exclude responsibility for "immaterial" errors in its representations and warranties (e.g., if a parking ticket for the plant manager's car has not been paid, does this mean the Project Company is not in compliance with the law?). Lenders are unlikely to accept any significant watering down of their requirement for the Project Company to take full responsibility for the basis behind the financing.

The Sponsors themselves may also be required to provide similar representations and warranties directly to the lenders; if so, the debt becomes a limited-recourse loan, in the sense that the Sponsors may be liable for a loss suffered by the lenders relying on a representation that is not correct. The Sponsors should therefore ensure that their liability in this respect relates only to things under their direct control (e.g., their ownership of the Project Company).

These representations and warranties are made on signing of the financing documentation and are usually deemed to be repeated at Financial Close; they may also be deemed to be repeated when each drawing is made, and on each interest payment or loan repayment date: if they are found incorrect at any of these times, it will be an event of default.

§13.10 COVENANTS

Covenants are undertakings by the Project Company either to take certain actions ("positive" or "affirmative" covenants), or not to do certain things ("negative" or "protective" covenants). These undertakings by the Project Company are a characteristic of project finance, being more comprehensive and detailed than usually found in other types of financing. (These controls are typically less stringent for a bond issue—cf. §5.3.) It is through the covenants that the lenders exercise their continuing control over the construction and operation of the project, but they may need to take care that this control does not also make them liable for Project Company obligations to third parties; for example, in the United Kingdom, if lenders are deemed to have acted as "shadow directors" of an insolvent company, this could create liability for them towards other creditors.

The main purposes of the covenants are:

- To ensure that the project is constructed and operated as agreed with the lenders
- To give lenders advance warning of any problems that might affect the Project Company
- To protect the lenders' security

If the Project Company is not able to comply with a covenant, for what the lenders consider to be a good reason, a temporary or permanent waiver of the requirement can be given (cf. §13.12). Since many lenders have to go through a formal credit approval procedure for even quite small waivers of this type, the covenants on the Project Company should not be so restrictive that it has to keep requesting such waivers.

§13.10.1 POSITIVE COVENANTS

Typical positive covenants by the Project Company include obligations to:

- Maintain its corporate existence, make all required corporate filings, and pay taxes when due
- Construct, operate and maintain the project in accordance with the Project Contracts, applicable law, and good industry practice
- Provide the agent or security trustee and lenders' advisers with reasonable access to the project and its records
- Maintain the management structure agreed with the lenders
- Obtain and maintain the agreed project insurances (cf. §7.6)
- Supply copies of management accounts (usually quarterly) and annual audited financial statements
- Supply reports (usually monthly) on the progress of construction, including achievement of milestone dates, percentage completion, critical-path issues, and expected completion date (these reports are usually produced by, or based on information from, the EPC Contractor)
- Apply funding (equity and debt) in the agreed order (cf. §13.3.1) and only for the purposes agreed in the construction and funding budget (cf. §8.5.4 / §12.4)
- Ensure that COD is achieved by the agreed date (cf. §8.5.6). The definition of project completion for this purpose may be wider than that in the EPC Contract, or a Project Agreement, especially if there is a limited-recourse completion guarantee from Sponsors (cf. §8.12); in such cases, beside physical completion as required under the Project Contracts, the Project Company may also, e.g., have to achieve a minimum ADSCR to denominate that it can operate profitably.)
- Achieve the agreed debt : equity ratio at the end of the construction period (cf. §13.1.4)
- Provide annual budgets in advance of each operating year (cf. §8.7.3)
- Apply all revenues in accordance with the cash flow cascade (cf. §13.5.1)
- Supply reports (usually quarterly) on the operating performance of the project (covering issues such as availability and output for a process plant, traffic

flows for an infrastructure project, any unscheduled maintenance, *force majeure* events, etc.)

- Supply revised financial projections (usually every half-year during operation of the project) (cf. §12.10)
- Notify the agent bank or security trustee of any significant interruption in the operation of the project or supply of fuel, raw materials or other essential utilities
- Notify the agent bank or security trustee of any insurance claims
- Notify the agent bank or security trustee of any event of default (cf. §13.11), dispute under the Project Contracts, or litigation or other claims
- Enforce all its rights under the Project Contracts
- Indemnify the lenders against any claim arising from environmental liabilities related to the project
- Obtain all Permits required in future for construction and operation of the project (cf. §7.4)
- Notify the agent bank or security trustee of any change of law affecting the project (cf. §10.6) or withdrawal, failure to renew, or amendment of any Permit or license
- Take any action required to maintain the lenders' security interests (cf. §13.7)
- Pay for the costs of the lenders' advisers (cf. §5.4)

The Sponsors may also give separate undertakings to the lenders as to the maintenance of their ownership of the Project Company, provision of technical support, etc. (cf. §8.7.2).

§13.10.2 NEGATIVE COVENANTS

Typical negative covenants by the Project Company include undertakings not to:

- Undertake any business other than the project
- Amend its constitutional documents
- Merge or consolidate with any other entity
- Agree to any amendment, waiver, or change order in the Project Contracts, or any changes in the project itself (some scope may be given for *de minimis* amendments and waivers)
- Enter into any contracts (other than the agreed Project Contracts), subject to a *de minimis* exception
- Use its cash balances to make any investment (surplus funds are normally held in interest-bearing Reserve Accounts, although in more sophisticated markets the Project Company may be able to invest in an agreed list of short-term money market instruments if this does not jeopardize the lenders' security)

- Incur any additional debt or issue guarantees for third parties
- Enter into any hedging contracts other than the agreed hedging of interest rate or exchange rate risks (cf. §9.2 / §9.3.1)
- Incur any capital expenditure not agreed to by the lenders (even if it is funded by equity—this is to ensure the specifications of the project are not changed without lender consent)
- Incur operating costs not provided for in the agreed annual budget (usually subject to an agreed tolerance level—cf. §8.7.3)
- Sell, lease, or otherwise transfer any of its assets (subject to a *de minimis* exception)
- Change its financial year end or auditors

It can be seen from the above that the difference between positive and negative covenants is often a matter of wording; a positive covenant to maintain the management structure agreed with the lenders is the same as a negative covenant not to change the management structure agreed with the lenders.

§13.11 EVENTS OF DEFAULT

Project finance lenders do not want to have wait to take action until the Project Company has run out of funds to service the debt; they therefore create a defined set of "triggers" that gives them the right to take action against the Project Company. These are "events of default"—once an event of default has occurred, the Project Company is no longer able to manage the project without lender involvement. Some of these events (such as failure to pay, insolvency, etc.) would apply to any corporate financing, but others (such as failure to complete the project) are peculiar to project finance.

It should be noted that these events do not of themselves put the project in default (i.e., bring the financing to an end and allow the lenders to enforce their security): a positive decision to take this next stage of action has to be made by the lenders after the event of default has occurred (cf. §13.12). The threat of moving to this next stage gives the lenders a lever that ensures that they can sit at the table with the Project Company and other project counterparts to find a way out of the problem, which either exists already or is indicated by the trigger events to be on the horizon.

Typical events of default are:

- The Project Company fails to make any payment under the financing documentation on its due date
- Any representation or warranty made by the Project Company (or any other party such as a Sponsor) proves to have been incorrect or misleading
- The Project Company does not fulfill any of its covenants or undertakings under the finance documentation

- The Sponsors fail to fulfill any of their obligations or undertakings to the lenders or the Project Company
- There is any change in the ownership or control of the Project Company prior to an agreed date
- The Project Company, any Project Contract counterpart, or any Sponsor or other guarantor fails to pay any of its debts when due, or is subject to a court judgment for more than a *de minimis* amount, or to insolvency proceedings that are not discharged within a specified time
- The project will not be able to achieve COD by an agreed "long stop" date
- Insufficient funding remains to complete construction of the project
- Any Permit or license is revoked
- The project is abandoned (for more than a specified period of time) or becomes a total loss
- Any party defaults under a Project Contract, or the contract ceases to be in full force and effect
- The Project Company loses title to the project site
- Any of the lenders' security becomes invalid or unenforceable
- The latest ADSCR falls below a certain level; thus the initial Base Case average ADSCR (cf. §12.9.1) might be 1.35:1, the dividend stop level (cf. §13.5.3) 1.2:1, and this "default ratio" level 1.1:1; as with dividend stops, there is the issue of whether forward-looking ratios should be used in this context
- The Host Government expropriates the project (including creeping expropriation), declares a moratorium on its foreign currency debt, or restricts the conversion or transfer of foreign currency (if the Project Company has borrowed in foreign currency)

Lenders may also wish to add a MAC clause as an event of default. As already mentioned, a MAC clause may be used as a condition precedent to prevent the project reaching Financial Close, or subsequent drawing on the loan (cf. §13.8). Adding this to events of default widens the uncertainty for the Project Company and its investors; lenders often take the view, however, that they cannot foresee everything that might go wrong with the project, and they need a catch-all provision to fill any gaps. If the Project Company agrees to such a provision, a material adverse change should be carefully defined; such an event should have a material adverse effect on the ability of any party to the Project Contract to discharge its obligations, or on the Project Company's operations, assets, or financial condition, *and* materially affect either the Project Company's ability to service its debt or the lenders' security interests.

Lenders may wish to include "potential events of default," i.e., an event of default that can be foreseen but has not yet occurred, thus allowing early action on the lenders' part. This should be acceptable to the Project Company provided that it is quite clear that the occurrence of the event is only a matter of time.

The Project Company needs to secure periods of grace to remedy the events of default, if remedy is possible. Nonpayment is not the kind of default that can be allowed to drift on, and therefore a grace period of more than 2–3 business days (to allow for any technical problems in transfer of the funds through the banking system) is the normal maximum here. A reasonable period (say 30 days) should be given for other defaults that can be remedied; for example, failure to fulfill an undertaking to provide financial information.

Similarly, some materiality limitation may be reasonable for some of the events of default: for example, a representation or warranty should have been misleading in a material respect to make it an event of default. This is usually an issue of much debate between Project Company and lenders. For example, the latter may argue that the whole loan should not be placed in default just because it does not fulfill the covenant to deliver the management accounts by a certain date; however, the lenders are likely to consider the failure to produce management accounts in a reasonable period of time a symptom of something seriously wrong with the Project Company's operations, and therefore this should give them a basis to intervene. Lenders always make the point that they will not automatically use events of default to destroy the project (which is seldom in their interests), and that they are just there to get everybody around the table, but obviously once an event of default occurs, the Sponsors and Project Company are at a disadvantage in any discussions that take place with the lenders.

It will be seen that there is considerable potential for overlap between representations and warranties, covenants, and events of default, especially as a breach of a representation, warranty, or covenant is itself an event of default. There is little merit in duplication between them.

§13.12 WAIVERS, AMENDMENTS, AND ENFORCEMENT ON DEFAULT

Various courses of action are open to the lenders after an event of default, partly depending on what stage the project has reached:

- To waive (i.e., ignore) the event of default
- If the project is still under construction, to freeze any further drawings of funds—known as a "drawstop"
- If the project is operating, to require that all net cash flow be applied to reduction of debt or held in a separate reserve or escrow account under the lenders' control
- To enforce the lenders' security

Once the event of default has occurred it is entirely within the lenders' discretion which of these actions they choose to take. The Project Company may also ask the lenders to waive or amend a particular term of the financing documentation so it does not fall into default in the first place.

If there is a syndicate of banks or a group of bond holders providing the loan, there has to be a decision-making process, or one rogue lender could pull the house down by taking individual action against the Project Company while the rest are trying to find a solution. (Indeed, it is not unknown for a small lender to blackmail the larger ones by threatening to do this, so that the larger lenders will buy out the smaller lender's loan.) The agent bank or security trustee also needs to have clear instructions from the lenders as a whole on what action is to be taken on their behalf. Voting mechanisms therefore have to be agreed to in advance between lenders; the Project Company also has an interest in these arrangements, to try to ensure that one or two "hostile" lenders cannot dictate the action taken, against the wishes of the majority.

Voting arrangements need to cover:

- A decision to waive an event of default, so that no further action need be taken on the matter
- An advance waiver (i.e., permission to the Project Company to take an action that would otherwise be a default; e.g., to issue a change order to the EPC Contractor, sell an asset above the *de minimis* level set out in the covenants, or amend some aspect of the Project Contracts)
- Amendments to the financing documentation, both to correct errors and to change the provisions to avoid future defaults or allow the Project Company to make some change in the project
- Instructions to the agent bank or security trustee (e.g., to enforce security after an event of default)

Typical voting arrangements on such issues could be:

Waivers and permissions. These usually require a "normal" majority, usually 66⅔–75% of the lenders (by value of their participation in the finance), except for "fundamental" defaults such as nonpayment (and possibly fundamental changes to Project Contracts), for which 100% majority would be needed. (Individual banks may, however, retain the right to withhold further drawdowns if the Project Company is in default in the construction period, i.e., without a syndicate vote.)

Amendments to financing documents. Amendments that amend the lenders' security, repayment dates, repayment amounts, or interest rate require 100% consent; other amendments may be made with a 66⅔–75% vote.

Enforcement. If the required majority is not achieved for a waiver, the agent bank or security trustee issues a notice of default: the next stage is enforcement action against the project security; there can be a sliding scale of voting for this: 75% of the lenders must vote for enforcement within, say, 90 days of the notice of default, 66⅔% for the next 90 days, and 51% thereafter; however, some lenders may insist on the right to take individual enforcement action if the agent bank or security trustee does not do so once a notice of default has been issued, especially if the default is caused by nonpayment.

The main practical problem with any voting arrangement is that usually a bank lending as a relatively small participants in a syndicate does not want to be bothered with voting on small issues: for most banks, this means the loan officer having to prepare and explain a paper on the issue to the bank's credit department, and for a minor or technical waiver this is not a very productive use of the loan officer's time. Therefore, actually getting banks to vote at all is difficult. As a result, if the hurdles for voting majorities on day-to-day amendments and waivers are set too high, the Project Company's business can be paralyzed.

One solution to this problem of inertia in voting is the "silence equals consent" route; if, for example, a 75% majority is required, this can be achieved by getting a 75% majority of those lenders who actually vote by a defined deadline, not of all lenders. This approach is not just beneficial to the Project Company, since paralyzing the Project Company's business through voting inertia is seldom in the interests of the lenders as a whole. The issue becomes even more acute where there are a large number of bond investors involved, who are likely to be less concerned about such issues than banks. In such cases some decisions may be delegated to the agent for the commercial banks, if any, or a special agent for the bond holders.

If a commercial bank's loan has full cover from an ECA (cf. §11.3.1), the bank has to vote as the ECA directs, but if there is political risk cover only, the bank should be free to vote as it wishes because such votes normally deal with commercial issues. A similar principle applies where there is a guarantee from an IFI.

Having said this, however, an ECA or IFI will still expect to have a vote on any change in the project that could affect the risk it has agreed to take on. For example, if an ECA or IFI is relying on private-sector banks taking on the completion risks, these banks should have the right to make decisions on issues arising during the construction of the project, but not if these issues may affect the project's operation after completion. Thus drawing precise dividing lines between when the lenders can make their own decision and when the ECA or IFI's decision applies, may be a matter of some debate.

§13.13 INTERCREDITOR ISSUES

If the Project Company has one syndicate of lenders, they can act as a single block through the voting arrangements described above. But it is quite common to have more than one group of lenders, for example, a bank syndicate and bond investors, an ECA-backed loan and a bank syndicate lending without ECA cover, domestic banks and foreign banks.

Each of these groups will have their own loan agreement with the Project Company, but the lending groups also need to establish machinery for working together, or the Project Company will soon find itself like a bone between two dogs, with the project in pieces after being pulled in different directions by different lenders. Although the Project Company may not be a direct party to these intercreditor arrangements, it has a strong interest in ensuring that they are practical and workable.

As a minimum, the intercreditor arrangements need to establish:

- Common arrangements for Financial Close (usually Financial Close cannot be reached in one loan if it is not also simultaneously reached in the other)
- *Pro rata* sharing of security
- Common voting arrangements for waivers, amendments, and enforcement action: voting in such cases is normally by lending group; each group of lenders decides on its own voting rules, and then the decision of each group becomes one block of votes (*pro rata* to that group's exposure) in the intercreditor voting, although it should be noted that commercial banks are reluctant to get into a position where their ability to take action can be blocked by public-sector lenders or others who may not be motivated by purely commercial factors

It is preferable for the intercreditor arrangements to extend well beyond this, through the signature of a much wider-ranging Common Terms Agreement (the agreement has a variety of other names, such as Project Co-ordination Agreement or Co-financing Agreement). Under this arrangement, the individual loan agreements cover little more than the amount of the loan, and perhaps the interest rate. All the other provisions are set out in the Common Terms Agreement, e.g.:

- A common repayment schedule
- Conditions precedent to Financial Close and drawings
- Agreement on priority of drawings on each loan and adjustments between lenders at the end of construction, or if there is a default, to keep the loans on an agreed *pro rata* basis
- Representations and warranties
- Covenants
- The cash flow cascade and Reserve Accounts
- Events of default
- Appointment of an intercreditor agent as a central conduit for payments and voting
- Voting and enforcement procedures
- Security documentation

If these issues are not covered in a common agreement, the Sponsors will have difficulty negotiating exactly parallel terms in separate financing agreements, and if exactly parallel terms are not negotiated, the Project Company is likely to have great difficulty keeping the different groups of lenders from moving in different directions, to the detriment of both lenders and investors.

There is also a legal benefit to a Common Terms Agreement, as lending groups may be from different countries and wish their loan documentation to be governed by the laws and jurisdiction of their group's country. Even if the loan documentation is exactly parallel between the different groups, the differing legal systems may produce different interpretations of what it means. This problem is largely solved by signing loan agreements with a limited scope as above, and then signing the Common Terms Agreement based on one convenient law and jurisdiction.

Further intercreditor issues arise if groups of lenders are not on a similar footing:

- Interest swap providers (cf. §13.13.1)
- Fixed-rate lenders (cf. §13.13.2)
- Lenders with different security (cf. §13.13.3)
- Lessors (cf. §13.13.4)
- Subordinated or mezzanine lenders (cf. §13.13.5)

§13.13.1 INTEREST RATE SWAP PROVIDERS

If an interest rate swap (cf. §9.2.1) is provided *pro rata* by all the banks in a lending syndicate, there is obviously no need for any special intercreditor arrangements to take account of this, but if—as is commonly the case—the swap is being provided just by one or two banks (either for their own account or acting as a fronting bank), their voting and enforcement rights vis à vis the rest of the syndicate need to be considered. Because their breakage costs at any one time cannot be predicted (and may be zero if rates move the right way), the extent of their risk—if any—on a default by the Project Company cannot be fixed in advance. Theoretically, the swap provider would wish to have a vote in the syndicate equal to whatever proportion the breakage cost at the time of the vote bears to the rest of the debt: this uncertainty is usually not acceptable to the other lenders. The end result is often that:

- The swap provider does not take part in voting on waivers and amendments (the swap provider is usually also a lending bank and thus still has a voice that can be heard in this way)
- The swap provider may terminate the swap independently if the Project Company is in default under a limited number of categories (such as non-payment and insolvency)
- Once the claim has been crystallized by termination of the swap, the swap provider's vote on enforcement is also fixed *pro rata* to this

However the voting rights are structured, the swap provider shares *pro rata* in any enforcement proceeds based on the crystallized breakage cost.

§13.13.2 FIXED-RATE LENDERS

Fixed-rate lenders are in a similar position to interest swap providers when a default takes place: they may also have a breakage cost. This does not normally give them any extra voting rights, but is taken into account in determining their *pro rata* share of any enforcement proceeds.

A problem may arise, however, if the fixed-rate lender charges a very large penalty for terminating the loan; for example, the amount due on early repayment may include not just the principal and interest amounts outstanding and breakage costs, but also the discounted NPV of the future profits for investors—i.e., the principal amount due is calculated as the NPV of future payments due on the bond, discounted at a rate below the coupon (interest rate) on the bond. Floating rate lenders usually do not claim future loss of profit in this way. This may lead to a large discrepancy in the relative size of the claim that the different groups of lenders have on a default. (Similar problems may arise where one group of lenders is lending on an inflation-indexed basis.)

§13.13.3 LENDERS WITH DIFFERENT SECURITY

If one lender group has, for example, a Sponsor guarantee that another group has not, then it is evident that the former cannot be inhibited by the latter from enforcing their security after a Project Company default, and *vice versa*.

§13.13.4 LESSORS

If the Project Company finances part of the project costs through leasing, the equipment financed is legally owned by the lessor (leasing company), who are likely to be reluctant to share the value of this security *pari passu* with other lenders. But any other lenders will not wish the lessor to deal separately with key components of the project. Therefore, an agreement will be needed both to coordinate on foreclosure and probably to share the benefits of a sale.

A similar position may arise if the Project Company uses Islamic financing to fund part of the project costs (cf. §11.6.11). The key characteristic of Islamic financing is that it eschews charging interest (as being contrary to provisions in the Koran), and therefore may charge for the use of an asset—much the same as leasing—instead. In such cases the ownership of the asset may remain with the Islamic lender, giving rise to the same "sharing" issues as for a lease.

§13.13.5 SUBORDINATED OR MEZZANINE LENDERS

Subordinated debt provided by the investors in lieu of equity (cf. §3.3, §12.7.2) cannot be used to give them any extra rights either before or after a default. The lenders will require them to agree that they have no security rights and cannot take any enforcement action to recover this debt, or otherwise obstruct the senior lenders, until all the senior lenders' debt has been fully repaid.

Mezzanine debt may be provided by third parties unconnected with the Sponsors or other investors (cf. §3.3), usually secured by a second mortgage or junior position on the senior lenders' security. Such mezzanine lenders are placed in the cash flow cascade (cf. §13.5.1) above distributions to investors, and so are repaid if sufficient cash flow is available after prior payments have been made. They accept that if the financing package as a whole is in default, and enforcement action is taken, they will only be repaid if the senior lenders are fully repaid. But there are a number of potentially difficult issues with mezzanine lenders.

In general, these issues revolve around the concern that senior lenders have of "Samson in the temple" behavior by mezzanine lenders; if the project goes wrong and there is only enough money to repay the senior lenders, as the mezzanine lenders have nothing to lose they can threaten to pull the whole project to pieces unless the senior lenders share some of the value that their loans still have.

Senior lenders therefore restrict the rights of mezzanine lenders in a number of ways to try to avoid this happening:

Timing of drawings. Senior lenders may wish mezzanine loans to be drawn first by the Project Company, in a similar way to equity funding; mezzanine lenders may only be willing to fund *pro rata* with senior lenders.

Conditions precedent to drawings. If funding is being provided on a *pro rata* basis, senior lenders will want there to be only very limited conditions precedent to funding by mezzanine lenders.

Amendments to senior loan terms. Senior lenders want freedom to make amendments to their loan terms, including the repayment schedule and interest rate, and the ability to increase the amount of senior debt if the project gets into trouble. Obviously this may make the mezzanine lenders' position worse: a compromise may be to limit the amount of extra debt or other costs that can be added on to the senior debt at various points in the project life.

Amendment to Project Contracts. Any amendments to the Project Contracts require senior lenders' consent; they normally require freedom to allow such amendments without interference by mezzanine lenders, unless the result is to increase the senior debt amount, as discussed above.

Blocking of payments. The place of the payments to mezzanine lenders in the cash flow cascade may raise issues: do the senior lenders' DSRA, or the Maintenance Reserve Account, have to be filled up before mezzanine lenders can be paid; can payments to mezzanine lenders be blocked in a similar way to payments to investors (e.g., if cover ratios fall below certain levels)?

Default. Mezzanine lenders want to have the right to take enforcement action if they are not paid when due. It is difficult for senior lenders to exclude the mezzanine lenders completely from taking action; a common compromise is to require the mezzanine lenders to wait, say, six months after a payment default before they can take action (and of course such action will trigger action by the senior lenders, so ensuring that any enforcement proceeds still accrue to them first).

Glossary and Abbreviations

Technical terms used in this book which are mainly peculiar to project finance are capitalised, and briefly explained in this Glossary, with cross-references to the places in the main text where a fuller explanation can be found; other financial terms used in the book are also explained and cross-referenced in the Glossary, as are the various abbreviations used.

abandonment   Failure by the Sponsors to continue with the construction or operation of the project. *See* §6.8.1

accreting swap   An interest rate swap drawn in installments to match drawing of the notional principal amount. *See* §9.2.1

acknowledgements and consents *see* Direct Agreement(s)

ADB   Asian Development Bank, a regional IFI. *See* §11.6.5

ADSCR   Annual Debt Service Cover Ratio, the ratio between operating cash flow and debt service over any one year of the project. *See* §12.9.1

advance payment guarantee   Security provided by the EPC Contractor for amounts paid in advance under the EPC Contract by the Project Company. *See* §7.1.10

AfDB   African Development Bank, a regional IFI. *See* §11.6.6

agent bank   The bank liasing between the Project Company and its lenders. *See* §5.1.8; §13.12

All Risks insurance   Insurance against physical damage to the project during operation. *See* §7.6.2

ALOP insurance   Advance Loss of Profits insurance. *See* DSU insurance.

amortizing swap   An interest rate swap reduced in installments to match reductions in the notional principal amount. *See* §9.2.1

annuity repayment   A debt repayment schedule that produces level debt service payments. *See* §13.2.3

arranger   *See* Lead Manager.

assumptions book   The source data for the financial model. *See* §12.1

availability   The period(s) when the project is able to operate. *See* §6.1.4; §6.2.1; §8.7.4

Availability Charge   The fixed charge element of a Tariff, payable whether or not the product or service is required. *See* §6.1.5

average life (of a loan)   The average period that the loan principal is outstanding. *See* §13.2.2

B Loans   Loans provided by private-sector banks in parallel with IFIs. *See* §11.6.2; §11.6.8

BAFO   Best and Final Offer, a second stage bid in a public procurement. *See* §4.6.3

balloon repayment   A large final principal repayment of a loan (after a series of smaller payments); cf. bullet repayment

banker's clauses   Additional lender requirements on insurances. *See* §7.6.4

banking case   *See* Base Case.

Base Case   The lenders' projections of project cash flow at or shortly before Financial Close. *See* §12.10

bbl   Barrel (of oil)

benchmarking   Adjustment to the Unitary Charge based on regular review of the costs of services provided to the Project Company. *See* §6.2.1

Berne Union   International Union of Credit and Investment Insurers. *See* §11.2

BI insurance   Business Interruption insurance, i.e., insurance against the loss of revenue after damage to the project. *See* §7.6.2

BLOT   Build-Lease-Operate-Transfer. *See* BLT.

BLT   Build-Lease-Transfer. *See* §2.3

bond   A tradable debt instrument. *See* §3.2; §5.2

bonding   Security provided by the EPC Contractor. *See* §7.1.10

BOO   Build-Own-Operate. *See* §2.3

BOOT   Build-Own-Operate-Transfer. *See* §2.3

BOT   Build-Operate-Transfer. *See* §2.3

breach of contract   Failure by a public-sector body to fulfil its obligations under a Project Contract or by a Host Government to fulfill its obligations to compensate for this under a Government Support Agreement. *See* §10.7.1

breach of provision clause   *See* nonvitiation clause.

breakage cost   The cost of early termination of an interest rate swap or fixed-rate loan. *See* §9.2.1; §13.13.1; §13.13.2

BTO   Build-Transfer-Operate. *See* §2.3

bullet repayment   Repayment of a loan in one final installment rather than a series of principal repayments.

Capacity Charge   *See* Availability Charge.

CAR insurance   Contractor's All Risks insurance. *See* CEAR insurance.

cash clawback   Requirement for investors to repay distributions received if the Project Company is later short of cash. *See* §13.5.5

cash flow cascade   The order of priorities under the financing documentation for the application of the Project Company's cash flow. *See* §13.5.1

cash flow waterfall   *See* cash flow cascade.

cash sweep   Dedication of surplus cash flow to debt prepayment. *See* §13.5.4

CEAR insurance   Construction &

Erection All Risks insurance, covering physical damage to the project during construction. *See* §7.6.1

change of law A change in the law affecting the Project Company or the project, which results in additional capital or operating costs. *See* §10.6

CIRR Commercial Interest Reference Rates, the interest rates charged on ECAs' subsidized export credits. *See* §11.3.2

CIS Commonwealth of Independent States, the former Soviet Union.

COD Commercial Operation Date, the date on which the project is complete and the Project Company is ready to begin operations. *See* §7.1.6; §8.5.6

COFACE Compagnie Française d'Assurance pour le Commerce Extérieur, the French ECA. *See* §11.5.5

collateral warranties Agreements under which parties providing services in connection with construction or operation of the project accept liability to the lenders for the performance of the service. *See* §7.7

comfort letter A letter of support for a subsidiary's liabilities which does not constitute a guarantee. *See* §8.11

commercial banks Private-sector banks, the main providers of debt to the project finance markets. *See* §3.1; §5.1

commercial risks Project finance risks inherent in the project itself or the market for its product or service; cf. completion, operating, revenue, input supply, and environmental risks. *See* Chapter 8

commitment fee Percentage fee charged on the available but undrawn portion of a bank loan. *See* §13.4

Common Terms Agreement Common lending conditions agreed between different groups of lenders. *See* §13.13

completion risks Commercial risks relating to the completion of the project. *See* §8.5

Concession Agreement A Project Agreement under which the Project Company provides a service to the Contracting Authority, or directly to the general public. *See* §6.2

conditions precedent Conditions to be fulfilled by the Project Company before drawing on the debt. *See* §13.8

construction phase insurances CEAR, Marine Cargo, DSU, Marine DSU and *Force Majeure* insurances. *See* §7.6.1

construction risks *See* completion risks.

contingency Unallocated reserve in the project cost budget, covered by contingency funding. *See* §8.5.4; §13.3.3

Contract for Differences A Project Agreement under which the Project Company sells its product into the market, but pays to or receives from the Offtaker the difference between the market price and an agreed price level. *See* §6.1.1; §8.8.4

contract repudiation *See* breach of contract.

Contracting Authority A public sector entity which is the Project Company's contractual counterpart under a Concession Agreement. *See* §6.2

corporate loan A loan against a company's balance sheet and existing business. *See* §2.2

country risk *See* political risks.

coupon swap *See* interest rate swap.

covenants Undertakings given by the Project Company to the lenders. *See* §13.10

cover ratios Ratios of the cash flows from the project against debt service, i.e., ADSCR, LLCR, PLCR, or Reserve Cover Ratio. *See* §12.9

CPI Consumer price index, an index of inflation.

creeping expropriation A series of actions by the Host Government or another public-sector body which, taken as a whole, have the effect of expropriation. *See* §10.7.3

cross-border Debt or investment made from one country to another.

CUP MIGA's Co-operative Underwriting Programme, based on similar principles to B Loans. *See* §11.6.4

cure period A period of time allowed to remedy a default under a contract. *See* §7.7

DBFO Design-Build-Finance-Operate. *See* BOT.

deal creep Gradual increases in the originally agreed Tariff or Unitary Charge by the Sponsors during Project Agreement negotiations, usually caused by the project requirements not being initially specified in enough detail by the Offtaker or Contracting Authority, or by changes in requirements. *See* §4.6.3

debt Finance provided by the lenders. *See* §2.2

debt service Payment of interest and debt principal installments. *See* §13.2

debt : equity ratio Ratio of debt to equity. *See* §9.3.2; §13.1

deductibles Initial loss amount borne before insurance claims are paid. *See* §7.6.3

default ratio Minimum cover ratio(s) below which an event of default occurs. *See* §13.11

degradation The decline in operating efficiency of a project caused by usage. *See* §8.7.6

delay LDs LDs payable by the EPC Contractor for failure to complete the project by the agreed date. *See* §7.1.8

depreciation Writing down the capital cost of the project. *See* §12.7.1

derivatives *See* hedging.

developers *See* Sponsors.

Development Agreement An agreement between Sponsors relating to the development of the project. *See* §4.2

development costs Costs incurred by the Sponsors before Financial Close. *See* §4.2; §8.5.4

DFI Development finance institution—a financial institution providing bilateral loans and equity investment for projects in developing countries. *See* §11.4.2

Direct Agreement(s) Agreement(s) between the lenders and the parties signing Project Contracts with the Project Company, protecting the lenders' interests under these contracts. *See* §7.7

Disbursement Account The Project Company's bank account into which equity and debt advances are paid and from which payments we made for the project's construction costs. *See* §13.3.2

discount rate   The rate used to reduce a future cash flow to a current value, and calculate its NPV. *See* §12.8.1

distributions   Net cash flow paid to the investors as dividends, subordinated debt interest or principal, or repayment of equity. *See* §13.5.3

dividend stop ratio(s)   Cover ratio(s) below which the lenders prevent payment of distributions to the investors. *See* §13.5.3

dividend trap   Inability of the Project Company to pay dividends, despite having cash available to do so, because of accounting losses. *See* §12.7.2

domestic   Relating to the country of the project. *See* §12.7.2

DPC Contract   Design, Procurement, and Construction Contract; *see* EPC Contract.

drawing request   The formal procedure for drawings on the debt by the Project Company. *See* §13.3.2

drawstop   Suspension of drawings (loan advances) by the lenders after an event of default. *See* §13.12

DSRA   Debt Service Reserve Account, a Reserve Account with a cash balance sufficient to cover the next scheduled debt service payment. *See* §13.5.2

DSU insurance   Delay in Start-up insurance, i.e., insurance against the loss of revenue or extra costs caused by a delay in completion after damage to the project. *See* §7.6.1

due diligence   Review and evaluation of Project Contracts and commercial, financial, and political risks. *See* §2.5; §8.2

easement   A right to use adjacent land, e.g., for discharge of water. *See* §7.4.3

EBRD   European Bank for Reconstruction and Development, an IFI covering Central and Eastern Europe and the CIS. *See* §11.6.8

ECA   export credit agency (or export–import bank). *See* §11.2; §11.5

ECGD   Export Credits Guarantee Department, the U.K. ECA. *See* §11.5.8

EDC   Export Development Corporation, the Canadian ECA. *See* §11.5.3

Effective Date   *See* Financial Close.

EIA   Environmental Impact Assessment, a study of the effect of the construction and operation of the project on the natural and human environment. *See* §7.4.1

EIB   European Investment Bank, the long-term lending institution of the European Union. *See* §11.6.9

EID/MITI   Export–Import Insurance Division of the Ministry of International Trade and Industry of Japan, now superseded by NEXI. *See* §11.5.4

EIF   European Investment Fund, a partnership between EIB and private-sector financial institutions to provide support for European projects. *See* §11.6.9

emergency step-in   The right of the Offtaker or Contracting Authority to take over the running of the project for reasons of safety or public security. *See* §6.7

enclave project A project whose products are exported, for which payment is received outside the Host Country. *See* §10.3.1; §11.6.1

Energy Charge The element of a Tariff intended to cover fuel costs. *See* §6.1.5

environmental risks Risk relating to the environmental effect of the construction or operation of the project. *See* §8.6

EPC Contract Engineering, Procurement, and Construction Contract, a fixed-price, date-certain, turnkey contract under which the project is designed and engineered, equipment procured or manufactured, and the project constructed and erected. *See* §7.1

EPC Contractor The contractor under the EPC Contract. *See* §8.5.3

equity The portion of the project's capital costs contributed by the investors, which may be provided as share capital or subordinated debt. *See* §2.2

equity bridge loan Finance provided by lenders during the construction period for the amount of the equity investment. *See* §13.3.1

equity IRR The IRR on the equity paid in by the investers, derived from distributions. *See* §12.12.1

escrow account A bank account under the joint control of two parties; cf. Reserve Accounts. *See* §8.8.1; §10.3.1

European Bank *See* EBRD.

events of default Events that give the lenders the right to drawstop or terminate the financing (or parties to Project Contracts the right to terminate them after due notice). *See* §13.11

exchange rate risks Macroeconomic risks resulting from changes in currency exchange rates. *See* §9.3; §12.3.4; §12.7.7

export credits Guarantees or insurance to lenders or direct loans to the Project Company, linked to export sales, provided by ECAs. *See* §11.3

expropriation Illegal takeover of the project or the Project Company by the Host Government. *See* §10.4

fare box guarantee Guarantee by the Contracting Authority of a minimum level of usage or real toll payments in a transportation project. *See* §6.2.2

FIM Final Information Memorandum, the information memorandum on the Project Company used for syndication. *See* §5.1.7

Financial Adviser The Sponsors' adviser on arranging finance for the Project Company. *See* §5.1.2

Financial Close The date on which all Project Contracts and financing documentation are signed, and conditions precedent to initial drawing of the debt have been fulfilled. *See* §13.8

financial model The financial model used by lenders to review and monitor the project. *See* §5.1.5; Chapter 12

financial risks *See* macroeconomic risks.

Fixed Charge *See* Availability Charge.

floating interest rate An interest rate revised at regular intervals to the current market rate; cf. LIBOR, rate-fixing date. *See* §9.2

force majeure A natural or political event that affects the ability of one party to fulfil its contract, but that is not the fault of, and could not reasonably have been foreseen by, that party. *See* §6.6; §7.1.7; §8.10

Force Majeure **insurance** Insurance against the loss of revenue or extra costs caused by a delay in completion or interruption in operation due to *force majeure* not covered by DSU or BI insurances. *See* §7.6.1

forward-looking ratios Projection of future ADSCRs, or the LLCR, once a project has begun operation, for the purposes of a dividend stop or default ratio calculation. *See* §13.5.3

fronting bank A bank acting as a channel for an interest rate swap. *See* §9.2.1

Fuel Supply Contract An Input Supply Contract to supply the fuel for a project. *See* §7.3

full cover Guarantees or insurance for both political and commercial risks, provided to a lender by an ECA or IFI. *See* §11.1.

gearing *See* leverage.

GIC Guaranteed Investment Contract, a fixed rate of interest paid by a depository bank on the proceeds of a bond issue until these are required to pay construction costs for a project. *See* §9.2.5

governing law The law governing a Project Contract or the financing documentation. *See* §10.7.1

government The central government of the country in which the project is located.

Government Support Agreement A Project Contract that establishes the legal basis for the project, or under which the government agrees to provide various kinds of support or guarantees. *See* §7.5

gross up Increase a payment to allow for tax deductions. *See* §6.8.5; §9.2.4

heat rate The amount of fuel required to produce a set amount of electrical power.

hedging An arrangement in the financial or commodity markets to protect the Project Company against adverse movements in interest rates, currency exchange rates, or commodity prices. *See* §6.1.1; §8.8.3; Chapter 9

Hermes Hermes Kreditversicherungs A.G., the German ECA. *See* §11.5.6

host country The country in which the project is located (usually used in connection with a cross-border investment). *See* §10.2

host government The government of the host country.

IADB Inter-American Development Bank, a regional IFI. *See* §11.6.7

IBRD *See* World Bank.

ICB International competitive bidding procedures of the World Bank; *See* public procurement.

IDA International Development Association, an affiliate of the World Bank providing development finance to the poorest countries. *See* §11.6.3

IDB Islamic Development Bank, an Islamic financing institution. *See* §11.6.11

IDC Interest during construction, which is capitalized and forms part of the project cost budget. *See* §9.2

IFC International Finance Corporation, an affiliate of the World Bank dealing with the private sector. *See* §11.6.2

IFIs International financing institutions. *See* §11.6

Implementation Agreement *See* Government Support Agreement.

Independent Checker An engineering firm not linked to any party to the Project Contracts, who confirms that project construction has been carried out as required by the Project Agreement and EPC Contract. *See* §7.1.5

Independent Engineer *See* Lenders' Engineer.

inflation risks Macroeconomic risks resulting from changes in the rate of price inflation. *See* §9.1; §12.3.1; §12.7.8

Input Supplier The contractor under the Input Supply Contract.

Input Supply Contract A Project Contract for the supply of fuel or raw materials to the Project Company. *See* §7.3; §8.9.1

input supply risks Commercial risks relating to the availability and cost of input supplies for the project. *See* §8.9

insurance *See* §7.6; §8.10.1

intercreditor Relationship between different groups of lenders. *See* §13.13

Intercreditor Agreement *See* Common Terms Agreement.

interest rate cap A hedging contract that sets a maximum interest rate for the Project Company's debt. *See* §9.2.2

interest rate collar A hedging contract that sets a floor (minimum) and ceiling (maximum) on the interest rate payable by the Project Company. *See* §9.2.2

interest rate risks Macroeconomic risks resulting from increases in interest rates. *See* §9.2; §12.3.3

interest rate swap A hedging contract to convert a floating interest rate into a fixed rate. *See* §9.2.1

investment bank A bank arranging but not providing debt. *See* §3.2; §5.2.1

investment grade rating A rating of BBB- / Baa3 or above. *See* §5.2.1

investment insurance Insurance against political risks, provided to investors or lenders by ECAs, IFIs, or private-sector insurers. *See* §11.4

investment risks Political risks relating to currency convertibility and transfer, expropriation, and political *force majeure. See* §10.2

investors Sponsors and other parties investing equity into the Project Company. *See* §4.1

IPP Independent power plant. *See* §6.1.2

IRR Internal rate of return, the rate of return on an investment derived from future cash flows. *See* §12.8.2; §12.12.2

ISACE Istituto per i Servizi Assicurativi e il Credito all'Esportazione, the Italian ECA. *See* §11.5.7

ISDA International Swap and Derivatives Association, which produces standard form documentation for interest rate swaps. *See* §9.2.1

Islamic financing Finance without payment of interest. *See* §11.6.11; §13.13.3

ITN Invitation to Negotiate. *See* RFP.

ITT Invitation to Tender. *See* RFP.

JBIC Japan Bank for International Co-operation, which provides export credits and untied financing. *See* §11.5.4

JEXIM Export–Import Bank of Japan, now superseded by JBIC.

KfW Kreditanstalt für Wiederaufbau, which provides CIRR funding for German exports and untied financing. *See* §11.5.6

L/C Letters of credit, a form of payment guarantee issued by a bank.

LDs Liquidated damages, i.e., the agreed level of loss when a party does not perform under a contract. *See* §6.1.7; §7.1.8

Lead Manager(s) Bank(s) arranging and underwriting the debt. *See* §5.1.1; §5.1.4

lease A form of debt in which the equipment being financed is owned by the lessor. *See* §3.4; 13.13.4

lenders Banks or bond investors. *See* Chapters 3 and 5

lenders' advisers External advisers employed by the lenders. *See* §5.4

Lenders' Engineer An engineering firm advising the lenders. *See* §5.4.2

lessee The obligor under a lease (i.e., the Project Company). *See* §3.4

lessor The provider of finance under a lease (equivalent to a lender). *See* §3.4; §13.13.4

leverage The debt:equity ratio. *See* §13.1

LIBOR London interbank offered rate, one of the leading floating interest rates. *See* §9.2

limited-recourse Finance with limited guarantees from the Sponsors. *See* §8.12

LLCR Loan Life Cover Ratio, the ratio of the NPV of operating cash flow during the remaining term of the debt and the debt principal amount. *See* §12.9.2

LNG Liquefied natural gas.

lock-up ratio *See* dividend stop ratio.

LOI Letter of Intent, heads of terms for a Project Agreement or other Project Contract.

MAC clause Material adverse change clause(s) in the financing documentation that give the lenders discretion to refuse to allow further drawings or to require repayment of the debt followings a material adverse change in the project. *See* §13.8; §13.11

macroeconomic risks Project finance risks related to inflation, interest rates, or currency exchange rates. *See* Chapter 9; §12.3

maintenance bond *See* warranties.

Maintenance Reserve Account A Reserve Account that builds up a cash balance sufficient to cover the major maintenance of the project. *See* §8.7.5; §13.5.2

Maître d'Oeuvre *See* Independent Checker.

Marine Cargo insurance   Insurance against damage to equipment in transit to the project site during construction. *See* §7.6.1

Marine DSU insurance   Insurance against the loss of revenue or extra costs caused by a delay in completion after damage to the equipment in transit to the project. *See* §7.6.1

mark-to-market   Calculating the breakage cost. *See* §9.2.1

MDB   Multilateral development bank. *See* IFI

merchant power plant   A power project that does not have a PPA, but relies on selling its power into a competitive market. *See* §8.8.6

mezzanine debt   Subordinated debt provided by third parties other than the investors. *See* §3.3; §13.13.5

MIGA   Multilateral Investment Guarantee Agency, an affiliate of the World Bank providing cover to lenders and investors against political risks. *See* §11.6.4

mini-perm   A loan for the construction period and first few years of operation of a project, to be refinanced in due course by longer term debt. *See* §13.6.3

MIRR   Modified IRR, an IRR calculation with a reduced reinvestment rate for cash taken out of the project. *See* §12.8.3

MLA   Multilateral lending agency. *See* IFI.

MLAs   Minimum liquid asset requirements; *see* MLRs.

MLRs   The cost of banks' minimum liquidity ratio requirements, if any. *See* §9.2.4

mobilization   The transition from the construction phase to the operating phase of the project.

Model Auditor   An independent firm of accountants that reviews and certifies the financial model. *See* §5.4.4

monoline insurance   Insurance of an individual financial risk (rather than general casualty insurance). *See* 5.2.3

MOU   Memorandum of Understanding. *See* LOI.

Natural *force majeure*   An unforeseeable natural event affecting the project, e.g., fire, explosion, flood, unusual weather conditions. *See* §6.6

negative arbitrage   The loss of interest caused by having to draw the whole of a bond financing and then redeposit the funds until required. *See* §5.3; §9.2.5

negative equity   An cumulative accounting loss exceeding the amount of the Project Company's share capital. *See* §12.7.3

NEXI   Nippon Export and Investment Insurance, the Japanese ECA. *See* §11.5.4

NIB   Nordic Investment Bank, the long-term lending institution of the Nordic countries. *See* §11.6.10

nominal return   The return on a project or investment including inflation (cf. real return). *See* §9.1

nonrecourse   Finance with no guarantee from the Sponsors; cf. limited-recourse.

nonvitiation clause   Provision in an insurance policy that the rights of lenders will not be affected by action by the Project Company that invalidates the insurance. *See* §7.6.4

notional principal amount The amount of debt that is the subject of an interest rate swap. *See* §9.2.1

NPV Net Present Value, the discounted present value of a stream of future cash flows. *See* §12.8.1

NTP Notice to Proceed, a notice from the Project Company to the EPC Contractor to begin the project works. *See* §7.1.2

O&M Operation and maintenance

O&M Contract Operation & Maintenance Contract, a Project Contract to operate and maintain the project on behalf of the Project Company. *See* §7.2; §8.7.2

O&M Contractor The contractor under the O&M Contract.

OECD Organisation for Economic Co-operation and Development.

OECD Consensus An agreement under the ægis of OECD to regulate credit terms offered by ECAs. *See* §11.3.2

Offtake Contract A Project Agreement under which the Project Company produces a product and sells it to the Offtaker. *See* §6.1

Offtaker The purchaser of the product under an Offtake Contract.

operating cost budget The budget for operating costs (where these are under the Project Company's control). *See* §8.7.3; §12.5

operating phase insurances All Risks, BI, and *Force Majeure* insurances. *See* §7.6.2

operating risks Commercial risks relating to the operation of the project. *See* §8.7

OPIC Overseas Private Investment Corporation, a U.S. government agency. *See* §9.3.5; §11.5.2

Owner's Engineer The engineer supervising the EPC Contractor on behalf of the Project Company. *See* §7.1.5; §8.5.3

Owner's Risks The responsibilities of the Project Company under the EPC Contract. *See* §7.1.3; §8.5.4

p.a. *per annum.*

***pari-passu* security** Security shared by different lenders on an equal and *pro rata* basis.

payback period The period of time in which distributions to investors equal their original investment. *See* §12.8.3

paying agent A company distributing debt service payments from the Project Company to bond investors. *See* §5.2.4

penalties LDs payable under the Project Agreement. *See* §6.1.7

performance bond Security provided by the EPC Contractor for performance under the EPC Contract. *See* §7.1.10

performance LDs LDs payable by the EPC Contractor if the completed project does not meet minimum required performance standards. *See* §7.1.8; §8.5.7

performance risks Completion risks relating to the performance of the project. *See* §8.5.7

Permits The rights or permissions required to construct and operate the project, invest in the project Company, or for the Project Company to borrow its debt. *See* §7.4; §8.5.2

PFI Private Finance Initiative, the United Kingdom's PPP program.

PIM Preliminary Information Memorandum, the information memorandum on the project used as a basis for obtaining financing bids from prospective Lead Managers. *See* §5.1.7

PLCR   Project Life Cover Ratio, the ratio of the NPV of operating cash flow and debt service during the remaining life of the project. *See* §12.9.4

Political *force majeure*   Political violence affecting the project, e.g., war, terrorism, or civil unrest. *See* §6.6; §10.5

political risk cover   Guarantees or insurance for political risks. *See* §11.1

political risks   Project finance risks related to political *force majeure* and other investment risks, change of law, and quasi-political risks. *See* §13.5.2

Power Purchaser   The Offtaker under a PPA.

PPA   Power Purchase Agreement, a type of Offtake Contract. *See* §6.1.2

PPP   Public–private partnership, a contracts under which a private-sector party provides a service to or on behalf of the public sector. *See* §2.3; §2.5.2; §6.2

pre-NTP works   Preliminary works on the project (e.g., design) carried out by the EPC Contractor before issuance of the NTP. *See* §7.1.2

prepayment   Early repayment of the debt, which may be in connection with a refinancing. *See* §13.6

prequalification   The first stage of a procurement process. *See* §4.6.1; §8.5.3

private placement   Bonds not quoted on a stock exchange. *See* §5.2.2

Project Agreement   A contract that provides the Project Company with revenues over the project's life, usually in the form of an Offtake Contract or Concession Agreement. *See* Chapter 6

Project Company   The SPV created to construct and operate a project. *See* §4.5

Project Company costs   Costs of running the Project Company itself. *See* §8.5.4

Project Contracts   Contracts signed by the Project Company, which may include a Project Agreement, EPC Contract, Input Supply Contract, O&M Contract, Government Support Agreement, and insurance. *See* Chapter 7

Project Coordination Agreement   *See* Common Terms Agreement.

project cost budget   The budget for construction, finance, and other capital costs of the project. *See* §8.5.4; §12.4.1

project finance   A method of raising long-term debt financing for major projects through "financial engineering," based on lending against the cash flow generated by the project alone; it depends on a detailed evaluation of a project's construction, operating and revenue risks, and their allocation between investors, lenders, and other parties through contractual and other arrangements. *See* §2.2

project finance risks   *See* commercial risks, macroeconomic risks and political risks.

Project IRR   The IRR of the Project Company's cash flow before allowing for debt service and distributions. *See* §12.8.2

project risks *See* commercial risks.

promoters *See* Sponsors.

public procurement Competitive bidding for a Project Agreement. *See* §4.6

pull tolling A Tolling Contract with an Offtaker supplying the fuel or raw materials (cf. push tolling). *See* §7.3.1

purchasing power parity The assumption that the future exchange rate between two currencies will reflect their inflation rate differentials. *See* §12.3.4

push tolling A Tolling Contract with an Input Supplier (cf. pull tolling). *See* §7.3.1

Put-or-Pay Contract An Input Supply Contract on a Take-or-Pay basis. *See* §7.3.1

QIB Qualified Institutional Buyer, an institutional investor to whom Rule 144a bonds can be sold. *See* §5.2.2

quasi-political risks Risks on the boundary between commercial and political risks, namely breach of contract (by a host government or public sector body), sub-sovereign risks, and creeping expropriation. *See* §10.7

rate-fixing date The date on which a floating interest rate is refixed to the current market rate. *See* §9.2

rating agency A company providing an independent view on the creditworthiness of the Project Company. *See* §5.2.1

real interest rate The interest rate excluding of inflation. *See* §12.3.3

real return The return on a project or investment excluding inflation (cf. nominal return). *See* §9.1

real tolls Tolls or fares paid in cash by the users of the project (cf. shadow tolls). *See* §6.2.2; §8.8.7

refinancing Prepayment of the debt and substitution of new debt on more attractive terms (e.g., lower cost or longer maturity). *See* §6.9.1; §12.12.4; §13.6.3

reinsurance Reinsurance of liability by an insurance company. *See* §7.6.5

relief events Temporary *force majeure* preventing the completion or continuous operation of the project. *See* §6.6; §8.10.2

representations and warranties Confirmation by the Project Company of the facts on which the financing is based. *See* §13.9

Reserve Accounts Accounts controlled by the lenders (or their trustee or escrow agent) in which part of the Project Company's cash flow is set aside to provide security for the debt or to cover future costs; cf. DSRA, Maintenance Reserve Account. *See* §10.3.3; §13.5.2

Reserve Cover Ratio The equivalent of LLCR for a natural resources project. *See* §12.9.5

reserve risk The risk of insufficient extraction of supplies of natural resources required for the project. *See* §8.9.4

reserve tail Proven reserves available after the final maturity of the debt. *See* §12.9.5

retainage The proportion of each payment under the EPC Contract retained by the Project Company as security until COD. *See* §7.1.10

revenue risks Commercial risks relating to generation of revenue by the Project Company, derived from volume and price of product sales, or level of usage of the project. *See* §8.8

RFP   Request for Proposals, an invitation to bid in a public procurement. *See* §4.6.2

right of way   A right of access to adjacent land (e.g. for a pipeline bringing fuel to the project). *See* §7.4.3

risk matrix   Schedule of project finance risks and mitigations. *See* §8.3

rollover risk   The risk that an interest rate swap contract may not be amended on acceptable terms if the amount of debt or repayment schedule changes. *See* §9.2.1

RPI   Retail price index. *See* CPI.

Rule 144a   SEC provisions that allow trading in bond private placements with QIBs. *See* §5.2.2

SACE   Sezione Speciale per l'Assicurazione del Credito all'Esportazione, now superseded by ISACE.

SEC   Securities and Exchange Commission (of the United States), which regulates the investment markets. *See* §5.2.2

senior lenders   Lenders whose debt service comes before debt service on mezzanine or subordinated debt, or distributions to investors, and who are repaid first in a liquidation of the project Company. *See* §13.13.5

sensitivities   Variations on the Base Case assumptions calculated by the lenders. *See* §12.11

SFF   EIB's Structured Finance Facility, under which it will assume various project risks. *See* §11.6.9

shadow tolls   Tolls based on usage of the project, but payable by the Contracting Authority rather than the general public (cf. real tolls). *See* §6.2.2; §8.8.7

Shareholder Agreement   An agreement between Sponsors relating to their investment in and management of the Project Company. *See* §4.5.2

Simest   Società Italiana per le Imprese all'Estero, which provides Italian CIRR interest subsidies and untied financing. *See* §11.5.7

site legacy risk   The risk of preexisting contamination on the project site. *See* §7.1.4

site risks   Risks related to the acquisition or condition of the project site. *See* §7.1.4: §8.5.1; §8.5.4; §8.5.6

sovereign risk   A risk carrying the full faith and credit of a country (cf. sub-sovereign risks). *See* §10.7.2

Sponsors   The investors who develop and lead the project through their investment in the Project Company. *See* §4.1

SPV   Special Purpose Vehicle, a separate legal entity with no activity other than those connected with its borrowing. *See* §2.4

step-in rights   Rights under a Direct Agreement for the lenders to take over management of a Project Contract to protect their security; cf. emergency step-in, substitution. *See* §7.7

subordinated debt   Debt whose debt service comes after amounts due to senior lenders, but before distributions of dividends to investors; cf. mezzanine debt. *See* §3.3; §12.7.2; §13.13.5

subrogation   Right of an insurer or

guarantor to take over an asset on which an insurance claim or guarantee has been paid. *See* §7.6.4; §11.3.4; §11.4.1

subsovereign risks Risks relating to a public-sector body other than the Host Government. *See* §10.7.2

substitution Right under a Direct Agreement for the lenders to substitute a new entity to take over the Project Company's rights and obligations under a Project Contract. *See* §7.7

Support Services Agreement A contract between the Project Company and one or more Sponsors to provide back-up technical support, spare parts, etc. *See* §8.7.2

swap provider A bank providing an interest rate swap to the Project Company. *See* §9.2.1; §13.13.1

syndication The process by which the Lead Managers reduce their underwriting by placing part of the loan with other banks. *See* §5.1.7

synthetic lease A form of lease (mainly in the United States) in which ownership of the equipment remains with the lessee for tax purposes, but with the lessor for accounting purposes. *See* §3.4

TA Technical Adviser. *See* Lenders' Engineer.

tail Continuing project revenues after repayment of the debt; cf. reserve tail. *See* §12.9.4; §13.2

Take-and-pay contract A contract under which the purchaser pays an agreed price for the product purchased, but is not obliged to purchase. *See* §6.1.1; §7.3.1

Take-or-pay contract A contract

under which the purchaser must buy the product or make a payment in lieu. *See* §6.1.1; §7.3.1

target repayments A flexible repayment structure to allow for temporary cash flow deficiencies. *See* §13.2.4

Tariff Payments under a Project Agreement; *see* Availability Charge and Variable Charge, or Unitary Charge. *See* §6.1.5: §6.1.6

term Duration of a Project Contract or the period until the final repayment date of the debt. *See* §6.3; §13.2.1

term sheet Heads of terms for the project finance. *See* §5.1.6

Termination Sum The compensation payable by the Offtaker or Contracting Authority for the early termination of a Project Agreement. *See* §6.8

Third-Party Liability Insurance Insurance against damage or injury caused by the project to third parties. *See* §7.6.1; §7.6.2

third-party risks Risks that failures by parties not involved with the Project Contracts may affect the completion or operation of the project. *See* §8.5.8; §8.9.1; §8.9.5

Throughput Contract A Project Agreement for the use of a pipeline. *See* §6.1.1

tied financing *See* export credits.

Tolling Contract An Input Supply Contract in which the fuel or raw material is supplied free, and the Project Company is paid for processing it. *See* §7.3.1

Transportation Contract *See* Throughput Contract.

turnkey contract A contract for design and construction of a complete project

U.S. Exim Export–Import Bank of the United States. *See* §11.5.1

Unitary Charge A combined Availability and Variable Charge under a Concession Agreement. *See* §6.2.1

untied financing Financing or other support by ECAs or other public sector agencies not linked to exports. *See* §11.4

unwind cost *See* breakage cost.

Variable Charge The element of a Tariff intended to cover a project's variable costs (cf. Energy Charge). *See* §6.1.5

VAT Value added tax. *See* §12.7.5

vendor finance Debt provided by a supplier of equipment or services to the Project Company. *See* §3.5

warranties Guarantees against failure of equipment, provided by the EPC Contractor. *See* §7.1.10

withholding taxes Host Country taxes deducted by the Project Company before paying interest or dividends. *See* §9.2.4; §12.7.6

working capital The amount of funding required for inventories and other costs incurred before receipt of sales revenues. *See* §12.4.1

working capital loan A loan to cover working capital requirements. *See* §12.4.2

World Bank International Bank for Reconstruction and Development, an IFI providing finance to governments. *See* §11.6.1

wrapped bonds Bonds guaranteed by a monoline insurance company. *See* §5.2.3